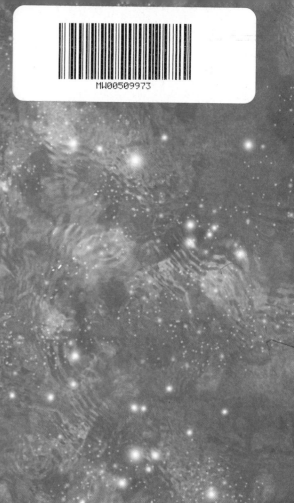

HOUGHTON MIFFLIN HARCOURT

# Tennessee
# Science

HOUGHTON MIFFLIN HARCOURT

Possession of this publication in print format does not entitle users to convert this publication, or any portion of it, into electronic format.

If you have received these materials as examination copies free of charge, Houghton Mifflin Harcourt School Publishers retains title to the materials and they may not be resold. Resale of examination copies is strictly prohibited.

## Program Authors

**William Badders**
Director of the Cleveland Mathematics
   and Science Partnership
Cleveland Municipal School District,
Cleveland, Ohio

**Douglas Carnine, Ph.D.**
Professor of Education
University of Oregon,
Eugene, Oregon

**Bobby Jeanpierre, Ph.D.**
Assistant Professor, Science Education
University of Central Florida,
Orlando, Florida

**James Feliciani**
Supervisor of Instructional Media and Technology
Land O' Lakes, Florida

**Carolyn Sumners, Ph.D.**
Director of Astronomy and Physical Sciences
Houston Museum of Natural Science,
Houston, Texas

**Catherine Valentino**
Author-in-Residence
Houghton Mifflin,
West Kingston, Rhode Island

### Contributing Author

**Michael A. DiSpezio**
Writer and Global Educator
JASON Project
Cape Cod, Massachusetts

## Tennessee Teacher Reviewers

**Melinda Carr**
West View School
Limestone, Tennessee

**Peggy Greene**
Gray Elementary School
Gray, Tennessee

**Loretta Harper**
Goodlettsville Elementary
Goodlettsville, Tennessee

**Donna Lachman**
Boones Creek Middle School
Johnson City, Tennessee

**Gloria R. Ramsey**
Science Specialist
Memphis City Schools
Memphis, Tennessee

**Richard Sherman**
Warner Enhanced Option School
Nashville, Tennessee

# Contents

## UNIT A
## Life Science

Tennessee Excursions . . . . . . . . . . . . . . . . . . . . 2

Technology and Engineering Project . . . . . . . . . . . . . . . 8

**Chapter 1** **Organization of Living Things** . . . . . . . . . . . . . . . 10

**Vocabulary Preview** . . . . . . . . . . . . . . . . . . . . . 12

Lesson 1    What Are the Parts of a Cell? . . . . . . . . . . . . . . . . . 14

Focus On: History of Science: History of the Microscope . . . 22

Lesson 2    How Are Animals Classified? . . . . . . . . . . . . . . . . . 24

Extreme Science: Living Fossils . . . . . . . . . . . . . . . . 36

**Links for Home and School** . . . . . . . . . . . . . . . . . 38

**Careers in Science** . . . . . . . . . . . . . . . . . . . . . 39

**Review and TCAP Prep** . . . . . . . . . . . . . . . . . . . 40

**Chapter 2** **Ecosystems, Communities, and Biomes** . . . . . . . . . . 42

**Vocabulary Preview** . . . . . . . . . . . . . . . . . . . . . 44

Lesson 1    How Do Living Things Form Communities? . . . . . . . . . . 46

Lesson 2    What Are Biomes? . . . . . . . . . . . . . . . . . . . . . 52

Focus On: Reader's Theater: Mr. Wayne's Way Cool
Science Podcast . . . . . . . . . . . . . . . . . . . . . 62

Lesson 3    What Is a Food Web? . . . . . . . . . . . . . . . . . . . . 66

Extreme Science: Leaping Teeth! . . . . . . . . . . . . . . . 74

**Links for Home and School** . . . . . . . . . . . . . . . . . 76

**People in Science** . . . . . . . . . . . . . . . . . . . . . 77

**Review and TCAP Prep** . . . . . . . . . . . . . . . . . . . 78

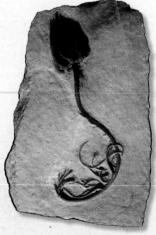

This Agaricocrinites is a type
of fossil found in Tennessee.

**Chapter 3**

**Energy and Matter in Ecosystems** . . . . . . . . . . . . . . . . . 80
**Vocabulary Preview** . . . . . . . . . . . . . . . . . . . . . . . . 82

**Lesson 1**    What Are Habitats and Niches? . . . . . . . . . . . . . . . 84
**Lesson 2**    What Factors Affect Ecosystems? . . . . . . . . . . . . . . 92
            Focus On: Primary Source: Fossils in Tennessee . . . . . . .102
**Lesson 3**    How Can Humans Change Ecosystems? . . . . . . . . . .104
            Extreme Science: A World In Your Hands . . . . . . . . . . .112

**Links for Home and School** . . . . . . . . . . . . 114
**Careers in Science** . . . . . . . . . . . . . . . . . . 115
**Review and TCAP Prep** . . . . . . . . . . . . . . 116

**Chapter 4**

**Traits of Living Things** . . . . . . . . . . . . . . . . . 118
**Vocabulary Preview** . . . . . . . . . . . . . . . . . . . . . 120

**Lesson 1**    How Are Traits Inherited? . . . . . . . . . . . . . . . . . . .122
            Focus On: History of Science: Rosalind Franklin/Lynn
                Margulis . . . . . . . . . . . . . . . . . . . . . . . . . . 132
**Lesson 2**    Why Are Some Traits Very Common? . . . . . . . . . .134
            Extreme Science: Let's Dance! . . . . . . . . . . . . . . .146

**Links for Home and School** . . . . . . . . . . . . 148
**People in Science** . . . . . . . . . . . . . . . . . . . 149
**Review and TCAP Prep** . . . . . . . . . . . . . . 150

**Unit TCAP Prep** . . . . . . . . . . . . . . . . . . . . 152
**Digital Center** . . . . . . . . . . . . . . . . . . . . . . 154

Zebra swallowtail
butterfly

# Contents

## UNIT B
## Earth Science

Tennessee Excursions . . . . . . . . . . . . . . . . . . . . . . . 156
Technology and Engineering Project . . . . . . . . . . . . . . 162

**Chapter 5**    **Exploring Space** . . . . . . . . . . . . . . . . . . . . . 164
Vocabulary Preview . . . . . . . . . . . . . . . . . . . . . . . . 166

Lesson 1    What Orbits the Sun? . . . . . . . . . . . . . . . . . . . 168
Lesson 2    What Are the Planets Like? . . . . . . . . . . . . . . . 176
     Focus On: Literature: Earth Charged in Meteor's
     Fiery Death/Meteors . . . . . . . . . . . . . . . . . . . . . 184
Lesson 3    What Are Constellations? . . . . . . . . . . . . . . . . 186
     Extreme Science: Out With a Bang! . . . . . . . . . . . . 192

Links for Home and School . . . . . . . . . . . . . . . 194
Careers in Science . . . . . . . . . . . . . . . . . . . . . . 195
Review and TCAP Prep . . . . . . . . . . . . . . . . . . 196

**Chapter 6**    **Earth's Structure** . . . . . . . . . . . . . . . . . . . . 198
Vocabulary Preview . . . . . . . . . . . . . . . . . . . . . . . . 200

Lesson 1    What Is Earth's Structure? . . . . . . . . . . . . . . . . 202
Lesson 2    What Are Earthquakes and Volcanoes? . . . . . . . . 212
     Focus On: Reader's Theater: Look Out! It's
     an Earthquake! . . . . . . . . . . . . . . . . . . . . . . . . 222
Lesson 3    How Do Mountains Form? . . . . . . . . . . . . . . . . 226
     Extreme Science: Sleeping Giant Erupts! . . . . . . . . 234

Links for Home and School . . . . . . . . . . . . . . . 236
People in Science . . . . . . . . . . . . . . . . . . . . . . 237
Review and TCAP Prep . . . . . . . . . . . . . . . . . . 238

**Chapter 7**    **Weather and Climate** . . . . . . . . . . . . . . . . . . . . . . . 240

**Vocabulary Preview** . . . . . . . . . . . . . . . . . . . . . . . 242

**Lesson 1**    What Factors Affect Climate? . . . . . . . . . . . . . . . . . . . 244

**Extreme Science:** Twister! . . . . . . . . . . . . . . . . . . . 252

**Lesson 2**    How Are Weather Forecasts Made? . . . . . . . . . . . . . . 254

**Focus On: Primary Source:** Drought in Tennessee . . . . . 264

**Links for Home and School** . . . . . . . . . . . . . . . . . . . 266

**Careers in Science** . . . . . . . . . . . . . . . . . . . . . . . . 267

**Review and TCAP Prep** . . . . . . . . . . . . . . . . . . . . . 268

**Unit TCAP Prep** . . . . . . . . . . . . . . . . . . . . . . . . . 270

**Digital Center** . . . . . . . . . . . . . . . . . . . . . . . . . . . 272

**Cornfield in Tennessee
during a drought**

# Contents

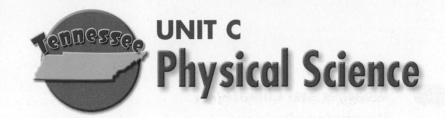

## UNIT C
## Physical Science

Tennessee Excursions . . . . . . . . . . . . . . . . . . . . . . . . . . . .274

Technology and Engineering Project . . . . . . . . . . . . . .280

**Chapter 8**

**Properties of Matter** . . . . . . . . . . . . . . . . . . . . . 282

**Vocabulary Preview** . . . . . . . . . . . . . . . . . . . . . . . . . 284

**Lesson 1**　What Makes Up Matter? . . . . . . . . . . . . . . . . . . . . .286

**Lesson 2**　What Are Physical and Chemical Properties? . . . . . . . . . . .294

Extreme Science: Vanishing Bottles . . . . . . . . . . . . . . . .304

**Lesson 3**　How Does Matter Change State? . . . . . . . . . . . . . .306

Focus On: Technology: Cooling Off . . . . . . . . . . . . . . . .314

**Links for Home and School** . . . . . . . . . . . . . . . . 316

**People in Science** . . . . . . . . . . . . . . . . . . . . . . . . . . 317

**Review and TCAP Prep** . . . . . . . . . . . . . . . . . . . . . . 318

**Chapter 9**

**Energy** . . . . . . . . . . . . . . . . . . . . . . . . . . . . . . . . 320

**Vocabulary Preview** . . . . . . . . . . . . . . . . . . . . . . . . . 322

**Lesson 1**　What Are Kinetic and Potential Energy? . . . . . . . . . . . . .324

Extreme Science: Extreme Drop! . . . . . . . . . . . . . . . . . .332

**Lesson 2**　How Does Thermal Energy Spread? . . . . . . . . . . . . .334

Focus On: Technology: Space Blankets . . . . . . . . . . . . . .342

**Links for Home and School** . . . . . . . . . . . . . . . . 344

**Careers in Science** . . . . . . . . . . . . . . . . . . . . . . . . . 345

**Review and TCAP Prep** . . . . . . . . . . . . . . . . . . . . . . 346

Dizzy Disk ride
at Dollywood

**Chapter 10**  **Forces, Motion, and Work** . . . . . . . . . . . . . . . . . . 348
**Vocabulary Preview** . . . . . . . . . . . . . . . . . . . . . . . . 350

**Lesson 1**   What Can Change an Object's Motion? . . . . . . . . . . . . . . 352
**Lesson 2**   How Do We Use Simple Machines? . . . . . . . . . . . . . . . . 362
**Focus On: History of Science:** Transportation . . . . . . . . 374
**Lesson 3**   What Forces Come from Magnets? . . . . . . . . . . . . . . . . 376
**Extreme Science:** From the Inside Out! . . . . . . . . . . . . . 384

**Links for Home and School** . . . . . . . . . . . . . . . . . . . . 386
**People in Science** . . . . . . . . . . . . . . . . . . . . . . . . . . 387
**Review and TCAP Prep** . . . . . . . . . . . . . . . . . . . . . . 388

**Unit TCAP Prep** . . . . . . . . . . . . . . . . . . . . . . . . . . . 390
**Digital Center** . . . . . . . . . . . . . . . . . . . . . . . . . . . . 392

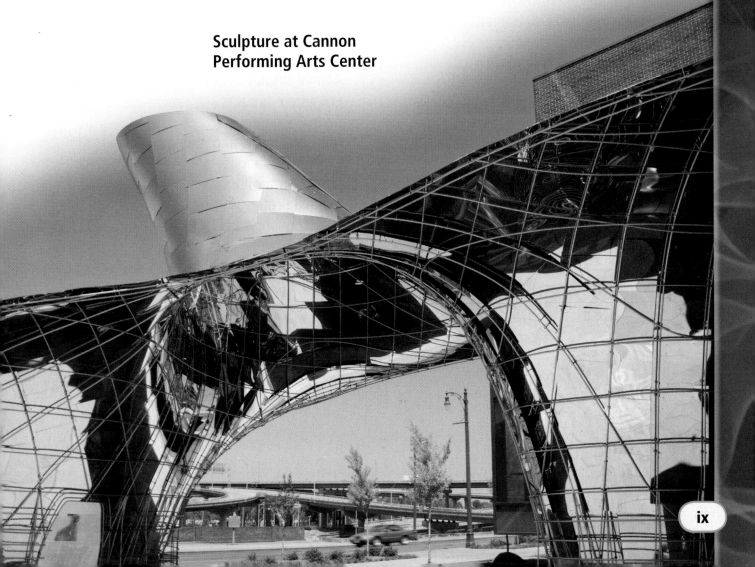

Sculpture at Cannon
Performing Arts Center

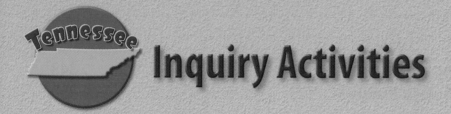

# Inquiry Activities

## LIFE UNIT A SCIENCE

**Technology and Engineering:** Build a Fish Transport

### Directed Inquiry

Get Closer! . . . . . . . . . . . . . . . . . . . . 15
Organizing Animals . . . . . . . . . . . . . 25
Look at Life . . . . . . . . . . . . . . . . . . . . 47
Compare Climates . . . . . . . . . . . . . . 53
Model Energy Flow . . . . . . . . . . . . . 67
Worm and Fish Habitats . . . . . . . . . 85
Limits to Growth . . . . . . . . . . . . . . . 93
Rising Sea Level . . . . . . . . . . . . . 105
Trait Tabulation . . . . . . . . . . . . . . 123
Chromosome Combinations . . . . . . 135

Identify Interspecific Relationships . . . 90
Make a Model Fossil . . . . . . . . . . . . 100
Protect Wildlife . . . . . . . . . . . . . . . 109
Compare Parents and Offspring . . . . 129
Compare Adaptations . . . . . . . . . . 144

### Express Lab

Model Cells . . . . . . . . . . . . . . . . . . . 20
Observe an Animal . . . . . . . . . . . . . 32
Model Interactions in Ecosystems . . . 49
Observe Ecosystems . . . . . . . . . . . . 58
Analyze a Food Web . . . . . . . . . . . . 71

### Check for Understanding

Compare Plant and Animal Cells . . . . 21
Animal Display . . . . . . . . . . . . . . . . 35
Ecosystem Impacts . . . . . . . . . . . . . 51
Animal Features . . . . . . . . . . . . . . . 61
Compare Plants and Animals . . . . . . 73
Evaluate Relationships . . . . . . . . . . . 91
Match Organisms . . . . . . . . . . . . . . 101
Make a Poster . . . . . . . . . . . . . . . . 111
The Story of You . . . . . . . . . . . . . . 131
New Plants . . . . . . . . . . . . . . . . . . 145

**Technology and Engineering:** Build a Safe Clubhouse

### Directed Inquiry

A Very Long Trip! . . . . . . . . . . . . . 169
Scaling the Solar System . . . . . . . . 177
Star Search! . . . . . . . . . . . . . . . . 187
A Model World . . . . . . . . . . . . . . 203
Picking Out a Pattern . . . . . . . . . 213
Make a Mountain! . . . . . . . . . . . . 227
Lighten Up! . . . . . . . . . . . . . . . . 245
The Pressure's On! . . . . . . . . . . . . 255

Make a Mountain Type . . . . . . . . . . 231
Investigate Climate . . . . . . . . . . . . 249
Compare Regions . . . . . . . . . . . . . 259

### Check for Understanding

Defend the Planet . . . . . . . . . . . . . 175
Describe the Planets . . . . . . . . . . . 183
Research a Constellation . . . . . . . . 191
Plate Boundary Model . . . . . . . . . . 211
Constructive and Destructive . . . . . . 221
Earth's Surface Features . . . . . . . . . 233
Climate Factors . . . . . . . . . . . . . . 251
Varying Climates . . . . . . . . . . . . . 263

### Express Labs

Explore Distant Planets . . . . . . . . . 171
Compare the Outer Planets . . . . . . . 180
Use a Star Chart . . . . . . . . . . . . . 190
Make an Earth Model . . . . . . . . . . 210
Model Plate Motion . . . . . . . . . . . 218

**Technology and Engineering:** Build a Solar Oven

### Directed Inquiry

Compare Matter . . . . . . . . . . . . . . 287
Oil and Water . . . . . . . . . . . . . . . 295
Making Rain . . . . . . . . . . . . . . . . 307
Rollerball . . . . . . . . . . . . . . . . . . 325
The Melting Point . . . . . . . . . . . . 335
Monster Trucks . . . . . . . . . . . . . . 353
Ramping it Up . . . . . . . . . . . . . . . 363
Exploring Magnets . . . . . . . . . . . . 377

Transfer Thermal Energy . . . . . . . . . 339
Test Shapes . . . . . . . . . . . . . . . . . 360
Use Simple Machines . . . . . . . . . . . 371
Sort Objects . . . . . . . . . . . . . . . . 380

### Check for Understanding

Magnification Review . . . . . . . . . . . 293
Shining Pennies . . . . . . . . . . . . . . 303
Investigate Evaporation . . . . . . . . . 313
Energy Organizer . . . . . . . . . . . . . 331
Movement of Thermal Energy . . . . . 341
Force, Mass, and Distance . . . . . . . . 361
Design an Investigation . . . . . . . . . 373
At a Distance . . . . . . . . . . . . . . . . 383

### Express Labs

Investigate Scents . . . . . . . . . . . . . 291
Observe Chemical Reactions . . . . . . 301
Observe Condensation . . . . . . . . . . 311
Store and Release Energy . . . . . . . . 329

## Grade 5 Embedded Inquiry

**GLE 0507.Inq.1** Explore different scientific phenomena by asking questions, making logical predictions, planning investigations, and recording data.

**GLE 0507.Inq.2** Select and use appropriate tools and simple equipment to conduct an investigation.

**GLE 0507.Inq.3** Organize data into appropriate tables, graphs, drawings, or diagrams.

**GLE 0507.Inq.4** Identify and interpret simple patterns of evidence to communicate the findings of multiple investigations.

**GLE 0507.Inq.5** Recognize that people may interpret the same results in different ways.

**GLE 0507.Inq.6** Compare the results of an investigation with what scientists already accept about this question.

**Coverage of these standards occurs in Directed Inquiry, Guided Inquiry, and other features.**

# Grade 5 Embedded Technology & Engineering

**GLE 0507.T/E.1** Describe how tools, technology, and inventions help to answer questions and solve problems.

**GLE 0507.T/E.2** Recognize that new tools, technology, and inventions are always being developed.

**GLE 0507.T/E.3** Identify appropriate materials, tools, and machines that can extend or enhance the ability to solve a specified problem.

**GLE 0507.T/E.4** Recognize the connection between scientific advances, new knowledge, and the availability of new tools and technologies.

**GLE 0507.T/E.5** Apply a creative design strategy to solve a particular problem generated by societal needs and wants.

**Coverage of these standards occurs in Directed Inquiry, Guided Inquiry, Focus On, Technology and Engineering Projects, and other features.**

**New technologies were used by engineers to design thermal tiles to protect astronauts on the space shuttle.**

# Grade 5 Life Science

## Standard 1—Cells

**GLE 0507.1.1** Distinguish between the basic structures and functions of plant and animal cells.

**Chapter 1: Organization of Living Things**

## Standard 2—Interdependence

**GLE 0507.2.1** Investigate different nutritional relationships among organisms in an ecosystem.

**GLE 0507.2.2** Explain how organisms interact through symbiotic, commensal, and parasitic relationships.

**GLE 0507.2.3** Establish the connections between human activities and natural disasters and their impact on the environment.

**Chapter 2: Ecosystems, Communities, and Biomes**
**Chapter 3: Energy and Matter in Ecosystems**

## Standard 3—Flow of Matter and Energy

**GLE 0507.3.1** Demonstrate how all living things rely on the process of photosynthesis to obtain energy.

**Chapter 2: Ecosystems, Communities, and Biomes**

## Standard 4—Heredity

**GLE 0507.4.1** Describe how genetic information is passed from parents to offspring during reproduction.

**GLE 0507.4.2** Recognize that some characteristics are inherited while others result from interactions with the environment.

**Chapter 4: Traits of Living Things**

## Standard 5—Biodiversity and Change

**GLE 0507.5.1** Investigate physical characteristics associated with different groups of animals.

**GLE 0507.5.2** Analyze fossils to demonstrate the connection between organisms and environments that existed in the past and those that currently exist.

**Chapter 1: Organization of Living Things**
**Chapter 3: Energy and Matter in Ecosystems**

# Grade 5 Earth and Space Science

**Standard 6—The Universe**

**GLE 0507.6.1** Compare planets based on their known characteristics.

**GLE 0507.6.2** Recognize that charts can be used to locate and identify star patterns.

**Chapter 5: Exploring Space**

**Standard 7—The Earth**

**GLE 0507.7.1** Compare geologic events responsible for the earth's major geological features.

**Chapter 6: Earth's Structure**

**Standard 8—The Atmosphere**

**GLE 0507.8.1** Analyze and predict how major landforms and bodies of water affect atmospheric conditions.

**Chapter 7: Weather and Climate**

**The Cumberland Plateau in Tennessee**

# Grade 5 Physical Science

### Standard 9—Matter

**GLE 0507.9.1** Observe and measure the simple chemical properties of common substances.

**GLE 0507.9.2** Design and conduct an experiment to demonstrate how various types of matter freeze, melt, or evaporate.

**GLE 0507.9.3** Investigate factors that affect the rate at which various materials freeze, melt, or evaporate.

**Chapter 8: Properties of Matter**

### Standard 10—Energy

**GLE 0507.10.1** Design an experiment to illustrate the difference between potential and kinetic energy.

**GLE 0507.10.2** Conduct experiments on the transfer of heat energy through conduction, convection, and radiation.

**Chapter 9: Energy**

### Standard 11—Motion

**GLE 0507.11.1** Design an investigation, collect data and draw conclusions about the relationship among mass, force, and distance traveled.

**Chapter 10: Forces, Motion, and Work**

### Standard 12—Forces in Nature

**GLE 0507.12.1** Recognize that the earth attracts objects without directly touching them.

**GLE 0507.12.2** Investigate how the shape of an object influences the way that it falls toward the earth.

**GLE 0507.12.3** Provide examples of how forces can act at a distance.

**Chapter 10: Forces, Motion, and Work**

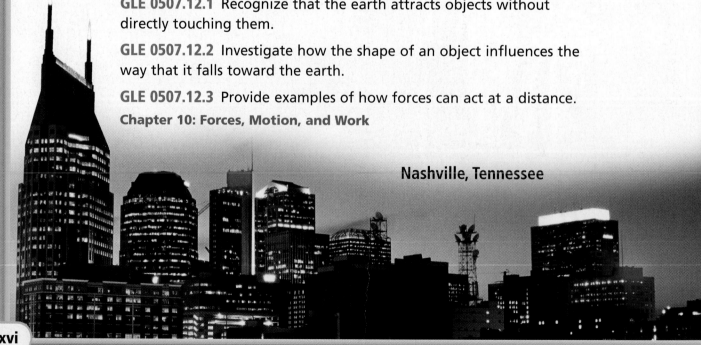

Nashville, Tennessee

# The Nature of Science

You Can Do What Scientists Do . . . . S2

You Can Think Like a Scientist . . . . S4

You Can Be an Inventor . . . . . . . . S10

You Can Make Decisions . . . . . . . S14

Science Safety . . . . . . . . . . . . . . . S16

# You Can...

# Do What Scientists Do

Meet Dr. Dale Brown Emeagwali. She works as a teacher and researcher at Morgan State University in Baltimore, Maryland. Dr. Emeagwali is a microbiologist, which is a biologist who specializes in studying single-celled organisms, or microorganisms. The goal of her investigations is to gain a better understanding of the processes that take place inside cells. Depending on the question she is investigating, Dr. Emeagwali may observe these living things in nature or conduct an experiment in the laboratory.

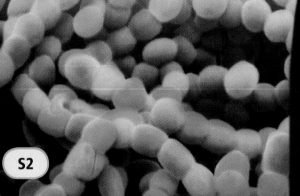

Scientists ask questions. Then they answer the questions by investigating and experimenting. Dr. Emeagwali has asked many questions about how microorganisms carry out their life processes, as well as how they affect human health.

In one investigation, she demonstrated that a certain chemical exists in a type of bacteria called *Streptomyces parvulus*. Such discoveries add to the basic knowledge of microbiology. Dr. Emeagwali is pleased, though, when her work has practical applications in medicine. In another experiment, she demonstrated that certain molecules could be used to stop the formation of tumors in people with cancer.

Dr. Emeagwali understands that for each investigation she carries out she must repeat the procedure many times and get the same results before she can conclude that her results are true.

## Science investigations involve communicating with other scientists.

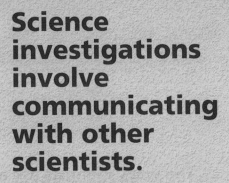

In addition to laboratory research, Dr. Emeagwali spends time writing papers about her work in order to communicate with other scientists. She wants other scientists to be able to repeat her investigations in order to check that her results are valid. Dr. Emeagwali also spends time reading about the work of other scientists to keep informed about the progress others have made in microbiology.

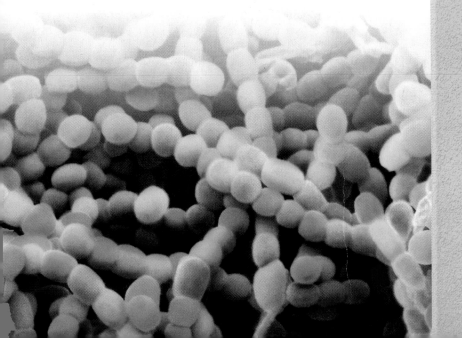

# Think Like a Scientist

The ways scientists ask and answer questions about the world around them is called **scientific inquiry.** Scientific inquiry requires certain attitudes, or approaches to thinking about a problem. To think like a scientist you have to be:

- curious and ask a lot of questions.

- creative and think up new ways to do things.

- able to keep an open mind. That means you consider the ideas of others.

- willing to use measurement, estimation, and other mathematics skills.

- open to changing what you think when your investigation results surprise you.

- willing to question what other people tell you.

**What kind of rock is this? How did this rock form? Where did the different materials that make up the rock come from?**

# Use Critical Thinking

When you think critically, you make decisions about what others tell you or what you read. Is what you heard on TV or read in a magazine a fact or an opinion? A *fact* can be checked to make sure it is true. An *opinion* is what someone thinks about the facts.

Did you ever hear a scientific claim that was hard to believe? When you think, "What evidence is there to support that claim?" you are thinking critically. You'll also think critically when you evaluate investigation results. Observations can be interpreted in many ways. You'll judge whether a conclusion is supported by the data collected.

The book states that a sedimentary rock forms when rock fragments and other sediments are pressed and cemented together.

It looks like fragments of different kinds of rock came together to make this rock. This must be a type of sedimentary rock.

# Science Inquiry

Applying scientific inquiry helps you understand the world around you. Suppose you have decided to investigate which color is easiest to see clearly in the dimmest light.

**Observe** In the evening, as daylight fades, you observe the different colored objects around you. As the light becomes dimmer and dimmer, you notice which color remains clear to your eyes.

**Ask a Question** When you think about what you saw, heard, or read, you may have questions.

**Hypothesis** Think about facts you already know. Do you have an idea about the answer? Write it down. That is your *hypothesis*.

**Experiment** Plan a test that will tell if the hypothesis is true or not. List the materials you will need. Write the steps you will follow. Make sure that you keep all conditions the same except the one you are testing. That condition is called the *variable*.

**Conclusion** Think about your results. What do they tell you? Did your results support your hypothesis or show it to be false?

Describe your experiment to others. Communicate your results and conclusion.

# My Color Experiment

**Observe** As the light dims, dark colors such as dark blue seem to disappear from sight first.

**Ask a question** I wonder which color can be seen most clearly in the dimmest light?

**Hypothesis** Yellow is the color that can be seen most clearly in the dimmest light.

**Experiment** I'm going to observe several differently colored objects as I dim the light. Then I'm going to observe which color I can see most clearly in the dimmest light.

**Conclusion** The results support my hypothesis. Yellow is the color that can be seen most clearly in the dimmest light.

# Inquiry Process

The methods of science may vary from one area of science to another. Here is a process that some scientists follow to answer questions and make new discoveries.

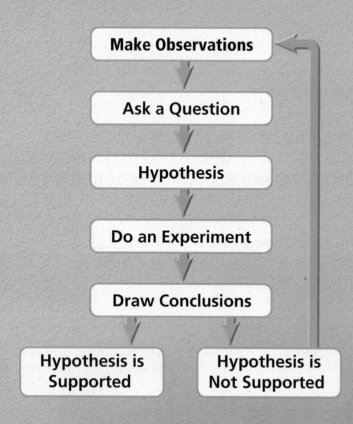

Make Observations

Ask a Question

Hypothesis

Do an Experiment

Draw Conclusions

Hypothesis is Supported

Hypothesis is Not Supported

# Science Inquiry Skills

You'll use many of these skills of inquiry when you investigate and experiment.

- Ask Questions
- Observe
- Compare
- Classify
- Predict
- Measure

- Hypothesize
- Use Variables
- Experiment
- Use Models
- Communicate
- Use Numbers

- Record Data
- Analyze Data
- Infer
- Collaborate
- Research

# Try It Yourself!

## Experiment With Energy Beads

When you hold Energy Beads in your fist for a while and then go outdoors and open your hand, the beads change from off-white to many different colors.

1 What questions do you have about the Energy Beads?

2 How would you find out the answers?

3 How could you use Energy Beads to test a hypothesis?

4 Write your plan for an experiment with one variable using Energy Beads. Predict what will happen.

# You Can...

## Be an Inventor

Cassandra "Cassie" Wagner became an inventor when she was 11 years old. At that time, she was in middle school. During the summer, she wanted to make a toy for her pet cat. Cats are attracted to catnip, a plant with a strong odor. Cassie considered including catnip as part of her toy.

When Cassie researched about catnip on the Internet, she discovered that some people thought an oil in the plant will repel insects. She could find no proof of that hypothesis, and so she decided to test it herself. In her first experiment, Cassie put a small amount of the oil from catnip onto a cotton ball. She then observed whether mosquitoes were repelled by the ball. They were.

With the help of a University of Florida professor, Cassie ran further experiments in a laboratory. She proved that the spray she made with the catnip oil repelled insects just as well as bug sprays sold in stores.

Cassie called her bug repellent Bugnip, and she planned to have it produced and sold to consumers. In the future, her efforts may lead to other inventions and better ways of repelling bothersome bugs.

"It was over the summer, and I didn't have much going on. I was just fooling around."

# What Is Technology?

The tools people make and use, the things they build with tools, and the methods used to accomplish a practical purpose are all **technology**. A toy train set is an example of technology. So is a light rail system that provides transportation in a major city.

Scientists use technology, too. For example, a telescope makes it possible for scientists to see objects far into space that cannot be seen with just the eyes. Scientists also use measurement technology to make their observations more exact.

Many technologies make the world a better place to live. Sometimes, though, a technology that solves one problem can cause other problems. For example, burning coal in power plants provides power for generators that produce electricity for homes, schools, and industries. However, the burning of coal also can cause acid rain, which can be very harmful to living things.

# A Better Idea

"I wish I had a better way to _____." How would you fill in the blank? Everyone wishes he or she could do a job more easily or have more fun. Inventors try to make those wishes come true. Inventing or improving an invention requires time and patience.

A company in Canada had a better idea in 1895. It invented the first power tool. Today, many other tools are powered by electricity—including this cordless power screwdriver. Today, inventors are still improving power tool technology, including using lasers and microwaves to drill into steel, stone, and glass. Maybe, someday, you will have a better idea for a new power tool.

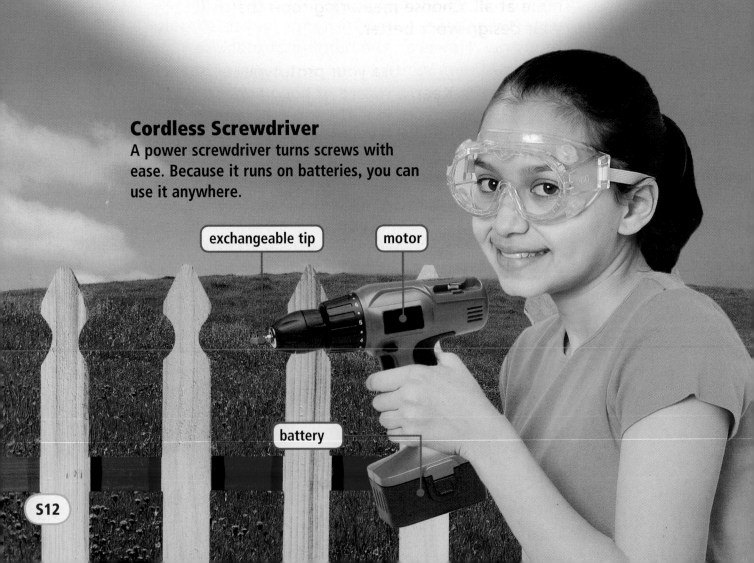

**Cordless Screwdriver**
A power screwdriver turns screws with ease. Because it runs on batteries, you can use it anywhere.

exchangeable tip

motor

battery

# How to Be an Inventor

1. **Identify the problem.** It may be a problem at school, at home, or in your community.

2. **Think of a solution.** Sometimes the solution is a new tool. Other times it may be a new way of doing an old job or activity. Decide which idea you predict will work best. Think about which one you can carry out.

3. **Plan and build.** A sample, called a *prototype*, is the first try. Your idea may need many materials or none at all. Choose measuring tools that will help your design work better.

4. **Test and improve.** Use your prototype, or ask some else to try it. Keep a record of how it works and what problems you find. The more times you try it, the more information you will have. Improve your invention. Use what you learned to make your design work better. Draw or write about the changes you made and why you made them.

5. **Communicate.** Show your invention to others. Explain how it works. Tell how it makes an activity easier or more fun. If it did not work as well as you wanted, tell why.

# Make Decisions

## Trouble for Manatees

Manatees are large, slow-moving marine mammals. An average manatee is about 3 meters long and has a mass of about 500 kilograms. Manatees are gentle plant eaters.

In summer, manatees can be seen along the ocean coasts of Alabama, Georgia, Florida, and South Carolina. In winter, they migrate to the warm waters of bays and rivers along the Gulf Coast of Florida. Living near the coast protects the manatees from diseases they might catch in colder waters. However, there are dangers in living so close to land. The great majority of manatee deaths are caused by collisions with boats. Almost all manatees have scars on their backs from being hit by fast-moving boats.

# Deciding What to Do

What can be done to protect manatees from harm?

Here's how to make your decision about the manatees. You can use the same steps to help solve problems in your home, in your school, and in your community.

**1 LEARN** Learn about the problem. Take the time needed to get the facts. You could talk to an expert, read a science book, or explore a website.

**2 LIST** Make a list of actions you could take. Add actions other people could take.

**3 DECIDE** Think about each action on your list. Identify the risks and benefits. Decide which choice is the best one for you, your school or your community.

**4 SHARE** Communicate your decision to others.

Boat Slow
Speed Zone!

# Science Safety

- ☑ Know the safety rules of your school and classroom and follow them.

- ☑ Read and follow the safety tips in each Directed Inquiry activity.

- ☑ When you plan your own investigations, write down how to keep safe.

- ☑ Know how to clean up and put away science materials. Keep your work area clean, and tell your teacher about spills right away.

- ☑ Know how to safely plug in electrical devices.

- ☑ Wear safety goggles when your teacher tells you.

- ☑ Unless your teacher tells you to, never put any science materials in or near your ears, eyes, or mouth.

- ☑ Wear gloves when handling live animals.

- ☑ Wash your hands when your investigation is done.

## Caring for Living Things

- ☑ Learn how to care for the plants and animals in your classroom so that they stay healthy and safe. Learn how to hold animals carefully.

# LIFE UNIT A SCIENCE

# TENNESSEE

## Tennessee Excursions and Engineering Project

Hubbard's Cave. . . . . . . . . . . . . . . . . . . . . . . . .2

Honeybees in Tennessee . . . . . . . . . . . . . . . . . .4

Norris Dam . . . . . . . . . . . . . . . . . . . . . . . . . . .6

Build a Fish Transport. . . . . . . . . . . . . . . . . . . .8

**UNIT A**
**Life Science**. . . . . . . . . . . . . . . . . . . . . . . . . . . .9

**CHAPTER 1**
  Organization of Living Things . . . . . . . . . . . .10

**CHAPTER 2**
  Ecosystems, Communities, and Biomes . . . . .42

**CHAPTER 3**
  Energy and Matter in Ecosystems . . . . . . . . .80

**CHAPTER 4**
  Traits of Living Things. . . . . . . . . . . . . . . . . .118

# Hubbard's CAVE

Caves can be scary places. They are cool, dark, and damp, with narrow passageways and steep drops. Caves can also be beautiful places. Many have interesting rock formations and animals that live nowhere else on Earth. Some of these animals are endangered.

Tennessee has more than 8,700 caves—more than any other state! Blue Spring Cave in White County is more than 53 km (33 mi) long. It's the longest cave in Tennessee. A few of Tennessee's caves are visitor attractions. Many caves have gates to keep people from entering because caves can be dangerous.

GLE 0507.2.1 Investigate different nutritional relationships among organisms in an ecosystem.

ENGAGE

## Food Sources in Caves

In caves, there is no sunlight and there are no plants. However, there are animals. What do these animals eat?

Many cave food chains rely on bats and other animals that enter and exit the cave regularly. These animals bring food into the cave with them. Their waste products provide food for small animals and bacteria. For example, some cave ecosystems depend entirely on bat droppings, called guano.

**Gray bats eat insects such as moths and mosquitoes.**

## The Gray Bat Food Chain

The gray bat is an endangered species found in some Tennessee caves, such as Hubbard's Cave in McMinnville. Gray bats leave the cave at night in warm months. They eat insects such as mosquitoes. Adult female mosquitoes feed on blood from mammals, such as mice. Mice eat grasses and other plants, which use energy from the sun to make their own food.

### Think and Write

1. **Scientific Inquiry** Choose an animal in Tennessee that eats other animals. Make a drawing that represents the food chain for the animal you chose.

2. **Scientific Thinking** Gray bats are protected because there are very few remaining. What might happen to the cave ecosystem in Hubbard's Cave if gray bats no longer lived there?

**Most adult moths sip liquids, such as nectar from flowers.**

3

# Honeybees in Tennessee

At the West Tennessee Agricultural Museum in Milan, you can learn a lot about the history of farming. On a warm afternoon in the nearby fields, you're sure to hear honeybees. Observe a bee for a few minutes, and you'll probably see it flying from one flower to another.

You may know that honey is made by honeybees. They visit flowers and sip a sweet liquid there called nectar. Then they carry the nectar back to the hive and use it to make honey. Bees also collect a powdery substance called pollen. On the back legs, a part called the pollen basket helps hold the pollen. Bees use pollen for food in the hive.

This bee has collected pollen from several apple blossoms.

**GLE 0507.2.2** Explain how organisms interact through symbiotic, commensal, and parasitic relationships.

**ENGAGE**

**These beehives were placed in this apple orchard so the bees will pollinate the flowers.**

## Bees Are Important

Flowers are important to bees because they provide bees with food. Bees are also important to plants because they help plants reproduce.

To make seeds, pollen must move between flowers. Bees carry pollen between flowers. Farmers often rely on honeybees to pollinate some crops. Apples, watermelons, sunflowers, squash, cotton, and soybeans are just a few of the plants that bees pollinate. Many farmers pay beekeepers to place beehives in their fields when their crops are flowering. Bees and flowering plants have a relationship called *mutualism.* Both living things benefit from the relationship.

## Other Kinds of Relationships

Other kinds of relationships exists between living things. In *parasitism,* one of the living things is harmed. Fleas, ticks, and heartworms are parasites of dogs. Mites are tiny animals that suck blood from bees. The mites benefit from the relationship, but the bees are harmed.

### Think and Write

❶ **Scientific Thinking** Why isn't the relationship between honeybees and mites mutualism?

❷ **Scientific Inquiry** Gregor Mendel studied pea plants in a large outdoor garden. He wanted to know what kind of offspring were produced when pollen from a purple flower was transferred to white flowers. Why was it important for Mendel to remove the flower parts that produce pollen?

Norris Dam

# Norris Dam

**B**eavers build their lodges in ponds. When a pond isn't available, beavers form their own pond by building a dam on a stream. The dam causes the water to back up, and a fast-flowing stream forms a still pond.

Like beavers, people build dams on rivers. The oldest dams were built to provide water to farmers. Today, there are hundreds of dams in Tennessee; many of them are small. However, some of them, such as the Norris Dam, are large. Norris Dam is 81 m (265 ft) high, which is as high as a 26-story building. It was completed in 1936.

## Effects on the Environment

When a dam is built, it changes the environment. Often there are forests and grasslands along a river. As river water backs up behind a dam, a large lake forms. The forests and grasslands disappear under the lake. Plants and animals that lived there must find new places to live or they may die. Many dams have fish ladders that help fish travel up a river.

Water stored in Norris Lake is available during droughts.

**GLE 0507.2.3** Establish the connections between human activities and natural disasters and their impact on the environment.

**ENGAGE**

# Floods and Droughts

Building a dam has good effects. Floods can occur when there is a lot of rain. Dams can be used to control how much water flows down a river, which can keep flooding from happening. On the other hand, the lake formed behind a dam can provide water during droughts. Droughts occur when an area has much less rain than usual.

Norris Lake formed after Norris Dam was completed in 1936.

## Think and Write

**1** **Science and Technology** How would a dam affect fish that migrate up and down a river? What technology helps solve this problem?

**2** **Scientific Thinking** What are two ways that dams can help control the effects of natural disasters?

# Build a Fish Transport

**Identify the Problem** You enjoy fishing on a river near your home. Now a dam is to be built on the river. The fish will be trapped on the other side of the dam, and there will be no more fish for you to catch.

**Think of a Solution** Design a fish-transport model that will allow fish to get past this barrier so that you can keep fishing. List the characteristics the transport must have to allow fish to cross through or pass by the dam. For example, it must enable fish to pass through the dam without letting all the water through, too.

**Plan and Build** Using your list of ideas, sketch and label a design for your fish-transport model. Think about materials you could use. Then build your model.

**Test and Improve** Test your fish-transport model. Improve it, if necessary. Provide sketches and explanations of what you did.

## Communicate

1. How did you decide whether your fish-transport design was a success?

2. Describe how your list helped you build your model.

3. If constructed as part of a dam, how would your fish-transport device affect fish and other organisms in the river?

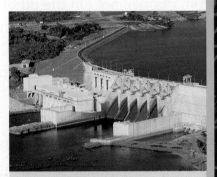

**Possible Materials**

- masking tape
- cardboard tubes
- scissors
- craft sticks
- glue
- scrap cardboard
- paper clips
- string
- rubber bands
- balloons
- straws

GLE 0507.T/E.2 Recognize that new tools, technology, and inventions are always being developed.

# TENNESSEE  UNIT A  SCIENCE

# Life Science

 **Guiding Question**

How do living things survive, obtain energy, and interact with other living things?

# Chapter 1

# Organization of Living Things

**LESSON 1**

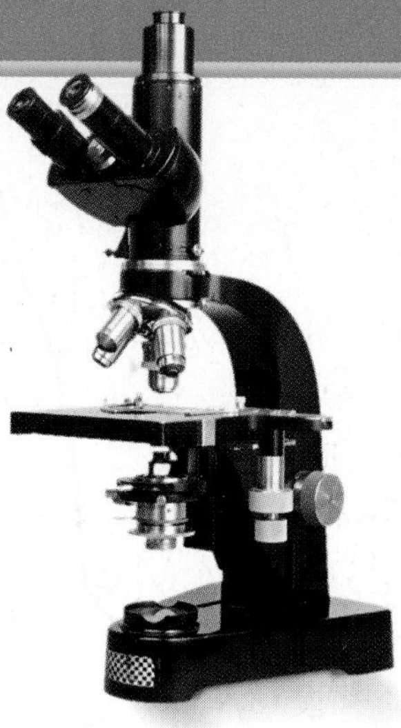

Cells are tiny fluid-filled chambers with parts that never stop moving. Why are cells so important?

**LESSON 2**

Animals crawl, fly, swim, and scurry all over the world. What does this salamander have in common with all other animals?

**Fun Facts**

All birds have feathers. Feathers make up about 45% of a bird's volume but only about 5% of a bird's weight.

amphibians
cell
cnidarians
invertebrates
nucleus
organelle
symmetry
vertebrates

 ## Vocabulary Strategies

Have you ever seen any of these terms before? Do you know what they mean?

State a description, explanation, or example of the vocabulary in your own words.

Draw a picture, symbol, example, or other image that describes the term.

**Glossary** p. H18

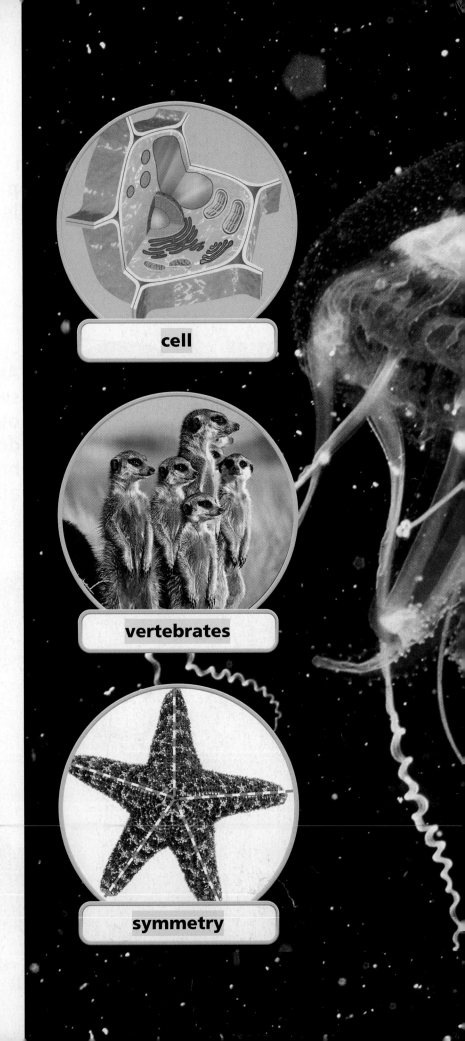

cell

vertebrates

symmetry

invertebrate

## Start with Your Standards

### Inquiry

**GLE 0507.Inq.3** Organize data into appropriate tables, graphs, drawings, or diagrams.

**GLE 0507.Inq.5** Recognize that people may interpret the same results in different ways.

### Technology & Engineering

**GLE 0507.T/E.1** Describe how tools, technology, and inventions help to answer questions and solve problems.

**GLE 0507.T/E.2** Recognize that new tools, technology, and inventions are always being developed.

### Life Science

**Standard 1—Cells**

**GLE 0507.1.1** Distinguish between the basic structures and functions of plant and animal cells.

**Standard 5—Biodiversity and Change**

**GLE 0507.5.1** Investigate physical characteristics associated with different groups of animals.

**Interact with this chapter.**

 www.eduplace.com/tnscp

13

**TENNESSEE STANDARDS**

**GLE 0507.Inq.5** Recognize that people may interpret the same results in different ways.
**GLE 0507.1.1** Distinguish between the basic structures and functions of plant and animal cells.

**Guiding Question**

# What Are the Parts of a Cell?

## Why It Matters...

All living things, from water plants to hippos, are made of cells. When you learn about the parts of cells and their functions, you can better understand how organisms like this hippopotamus live and interact with their environments.

## PREPARE TO INVESTIGATE

### Inquiry Skill

**Communicate** You can share science results by making sketches, charts, graphs, or models, and by speaking and writing.

### Materials

- microscope
- prepared slides of various plant and animal tissues

### Science and Math Toolbox

For step 2, review **Using a Microscope** on page H2.

# Get Closer!
## Procedure

STEP 1

1. **Observe** Work in a small group. Take turns looking through a microscope at each slide. Note the titles of the slides, which tell the sources of the samples.

2. **Communicate** Draw a picture of the cells in each sample. Next to the picture write the name of the sample, and whether it comes from a plant or an animal.

STEP 2

3. **Compare** Compare drawings with the other members of your group. Discuss how all the plant cells are similar. Discuss how all the animal cells are similar.

4. **Use Models** After you discuss the cells with your group, draw a diagram of a typical plant cell and a diagram of a typical animal cell.

# Think and Write

1. **Communicate** Discuss how your diagrams of typical cells show the differences between plant and animal cells.

2. **Infer** Compare the outer boundaries of an animal cell and a plant cell. What differences between plants and animals do the cell boundaries help explain?

3. **Hypothesize** Do you think the cells of all plants and animals share the characteristics you identified? How could you test your hypothesis?

0507.1.1

**Guided Inquiry**

**Use Models** Cells vary a great deal in size. Your cells are almost 100 times bigger than a bacteria cell. Build or draw a model to show the difference in size between a human and a bacteria cell.

# Cells

**VOCABULARY**

cell

nucleus

organelle

**GRAPHIC ORGANIZER**

**Compare and Contrast**
Use a Venn diagram to list similarities and differences between animal cells and plant cells.

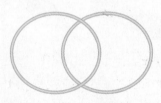

**GLE 0507.1.1** Distinguish between the basic structures and functions of plant and animal cells.

## Building Blocks of Life

The basic unit that makes up living things is the **cell.** All living things, from tiny bacteria to the largest whale, are made of cells.

When you look at most living things, you cannot see individual cells. That is because most cells are much too small to be seen with the unaided eye. The invention of the microscope made it possible for scientists to discover cells and the structures within them.

In 1665, English scientist Robert Hooke studied a slice of cork under a microscope. He observed that cork was divided into many tiny, box-shaped sections. Hooke called these sections cells because they reminded him of the small rooms in which monks of the time lived.

All of Hooke's observations about cells involved the remains of dead cells. Dutch microscope maker Anton van Leeuwenhoek became the first person to observe living cells. He observed tiny living things within a drop of water.

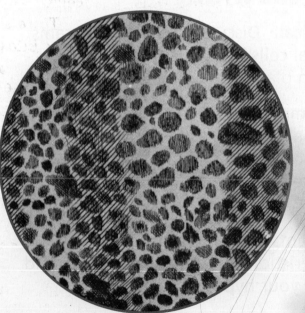

**Year 1665 ▶**
Hooke used a microscope to study thin slices of cork. He observed thin, boxy sections that he called cells.

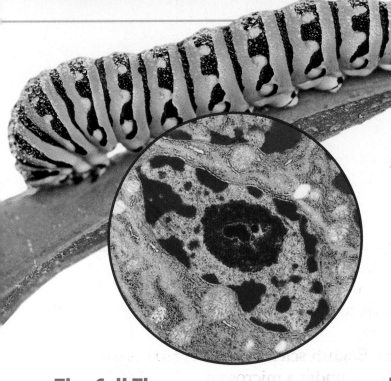

◀ **Today**
Scientists know that all living things are made of cells. This image from an electron microscope shows a nerve cell nucleus magnified 3,980 times (3,980X).

## The Cell Theory

By using new and improved microscopes, scientists were able to observe cells in more detail. In 1838, German scientist Matthias Schleiden compared different plants and plant parts. He concluded that all plants are made of cells. Another scientist drew the same conclusion about animals. Twenty years later, German physician Rudolf Virchow reasoned that cells come only from other cells.

These conclusions were eventually organized into a single theory known as the cell theory. The theory states:

* All living things are made of one or more cells.
* The cell is the smallest unit of a living organism.
* Cells come from other cells.

Today, scientists continue to use new equipment and techniques to study cells. The additional evidence continues to support the cell theory.

## Microscope Development

The earliest microscopes used a single lens to collect and focus light. In time, two lenses were combined to form a compound light microscope. Its magnifying power is the power of each lens multiplied together.

Modern light microscopes can magnify objects up to 2,000 times, or 2,000X. That's powerful enough to see not just cells, but structures within cells.

The electron microscope (EM) came into use during the 1930s. EMs use rapidly moving electrons instead of light to make images of objects. EMs may magnify objects 40,000X or more. Today, the scanning electron microscope (SEM) has taken this technology still further. SEMs allow scientists to study the three-dimensional structure of the surfaces of cells and other tiny things.

◎ **FOCUS CHECK** How does Hooke's microscope compare to microscopes today?

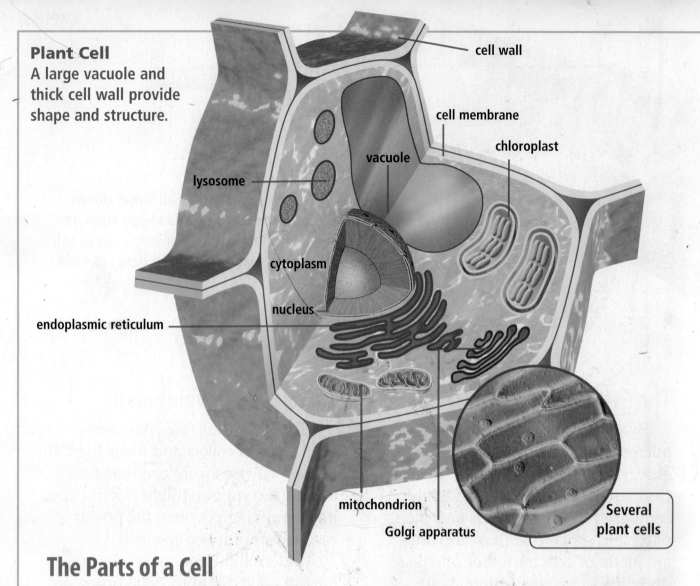

**Plant Cell**
A large vacuole and thick cell wall provide shape and structure.

cell wall

cell membrane

chloroplast

vacuole

lysosome

cytoplasm

nucleus

endoplasmic reticulum

mitochondrion

Golgi apparatus

Several plant cells

# The Parts of a Cell

Cells contain even smaller structures called **organelles.** These structures perform specific functions in the cell.

Animal cells and plant cells have many of the same organelles, but some are quite different. As you read through this section, refer to the organelle or cell part in the illustrations.

**Nucleus** The **nucleus** directs the activities of the cell. It stores a molecule called DNA, which determines an organism's traits. DNA stores genetic information, which is passed from parents to their offspring.

**Cell Membrane** The cell membrane is a thin, flexible covering that surrounds all types of cells. It allows food, water, and gases to enter the cell and wastes to leave.

**Cell Wall** In plant cells only, the cell wall is a rigid outer layer that surrounds the cell membrane. The cell wall protects the cell and helps the plant stand upright. Pores in the cell wall allow materials to pass in and out.

**Cytoplasm** Between the nucleus and the cell membrane is the cytoplasm. All of the remaining organelles are located within the cytoplasm. They are suspended there in a thick fluid.

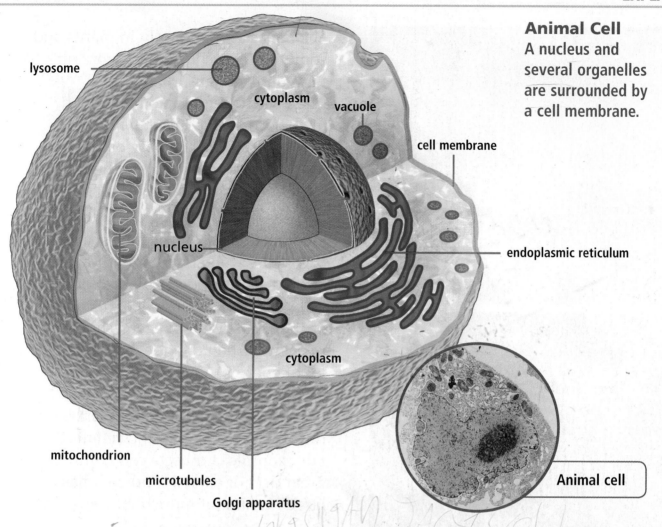

lysosome

cytoplasm

vacuole

**Animal Cell**
A nucleus and several organelles are surrounded by a cell membrane.

cell membrane

nucleus

endoplasmic reticulum

cytoplasm

mitochondrion

microtubules

Golgi apparatus

Animal cell

**Ribosomes** Tiny ribosomes are scattered throughout the cell. Unlike organelles, ribosomes are not surrounded by membranes. Ribosomes assemble compounds called proteins. Proteins make up the structural components of cells, and they allow the cell to perform nearly all chemical reactions.

**Lysosomes** Lysosomes are small, ball-shaped organelles that help the cell break down nutrients and old cell parts. Lysosomes are common in animal cells, but rare in plants.

**Vacuoles** Vacuoles are membrane-bound sacs that are filled with fluid. They store water, food, waste, and other substances the cell processes.

Animal cells may have small vacuoles. Plant cells, however, often have one large, central vacuole. When the vacuole in a plant cell is full, the cell is rigid. If the vacuoles in many cells lose water, the plant will wilt.

**Golgi apparatus** The Golgi apparatus receives proteins, then processes them for "shipment" outside the cell. This organelle is a system of membranes. It modifies and refines proteins, sometimes adding compounds that will protect them from being broken apart.

**FOCUS CHECK** Compare and contrast vacuoles in plant cells to vacuoles in animal cells.

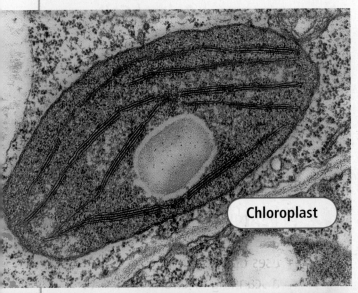

**Chloroplast**

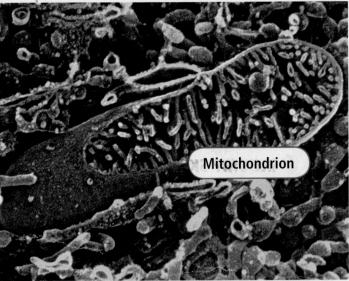

**Mitochondrion**

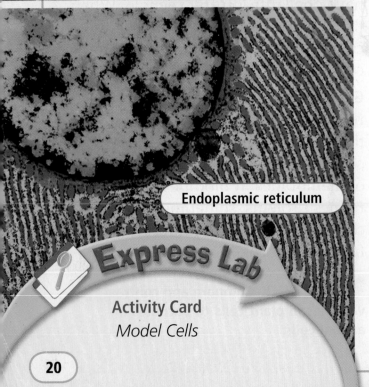

**Endoplasmic reticulum**

**Chloroplasts** Found only in plants and some protists, chloroplasts contain pigments that absorb sunlight. They use the energy to make food in a process called *photosynthesis*. Chloroplasts are the only organelles that can perform photosynthesis. The pigment chlorophyll gives plants their green color.

**Mitochondria** Large, peanut-shaped organelles, called mitochondria, are known as the "power plants" of the cell. Inside them, sugars break apart as they react with oxygen. The process releases carbon dioxide, water, and a lot of energy.

In both plant and animal cells, the number of mitochondria depends on the amount of energy the cell needs. For example, a muscle cell requires a great deal of energy, and so it has a large number of mitochondria.

**Endoplasmic reticulum** The endoplasmic reticulum (ER) is a system of membranes and tubes. The membranes twist and turn through the cell, creating passages through which materials can pass.

A cell usually contains two kinds of ER, called rough and smooth. Rough ER is dotted with ribosomes. This type of ER is common in cells that secrete lots of proteins. Smooth ER is not covered by ribosomes. Its activities include breaking down toxic substances and controlling the levels of certain chemicals.

**FOCUS CHECK** Compare and contrast chloroplasts and mitochondria.

**Express Lab**

**Activity Card**
*Model Cells*

# Lesson Wrap-Up

## Visual Summary

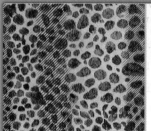

Cells were first discovered more than 300 years ago.

Microscopes enable scientists to look at and study cells.

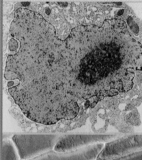

Cells contain smaller structures called organelles. Each performs a specific function.

Unlike animal cells, plant cells are surrounded by cell walls. They typically have a boxy shape.

## Check for Understanding

**COMPARE PLANT AND ANIMAL CELLS**
Make a large Venn diagram that compares and contrasts plant cells and animal cells. Make sure your diagram identifies the cell structure in which photosynthesis occurs.

✔ 0507.1.2
✔ 0507.3.1

# Review

❶ **MAIN IDEA** What are the three main points of the cell theory?

❷ **VOCABULARY** Write a sentence using the terms *cell* and *nucleus*. Explain the role of the nucleus in the cell.

❸ **READING SKILL: Compare and Contrast** How are the uses of a light microscope and a scanning electron microscope similar? How are they different?

❹ **CRITICAL THINKING: Evaluate** How would you determine whether a cell came from an animal or a plant? Discuss cell parts in your answer.

❺ **INQUIRY SKILL: Communicate** Write a paragraph explaining how a cell membrane is similar to a cell wall. How is it different?

## TCAP Prep

Which of these organelles is part of a plant cell but not an animal cell?

**A** mitochondria
**B** cell membrane
**C** chloroplast
**D** nucleus

SPI 0507.1.1

## Technology

Visit **www.eduplace.com/tnscp** to learn more about the parts of a cell.

# History of the Microscope

Today's microscopes are much more complex and powerful than those used hundreds of years ago. As you read about the different microscopes, compare them to the ones you use in your classroom.

**Egyptians polish rock crystals in the shape of convex lenses.**

**Eyeglasses are invented in Italy.**

**Anton van Leeuwenhoek uses a microscope to observe free-living protists, which he calls "animalcules."**

| ~2600 B.C. | ~1285 | 1665 | 1673 |

**Robert Hooke uses a microscope of magnification 30× to observe cells in cork.**

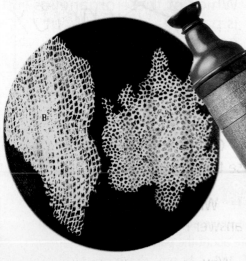

▲ Drawing of cork cells made by Robert Hooke

**GLE 0507.T/E.1** Describe how tools, technology, and inventions help to answer questions and solve problems. **GLE 0507.T/E.2** Recognize that new tools, technology, and inventions are always being developed.

EXTEND

## Modern Microscopes

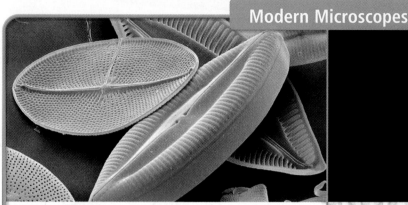

**SEM (3-D)**
This scanning electron micrograph (SEM) shows two kinds of diatoms, magnified 1,750×.

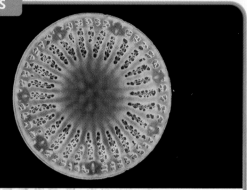

**TEM (cross-section)**
This transmission electron micrograph (TEM) shows a diatom that lives in fresh water.

Carl Zeiss produces the first commercial microscope that forms images from ultraviolet (UV) light.

The scanning probe microscope is invented. It works by measuring current. It produces highly detailed images of surfaces.

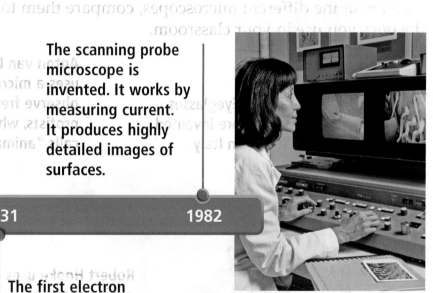

**1904        1931              1982**

The first electron microscope is built.

 **Sharing Ideas**

1. **READING CHECK** Compare the microscopes of the past to those that scientists use today.

2. **WRITE ABOUT IT** Write three questions that a scientist could answer by using a microscope.

3. **TALK ABOUT IT** Why do you think many scientists name the microscope as the most important tool for studying living things?

23

⚡ **TENNESSEE STANDARDS**

**GLE 0507.Inq.3** Organize data into appropriate tables, graphs, drawings, or diagrams.
**GLE 0507.5.1** Investigate physical characteristics associated with different groups of animals.

# How Are Animals Classified?

## Why It Matters...

Eagles, snakes, whales, and humans: all are examples of animals. Classifying animals shows what humans share with all other animals and what makes humans unique. It also helps scientists understand the animal kingdom.

## PREPARE TO INVESTIGATE

### Inquiry Skill

**Communicate** You can share the results of investigations through words, sketches, charts and graphs, or physical models.

### Materials

- hand lens
- preserved animals or parts, such as a clam shell, snail shell, or starfish
- pictures of various animals

### Science and Math Toolbox

For step 4, review **Making a Chart to Organize Data** on page H11.

## Directed Inquiry

STEP 1

# Organizing Animals

## Procedure

1. **Observe** Use the hand lens to carefully examine each animal specimen and picture. Pay close attention to how they are alike and how they are different.

2. **Record Data** In your *Science Notebook*, record each specimen's characteristics in a table like the one at right. Describe the similarities and differences as you record your observations.

STEP 2

| Specimen | Characteristics |
|----------|-----------------|
|          |                 |
|          |                 |
|          |                 |
|          |                 |
|          |                 |

3. **Classify** Look at the characteristics you recorded. Are there two main groups into which you can sort all the specimens? Sort them and name the two groups.

4. **Classify** How are the specimens in each group similar to each other? How are they different? Sort the specimens into additional groups based on characteristics they share. Organize your groups into a chart.

STEP 3

## Think and Write

1. **Infer** All of the specimens you studied are animals. What characteristics do you think all animals have in common?

2. **Communicate** Make a poster showing the animal specimens you have grouped. Explain to your teacher and class why you organized the groups as you did.

### Guided Inquiry

**Design an Experiment**
How picky are the wild birds in your neighborhood? Will they eat any kind of birdseed, or only certain kinds? Design an experiment to find out. Ask your teacher to approve your procedure.

0507.5.1

# Classifying Animals

## GRAPHIC ORGANIZER

**Main Idea and Details**
Use the chart to write down the heading of each section and its main points.

**GLE 0507.5.1** Investigate physical characteristics associated with different groups of animals.

## The Animal Kingdom

The Kingdom Animalia includes an amazing variety of creatures. Some of these creatures swim, some fly, many walk. Some do all of these things. There are animals that you can see only with a microscope. Others are as tall as a house. Humans belong to the animal kingdom. They share several characteristics with all animals.

Animals have some of the same characteristics as organisms from other kingdoms as well. Like plants, animals have many cells. Yet unlike plants, animals do not take in energy from the Sun as plants do. Animals take in food from their environment by eating. They break down and digest food for its energy and nutrients.

radial symmetry

bilateral symmetry

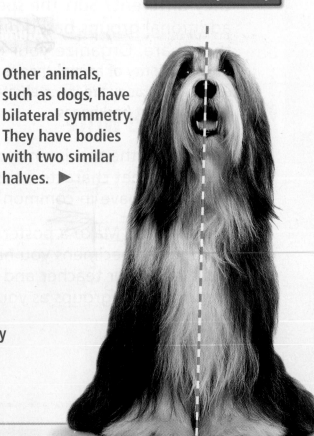

Other animals, such as dogs, have bilateral symmetry. They have bodies with two similar halves. ▶

▲ Animals with radial symmetry have body parts arranged equally around a middle point, such as the starfish shown here.

# Characteristics of Animals

Biologists study many characteristics to classify animals. These are the most common:

- Animals are multicellular with specialized cells. In most animals, cells form tissues and organs.
- Animals require oxygen to breathe.
- Animals consume other organisms to get the nutrients and energy they need.
- Most animals are able to move at some point in their lives.
- Most animals reproduce sexually.

Once an organism has been identified as an animal, it can be further classified into phylum, class, order, family, genus, and species.

**FOCUS CHECK** How do animals get their food?

**ANIMAL KINGDOM**
- **Many-celled**
- **Require oxygen**
- **Eat food**
- **Most move from place to place**
- **Reproduce sexually**

**Meerkats** live in the Kalahari Desert in Africa. They live in family groups in which all members share in caring for the young, watching out for predators, and getting food.

## Animal Species

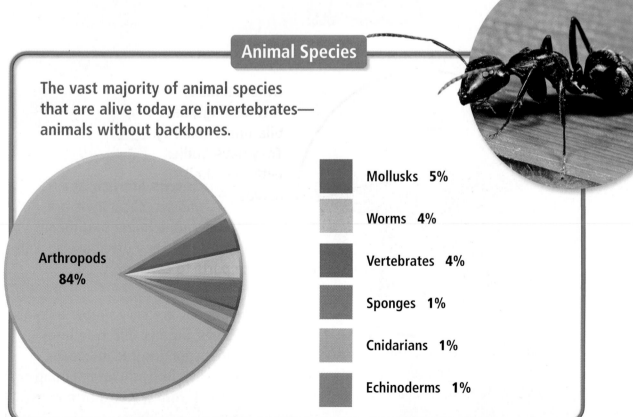

The vast majority of animal species that are alive today are invertebrates—animals without backbones.

Arthropods 84%

Mollusks 5%

Worms 4%

Vertebrates 4%

Sponges 1%

Cnidarians 1%

Echinoderms 1%

## Invertebrates

All animals without backbones are called **invertebrates** (ihn VUR tuh brihts). Invertebrates are very diverse and include the largest number of animal species.

As you study the photos of invertebrates, note the different types of body symmetries. **Symmetry** is a matching pattern of body shape.

**FOCUS CHECK** How are invertebrates alike and different?

Jellyfish

▲ **Cnidarians** Jellyfish and coral are **cnidarians** (ny DAIR ee uhns). They have simple digestive systems that include mouths. They have radial symmetry, meaning their parts repeat around a center.

Sea Cucumber

▲ **Echinoderms** Starfish, sea urchins, and sea cucumbers are echinoderms, a name that means "spiny skin." They often use sucker-like parts to catch prey.

Sponge

◄ **Sponges** Sponges are very simple animals. They lack tissues, organs, and true body symmetry. Most sponges live in oceans, although a few live in freshwater. Sponges filter bits of food from water that passes through them.

Lobster

Scorpion

◄ **Arthropods** Lobsters, crabs, spiders, and insects are all types of arthropods, the animal group with the most species. Arthropods have jointed parts surrounded by a hard covering called an exoskeleton. They have bilateral symmetry, meaning mirror-image left and right halves.

Squid

Snail

◄ **Mollusks** Clams and oysters are mollusks, as are snails, squids, and octopuses. Mollusks have soft bodies, and most have shells. They live, eat, and move in many different ways. For example, adult clams stay put, snails move very slowly, while squids and octopuses are some of the fastest creatures in the water!

**Worms** Different groups of worms include flatworms, roundworms, and a group that includes earthworms. All have bilateral symmetry, with clearly defined heads and simple organ systems. Some are parasites, meaning they live and feed off the body of a host. ▶

Bristleworm

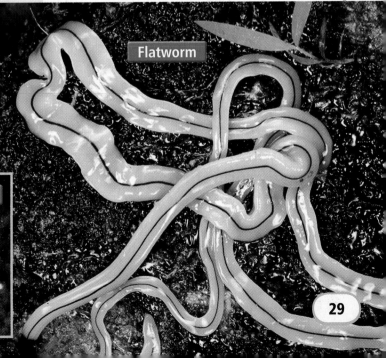

Flatworm

29

**Fish** Most fish have streamlined bodies that allow them to swim easily. What other characteristics do these fish share?

## Cold-blooded Vertebrates

All animals that have a backbone are called **vertebrates** (VUR tuh brihts). A backbone is a series of bones joined together with a flexible material called cartilage.

Vertebrates may be warm-blooded or cold-blooded. This doesn't refer to the actual temperature of the blood but rather to how the body temperature is maintained.

Reptiles, amphibians, and most fish are called cold-blooded. The body temperature of cold-blooded animals depends on the temperature outside their bodies.

If you've seen snakes or lizards in early spring, for example, they probably were moving slowly. Low temperatures cool their bodies and slow down movement. In the warm weather of summer, though, reptiles might move very quickly.

**Fish** Animals called fish include a great number and variety of species. Most fish have a bony skeleton, but some, such as sharks, have a skeleton that is only cartilage.

Fish have gills that allow them to breathe in water. The gills take oxygen from the water. All animals breathe oxygen, even animals that live in water.

Most fish are cold-blooded and are covered in scales. A structure called a swim bladder helps them move up and down. Fish typically have very well-developed sensory systems, including a good sense of smell.

**Amphibians** Frogs and toads are amphibians. **Amphibians** (am FIHB ee uhns) usually need to live close to water but do not spend their entire lives in it. Some have lungs that allow them to breathe outside of water. Others don't have lungs, and instead use the smooth surface of their skin to exchange gases with the air.

Amphibians need water to reproduce. Most species have eggs that would dry out on land, so they must lay their eggs in water or moist places. Many begin their early lives in water. For example, a tadpole is a young frog. It lives in the water until it is old enough to live on land.

Salamanders and newts are amphibians with tails. Like frogs, they have smooth, moist skin. Most of these animals live in moist areas where they can easily get to water. There are some, though, that live close to deserts.

**Reptiles** Snakes are reptiles, as are turtles, tortoises, lizards, crocodiles, and alligators. All reptiles have tough outer skin, and most lay eggs.

### Amphibians
More than 500 species of salamanders have been identified. Other amphibians include frogs and toads. ▼

### Reptiles
Almost 8,000 reptile species are known. Scientists discover about 60 more each year.

The dry, flexible, scaly skin of reptiles provides them with a waterproof coating. Their skin helps them conserve water. Many reptiles live near water and spend time in it, but they reproduce on land. Reptile eggs have a tough outer covering that prevents them from easily drying out.

Reptiles are cold-blooded, but some are very good at keeping their internal body temperatures steady. A lizard may sit on a rock in the sun to warm its body. If it gets too warm, it will move to the shade.

Snakes rely on their sense of smell and their tongues to know what's going on around them. When a snake flicks its tongue, it's sampling the air or the soil.

**FOCUS CHECK** Compare animals that are cold-blooded and warm-blooded.

▲ Some birds, such as swifts and swallows, spend almost all of their waking time in the air.

▲ Water birds usually use webbed feet to paddle water. Ducks, geese, and other plant-eaters have flat beaks or bills that help them pick up slippery food.

## Warm-blooded Vertebrates

Birds and mammals are warm-blooded. They maintain constant internal body temperatures. Their body cells produce enough heat to keep their bodies warm even when the temperature outside their bodies is very low.

**Birds**  Different bird species have adapted to live almost anywhere in the world. Some birds even migrate, or travel from one place to another at different times of the year.

Birds are the only group of animals living today that have feathers. For most birds, the feathers on their wings help them to fly.

Birds have beaks instead of teeth. How do you think this affects the types of foods birds eat? Some birds eat mammals, fish, and other birds. These are the birds of prey like eagles, falcons, and owls. Birds of prey have sharp, hooked beaks. Birds like woodpeckers have long, thin beaks that allow them to dig into tree bark for their favorite food—insects.

All birds have feathers and wings, but not all birds can fly. Ostriches can run as fast as 70 kilometers per hour (45 mph).

**Express Lab**

**Activity Card**
*Observe an Animal*

**Mammals** Mammals have the most complex organs and nervous systems in the animal kingdom. A mammal's brain is relatively large. This helps mammals to learn and to perform complex behaviors.

Compare the appearance of a polar bear and a bat. Or of a dog, leopard, or human. What do they all have in common? They all have hair. Indeed, all mammals have hair at some point in their lives. The hair may be fine or thick. It may cover the entire body or only certain parts of it. Even a whale has whiskers!

All mammals feed milk to their young. Most mammals give birth to live young. The exceptions are the duck-billed platypus and two species of spiny anteater. These mammals lay leathery eggs. However, once the young hatch, they suckle milk from their mothers.

Most mammals have teeth. Some mammals, such as mountain lions, have sharp teeth that allow them to tear the flesh they need to survive. Other animals, such as horses, have flat teeth that are better for grinding the grass that they eat.

Mammals move to find food, to escape from a predator, and for many other reasons. They may move on two legs or four. Or, in the case of whales and dolphins, they move using powerful flukes.

**FOCUS CHECK** What characteristics do mammals share?

▲ Kangaroos are a type of mammal called a marsupial. They use a pouch to carry their developing young.

Some mammals are herbivores. They eat only plants. Other mammals are carnivores. They eat other animals. Bears are examples of omnivores. They eat both animals and plants. ▼

**Kingdom:** What organisms have many cells and obtain energy by ingesting food? Answer: Animalia

**Phylum:** What animals have a cord of nerves down their backs? Answer: Chordata

**Class:** What chordates have body hair and nourish their young on milk? Answer: Mammalia

**Order:** What mammals are meat-eating land predators? Answer: Carnivora

**Family:** What carnivores have a short muzzle and retractable claws? Answer: Felidae

**Genus:** What cats are large and can roar? Answer: Panthera

**Species:** What cat is the largest and usually has an orange coat with black stripes? Answer: *Panthera tigris*

# Classification System

As you have seen, each kingdom contains a huge number of species. To organize them, scientists divide the kingdoms into smaller groups.

For example, consider tigers, members of the animal kingdom. Like many animals, tigers are members of the *phylum* Chordata. The phylum is the next level of classification after kingdom.

A group called a *class* comes next. Classes of chordates include Reptilia, Amphibia, and Mammalia.

The next group is called the *order*. The food a mammal eats helps determine its order. Tigers are grouped with cats, dogs, skunks, and other animals in the order Carnivora.

*Family* and *genus* are the next levels. Animals in the same family share many characteristics. Animals in the same genus share even more. Tigers belong to the same family and genus as lions.

The most specific group is the species. Organisms of the same species are able to breed with one another. Tigers belong to the species *Panthera tigris*.

**FOCUS CHECK** To which phylum do tigers belong?

# Lesson Wrap-Up

## Visual Summary

**Animal Kingdom**

| Invertebrates | Vertebrates |
| --- | --- |
| Sponges | Fish |
| Cnidarians | Birds |
| Roundworms | Amphibians |
| Arthropods | Reptiles |
| Mollusks | Mammals |
| Echinoderms | |
| Other groups | |

## Check for Understanding

### Animal Display

Choose an animal that you would like to learn more about. Research the scientific classification of the animal, as well as its close relatives. Make a poster, diorama, or multimedia report to teach others what you learned.

 0507.5.1

Atlantic Bottlenose Dolphin
(Tursiops truncatus)

# Review

**1 MAIN IDEA** Describe the diversity of the animal kingdom.

**2 VOCABULARY** Define *invertebrate* and *vertebrate*. Compare and contrast the two groups of animals.

**3 READING SKILL: Main Idea and Details** Describe six different kinds of invertebrates.

**4 CRITICAL THINKING: Synthesize** What could you conclude if you observed an animal with feathers that couldn't fly? Is the animal a bird? Explain.

**5 INQUIRY SKILL: Communicate** Draw a chart or diagram to show how vertebrates are classified.

## TCAP Prep

Which of these structures enables fish to move up and down in water?

**A** gills
**B** scales
**C** swim bladder
**D** bony skeleton

SPI 0507.5.1

## Technology

Visit **www.eduplace.com/tnscp** to learn more about the animal kingdom.

# Living FOSSILS

You don't need a time machine to e a prehistoric creature. Just go the beach and look for a horseshoe crab. st prehistoric animal species changed er time or became extinct. But horseshoe bs have existed basically unchanged for er 400 million years!

Their survival record isn't all that's treme about them. For one thing, rseshoe crabs aren't really crabs. They long to the same class of invertebrates spiders and scorpions.

Here is another curious fact about rseshoe crabs: Their blood is blue! man blood is red because of the iron it. The blue blood comes from a copper mpound. This compound turns blue en exposed to air.

Turn over a horseshoe crab, and you can see its similarity to spiders and scorpions.

**GLE 0507.5.1** Investigate physical characteristics associated with different groups of animals.

EXTEN

# Invasion!

Every spring, millions of horseshoe crabs come ashore on the mid-Atlantic coast to mate and lay billions of eggs. Birds and other predators eat most of the eggs, but enough survive to allow the species to thrive.

**GLE 0507.5.1** Investigate physical characteristics associated with different groups of animals.
**Math GLE 0506.2.3** Develop fluency with division of whole numbers. Understand the relationship of divisor, dividend, and quotient in terms of multiplication and division. **ELA GLE 0501.3.2** Write in a variety of modes and genres, including narration, literary response, personal expression, description, and imaginative.

## Math  Types of Microscopes

The science teachers of Sheldon Elementary School want to purchase hand lenses and microscopes for a new laboratory. They researched data on the Internet, and the results are shown in the table below.

| Product | Maximum Magnification | Cost |
|---|---|---|
| Hand lens, small | 5x | $1.30 |
| Hand lens, large | 10x | $8.90 |
| Light microscope, student model | 100x | $18.20 |
| Light microscope, lab model | 400x | $256.00 |
| Light microscope, advanced model | 2,000x | $620.00 |
| Scanning electron microscope | 40,000x | $162,600 |

1. How many small hand lenses could they purchase for the cost of the least expensive microscope?

2. The teachers have budgeted $3,000 to spend on hand lenses and microscopes. Propose one way to spend this money. Describe why you think your plan makes sense.

3. How many times more powerful is the scanning electron microscope than the light microscope, advanced model? How many times more costly is it?

 **Writing**   **Narrative/Tell a Story**

Write a story about taking a trip to a place that no one has ever visited. Describe an animal you discovered, and tell how you would classify it.

## Chef

Chefs prepare all kinds of creative and tasty dishes for restaurants. They also work at schools, office buildings, and other places that serve food.

Good chefs know all about the food they serve! Because foods come from living things, chefs need to know the nutritional value of different plants, animals, and fungi. They also need to know how to make different foods look appealing and taste delicious.

### What It Takes!

- A certificate from a cooking school or training on the job
- Keen senses of taste and smell
- An artistic flair, to prepare attractive dishes

## Botanist

Botany is the scientific study of plants. Botanists may work to develop heartier crops or cures for plant diseases. Or they may research new drugs from plants.

Some botanists travel the world to study unusual plants. Others work in laboratories, conducting experiments on plant parts and plant cells. Still others work with farmers, dieticians, landscape designers, or other people who work with plants.

### What It Takes!

- A degree in botany, biology, or ecology
- An interest in plants
- An appreciation for nature

### Vocabulary

**Complete each sentence with a term from the list.**

1. Animals, such as worms, that do not have a backbone are _____.

2. Every living thing is made of at least one _____.

3. Frogs and salamanders are examples of _____.

4. Jellyfish with stinging tentacles are classified as _____.

5. In plant and animal cells, genetic information is stored in the _____.

6. The bodies of many animals have two equal halves, which is called bilateral _____.

7. Even though a shark's backbone is made of cartilage, sharks are still classified as _____.

8. Tiny structures that perform a certain function inside a cell are _____.

**amphibians**

**cell**

**cnidarians**

**invertebrates**

**nucleus**

**organelles**

**symmetry**

**vertebrates**

### TCAP Inquiry Skills

9. **Classify** How do microscopes help scientists classify organisms?
   GLE 0507.Inq.2

10. **Communicate** Draw a sketch of an organism you studied. List three facts about this organism.   GLE 0507.Inq.3

11. **Predict** What do you predict would happen to a plant if all of its chloroplasts were removed?   GLE 0507.Inq.1

12. **Infer** Mammals that live in cold environments usually have more hair than mammals in warm environments. Infer how hair benefits a mammal in an cold environment.   GLE 0507.5.1

### Map the Concept

Copy the concept map below. Use it to identify the five types of vertebrates.   GLE 0507.5.1

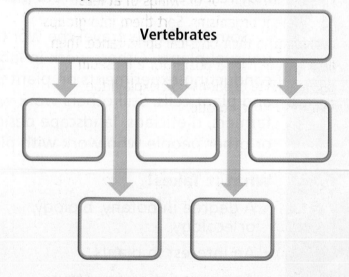

Vertebrates

## Critical Thinking

**13. Synthesize** How could new knowledge change the way that scientists classify organisms?  **GLE 0507.5.1**

**14. Evaluate** What physical characteristics help fish live in water?  **GLE 0507.5.1**

**15. Apply** Suppose you want to use your school as a model of a single cell. Choose three organelles, and explain what parts of your school would be best to represent these organelles.  **GLE 0507.1.1**

**16. Analyze** A student counts 15 chloroplasts in a leaf cell. She can find no chloroplasts in a root cell. Explain the difference.  **GLE 0507.1.1**

## ✔ Check for Understanding

### Museum Display

Find photographs or drawings of at least 15 different organisms. Sort them into groups according to their physical appearance. Then arrange them on a poster for a museum display. Write captions that explain the features of each group.

✔ 0507.5.1

## TCAP TCAP Prep

**Answer the following questions.**

**17** Which animal has gills and fins that enable it to survive under water?

 **A** largemouth bass

 **B** snapping turtle

 **C** bottlenose dolphin

 **D** green sea turtle  **SPI 0507.5.1**

**18** Which observations could have been made while looking at an animal cell?

 **F** has a cell wall and mitochondria

 **G** has a nucleus and chloroplasts

 **H** has a cell membrane and a nucleus

 **J** has a cell wall and a nucleus  **SPI 0507.1.2**

**19** Which trait would you expect to find in most birds that swim?

 **A** a sharp beak

 **B** webbed feet

 **C** strong claws

 **D** long legs  **SPI 0507.5.1**

**20** Which cell part controls the activities of the rest of the cell?

 **F** cell membrane

 **G** cell wall

 **H** cytoplasm

 **J** nucleus  **SPI 0507.1.1**

# Ecosystems, Communities, and Biomes

# Lesson Preview

Note Book

## LESSON 1

**Sunlight, water, air, plants, animals, and you—how do you and other living things interact with the environment?**

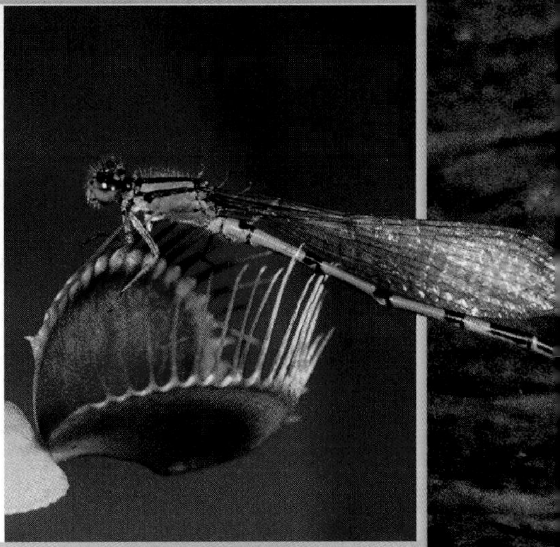

## LESSON 2

**Lots of rain or plenty of sunshine—in which type of biome do you live?**

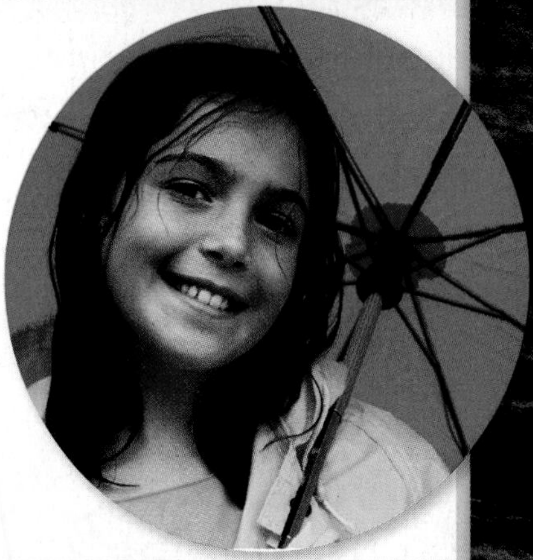

## LESSON 3

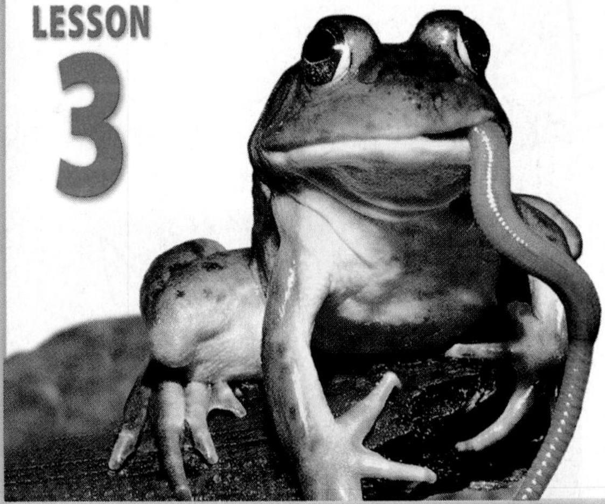

**Producers, consumers, decomposers—can you find your way around a food web?**

## Fun Facts

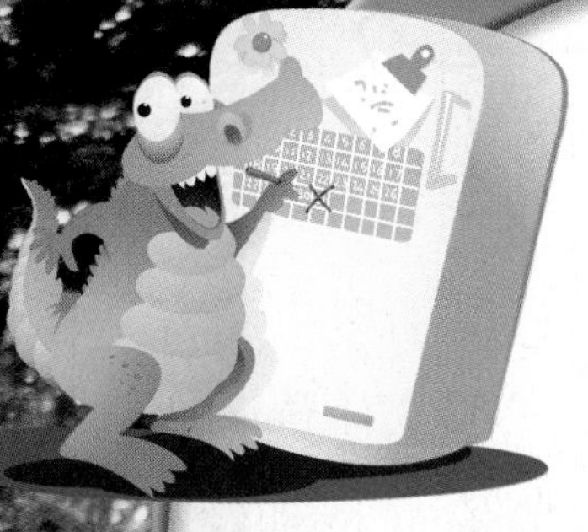

Alligators have a very slow metabolism. Some alligators can go six months without eating!

biome
climate
community
desert
★ ecosystem
food chain
food web
grasslands
population
taiga
temperate forest
tropical rain forest
tundra

★ = Tennessee Academic Vocabulary

 **Vocabulary Strategies**

Have you ever seen any of these terms before? Do you know what they mean?

State a description, explanation, or example of the vocabulary in your own words.

Draw a picture, symbol, example, or other image that describes the term.

**Glossary** p. H18

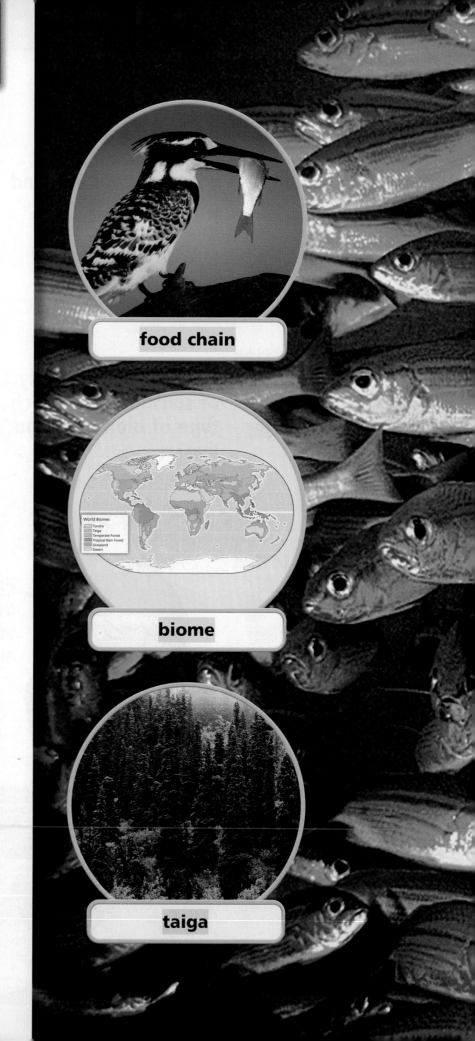

food chain

biome

taiga

population

# Start with Your Standards

## Inquiry

**GLE 0507.Inq.1** Explore different scientific phenomena by asking questions, making logical predictions, planning investigations, and recording data.

**GLE 0507.Inq.3** Organize data into appropriate tables, graphs, drawings, or diagrams.

## Life Science

### Standard 2—Interdependence

**GLE 0507.2.1** Investigate different nutritional relationships among organisms in an ecosystem.

### Standard 3—Flow of Matter and Energy

**GLE 0507.3.1** Demonstrate how all living things rely on the process of photosynthesis to obtain energy.

### Standard 5—Biodiversity and Change

**GLE 0507.5.1** Investigate physical characteristics associated with different groups of animals.

## Earth and Space Science

### Standard 8—The Atmosphere

**GLE 0507.8.1** Analyze and predict how major landforms and bodies of water affect atmospheric conditions.

## Interact with this chapter.

 www.eduplace.com/tnscp

Lesson 1

**TENNESSEE STANDARDS**

**GLE 0507.Inq.3** Organize data into appropriate tables, graphs, drawings, or diagrams.
**GLE 0507.2.1** Investigate different nutritional relationships among organisms in an ecosystem.

Guiding Question

# How Do Living Things Form Communities?

## Why It Matters...

You live in a community made up of trees and grasses, pets and people, and all the other living things in your area. Living things interact with one another and with nonliving things. In nature, everything an animal needs to survive—including food, air, and shelter—comes from the living and nonliving things in its environment.

## PREPARE TO INVESTIGATE

### Inquiry Skill

**Observe** When you observe, you use your senses to determine and describe the properties of objects and events.

### Materials

- soil
- 500 mL beaker
- terrarium
- organic matter, such as peat moss or decayed leaves
- food scraps
- water
- earthworms

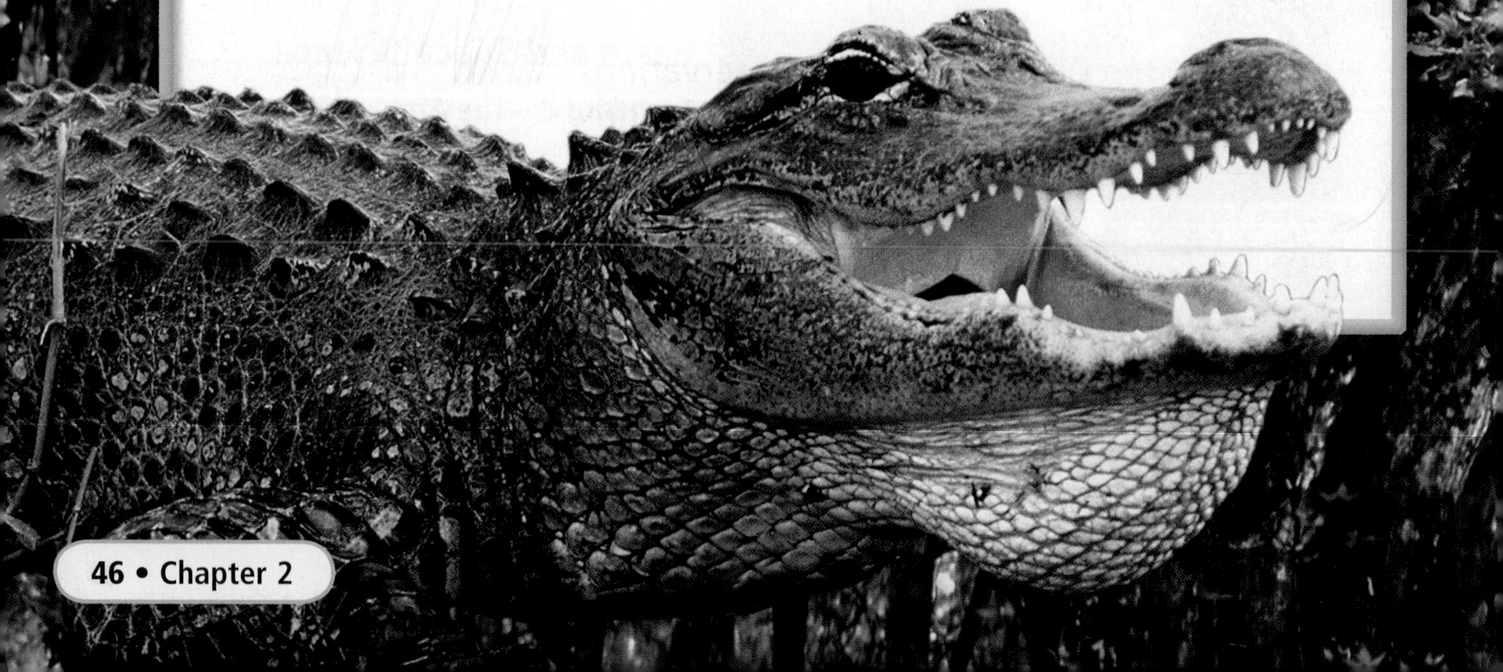

# Directed Inquiry

## Look at Life

### Procedure

**Safety:** Wash your hands after setting up the terrarium.

1. **Collaborate** Work in a small group. Measure 500 mL of soil in the beaker. Pour the soil into the terrarium. Spread a thin layer of organic matter over the soil. Add earthworms and a handful of food scraps, such as apple peels, to the terrarium.

2. **Predict** Add water to one side of the terrarium until the soil is slightly wet. In your *Science Notebook*, predict how the earthworms will react to the water. Loosely place the lid on the terrarium. Place it out of the sunlight.

3. **Classify** Make a chart in your *Science Notebook* like the one shown. Classify the things in the terrarium as living or nonliving.

4. **Observe** Each day for one week, carefully observe the earthworms and their environment.

5. **Record Data** Write down your observations in your *Science Notebook*. Include the time and day of each observation.

### Think and Write

1. **Observe** What interactions did you observe between the earthworms and their environment?

2. **Infer** Based on your observations, what do earthworms need to survive?

STEP 1

STEP 3

| Terrarium Ecosystem | |
| --- | --- |
| Living Things | Nonliving Things |
| | |

STEP 4

### Guided Inquiry

**Design an Experiment**
Predict whether earthworms grow largest in fine, coarse, or rocky soil. How could you test your prediction? Run an experiment with your teacher's approval.

✔ 0507.Inq.1

# Ecosystems

## GRAPHIC ORGANIZER

**Main Idea and Details**
As you read, write down details that describe ecosystems.

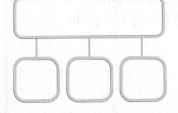

GLE 0507.2.1 Investigate different nutritional relationships among organisms in an ecosystem.

## What Is an Ecosystem?

If you put your head on the ground of a forest, what would you see? You might notice ants marching in line, or worms burrowing through the soil. Fuzzy mosses might tickle your nose, and twigs and bits of leaves might stick in your hair.

A section of forest floor is one example of an ecosystem. An **ecosystem** is made up of all the living and nonliving things that interact in one place. In a forest, the living things range from tiny bacteria and earthworms to trees towering above. Nonliving things include sunlight, soil, water, and air.

Scientists define and study small ecosystems, such as a rotting log or a patch of soil under a tree. They also study large ecosystems, such as a large forest or prairie. Regardless of size, everything in an ecosystem interacts.

**Small Ecosystems**
Soil, a rotting log, fungus, moss, and a lizard are all part of this small ecosystem.

The Florida Everglades is a large ecosystem in southern Florida. The land is swampy, covered by a thin layer of muddy water. Grasses grow tall because only a few **cypress trees** block the sunlight.

Closer to the ocean, salt water mixes with fresh water in shallow lands called estuaries. Mangrove trees thrive in estuaries, as do newly hatched fish and shrimp. Many birds nest in the mangroves and fish the waters for food.

The plants, birds, fish, and other organisms of the Everglades make up a community. A **community** is the group of living things found in an ecosystem. These living things depend upon one another for food, shelter, and other needs. They also depend upon the nonliving things in the ecosystem.

Organisms that live well in one ecosystem might not survive in another. Alligators, for example, find food and shelter only in warm, wet places. They also must drink lots of water to flush wastes from their blood.

Like the alligator, the roseate spoonbill is well suited for life in the Everglades. Its long legs and strong feet are ideal for wading. It shakes its open bill through the water to capture small fish and other animals.

**FOCUS CHECK** Describe some interactions among living things in the Everglades.

**Large Ecosystem**
The Florida Everglades includes a community of many living things, including palm trees, birds, panthers, and alligators.

Alligator

Roseate spoonbill

Florida panther

**Express Lab**

**Activity Card**
*Model Interactions in Ecosystems*

49

## Populations

You can learn a great deal by studying an individual plant, animal, or other organism. But to understand how an ecosystem functions, you need to study populations. A **population** consists of all the members of the same type of organism that live in an ecosystem.

The Everglades ecosystem includes populations of mangrove and cypress trees, alligators and spoonbills, and a wide variety of other species. The birth or death of one plant or animal is not likely to change the Everglades very much. But what if a disease killed all the mangrove trees? Or a new animal species began nesting where the spoonbills nest? Events like these can affect the entire community.

To evaluate ecosystems, scientists consider factors that affect the whole community. One major concern for the Everglades is the water supply. The Everglades depends on fresh water flowing from the north. Yet human needs are draining that supply, and those needs are growing every year.

In an ocean ecosystem, which fish would you suspect are most important in the community? Arguably, the answer is the smallest fishes, including herring and mackerel. These fish are food for bigger fish, which in turn are food for sharks, killer whales, and other big animals. Without large numbers of small fish, many other animals would starve.

**FOCUS CHECK** Why are small fish important in ocean ecosystems?

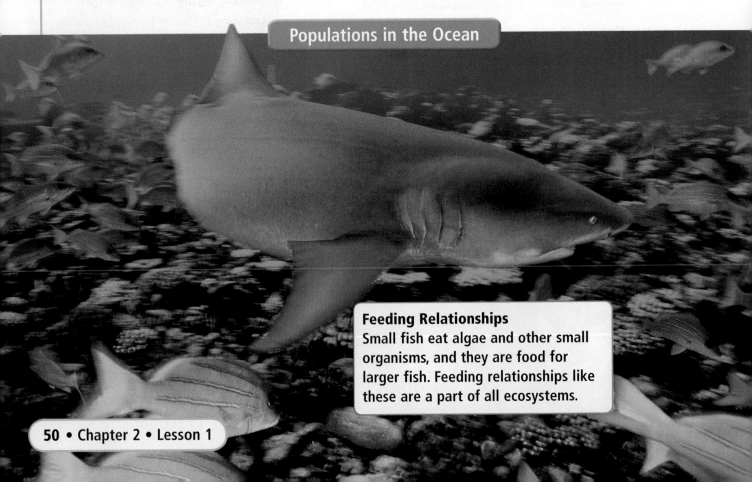

Populations in the Ocean

**Feeding Relationships**
Small fish eat algae and other small organisms, and they are food for larger fish. Feeding relationships like these are a part of all ecosystems.

## Lesson Wrap-Up

### Visual Summary

Ecosystems are made up of all the living and nonliving things that interact in a given place.

A community is made up of different populations of living things in an ecosystem.

A population consists of all the members of the same type of organism that live in a community.

### Check for Understanding

**ECOSYSTEM IMPACTS**

Think about all the living things in a forest. How would the forest community be affected if all the trees were blown down by a tornado? Draw a detailed graphic organizer that shows the sequence of events that would happen.

✔ 0507.2.1

## Review

**❶ MAIN IDEA** How do scientists classify the parts of an ecosystem?

**❷ VOCABULARY** Use the terms *ecosystem, community,* and *population* to describe the area where you live.

**❸ READING SKILL: Main Idea and Details** What nonliving things are found in ecosystems? Why are they important?

**❹ CRITICAL THINKING: Apply** What might happen if one population in an ecosystem disappeared? Give an example.

**❺ INQUIRY SKILL: Observe** Go outside with a partner and carefully observe a small patch of grass. Classify the things you observe as living or nonliving.

### TCAP Prep

Why are small fish important in a pond?

**A** They can survive in any ecosystem.

**B** They can survive without plants and algae.

**C** They can make their own food.

**D** They are food for many larger animals.

SPI 0507.2.1

### Technology

Visit **www.eduplace.com/tnscp** to learn more about ecosystems.

**TENNESSEE STANDARDS**

GLE 0507.Inq.3 Organize data into appropriate tables, graphs, drawings, or diagrams.
GLE 0507.8.1 Analyze and predict how major landforms and bodies of water affect atmospheric conditions.

Guiding Question

# What Are Biomes?

## Why It Matters...

Is your area usually hot and wet, or cold and dry? Are there thick forests or tall grasses? These types of factors affect many parts of your life, including the kind of home you live in and the clothes that you wear.

All plants and animals are affected by their environments. The prairie dogs shown below live very well on the grasslands, but would not survive on the tundra or in a rainforest. Earth's different regions support different kinds of living things.

## PREPARE TO INVESTIGATE

### Inquiry Skill

**Analyze Data** When you analyze data, you look for patterns in the information to make inferences, predictions, and other generalizations.

### Materials

- different-colored pencils
- calculator

### Science and Math Toolbox

For step 1, review **Making a Line Graph** on page H13.

# Directed Inquiry

# Compare Climates

## Procedure

**1** **Use Numbers** In your *Science Notebook* make a line graph using data in the temperature chart for Des Moines, Iowa and Iquitos, Peru. Plot the months on the *x*-axis and temperature on the *y*-axis.

**2** **Use Numbers** Use the data in the precipitation chart to make a bar graph in your *Science Notebook*. Plot the months on the *x*-axis and precipitation on the *y*-axis.

**3** **Use Numbers** Calculate average annual rates of precipitation and temperature for both places.

Des Moines, Iowa

Equator

Iquitos, Peru

| Average Temperature | | | | | | | | | | | | |
|---|---|---|---|---|---|---|---|---|---|---|---|---|
| | Jan. | Feb. | Mar. | Apr. | May | Jun. | Jul. | Aug. | Sep. | Oct. | Nov. | Dec. |
| Des Moines | −7°C | −5°C | −3°C | 3°C | 7°C | 21°C | 23°C | 22°C | 18°C | 11°C | 2°C | −4°C |
| Iquitos | 27°C | 26°C | 25°C | 25°C | 25°C | 24°C | 24°C | 25°C | 25°C | 25°C | 26°C | 26°C |

| Average Precipitation | | | | | | | | | | | | |
|---|---|---|---|---|---|---|---|---|---|---|---|---|
| | Jan. | Feb. | Mar. | Apr. | May | Jun. | Jul. | Aug. | Sep. | Oct. | Nov. | Dec. |
| Des Moines | 4 cm | 3 cm | 5 cm | 6 cm | 11 cm | 13 cm | 8 cm | 9 cm | 7 cm | 6 cm | 4 cm | 2 cm |
| Iquitos | 24 cm | 26 cm | 25 cm | 35 cm | 26 cm | 13 cm | 16 cm | 12 cm | 27 cm | 19 cm | 24 cm | 26 cm |

## Think and Write

1. **Analyze Data** Describe temperature and precipitation patterns in both places. Which place receives more precipitation? Is precipitation constant throughout the year?

2. **Compare** Use the data to compare Des Moines and Iquitos to your community.

0507.8.1

### Guided Inquiry

**Design an Experiment**
Study a map to find two cities, one inland and one near an ocean, that are at the same latitude. Research climate data for the cities, and make a chart or graph. Then draw a conclusion.

# Biomes

## VOCABULARY

biome
climate
desert
grasslands
taiga
temperate forests
tropical rain forests
tundra

## GRAPHIC ORGANIZER

**Draw Conclusions** As you read, draw conclusions about the living things in the different types of biomes.

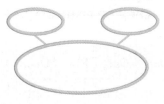

GLE 0507.5.1 Investigate physical characteristics associated with different groups of animals.

## Earth's Major Biomes

A **biome** is a large group of ecosystems that have similar characteristics. Study the map below to find the six major land biomes.

What makes biomes different from one another? The most important factor is climate. **Climate** refers to the type of weather that occurs in an area over a long period of time. Some climates are rainy, while others are quite dry. Some have a variety of temperatures, while others are almost always hot or cold.

Different climates support different populations of living things. The living things in each biome have body parts and features that help them survive in the biome. For example, the plants in a dry biome must have features for conserving or storing water.

Earth is home to six major land biomes. In each biome, climate affects the kinds of plants and animals that live there. ▼

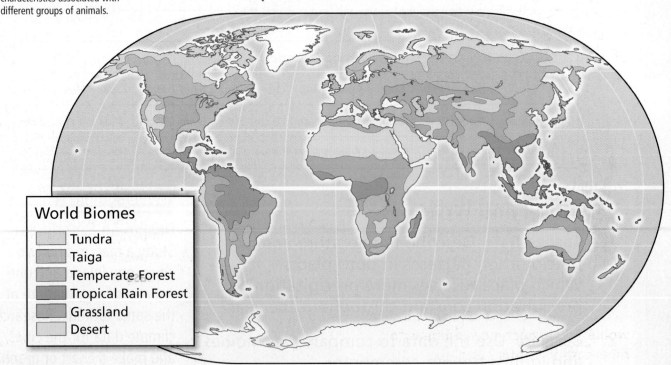

World Biomes
- Tundra
- Taiga
- Temperate Forest
- Tropical Rain Forest
- Grassland
- Desert

# Forest Biomes

Forests are home to tall trees and the animals that live in them. Forests are part of three biomes. **Tropical rain forests** are very rainy and hot. Some rain forests get more than 600 cm (240 in.) of rain each year! Temperatures range from about 18°C to 35°C (64°F to 95°F), which is like a hot summer that lasts all year.

Because of the moisture and warmth, tropical rain forests are teeming with life. In fact, more kinds of plants and animals live in this biome than in any other. Its huge mass of plants produces much of Earth's oxygen. Some of these plants might supply new medicines and other useful products.

The other type of forest biome, **temperate forests,** experiences four distinct seasons: summer, fall, winter, and spring. Temperatures range from a chilly −30°C (−22°F) to a warm 30°C (86°F). A temperate forest receives perhaps one-fifth the rainfall of a tropical forest.

These forests are home to animals such as white-tailed deer, rabbits, skunks, squirrels, and black bears. The trees include maple, oak, hickory, and beech. These trees lose their leaves in the fall and are dormant through winter. The fallen leaves decay on the ground and add nutrients to the soil.

**Tropical Rain Forest**

**Location:** near the equator
**Climate:** warm and wet

**Temperate Forest**

**Location:** eastern North America and other places
**Climate:** four distinct seasons

**⊚ FOCUS CHECK** In which forest biome would you expect more animals to hibernate in winter? Explain.

**Grasslands**

**Location:** central Africa, central U.S., and other regions
**Climate:** distinct dry season

**Desert**

**Location:** varies
**Climate:** extremely dry

## Grasslands and Deserts

Grasses cover the land in the **grasslands** biome. Trees are few and far between.

There are two main types of grasslands: prairies and savannas. Prairies are found in temperate regions, such as the central United States. Temperatures may dip as low as −40°C (−40°F) in winter and soar to 38°C (100°F) in summer. Prairie animals include prairie dogs, coyotes, hawks, and grouse.

Most savannas are found in warmer regions, such as central Africa. Yearly temperatures typically remain above 18°C (64°F). Elephants, giraffes, lions, and zebras call the savanna home.

A savanna receives as much as 100 cm (40 in.) of rain each year. But the savanna has a dry season, as do other grasslands. That's partly why trees are scarce in this biome—they do not thrive for long periods without water.

The **desert** is the driest biome. Most deserts receive less than 25 cm (10 in.) of rain each year. In fact, some deserts may not see a drop of rain all year long.

Cacti, sagebrush, and other plants are found in many deserts. Desert plants and animals are adapted to live with little water. Cacti, for example, have a waxy coating and spiny leaves to help reduce water loss. Earth's driest deserts contain little life. These deserts are filled with sandy dunes that stretch seemingly without end.

## Taiga and Tundra

The **taiga** biome has long, severe winters and short, cool summers. Temperatures may reach 10°C (50°F) during only one to three months each year. The taiga is fairly dry, each year receiving only about 50 cm (20 in.) of precipitation, mostly snow.

The most common trees in the taiga are conifers, such as pines, firs, and spruces. The leaves of these trees are thin, waxy needles that help keep in water. Their leaves do not fall all at once when the weather turns cold. Animals of the taiga include moose, deer, and wolves.

As harsh as the taiga can be, it is mild compared to the tundra. The **tundra** is Earth's coldest biome, having an average winter temperature of −34°C (−29°F). The ground is frozen for hundreds of meters down, and lower layers stay frozen all year long. This frozen ground is called permafrost.

In summer, temperatures hover just under 10°C (50°F). As the ground thaws, the tundra becomes swampy and covered with mosses, lichens, and dwarf-like trees. Mosquitoes thrive in the short summer.

Other tundra animals include polar bears, caribou, and reindeer. These animals have adaptations that help them survive in this cold biome. Polar bears, for example, have a thick layer of fat to keep them warm.

**FOCUS CHECK** How do temperatures compare in the taiga and tundra?

**Taiga**
**Location:** northern North America and Eurasia
**Climate:** severe winters and short, cool summers

**Tundra**
**Location:** near the Arctic Circle
**Climate:** extremely cold

## Marine Biomes

Look back at the map on page 54. Oceans cover about 70 percent of Earth's surface! They are home to the marine biomes.

Living things need special adaptations to live on or near the ocean shore. This is because the water level keeps changing with the tides. The intertidal zone is the area that ocean tides cover and uncover in a regular cycle. Sometimes this zone is under water, and other times it is exposed to the Sun and air.

In this zone, animals such as clams and mussels attach sticky threads to rocks so the waves won't wash them away. Other animals, including many kinds of crabs and some snails, can move about over land and underwater.

Just beyond the shore is the near-shore zone. In some places, this zone is home to an underwater forest of tall, brown seaweed called kelp. Otters and other animals live among the swaying stalks.

The presence of water and sunlight defines the zones of marine biomes. Different plants and animals live in each. ▼

**Intertidal Zone**

Mussels, sea stars, and crabs live in the constantly changing conditions of the intertidal zone.

**Near-Shore Zone**

Fish and other marine life live among the large kelp forests in some near-shore zones.

**Express Lab**

**Activity Card**
*Observe Ecosystems*

Still farther out to sea is the open ocean zone. Here, the water is deep and cold. Tiny algae float near the surface. Algae are plant-like organisms, and most are single-celled. Because algae are so numerous, they produce most of Earth's oxygen! They also provide food for ocean animals.

Even when the water is clear, sunlight mostly reaches a depth of only about 200 meters (660 ft). So, the floor of the open ocean is very cold and dark. Organisms here use special adaptations to survive in such a harsh environment. Some fish produce their own light, just as lightning bugs do on land. The light helps the fish to hunt for food.

Other unusual organisms include the giant tubeworms that live by vents on the ocean floor. These vents release heat and gases from Earth's interior. The tubeworms are unusual because the vents—not the Sun—are the source of their energy. Bacteria near the vents make food using heated chemicals, a process unlike any other on Earth. In turn, the worms get food from the bacteria.

**FOCUS CHECK** Compare the conditions in the three zones of the ocean.

Dolphins, whales, and jellyfish spend much of their time near the surface in open ocean zones.

Open Ocean Zone

Huge schools of herring, tuna, and other fish live in the middle depths of the open ocean.

Fangtooth fish and other creatures have adapted to the cold and darkness of the deepest parts of the ocean.

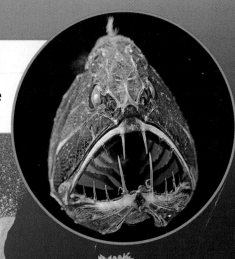

## Freshwater Ecosystems

Other bodies of water are made up of fresh water. These ecosystems include streams, rivers, ponds, lakes, and wetlands.

Streams and rivers contain flowing water. Near the beginning of a river, the current is usually fast and the water is clear. Trout and other fast-swimming fish live in this zone. Farther downstream, the current slows and the river widens. Plants are able to take root in the muddy bottom. Fish, beavers, and waterfowl may find homes here.

Kingfishers hunt for fish in fresh water. ▼

As the river flows, it picks up sediments. Near the end of the river, called the mouth, the water drops its sediments and becomes murky. Catfish and carp may live in these dark waters.

Ponds and lakes are made of still water. Some are small and may disappear during dry spells. Others, such as the Great Lakes, are huge.

Deep ponds and lakes have three different zones. Algae, plants, insects, and fish live near the sun-warmed surface. Farther down, the water is cooler, but some sunlight shines through. Here live plankton, which is a general term for many kinds of tiny organisms that live in water. Fish and other larger animals feed on the plankton.

Still farther down is a zone that is deep and cold. Bacteria and other decomposers break down dead plants and animals.

**FOCUS CHECK** What are three types of freshwater ecosystems?

# Lesson Wrap-Up

## Visual Summary

Different biomes have different climates and types of plants. Climate is influenced by temperature and precipitation.

Land biomes include tropical rain forests, temperate forests, grasslands, deserts, taiga, and tundra.

Water covers much of Earth's surface. Many organisms live in marine biomes and freshwater ecosystems.

## ✔ Check for Understanding

### ANIMAL FEATURES

Choose an animal that you think is interesting. Make a concept web about the animal. In the web, include several of the animal's characteristics. Think about how each characteristic helps the animal survive in a certain biome. Add this information to the web, connected to each characteristic. ✔ **0507.5.2**

## Review

❶ **MAIN IDEA** What factors distinguish one biome from another?

❷ **VOCABULARY** What is a biome? List six examples of biomes.

❸ **READING SKILL: Draw Conclusions** What nonliving factors are most important to include when describing a biome?

❹ **CRITICAL THINKING: Analyze** Why aren't marine algae found at depths below 200 meters? How does this influence life at these depths?

❺ **INQUIRY SKILL: Analyze Data** Which land biomes have a greater temperature range during the year, those near the equator or those in temperate regions?

### TCAP TCAP Prep

Which feature helps a cactus survive in the desert?

**A** becomes dormant in winter
**B** covered with a waxy coating
**C** loses its leaves in fall
**D** has leaves shaped like long, thin needles

**SPI 0507.5.1**

### Go Digital Technology

Visit **www.eduplace.com/tnscp** to learn more about biomes.

# Mr. Wayne's
# *Way Cool*
# Science Podcast

Each week, the students in Mr. Wayne's class host a podcast. Their discussion is broadcast over the Internet, and classes from around the country tune in to listen. This week, the class has decided to talk about biomes and how living things are adapted to live in different places. The students invited two experts, a professor and a zookeeper, to help answer the questions that listeners have.

## Characters

**Mr. Wayne**
teacher

**Dakota Dawson**
**Skyler Sparrow**
students and
podcast hosts

**Dr. Logan**
a professor

**Pat Silver**
a zookeeper

**Caller 1**
**Caller 2**
students
from
around the
country

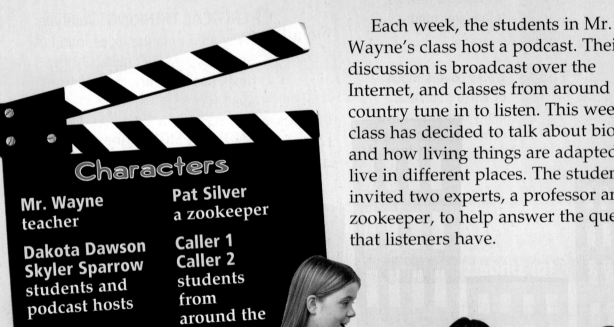

GLE 0507.5.1 Investigate physical characteristics associated with different groups of animals.

EXTEND

**Mr. Wayne:** Good afternoon and welcome to another edition of our Way Cool Science Podcast. Your hosts today are two of my students, Dakota Dawson and Skyler Sparrow.

**Dakota:** Thanks, Mr. Wayne. Hello everyone. I think we have a great show planned for you.

**Skyler:** That's right! Our class has been studying places that plants and animals live, and we wanted to share some of what we've learned.

**Dakota:** This week we're lucky to have two experts to help us answer your questions.

**Skyler:** I'd like to introduce everyone to Dr. Logan, from Upstate University, and Pat Silver, from City Zoo.

**Pat:** Thanks for inviting me to your show. At the zoo, I work with all kinds of animals from around the world.

**Dr. Logan:** I'm glad to be here, too. At the university, I study how plants are able to survive in extreme environments.

**Mr Wayne:** Let's dive right in. Our first caller is a student in Arizona. Go ahead caller, what's your question?

**Caller 1:** Hi. I just visited my grandparents in California. They have lots of trees there. Why aren't there many tall trees where I live in Arizona?

**Dakota:** I've never been to Arizona. What do you have instead of trees?

**Caller 1:** We have lots of small shrubs and cacti. There's also lots of bare soil and rock.

**Dakota:** So Arizona is part of the desert biome, right?

**Mr Wayne:** That's right, Dakota.

**Dr. Logan:** Tall trees grow only in a few biomes. A tree needs a lot more water than a cactus. They also need well-developed soil.

Desert in Arizona ▶

**Caller 1:** We have to be careful when we're playing outside. Cacti have sharp spines that hurt when you touch them.

**Dakota:** Is that so animals don't eat them?

**Dr. Logan:** That's one reason. Many cacti also have lots of spines to help shade them from the sun. That way they don't dry out.

**Caller 1:** My teacher told us that cacti also have waxy coatings on their stems to help hold in water.

**Dr. Logan:** Very good. They also have roots that spread out near the surface to grab every bit of rain they can.

**Caller 1:** Thanks for answering my question.

Polar bears have adaptations for living in the tundra.

**Dr. Logan:** You're welcome.

**Skyler:** I have another caller on Line 2. What would you like to know?

**Caller 2:** Hello. My favorite animal is the polar bear. I live in North Carolina, where we have black bears. Why can't polar bears live here, too?

**Skyler:** Good question. Let's see what our animal expert has to say.

**Pat Silver:** Who knows where polar bears live?

**Caller 2:** They live in the arctic, near the Arctic Circle and the North Pole.

**Skyler:** That biome is called the tundra.

**Pat Silver:** If you had to describe the tundra in one word, what would it be?

**Skyler and Caller 2** *(in unison):* Cold!

**Pat Silver:** Polar bears have adaptations for living in the tundra. For example, they have a thick coat of fur with two layers to help keep them warm.

**Caller 2:** Just like I wear a sweater and a jacket in winter?

**Pat Silver:** Exactly.

**Skyler:** Last year I tried to go ice-skating, and I fell down a lot! How do polar bears keep from slipping?

**Pat Silver:** Their paws are very large, and they have large claws. The pads on the bottom of their feet are also shaped like suction cups.

**Skyler:** Neat!

**GLE 0507.5.1** Investigate physical characteristics associated with different groups of animals.

EXTEND

**Caller 2:** Polar bears also use their paws to swim.

**Pat Silver:** And to catch their food—seals. Seals are larger than any food that black bears eat. Polar bears must be larger than black bears to be able to capture their food.

**Caller 2:** Since there are no seals and very warm summers in North Carolina, I guess it makes sense that polar bears don't live here.

**Skyler:** Black bears have better adaptations for living in North Carolina than polar bears do.

**Mr. Wayne:** We're getting close to the end of the show, so let's review what we've learned.

**Dakota:** Different biomes have different climates, or weather patterns.

**Skyler:** Plants and animals have adaptations to help them live in certain biomes.

**Dr. Logan:** Spines, long roots, and waxy stems are three adaptations that help a cactus live in the desert.

**Pat Silver:** Polar bears and black bears each have adaptations that are specific to the places they live.

**Mr. Wayne** (with excitement): Great job, everyone!

**Dakota:** Next week we will be talking about food chains and food webs.

**Skyler:** Don't forget to tune in and call us with your questions.

Black bears have paws and claws that are adapted for climbing trees.

## Note Book — Sharing Ideas

1. **READING CHECK** What biome do polar bears live in?

2. **WRITE ABOUT IT** How do adaptations help plants and animals?

3. **TALK ABOUT IT** Discuss the biome where you live and how living things are adapted to life there.

**TENNESSEE STANDARDS**

GLE 0507.Inq.1 Explore different scientific phenomena by asking
questions, making logical predictions, planning investigations, and
recording data.
GLE 0507.2.1 Investigate different nutritional relationships among
organisms in an ecosystem.

# What Is a Food Web?

## Why It Matters...

What did you have for breakfast?
Like this owl, you get the energy you
need from food. Food energy comes
ultimately from the Sun. It is then
passed through an ecosystem by
living things.

## PREPARE TO INVESTIGATE

### Inquiry Skill

**Use Models** When you use
models, you make and analyze a
structure or picture representing
a real-world process to better
understand how the process
works.

### Materials

- different-colored pencils
- Investigate photo card

---

**Science and Math Toolbox**

For step 2, review **Making a Chart
to Organize Data** on page H11.

---

# Directed Inquiry

## Model Energy Flow

### Procedure

1. **Hypothesize** Look at the photo card of living things. It includes grass, zebras, and a lion. Form a hypothesis about how each organism obtains its energy.

2. **Use Models** In an ecosystem, energy from food passes from one organism to another. Producers get their energy from the Sun. In your *Science Notebook*, make a chart like the one shown. Which organisms in the photo are producers? Draw the producers in the bottom level of the chart.

3. **Use Numbers** Producers get 100 units of energy from the Sun. Write this number of units on the chart. Note that producers use 90 percent of these units for their own life processes.

4. **Use Models** Which consumers eat the producers? Draw the consumers in the next level of the chart. Record the amount of energy available to them. They will use 90 percent of this energy.

5. **Use Models** Which consumer eats other consumers? Draw this consumer in the top level of the chart. Record its available energy.

STEP 1

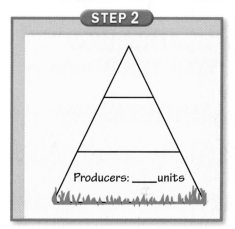

STEP 2

Producers: _____units

### Think and Write

1. **Use Numbers** How much energy is left for the living things that eat the producers? How much is left for the last consumer?

2. **Infer** Why aren't there more levels in the chart? Explain.

✔ 0507.2.1

**Guided Inquiry**

**Research** The model you used is called an energy pyramid. Use the Internet or library to research energy pyramids. What happens to energy as it is passed from one living thing to another?

# Energy Flow

## Energy from Food

Would you like to make food from a gas in the air and water from the ground? You could do that—if you were a plant. Plants are Earth's producers, as are algae and certain bacteria. A producer makes its own food from raw materials and energy.

Plants and other producers use the energy of sunlight, changing it into chemical energy. Water and carbon dioxide combine into sugars and oxygen. Sugars are the food for the plant. Plants use some of these sugars to grow, and store the rest in their tissues.

When you eat a plant, you take in energy the plant stored. You and all other animals are consumers. A consumer gets energy by eating food, not producing it.

**VOCABULARY**

food chain
food web

**GRAPHIC ORGANIZER**

**Classify** As you read, sort groups of living things according to their role in a food web.

GLE 0507.2.1 Investigate different nutritional relationships among organisms in an ecosystem.

GLE 0507.3.1 Demonstrate how all living things rely on the process of photosynthesis to obtain energy.

**First-Level Consumer**

The caterpillar is a first-level consumer that eats leaves.

**Producer**

Grass and other plants are producers. They make up the first link in most food chains.

## Food Chains

To better understand feeding relationships, scientists organize the living things of a community into food chains. A **food chain** describes how energy in an ecosystem flows from one organism to another.

Almost all food chains begin with the Sun. Producers, such as green grass, capture the Sun's energy to make food. Animals that eat plants, such as a caterpillar, are called first-level consumers or primary consumers. These animals eat plants or other producers.

The birds are second-level consumers. They eat other consumers. The cat is a third-level consumer. Notice that all the consumers rely on plants. Without plants, there would not be a food chain.

Which other organisms play a role in a food chain? If plants and animals die without being eaten, organisms called decomposers will break down the remains. Decomposers include bacteria, some protists, and fungi, as well as earthworms and other small animals. They serve to return an organism's tissues back to the soil for new organisms to use again.

In every ecosystem, different producers, consumers, and decomposers are constantly filling their roles in food chains. You, too, are part of food chains. When are you a primary consumer? Are you also a second-level consumer?

**FOCUS CHECK** Compare a producer and a consumer.

**Second-Level Consumer**

The bird is a second-level consumer that eats the caterpillar.

**Third-Level Consumer**

The cat is a third-level consumer that eats the bird.

**Decomposers**

Decomposers break down the decaying remains of dead producers and consumers.

## Food Webs

Like you, most animals take part in more than one food chain. For example, do cats eat only birds? No, cats also eat mice and fish.

A **food web** shows how food chains combine in an ecosystem. Look at the food web on the opposite page. The algae, trees, and smaller plants are producers. The mouse eats plant seeds, and it also eats insects. The snake eats insects, too, but it also eats mice. The hawk hunts both mice and snakes, and so does the fox.

By studying food webs, scientists can explain how ecosystems function. They also can predict the effects of changes to an ecosystem. If the hawks all left the ecosystem shown here, how do you think the other animals would be affected?

**Classifying Consumers** Most consumers play a similar role in every food chain they are a part of. A rabbit, for example, is always a primary consumer. It is an herbivore, meaning "plant eater."

Other consumers are second- or third-level consumers. Examples include hawks and snakes. These animals are called carnivores. The word *carnivore* means "meat eater." Many carnivores are predators, animals that hunt and kill prey.

A few animals, such as bears, eat both plants and animals. They are omnivores—the prefix *omni-* meaning "all." If you eat both plant and animal products, you are an omnivore, too.

## Cycles in Nature

Food chains and food webs show how energy flows through an ecosystem. Ecosystems have many other interactions, too.

For example, plants take up carbon dioxide from the air and release oxygen. Animals do just the opposite—they release carbon dioxide and take in oxygen. In this way, plants and animals provide one another with the gases each needs.

Another important cycle is the water cycle. All living things need water. Water leaves Earth's surface through evaporation. It returns through rain, sleet, and snow.

Nitrogen also cycles through ecosystems. Nitrogen is a gas that makes up almost four-fifths of Earth's atmosphere. All living things need nitrogen, but in a form different than nitrogen gas from the air. Fortunately, certain bacteria are able to "fix" nitrogen gas into a form that plants can use. Animals obtain nitrogen by eating plants.

**Bug-eating Plants** Marshy soils typically have little fixed nitrogen. To get the nitrogen they need, some plants take an interesting approach— they "eat" animals!

When an insect touches the hair-like structures inside a Venus flytrap, for example, the plant closes its leaves over it. These plants trap insects not for their energy, but for the nitrogen available in their bodies.

**FOCUS CHECK** How do consumers and producers interact in an ecosystem?

**Food Web**
Energy is transferred from one organism to another in a food web. The arrows show the direction of energy flow.

Express Lab

**Activity Card**
*Analyze a Food Web*

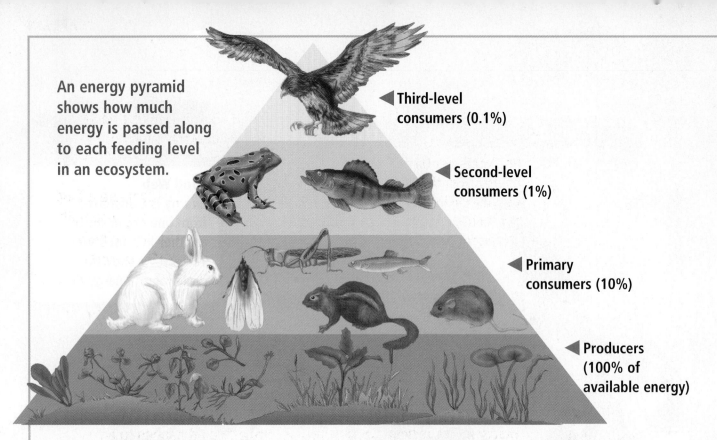

An energy pyramid shows how much energy is passed along to each feeding level in an ecosystem.

Third-level consumers (0.1%)

Second-level consumers (1%)

Primary consumers (10%)

Producers (100% of available energy)

# Energy Pyramid

What happens to the food you eat? You use the energy stored in food to walk, run, and engage in many other activities. A lot of this energy leaves your body in the form of heat. Any leftover energy is stored in your body tissues. You, like all living things, use some energy, lose some as heat, and store some energy in tissues.

An energy pyramid shows how energy flows through an ecosystem. Notice that each level is larger than the level above it. In general, only about 10 percent of the energy in one level is passed on to the next.

Producers, such as plants, make up the base of the energy pyramid. Primary consumers make up the next level. Second- and third-level consumers make up the next levels.

An energy pyramid explains a great deal about the populations of ecosystems. As a general rule, producers have the largest populations because they have the most energy available to them. Next in numbers are the primary and second-level consumers. An ecosystem can support only a few third-level consumers.

The higher an animal's level on the energy pyramid, the wider the range of land it must cover for food. This explains the large hunting ranges of animals such as eagles, lions, and snakes. These animals all have adaptations to move quickly and to catch smaller animals.

The energy pyramid also explains why food chains last only for three or four links. Beyond that, little energy remains for an animal to use.

⊙ **FOCUS CHECK** What is an energy pyramid?

# Lesson Wrap-Up

## Visual Summary

Producers get their energy from the Sun. All other living things get their energy from producers.

A food chain shows the flow of energy from one organism to another. A food web shows overlapping food chains in an ecosystem.

Energy is lost as heat at each step of a food chain. An energy pyramid shows how much energy is available for producers and consumers.

## ✓ Check for Understanding

### COMPARE PLANTS AND ANIMALS
Write a paragraph that compares and contrasts how plants and animals obtain energy.

✓ 0507.3.2

## Review

**1 MAIN IDEA** Describe how energy flows through an ecosystem.

**2 VOCABULARY** Compare a food chain with a food web. Use both terms to explain how animals interact and depend on one another.

**3 READING SKILL: Classify** Give one example each of a producer, herbivore, carnivore, omnivore, and decomposer.

**4 CRITICAL THINKING: Apply** What would happen to an ecosystem if a drought killed half of the plants that lived there?

**5 INQUIRY SKILL: Use Models** List the things you ate for breakfast today. Use the list to construct one or more food chains for each food.

### TCAP Prep

What does a producer do that a consumer does not?

**A** makes its own food
**B** eats only plants
**C** eats only animals
**D** eats both plants and animals

SPI 0507.2.1

## Go Digital Technology

Visit **www.eduplace.com/tnscp** to learn more about food webs.

# Leaping Teeth!

**Digestion begins with the teeth.** And nothing in the sea is more famous for its snapping, shredding bite than the great white shark.

The great white swallows down huge chunks of its prey—usually seals or sea lions—without chewing. It has a large, U-shaped stomach that takes over from there, dissolving the food until it is ready to be passed to the spiral-shaped intestines.

Great whites strike fast, eat a lot, and then take a break. Their digestion is so slow that this great fish may not need to eat another big meal for a month or two. Sometimes great whites swallow things they can't digest at all. Scientists have found a straw hat, a lobster trap, and even a cuckoo clock in great white stomachs!

**GLE 0507.2.1** Investigate different nutritional relationships among organisms in an ecosystem.

EXTEND

**The prehistoric shark** Megalodon was even bigger than the great white. The shark that owned this tooth may have been 15 meters long—nearly 50 feet!

**This shark seems to be trying** to leap at the camera. In fact, it is flying into the air after striking at a seal from below. This time the seal was lucky!

GLE 0507.2.1 Investigate different nutritional relationships among organisms in an ecosystem. **Math GLE 0506.5.2** Describe the shape and important features of a set of data using the measures of central tendency. **ELA GLE 0501.3.4** Write frequently across content areas.

# Math **Average Rainfall**

Tropical rain forests are biomes that are warm and receive a lot of rainfall. Most tropical rain forests are near the equator. Warm, moist air masses from the ocean move over land, bringing rain with them. In some rain forests, it rains almost every day! The yearly rainfall for a five-year period in a certain rain forest is shown in the table below.

| Rain Forest Rainfall | | | | |
|---|---|---|---|---|
| **Year 1** | **Year 2** | **Year 3** | **Year 4** | **Year 5** |
| 250 cm | 240 cm | 230 cm | 260 cm | 250 cm |

1. What was the average rainfall over the five-year period?

2. What was the range for that period? (Hint: Range is the difference between the largest and smallest number in a set.)

3. Which of the following is the most likely amount of rainfall for Year 6?
   **a.** 300 cm  **b.** 200 cm  **c.** 240 cm  **d.** 150 cm

**Writing** **Informational**

Use at least three different sources to research an ecosystem. Choose two plants or animals from that ecosystem. Find out about the food chains that these living things are part of. Then write a report that compares and contrasts the organisms and their roles in the ecosystem.

## Lou Gross

Dr. Gross uses computers to make models of the Everglades. ▼

You probably wouldn't want to live in Tennessee and study ecosystems in Florida—it would take a whole day to drive to Florida! Lou Gross, a professor at the University of Tennessee, studies the Everglades. However, he doesn't have to drive there every day. Dr. Gross uses mathematics and computers to make models of ecosystems.

Coastal lowlands, freshwater prairies, marshy rivers, and mangrove forests are some of the ecosystems found in the Everglades. People have built canals and ditches in the Everglades to help supply fresh water to large cities on Florida's coast. Many plants and animals in the Everglades are threatened and endangered because these wetland ecosystems have been drained.

Lou Gross is helping scientists who want to restore the Everglades. His computer models show the effects of making a change to one part of an ecosystem. For example, they show how filling a canal will change the flow of water and affect birds that breed in certain locations. With the help of many people, including Dr. Gross, several plants and animals that live only in the Everglades may be saved from extinction.

◄ Florida panthers have been affected by changes to the Everglades. Panthers need large areas to live in and a good supply of food.

## Vocabulary

**Complete each sentence with a term from the list.**

1. A(n) _____ shows overlapping food chains in an ecosystem.

2. Zebras are an example of a(n) _____ of living things in an ecosystem.

3. The flow of energy from producer to first-level consumer to second-level consumer can be shown using a simple _____.

4. Different populations of living things found in the same area at the same time form a(n) _____.

5. A(n) _____ includes living and nonliving things interacting together.

6. Ecosystems with similar climate and vegetation make up a(n) _____.

7. Temperature and precipitation determine the _____ of an area.

8. The _____ biome has long, severe winters and short, cool summers.

9. Prairies and savannas are the two main types of _____.

10. _____ has a layer of frozen ground called permafrost.

**biome**
**climate**
**community**
**desert**
★ **ecosystem**
**food chain**
**food web**
**grasslands**
**population**
**taiga**
**temperate forests**
**tropical rain forests**
**tundra**

## TCAP Inquiry Skills

11. **Classify** How do scientists classify a marine biome into three zones? In which zone must populations survive both above and below the water? What happens in this zone? **GLE 0507.5.1**

12. **Use Models** Make a list of your five favorite foods. Draw a food web that includes all of your food sources. Put a star next to each producer in the food web. **GLE 0507.2.1**

## Map the Concept

Fill the terms below into the concept map. Each box represents a larger group than the box inside it.

**Biome   Community   Ecosystem**
**Organism   Population**

**GLE 0507.2.2**

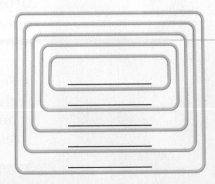

## Critical Thinking

**13.** **Apply** Describe four ways that you interacted with living and nonliving things in ecosystems today. **GLE 0507.2.1**

**14.** **Analyze** If you wanted to show energy flow in an ecosystem, would it be best to use a food chain or a food web? Explain your answer. **GLE 0507.2.1**

**15.** **Evaluate** Your friend comments that he does not eat vegetables and could survive without plants. Explain why you agree or disagree with him. **GLE 0507.3.1**

**16.** **Analyze** Which animal receives more energy from a producer: a first-level consumer or a second-level consumer? Explain. **GLE 0507.2.1**

## Check for Understanding

### Display a Biome

Make a display that shows a typical scene from a biome. Include at least four different types of living things. The display may be a detailed drawing, poster, or diorama. Write a paragraph or short essay to accompany the display. Be sure to explain the relationships between the producers and consumers you included in your display. **0507.2.1**

## TCAP Prep

Answer the following questions.

**17** Which of these is a primary consumer?

**A** a rabbit

**B** a cactus

**C** an owl

**D** a tiger **SPI 0507.3.2**

**18** Which process produces food for plants and gives off oxygen?

**F** burning

**G** photosynthesis

**H** respiration

**J** transpiration **SPI 0507.3.1**

**19** What is the source of all food energy on Earth?

**A** decomopsers

**B** herbivores

**C** carnivores

**D** producers **SPI 0507.2.1**

**20** In which biome would you find mammals with thick fur and a thick layer of fat?

**F** tropical rain forest

**G** temperate rain forest

**H** tundra

**J** desert **SPI 0507.5.1**

# Energy and Matter in Ecosystems

**LESSON 1**

Living things live on the highest mountains and in the deepest oceans. How do they survive in such different places?

**LESSON 2**

Decreases in food supply, changes in climate, relocated species—how do these factors upset the balance of an ecosystem?

**LESSON 3**

Swamps turn into meadows, meadows turn into forests—how do living things respond to changes in ecosystems?

START

## Fun Facts

The fastest animal in the world is the peregrine falcon. The fastest land animal is the cheetah.

# Vocabulary Preview

adaptation
endangered species
extinction
habitat
niche
pollution
population
predator
prey
symbiosis
threatened species

 ## Vocabulary Strategies

Have you ever seen any of these terms before? Do you know what they mean?

State a description, explanation, or example of the vocabulary in your own words.

Draw a picture, symbol, example, or other image that describes the term.

**Glossary** p. H18

pollution

predator

endangered species

habitat

# Start with Your Standards

## Inquiry

**GLE 0507.Inq.3** Organize data into appropriate tables, graphs, drawings, or diagrams.

**GLE 0507.Inq.4** Identify and interpret simple patterns of evidence to communicate the findings of multiple investigations.

**GLE 0507.Inq.5** Recognize that people may interpret the same results in different ways.

## Life Science

### Standard 2—Interdependence

**GLE 0507.2.1** Investigate different nutritional relationships among organisms in an ecosystem.

**GLE 0507.2.2** Explain how organisms interact through symbiotic, commensal, and parasitic relationships.

**GLE 0507.2.3** Establish the connections between human activities and natural disasters and their impact on the environment.

### Standard 5—Biodiversity and Change

**GLE 0507.5.1** Investigate physical characteristics associated with different groups of animals.

**GLE 0507.5.2** Analyze fossils to demonstrate the connection between organisms and environments that existed in the past and those that currently exist.

## Interact with this chapter.

 www.eduplace.com/tnscp

**TENNESSEE STANDARDS**

**GLE 0507.Inq.3** Organize data into appropriate tables, graphs, drawings, or diagrams.
**GLE 0507.5.1** Investigate physical characteristics associated with different groups of animals.

# Guiding ? Question What Are Habitats and Niches?

## Why It Matters...

How can a clownfish live so close to the stinging tentacles of a sea anemone? The fish rubs against the anemone, coating its scales with a kind of slime. The anemone doesn't recognize the coated fish as food.

Living things interact with one another in all sorts of ways. These interactions are key to understanding how they survive.

## PREPARE TO INVESTIGATE

## Inquiry Skill

**Observe** When you observe, you use your senses to describe the properties of objects and events.

## Materials

- safety goggles
- earthworms
- goldfish
- 2 aquariums
- soil
- organic matter
- apple peels
- fish food

# Directed Inquiry

# Worm and Fish Habitats

## Procedure

**Safety:** Wear goggles when handling soil.

STEP 1

1. **Collaborate** Work in a small group. Half fill one aquarium with soil. Spread a thin layer of decayed leaves or other organic matter over the soil. Add some earthworms and a handful of apple peels. Moisten the soil. Wash your hands afterwards.

STEP 2

2. **Measure** Fill the second aquarium with water at room temperature, almost to the top. Add the goldfish and fish food. You may also add small rocks and plastic plants. Wash your hands afterwards.

3. **Observe** Each day for a week, observe the earthworms and fish. How do they move? What do they eat? How do they affect their environment?

4. **Record Data** In your *Science Notebook,* write your observations in a chart like the one shown.

STEP 4

| Observations | | |
|---|---|---|
| | Worms | Fish |
| Physical Properties | | |
| Type of Food | | |
| Interactions | | |

## Think and Write

1. **Infer** What body parts make the fish well suited to their environment? How are the earthworms suited to their environment?

2. **Predict** Could the fish live in the earthworms' environment? Could the earthworms live in the fish's environment? Why or why not?

**Guided Inquiry**

**Research** Learn about an interesting plant or animal that lives in Tennessee. Where does it live? What role does it have in its ecosystem?

0507.5.2

# Habitats and Niches

**VOCABULARY**

adaptation
habitat
niche
symbiosis

**GRAPHIC ORGANIZER**

**Compare and Contrast**
As you read, compare and contrast relationships among different organisms and their environments.

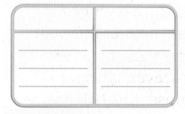

**GLE 0507.2.2** Explain how organisms interact through symbiotic, commensal, and parasitic relationships.

## Habitats

To tell people where you live, you probably use a street address. An address is a simple way to describe the location of your home.

All living things have an "address," a place they live in. This place is called a habitat. A **habitat** is the area where an organism lives, grows, and develops. Everything that an organism needs to survive can be found in its habitat.

Many different living things may live in the same habitat. The African savanna, for example, is home to zebras, lions, and many other animals.

Savanna Habitat

**Lion**
The niche of a lion in a savanna includes hunting zebras.

# Niches

Have you seen pictures or movies of workers at an automobile factory? Every worker has a place to be and a job to do. If one of them fails to do his or her job, everyone else's job is affected.

Organisms in a habitat have specific functions, too. A **niche** describes what an organism does in its habitat. You can think of a niche as a job at a factory or a role in a play. Each organism plays a certain role in its habitat.

Look at the savanna habitat shown below. The zebras are consumers. They eat producers, such as grass. They drink water from the watering hole. These are parts of their niche.

Zebras are also food for lions. That is another part of their niche. Zebras and lions share the same habitat, but have different niches.

Niches describe more than just feeding relationships. A niche includes exactly where in the habitat an organism lives, how it reproduces, how it protects itself, and how it behaves. For example, birds in the savanna may live in nests. They may use sticks, mud, and other materials. Part of their niche includes recycling such materials in their habitat.

Each group of organisms in a habitat uses resources in different ways. Zebras, for example, eat the grass. Lions do not eat grass, but they lie in the grass. Birds use the grass to build nests. Because each group uses the same resources in different ways, there are enough resources for everyone. However, changes in ecosystems can upset this balance, as you'll learn in the next lesson.

**⊙ FOCUS CHECK** **How do habitats and niches compare?**

**Zebra**
**The niche of a zebra in a savanna includes eating grass.**

## Adaptations

What if you see a drawing of a large, white polar bear crossing a hot, sandy desert? Something's wrong with this picture! Can you explain what it is?

The thick fur and heavy padding of a polar bear help it stay warm in its cold, arctic habitat. Desert animals, on the other hand, have body parts that help them stay cool. These characteristics are called adaptations. An **adaptation** is any characteristic that helps an organism survive.

Sometimes adaptations are physical. The turtles in the pictures on this page are good examples of similar animals with different adaptations. The desert tortoise has legs that help it move easily across the sand. The sea turtle has flippers that help it move through water. Each animal's body is physically adapted to its habitat.

Plants have adaptations, too. For example, a cactus's leaves are thin, pointed spines. Its body, or stem, has a very thick outer layer. These adaptations help the cactus conserve water in its dry habitat.

Other adaptations are behavioral. This means that the organism has certain behaviors that help it survive in its habitat. A bat, for example, might sleep through the winter. This adaptation, called hibernation, allows the bat to live in cold climates.

**Sea Turtle ▲**
The flippers of a sea turtle are adapted for swimming.

**Desert Tortoise ▲**
The feet of a desert tortoise are adapted for walking in sand.

### Cacti
Most plants would wilt and die in a hot desert. Cacti survive because of their waxy stems, long roots, and other adaptations. ▶

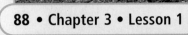

## Natural Selection

How do organisms develop adaptations? In the mid-1800s, British naturalist Charles Darwin proposed a theory to help explain the process. According to Darwin, some members of a species have characteristics better suited to the environment than other members. These individuals are more likely to survive and pass on their characteristics to their offspring.

This process is known as natural selection. Let's examine how it works.

Picture a rocky beach. A population of birds searches among the rocks for food. Some of the birds have long, pointed beaks and can easily pick up pieces of food from cracks between the rocks. Other birds have shorter, more rounded beaks and cannot reach food.

Which birds are more likely to survive on the rocky beach? Which birds are more likely to reproduce? The birds with the pointed beaks are more likely to do both. Thus, their characteristics are passed on to their offspring. After several generations, many more of the birds on the beach will have pointed beaks.

Most scientists believe that natural selection accounts for the amazing variety of living things and their adaptations. Scientists also use the theory to predict how species might change in the future.

▲ Why does a sandpiper have such a long, thin beak? According to the theory of natural selection, traits that help an animal survive become more common in the population.

The dense, shaggy hair of these yaks helps them survive the bitterly cold weather of the Himalayas. ▼

**FOCUS CHECK** What is an adaptation? Compare adaptations among different organisms.

89

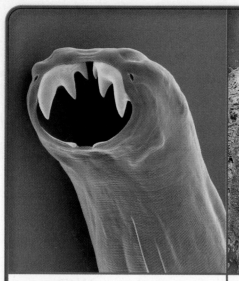

**Parasitism**
A hookworm takes blood and nutrients from its host. It benefits, and the host is harmed.

**Commensalism**
An elf owl makes its nest in a hole in a cactus. The owl benefits, and the cactus is not affected.

**Mutualism**
Cleaner shrimp eat parasites attached to fish. Both the shrimp and the fish benefit from this relationship.

## Symbiosis

All living things depend on and affect one another. Sometimes the relationship is very close. **Symbiosis** describes a close, long-lasting relationship between two different kinds of organisms. This word means "living together."

*Parasitism* is one type of symbiosis. One organism, called the parasite, benefits from living off the body of another organism, the host. For example, a hookworm benefits from living inside the digestive tract of a larger host, such as a dog. The dog may become ill, but it usually doesn't die. If it did, the hookworm would die, too.

In *commensalism*, one organism benefits and the other organism is not affected. Birds called cattle egrets, for example, follow cattle as they move through a field. The birds eat the insects that jump from the grass as the cattle graze. The birds benefit, while the cattle are neither harmed nor helped.

In *mutualism*, both organisms benefit. Cleaner shrimp, for example, eat parasites off fish. The shrimp get food and the fish stay healthy. This relationship helps both the shrimp and the fish.

**FOCUS CHECK** How do the three types of symbiosis compare?

## Express Lab

**Activity Card**
*Identify Interspecific Relationships*

# Lesson Wrap-Up

## Visual Summary

A natural habitat is the area where an organism lives. It provides everything the organism needs to survive. A niche describes the role of an organism in its habitat.

Adaptations are traits that help organisms survive in their habitats. Adaptations can be physical or behavioral.

Symbiosis is a close, long-lasting relationship between organisms. The three main types of symbiosis are parasitism, commensalism, and mutualism.

## Check for Understanding

### EVALUATE RELATIONSHIPS

Use the Internet to research two different types of parasites and their hosts. Evaluate how the parasites harm these hosts and if there is anything the host does to remove the parasite.

✔ 0507.2.1

## Review

**❶ MAIN IDEA** Describe two different niches in a savanna habitat.

**❷ VOCABULARY** Give an example of an adaptation. Describe how the adaptation helps the organism.

**❸ READING SKILL: Compare and Contrast** How does a parasitic relationship affect both the parasite and the host?

**❹ CRITICAL THINKING: Apply** How would you describe your niche in your family? How does it compare to an animal's niche in nature?

**❺ INQUIRY SKILL: Observe** Describe a type of symbiotic relationship that you have observed. Identify which organisms benefit and which are harmed, if any.

### TCAP TCAP Prep

Which is the type of relationship in which both organisms benefit?

**A** mutualism
**B** parasitism
**C** commensalism
**D** symbiosis

SPI 0507.2.2

### Go Digital Technology

Visit **www.eduplace.com/tnscp** to learn more about habitats and niches.

**TENNESSEE STANDARDS**

**GLE 0507.Inq.4** Identify and interpret simple patterns of evidence to communicate the findings of mulitple investigations.
**GLE 0507.2.3.** Establish the connections between human activities and natural disasters and their impact on the environment.

# ? What Factors Affect Ecosystems?

*Guiding Question*

## Why It Matters...

How many wolves can live in a forest? The answer depends on the size of the forest and the amount of food it provides for the wolves. Temperature can affect the population, and so can pollution. In any population—of wolves, trees, birds, or people—the size is limited by the available resources.

## PREPARE TO INVESTIGATE

### Inquiry Skill

**Hypothesize** When you hypothesize, you use prior knowledge or observations to suggest a cause-and-effect relationship that can be tested.

### Materials

- measuring cup
- 3 plastic cups
- 32 lima bean seeds
- soil
- water
- marker
- safety goggles

### Science and Math Toolbox

For step 4, review Making a Chart to Organize Data on page H11.

# Directed Inquiry

# Limits to Growth

## Procedure

**Safety:** Wear goggles while handling soil.

**STEP 1**

1. **Collaborate** Work with a partner. Label the three cups *A*, *B*, and *C*. Place soil into the cups until they are nearly full. Each cup should contain roughly the same amount of soil.

2. **Use Variables** Place 2 seeds in cup A. Place 10 seeds in cup B. Place 20 seeds in cup C.

**STEP 2**

3. **Measure** Measure and pour 25 mL of water into each cup.

4. **Record Data** Place all three cups in a sunny spot. In your *Science Notebook,* make a chart like the one shown for each cup.

**STEP 4**

| Cup ____ | | |
|------|--------|-------------|
| Date | Height | Observations |
| | | |
| | | |
| | | |
| | | |

5. **Observe** Over the course of the next three weeks, water the cups when the soil is dry and measure growth. Be certain that all the cups receive the same amount of water and sunlight. Record the date, height, and your observations at least twice a week.

## Think and Write

1. **Observe** What differences did you observe in the growing seeds?

2. **Hypothesize** What factor might have caused these differences?

3. **Use Variables** Why was it important to give each cup the same amount of sunlight and water?

### Guided Inquiry

**Design an Experiment**
Design an experiment to determine how sunlight affects plant growth. Remember to keep other variables constant and to include a control.

0507.Inq.4

# Changes in Population

## A Balanced Ecosystem

Different living things use the resources of an ecosystem in different ways. They take some resources from ecosystems and add others to it. A balanced ecosystem has enough resources for all of its living things.

Every ecosystem supports many populations. A **population** is all the organisms of a given species that live together in the same area. Any change in one part of an ecosystem can upset the balance. For example, suppose a fungus kills many of the plants that rabbits eat. Such an event could lower the rabbit population. This would affect the hawks, owls, and other animals that eat the rabbits.

On the other hand, if a population of rabbits becomes too large, they might crowd out other species that live in the area. Because ecosystems have limited resources, they can support only a limited number of living things.

### VOCABULARY

extinction
population
predator
prey

### GRAPHIC ORGANIZER

**Cause and Effect** As you read, look for cause-and-effect relationships in populations and ecosystems.

GLE 0507.2.1 Investigate different nutritional relationships among organisms in an ecosystem.

GLE 0507.2.3 Establish the connections between human activities and natural disasters and their impact on the environment.

GLE 0507.5.2 Analyze fossils to demonstrate the connection between organisms and environments that existed in the past and those that currently exist.

Predators that consume frog eggs help keep the frog population from growing too large.

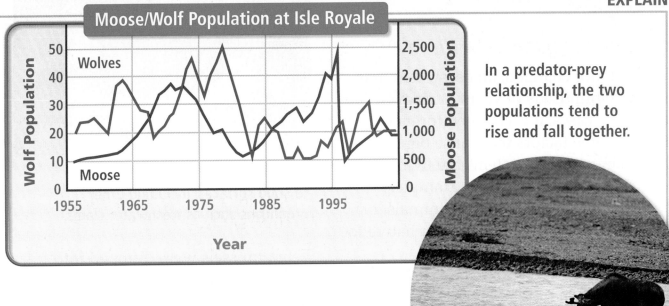

## Moose/Wolf Population at Isle Royale

In a predator-prey relationship, the two populations tend to rise and fall together.

## Limits on Populations

In any ecosystem, populations are always changing. Old animals die, and new ones take their place. When a tree falls, plants that thrive in sunlight can begin to grow. Other changes, however, can upset the balance of the ecosystem.

Consider the relationship between predators and their prey. **Predators** are animals that hunt and eat other animals. **Prey** are animals hunted and eaten by predators.

In a healthy ecosystem, the population densities of predators and prey are balanced. But certain factors can upset this balance. One example comes from an actual ecosystem—Isle Royale, an island in Lake Superior.

Moose first appeared on the island around 1900. They may have crossed on ice that formed a temporary bridge from the mainland. The island had plenty of plants for the moose to eat, and no predators.

The population of the moose had skyrocketed by 1930. Then it fell sharply. Why? The moose did not have enough food. Food is a limited resource in an ecosystem. So, the limited food supply on the island helped slow population growth.

In 1950, wolves appeared on the island. Wolves are predators of moose, so the moose population dropped while the wolves increased. Yet after a while, the wolf population dropped because not enough moose remained to support them. With fewer wolves, the moose population rose again. As the graph shows, the populations of these two species continued to rise and fall.

Lack of predators can make an ecosystem unbalanced as prey populations grow unchecked. Adding predators is one way to restore the balance.

**FOCUS CHECK** How might a decrease in predators affect prey?

# Changing the Balance

Once changed, an ecosystem may take hundreds of years to recover. In some cases, it is changed forever.

Some factors that cause big changes in ecosystems are living. Alien species are good examples. Alien species are plants, animals, or other organisms that are not native to a given ecosystem.

In some cases, an alien species has no natural predators in its new home. It may thrive and "steal" resources from native plants and animals, or feed directly off them.

How do alien species enter new ecosystems? Often, they are brought in by accident. Zebra mussels, for example, traveled from western Russia to North America during the 1980s in water stored on a boat. The

▲ Zebra mussels anchor themselves to solid surfaces, including other organisms such as freshwater clams.

zebra mussels were dumped into the Great Lakes with the water. By the 1990s, the mussels had spread throughout many lakes and rivers.

The tiny zebra mussels can clog water pipes used by power plants and water treatment facilities. Zebra mussels also harm native organisms. They grow in large groups on clams, mussels, and crayfish. This growth can smother the native species.

Another problem is that zebra mussels filter the water, clearing it of plankton. Plankton are tiny producers. With fewer plankton to eat and to provide oxygen, many native species die.

It can be very difficult to get rid of an alien species. However, many states are working together to control the spread of these troublesome organisms.

◀ The Asian long-horned beetle entered the United States in wooden shipping crates in the 1990s. Its larvae burrow under the bark of trees, slowly killing them.

Nonliving things can also change the balance of an ecosystem. These include natural events, such as volcanic eruptions.

For example, Mount St. Helens is a volcano in the state of Washington. For many years, it was like a sleeping giant—it caused no trouble. Hemlock and fir thrived on the mountainside, as did many animals.

Everything changed in May 1980, when the volcano violently erupted. In a matter of minutes, the explosion knocked down and burned trees over an area of 500 square kilometers. Thick deposits of ash covered ground hundreds of kilometers away. The area surrounding the volcano became almost barren.

Within a few years of the Mount St. Helens eruption, flowers bloomed again on nearby slopes.

Yet life slowly returned to the mountain and neighboring areas. Some plants survived the eruption. Wind blew in seeds for grasses and shrubs, which sprouted a year or so after the eruption. Then larger plants moved in, followed by animals that ate those plants.

In 2004, the volcano turned active once again, although the damage was not nearly as severe as before. If the volcano stays quiet for many more years, the forest will return as before.

Other natural events include forest fires, floods, and droughts. Each can cause long-lasting changes in ecosystems. What do you think animals do when ecosystems change?

**FOCUS CHECK** **Describe one way that a nonliving factor may change an ecosystem.**

1983

1980

When a new lizard moved into part of its habitat, the green anole of Florida moved to the treetops. ▲

## Adapting to Change

What if your home suddenly lost heat during a cold winter? What would you and your family do? You might move to a new home. Or you might adapt to the cold house, meaning you would find a way to still live there. Maybe you would build a fire or wear warm clothes.

In nature, living things also respond to dramatic changes in their environment. Sometimes they relocate, meaning they move to a new home.

The move need not be far. For example, in recent years a lizard from Cuba invaded part of the Florida habitat of another lizard, the green anole. The green anole used to live close to the ground. When it lost resources to the Cuban lizard, the green anole moved to the treetops.

A living thing can also adapt to changes in its environment. For example, many animals grow thicker coats when the weather turns cold.

If the change is too dramatic, however, the animal might perish, meaning it would die. Perishing is the consequence when living things can neither adapt nor relocate to survive a change.

Living things have relocated, adapted, and perished for as long as they have been on Earth. Fossils give clues to how this happened. *Fossils* are the remains or traces of once-living things.

Fossils may not show how individual organisms changed, but they do show that different species have lived at different times. Look at the fossil dinosaur shown below. No animal alive today has a skeleton just like this. Because dinosaurs could not survive changes in their environment, they perished.

Fossils help scientists determine how species have changed. ▶

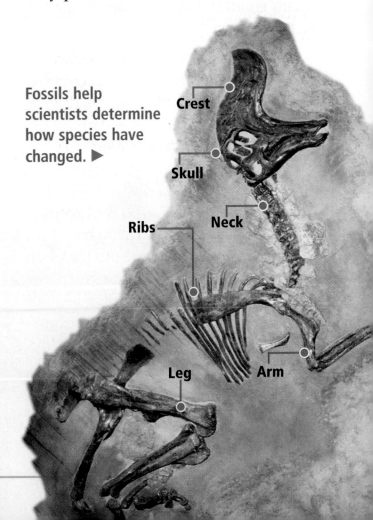

Crest

Skull

Neck

Ribs

Leg

Arm

Geologic Age

**Key**
- Limestone
- Shale
- Sandstone
- Shale
- Conglomerate

Exposed rock layers

Sedimentary rocks form in horizontal layers. When an organism is buried in a layer, fossils may form. Over time, the layers may bend, tilt, or remain flat. ▲

# Evidence in Rocks

Change in ecosystems can occur very rapidly and can affect vast areas. For many animals, perishing is often the result. Throughout Earth's history, not only have countless individual organisms perished, but so have entire species.

When this happens, the species becomes extinct. **Extinction** occurs when all members of a species die out. Many different events can cause extinction, even among very successful species.

How do scientists draw conclusions about species that went extinct long ago? They do so by studying both fossils and the rocks in which the fossils were found.

The illustration above, for example, shows layers of rocks from a hillside. These layers formed on top of one another over time. The oldest rocks are on the bottom, the youngest on top. Any fossils in the rocks must have formed at the same time as the rocks around them.

Taken together, fossils and rocks show that species and ecosystems have changed a great deal throughout Earth's history. For example, fossil shells or fish show the land once was underwater. Fossil ferns show a wet, warm climate. Both kinds of fossils have been found in mountains!

Scientists are also able to estimate the age of a fossil. The oldest fossils are billions of years old.

The absence of fossils can be key information. For example, Earth's rocks hold many dinosaur fossils, yet none in layers younger than 65 million years old. Scientists conclude that the last of the dinosaurs all became extinct at this time.

An event in which many species become extinct is called a mass extinction. Earth has experienced several mass extinctions throughout its history.

**FOCUS CHECK** What can scientists learn by studying fossils and rocks?

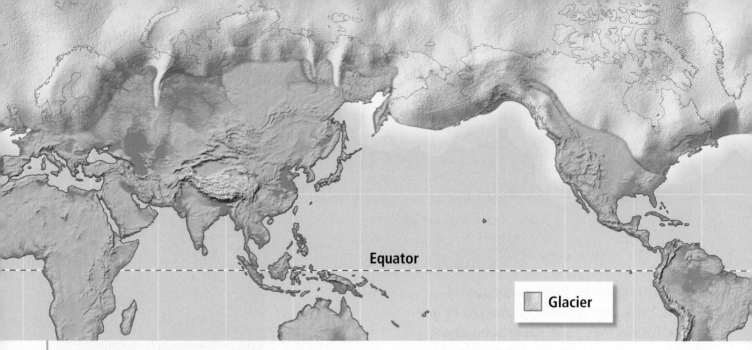

Equator

Glacier

▲ This map shows the extent of the glaciers in the Northern Hemisphere during the most recent ice age, from about 20,000 years ago.

## Climate Change

Have you ever been to New York? Or Minnesota or Michigan? If you could travel back in time—say, 20,000 years—you would not recognize these places. They would be covered under a thick sheet of ice.

Over the last two million years, large parts of North America and Europe have been covered several times by huge ice sheets, or glaciers. These periods are called ice ages. The last ice age ended about 11,000 years ago.

During an ice age, much of Earth's water is locked up in glaciers, causing sea levels to fall. During the last ice age, the drop in sea level exposed a land bridge between Asia and North America. Many living things, humans included, may have crossed this bridge to settle in North America.

Many animals were already in North America at this time. Some were very large, like the woolly mammoth and the saber-toothed cat. With their thick, furry coats, they were well adapted to the cold conditions. When the ice age ended, however, they became extinct.

Some scientists believe that these animals could not adapt to the warmer climate. Other scientists think that both climate and humans caused the extinctions. Humans may have overhunted the great animals.

The exact reasons why some animals became extinct may never be known. But Earth's climate does change periodically. These changes greatly affect the living things upon it.

**FOCUS CHECK** How might climate change affect living things in the future?

**Express Lab**

**Activity Card**
*Make a Model Fossil*

## Lesson Wrap-Up

### Visual Summary

Ecosystems have limited resources. A balanced ecosystem has enough resources to support all living things.

Both living things, such as alien species, and nonliving things, such as volcanic eruptions, can upset the balance of an ecosystem.

Living things can respond to changes in ecosystems by relocating, adapting, or perishing.

### Check for Understanding

**MATCH ORGANISMS**

Using the images provided by your teacher, make a list of animals that resemble each fossil. Be sure to tell how they resemble the animals in your list.

✔ 0507.5.5

## Review

❶ **MAIN IDEA** What factors can cause the size of a population of living things to change?

❷ **VOCABULARY** Use the terms *predator* and *prey* in a sentence.

❸ **READING SKILL: Cause and Effect** Why do alien species often thrive in their new ecosystems?

❹ **CRITICAL THINKING: Apply** What could you conclude if a dinosaur fossil and a bird fossil were found in the same layer of rocks?

❺ **INQUIRY SKILL: Hypothesize** What changes in living and nonliving things might be brought about by the onset of another ice age?

### TCAP Prep

A scientist found a woolly mammoth fossil. What could she conclude about the environment where she found the fossil?

**A** It was once hot.
**B** It was once under water.
**C** It was once windy.
**D** It was once cold.

SPI 0507.5.2

### Technology

Visit **www.eduplace.com/tnscp** to learn more about populations.

# Fossils in Tennessee

**When scientists want to learn facts about the past, they don't always look in a history book.** Sometimes they look in the ground! There are many places in Tennessee where scientists can find fossils that tell about Tennessee's past. Many of these fossils are displayed in museums. You can go to see the fossils and learn about Tennessee's past, just like the scientists that found them.

Scientists look in the ground for fossils because many fossils are formed when sediment settles over the body of a dead organism. This organism eventually decays, and minerals fill the space that is left. These minerals form one kind of fossil.

→ **GLE 0507.5.2** Analyze fossils to demonstrate the connection between organisms and environments that existed in the past and those that currently exist.

**EXTEND**

When scientists study fossils they can learn many things. Scientists can compare the fossils they find there to animals that live today. This helps them see the relationships between organisms and their environments. For example, fish have gills, so they can take in oxygen from the water. Aquatic mammals have fins or flippers to help them move around in water. When scientists find fossils of animals that have fins, flippers, or gills, they know that land was under water at some time in its history.

Studying fossils also helps scientist contrast the types of sea animals that lived in the past with those that are alive today. For example, you know from fossils that *Megalodon,* an extinct shark, was much larger than today's great white sharks.

Scientists can also learn which organisms lived at about the same time. If two fossils are found in the same rocks, scientists know that those two things lived at about the same time.

Studying fossils helps scientists learn about Earth's past environments and how they compare to environments today. The more fossils they find, the more complete their understanding of the past becomes.

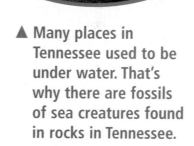

▲ **Many places in Tennessee used to be under water. That's why there are fossils of sea creatures found in rocks in Tennessee.**

**The animals that left these fossils used to live in what is now Tennessee.** ▼

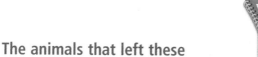 **Sharing Ideas**

1. **READING CHECK** How do fossils show the relationship between organisms and environments of the past to those of today?

2. **WRITE ABOUT IT** How do the fossils from Tennessee tell about Tennessee's past? Choose a Tennessee fossil. Research the organism that left it, and describe what the environment might have been like when it was alive.

3. **TALK ABOUT IT** Look at the fossil images on these pages. Discuss with your classmates how these fossils resemble animals that are alive today.

**TENNESSEE STANDARDS**

**GLE 0507.Inq.5** Recognize that people may interpret the same results in different ways.

**GLE 0507.2.3** Establish the connections between human activities and natural disasters and their impact on the environment.

*Guiding Question*

# ? How Can Humans Change Ecosystems?

## Why It Matters...

Huge numbers of bison once roamed the Great Plains of North America. Yet in the 1800s, humans hunted them almost to extinction. Hunting and other human activities changed not only the bison, but the ecosystems of which they were part.

Changes like this continue today. By understanding how and why ecosystems change, people can manage those changes wisely.

## PREPARE TO INVESTIGATE

### Inquiry Skill

**Predict** When you predict, you use observations, facts, or patterns to anticipate results.

### Materials

- plastic container with lid
- ice cubes
- modeling clay
- water
- metric ruler

### Science and Math Toolbox

For step 2, review **Measurements** on pages H16–H17.

# Directed Inquiry

## Rising Sea Level

### Procedure

**STEP 1**

1. **Use Models** Work with a partner. Use clay to make a model slope inside a shallow plastic container. The slope represents a coastal area. It should be placed at one end of the container.

**STEP 2**

2. **Measure** Add water to a depth of 2 cm inside the container. The water represents the ocean. It should cover only the edge of the slope.

3. **Predict** Add four ice cubes to the container. The ice cubes represent glaciers. Cover the container. In your *Science Notebook,* predict what will happen to the level of the water when the ice cubes melt.

**STEP 3**

4. **Record Data** The next day, measure the depth of the water in the container. Record your measurements in a chart.

### Think and Write

1. **Observe** What happened to the depth of the water in the container?

2. **Observe** How was the model land affected by the change in the depth of the water?

3. **Predict** How might a rise in sea level affect coastal areas?

**Guided Inquiry**

**Research** Is Earth's average temperature increasing? Research this question. Prepare a report that includes a graph or a map to display data. Find out if everyone agrees about global warming.

✔ 0507.Inq.3

# Human Impact on Ecosystems

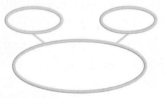
Tropical rain forests are being cleared for farming and logging. Many species are lost along with the forests. ▼

## Human Activities

Rain forests are among the most valuable resources on Earth. They are home to a vast variety of plants and animals. Yet rain forests are destroyed every day. By one account, almost 200,000 square kilometers (77,000 square miles) are lost each year. That's about 37 city blocks per minute!

People clear rain forests for land to grow crops, raise livestock, and build homes and businesses. Lumber that comes from the trees is valuable, too.

Why should you be concerned about the loss of rain forests? One reason is that plants and animals may become extinct when their habitats are destroyed. Scientists believe that some rain forest plants may contain substances that could be used as medicines. In addition, rain forest plants release oxygen and take in carbon dioxide from the atmosphere.

▲ In the United States alone, more than 4 billion kg (9 billion lbs) of fish are caught each year. Many popular fish are now threatened.

▲ Developers cut the top off a hillside to build these houses.

Humans have a huge effect on ecosystems by destroying habitats. In fact, habitat loss is the main reason why rates of extinction are rising. Not only rain forests are affected. Other ecosystems are impacted, too.

Wetlands, for example, are sometimes drained and filled in to provide land for farms, businesses, and housing developments. Until recently, people did not understand the importance of wetlands. These ecosystems help filter harmful chemicals from groundwater.

The spongy grasses in wetland areas also absorb excess water during heavy rains. This action helps reduce flooding. Many animal species hatch in wetlands. Later, as adults, they live in the sea. Wetlands are important nurseries for these animals.

Excessive hunting and fishing practices pose another threat to many ecosystems. In the early 1800s, for example, more than 60 million bison roamed the Great Plains. Yet by 1890, fewer than a thousand were left. Overhunting was the biggest reason. People killed the bison for their hides or tongues.

When a species is close to becoming extinct, it is called an **endangered species.** When a species is close to becoming endangered, it is called a **threatened species.** These categories are important. They let everyone know which species need the most protection.

**FOCUS CHECK** Is habitat destruction a serious problem? Explain.

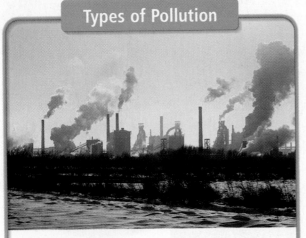

**Air Pollution**
Factories that burn fossil fuels can release harmful substances into the air.

**Water Pollution**
Oil spills can harm plants and animals that live in or near the water.

**Land Pollution**
Trash and garbage are often carelessly discarded, polluting the land.

## Pollution

What other human activities can impact ecosystems? Burning fossil fuels is one example. Fossil fuels include oil, gas, and coal. These fuels contain a lot of energy and are easy to use. However, burning them can cause pollution. **Pollution** is the addition of harmful substances to the environment.

When fossil fuels are burned, certain gases and solid particles are released into the air. These pollutants can make the air unhealthy to breathe. Some combine with water droplets to form acids. They fall to the ground as acid rain.

Fossil fuels don't have to be burned to pose a threat to the environment. Oil, for example, is often transported on big ships called tankers. Accidental spills can damage the environment and be expensive to clean. About 300,000 birds died following a major oil spill in Alaska in 1989.

Human activities can also pollute the land. Each year, people in the United States produce hundreds of millions of tons of solid waste, including paper, plastics, and metals. Most solid waste is buried in sanitary landfills, and some is burned. However, people sometimes carelessly dump solid waste along roadsides or in bodies of water.

Some farming and lawn-care practices can also cause pollution. Rain can wash fertilizers into rivers and streams, where they may damage the ecosystem.

## Good News

All around the world, people are working to reduce pollution and restore damaged ecosystems. Governments are passing laws. Industries are taking action. And people like you are making a difference everywhere!

**FOCUS CHECK** How can individual actions help protect the environment?

**Endangered Species Act**
This legislation protects endangered and threatened species from harm by human activities.

**Cleaner Cars**
The Clean Air Act, revised in 1990, limits the pollutants from new cars. Some manufacturers have designed cars that use alternative fuels.

**Wildlife Refuges**
In the United States, wildlife refuges cover nearly 39 million hectares (96 million acres). Development and hunting are limited, providing safe habitats for wildlife.

**Express Lab**

Activity Card
*Protect Wildlife*

## How to Help

People can help decrease their impact on the environment, too. They can reduce the amount of energy they use. People can also reuse items instead of throwing them away. Many materials can be recycled as well. Doing these things helps reduce pollution and conserve resources.

**FOCUS CHECK** How does reusing materials help the environment?

### Clean Technology
New technology reduces pollutants at coal-burning power plants.

### Community Actions
Many people work to clean up trash, plant trees, or carpool to school and work. Individuals can make a big difference!

FLORIDA APR 07446899
AYE CAPT
Save the Manatee

### Environmental Legislation
Many states have passed laws to protect or support local species. In Florida, funds from license plates help protect manatees.

### Protecting Wetlands
The Environmental Protection Agency (EPA) works with state and local governments to protect bogs, swamps, and other wet places.

# Lesson Wrap-Up

## Visual Summary

Many habitats are destroyed by logging, development, and other human actions. Overharvesting can reduce the populations of certain species.

Pollution affects air, water, and land. A growing human population means that more people are competing for limited resources.

Governments have passed laws to protect the environment. Many industries use new technology to reduce pollution. Individuals can help clean up ecosystems.

## Check for Understanding

### MAKE A POSTER

Work with a partner to make a poster that shows how human activities can affect the environment. Be sure to show both positive and negative effects.

✔ 0507.2.5

## Review

❶ **MAIN IDEA** What are some ways that people affect ecosystems?

❷ **VOCABULARY** What can happen to a threatened species if its population continues to decrease?

❸ **READING SKILL: Draw Conclusions** Can the actions of one person help the environment? Explain your answer.

❹ **CRITICAL THINKING: Synthesis** A plant in a tropical rain forest becomes extinct. Why should this concern you?

❺ **INQUIRY SKILL: Predict** How will Earth's resources be affected if the human population continues to grow?

### TCAP Prep

Predict how recycling aluminum would affect the environment.

**A** Pollution would increase.
**B** Pollution would decrease.
**C** Rainfall would decrease.
**D** Waste would increase.

SPI 0507.2.3

### Go Digital Technology

Visit **www.eduplace.com/tnscp** to learn more about pollution.

# A World In Your Hands

**What you see here is a world in a glass bubble.** Called the EcoSphere™, this sealed globe is a miniature ecosystem that is self-contained, self-renewing, and in almost perfect biological balance. This biosphere's physical environment is simple: gravel, seawater, some trapped air, and a small branch. The inhabitants of this little world are microorganisms, algae, and tiny red shrimp.

The EcoSphere's biological cycle is a simple version of Earth's. Carbon dioxide in the seawater and light enable the algae to produce oxygen by photosynthesis. The shrimp breathe the oxygen in the water while nibbling on the algae and bacteria. The bacteria break down the animal waste into nutrients, which the algae use. The shrimp and bacteria give off carbon dioxide, which the algae use to produce oxygen. And so the cycle repeats itself.

➡ **GLE 0507.2.1.** Investigate different nutritional relationships among organisms in an ecosystem.

EXTEND

**The first pictures of the whole Earth from outer space helped people realize that our planet is a self-contained biosphere too. Anything that disrupts the oxygen or carbon cycle threatens all life on Earth.**

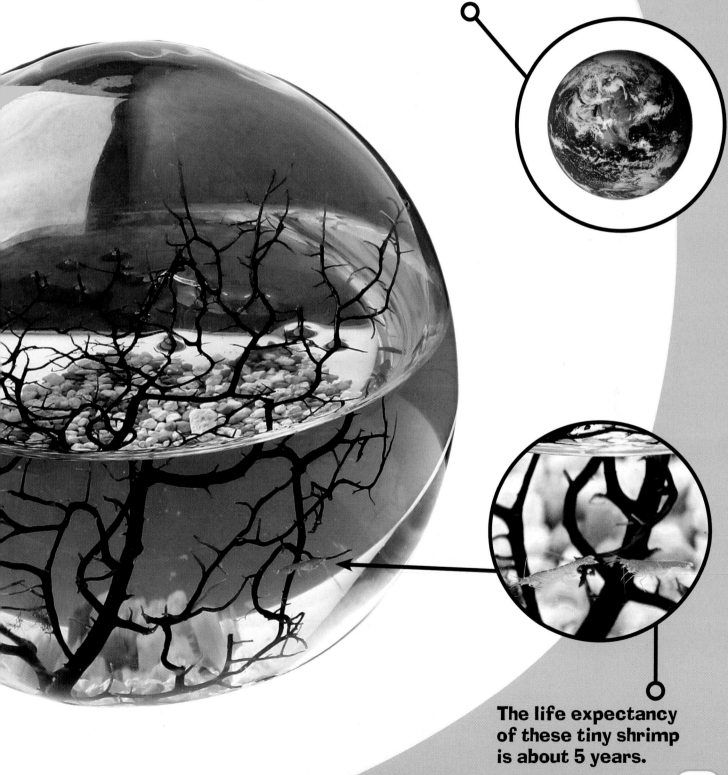

**The life expectancy of these tiny shrimp is about 5 years.**

# LINKS
## for Home and School

**GLE 0507.2.3** Establish the connections between human activities and natural disasters and their impact on the environment. **Math GLE 0506.5.1** Make, record, display and interpret data and graphs that include whole numbers, decimals, and fractions.
**ELA GLE 0501.3.2** Write in a variety of modes and genres, including narration, literary response, personal expression, description, and imaginative.

## Math  A Bird Population

A flock of birds arrived on an island on which birds have never lived. The bar graph shows the population of birds for 5 years.

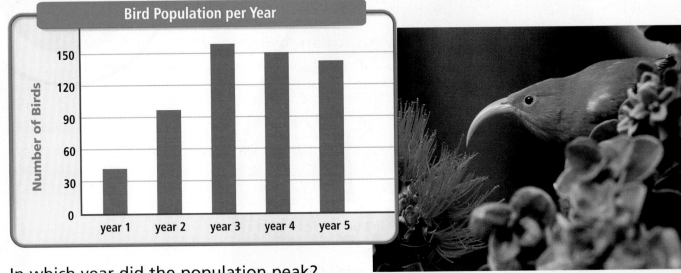

Bird Population per Year

1. In which year did the population peak?

2. Which of the following is a more likely cause for the decreasing population of birds between years 3 and 5?
   **a.** a sudden catastrophe, such as a volcanic eruption
   **b.** a slowly decreasing food supply

3. Explain your choice for question 2.

 **Writing**  **Persuasive Essay**

Suppose developers propose to fill in local wetlands to build a mall. They plan to move the animals that live in the wetlands to a forest. Identify the information you would need to form an opinion about the proposal. Then write a letter to the town council persuading them to vote for or against it.

## Wetlands Ecologist

Wetlands ecologists explore the unique ecosystems found in marshes, swamps, and low-lying areas near rivers. They study biodiversity, interactions among different species, and factors that contribute to environmental health.

Wetlands research is important for protecting water supplies. The fresh water from wetlands often becomes drinking water—maybe even in your community.

**What It Takes!**

- A degree in biology or ecology
- An interest in wild places

## Zookeeper

Part rancher, part veterinarian, part museum attendant—zookeepers care for zoo animals. They maintain the animals' diet and health and display them in ways that are safe for visitors and animals alike. Zookeepers also educate the public about animals, their ecosystems, and the issues they face in the wild.

**What It Takes!**

- Studies in biology and zoology
- Experience caring for animals

# Review and TCAP Prep

## Vocabulary

**Complete each sentence with a term from the list.**

1. The area where an organism lives is its _____.

2. There are very few giant pandas alive in the world today, so they are a(n) _____.

3. A sperm whale eats a giant squid, because giant squid are the whale's _____.

4. When a species that is headed toward extinction is not yet an endangered species, it is considered a(n)_____.

5. When an elephant eats grass, that is part of its _____.

6. Burning fossil fuels and dumping trash can cause _____.

7. A lion is an example of a(n) _____ that hunts zebras.

8. A giraffe's long neck is an example of a physical _____.

9. When all the members of a certain species are gone, _____ occurs.

10. Parasitism, commensalism, and mutualism are types of _____.

adaptation
endangered species
extinction
habitat
niche
pollution
population
predator
prey
symbiosis
threatened species

## TCAP Inquiry Skills

11. **Observe** Look around the area in which you live for examples of how humans have changed local ecosystems. Write a short paragraph describing these changes. **GLE 0507.Inq.4**

12. **Predict** A fire destroyed a forest. After a year, grasses began to grow back in the area. Soon after that, rabbits moved in to eat the grass. The rabbits had no major predators, so their population grew. Recently, foxes and hawks returned to the area. Predict how the population of the rabbits will change. **GLE 0507.Inq.1**

## Map the Concept

Fill in the concept map by listing types of symbiotic relationships, then write a definition for each term. **GLE 0507.2.2**

Symbiotic Relationships

Commensalism

## Critical Thinking

**13. Synthesize** What might be done to stop the spread of harmful alien species? List three ideas and discuss why they could work. GLE 0507.2.3

**14. Apply** What are some things you can do to help the environment? How could you encourage people to join you? GLE 0507.2.3

**15. Evaluate** Are symbiotic relationships beneficial or harmful to ecosystems? Explain your answer. GLE 0507.2.2

**16. Analyze** Scientists dig for fossils in an area of Tennessee. They find a fish fossil. After digging much deeper, they find a rhinoceros fossil. What does this tell the scientists about that area of land and its past? GLE 0507.5.2

 **Check** for Understanding

### Describe an Environment

Use the Internet to research fossil images. Examine the fossils to determine what the organisms that left them may have been like. After you have examined them, choose one. What can you infer about that organism's environment? Write a paragraph to describe that environment. 0507.5.4

## TCAP Prep

Answer the following questions.

**17** In which way can humans have a positive influence on the environment around them?

**A** drive cars more often

**B** recycle used cans

**C** leave the lights on

**D** dump trash SPI 0507.2.3

**18** What can scientists learn about Earth's past by studying fossils?

**F** how birds and dinosaurs interacted

**G** what color extinct animals were

**H** how sedimentary rock formed

**J** what environments existed on Earth SPI 0507.5.2

**19** Which symbiotic relationship is beneficial to one organism but is harmful to the other organism in the relationship?

**A** mutualism

**B** parasitism

**C** adaptation

**D** commensalism SPI 0507.2.2

**20** Which is an example of how people affect ecosystems?

**F** pollution

**G** volcanoes

**H** earthquakes

**J** hurricanes SPI 0507.2.3

# Traits of Living Things

**LESSON**

**1**

This flamingo was born with some traits and it acquired others. What determines traits?

**LESSON**

**2**

Certain traits help organisms to survive. Why are some traits more common than others?

**Fun Facts**

An alligator snapping turtle has a worm-like appendage on its tongue. The turtle uses it to attract fish.

FREE FOOD

acquired trait
adaptation
asexual reproduction
chromosome
DNA
dominant
gene
heredity
hybrid
mutation
nucleotide
recessive
selective breeding
sexual reproduction

## Vocabulary Strategies

Have you ever seen any of these terms before? Do you know what they mean?

↓

State a description, explanation, or example of the vocabulary in your own words.

↓

Draw a picture, symbol, example, or other image that describes the term.

**Glossary** p. H18

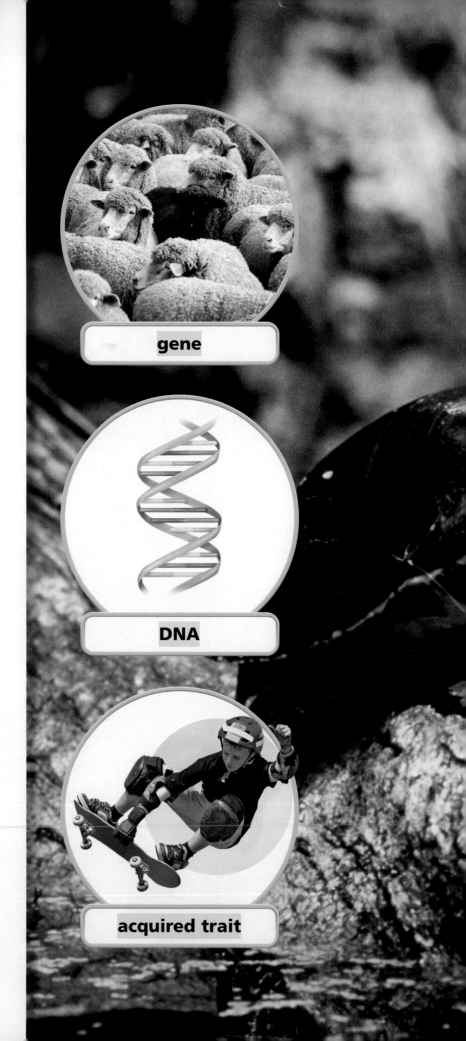

gene

DNA

acquired trait

adaptation

## Start with Your Standards

### Inquiry

**GLE 0507.Inq.1** Explore different scientific phenomena by asking questions, making logical predictions, planning investigations, and recording data.

**GLE 0507.Inq.4** Identify and interpret simple patterns of evidence to communicate the findings of multiple investigations.

### Life Science

#### Standard 4—Heredity

**GLE 0507.4.1** Describe how genetic information is passed from parents to offspring during reproduction.

**GLE 0507.4.2** Recognize that some characteristics are inherited while others result from interactions with the environment.

## Interact with this chapter.

**Go Digital** www.eduplace.com/tnscp

121

## Lesson
# 1

**TENNESSEE STANDARDS**

**GLE 0507.Inq.4** Identify and interpret simple patterns of evidence to communicate the findings of multiple investigations.
**GLE 0507.4.2** Recognize that some characteristics are inherited while others result from interactions with the environment.

*Guiding Question*

# How Are Traits Inherited?

## Why It Matters...

A trait is a physical or behavioral characteristic of an organism. Every person has a unique combination of traits. You have a set of traits that belongs to you alone. You also have traits you have acquired from interacting with your environment.

## PREPARE TO INVESTIGATE

### Inquiry Skill

**Analyze Data** When you analyze data, you look for patterns in information you have collected.

### Materials

- index cards
- pencils

---

**Science and Math Toolbox**

For step 2, review **Making a Chart to Organize Data** on page H11.

---

# Directed Inquiry

# Trait Tabulation

## Procedure

① **Collaborate** Work in a small group. Your team will get a letter. Assign a number to each person in your group. For example, your group letter might be C and your number might be 5, or C5.

② **Observe** Copy the chart shown at right onto an index card. Write your number-letter code, not your name, on your card. Answer the questions in the chart.

③ **Collaborate** Collect your team's cards and exchange them with the cards from another team. Then work with your team to count the number of people with each trait. Work in the same way with each of the other teams.

④ **Record Data** Tally the results for everyone in the class. Prepare a bar graph to show the data.

## Think and Write

1. **Use Numbers** How did the data change as you counted more people in the class? Why is it important that scientists use a large number of samples when doing research, such as you did in this activity?

2. **Evaluate** Of the five traits you studied, which could change as a person grows older? Which always stay the same?

3. **Analyze Data** For each trait, which form did you find to be the most common?

**STEP 2**

Letter and Number: _____

| Questions: | Answers: |
|---|---|
| 1. What color are your eyes? | |
| 2. Are your earlobes attached or detached? | |
| 3. Do you write with your left hand, right hand, or both? | |
| 4. Do you know how to ride a skateboard? | |
| 5. Can you recite the alphabet backwards very quickly? | |

**STEP 3**

Detached lobe    Attached lobe

**Guided Inquiry**

**Design an Experiment** With your teacher's permission, survey students in other classes about the five traits. What can you conclude from your results?

0507.4.2

# Traits

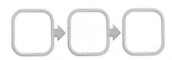
## Traits of Organisms

Do you look like anyone in your family? People tend to look like their parents and grandparents because of heredity. **Heredity** is the process through which traits are passed from parents to offspring.

Human traits that are passed by heredity—or inherited traits—include face shape, hair color, and blood type. The color of an animal's fur, the shape of its ears, and the arrangement of its teeth are also examples of inherited traits. The colors of a flower or the shape of a fruit are examples among plants. An inherited trait can also be a behavior, such as the way a spider spins a web.

Not every trait that you can observe is passed down by heredity. Some traits are acquired. An **acquired trait** is one that an organism develops after it is born. Some acquired traits come from the environment, others are learned, and still others are brought about purposely.

Inherited traits are passed on from generation to generation through chromosomes.

## Acquired Traits

Flamingos are known for their beautiful pink color, which sets them apart from other large, long-legged water birds. The color comes from pigments in shrimp and certain algae that flamingos eat.

The pink color of flamingos is an example of an acquired trait. This kind of trait comes from interactions with the environment. In a similar way, organisms can acquire traits from food, soil, water, and other elements in their environment.

Some acquired traits are learned. You were not born knowing how to ride a bicycle or a skateboard—you learned how to ride.

Other animals learn behaviors, too. Dogs learn to follow commands, lions learn to hunt, and birds learn how to sing songs. An acquired trait of this kind is called a learned trait.

Manipulated traits are traits that people deliberately change. Plants and animals have been manipulated for thousands of years. Breeders mate animals or cross plants with the most desirable traits. Gardeners also control the shape and design of a plant. They may keep some plants small, or give plants interesting shapes.

Some traits arise from both inherited and acquired features. For example, a person may inherit the capacity to be tall. However, the trait will show itself only if combined with proper nutrition and exercise.

**FOCUS CHECK** How might a plant develop an acquired trait?

**Learned** ▲
Organisms can acquire traits, like the ability to ride a skateboard, by learning and remembering skills and information.

**Environmental** ▲
Organisms can acquire traits from their environments. A flamingo is pink because it eats pink food.

**Manipulated** ▶
Manipulated traits, such as coiled bamboo, are created by human design. People can change both inherited and acquired traits.

## Chromosomes and Genes

What determines the inherited traits of an organism? The information is stored within the cell nucleus in a molecule called deoxyribonucleic acid, **DNA.** A DNA molecule consists of two long parallel strands. The strands coil around each other like edges of a twisted ladder.

Molecules of DNA are passed from one generation to the next during reproduction. Recall that reproduction is the process through which organisms make offspring. For DNA to be passed to offspring, a copy of it must first be made.

In cells that are not dividing, DNA and protein are found in a loose form that is spread out within the nucleus. This form of DNA, called chromatin, is difficult to see even with most microscopes.

As the cell gets ready to divide, however, the double strands of DNA coil tightly. These shorter, thicker coils of DNA form rod-shaped structures called **chromosomes.** Chromosomes are visible under a microscope.

As a cell is dividing, each chromosome consists of two identical halves called chromatids. The central region that holds the chromatids together is called the centromere.

In the bodies of most organisms, all cells have an even number of chromosomes. In fact, they form pairs. The chromosomes in each pair are similar, but not identical.

The number of chromosomes per cell is different in different species. Humans, for example, have 46 chromosomes in each cell. Dogs have 78, cats have 38, and fruit flies have 8 chromosomes.

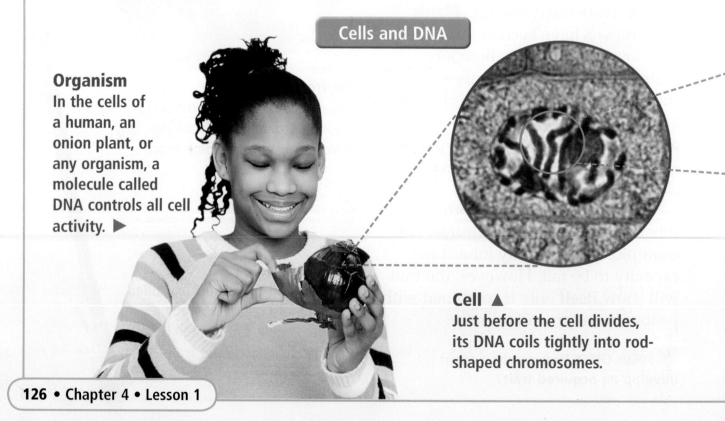

Cells and DNA

**Organism**
In the cells of a human, an onion plant, or any organism, a molecule called DNA controls all cell activity. ▶

**Cell** ▲
Just before the cell divides, its DNA coils tightly into rod-shaped chromosomes.

In every plant and animal, one type of cell is made with only half the chromosomes of other cells. These are the cells used for reproduction. They are called gametes, or egg and sperm cells. Human gametes, for example, contain only 23 chromosomes.

When two gametes combine, their chromosomes become part of the nucleus of a cell of a new individual. The cell has a complete set of chromosomes.

There are many more traits than there are chromosomes. The reason is that the information in one chromosome can determine many traits. Each trait of an organism is determined by a short segment of DNA known as a **gene.** One chromosome can have hundreds of genes on it.

## The Structure of DNA

A basic unit of DNA is called a **nucleotide**. Each nucleotide is made up of a phosphate, a sugar, and a nitrogen base. There are four possible nitrogen bases.

Recall that a molecule of DNA resembles a ladder. The phosphate groups and sugar molecules make up the sides of the ladder. Pairs of nitrogen bases make up the steps. Pairs form only between specific bases.

The order of the nitrogen bases determines the genes of the organism. Because the bases can be arranged in a great number of ways, a great number of genes are possible.

**FOCUS CHECK** **Why do body cells have twice as many chromosomes as gametes?**

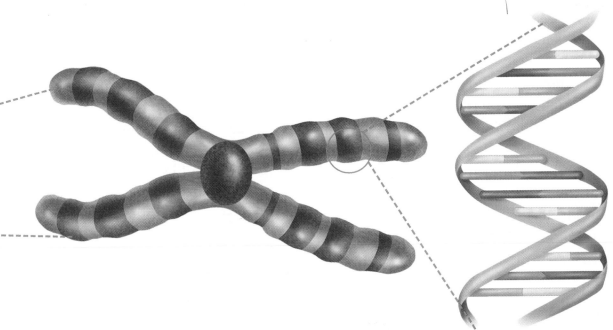

**Chromosome ▲**
A chromosome is made of two identical strands, called chromatids, joined at the centromere. The DNA is organized into units called genes.

**DNA ▲**
The information in DNA is coded by its arrangement of nitrogen bases. A single DNA molecule may have billions of base pairs!

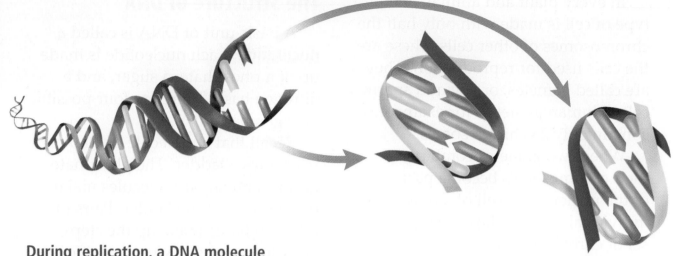

During replication, a DNA molecule separates. Each strand is used to form a new DNA molecule. ▲

The two new molecules are identical to the original. ▲

## DNA Replication

Before a cell divides, an exact copy of its DNA is made. This process is called DNA replication. To begin the process, the strands of the DNA molecule separate along their nitrogen bases. This part of the process resembles unzipping a zipper.

Quickly after, bases floating around the nucleus attach to the bases of unzipped strands of DNA. Remember that bases always pair up in the same combinations. That means that the same type of base that just separated from one strand attaches to take its place.

This process happens to both of the unzipped strands. When all the bases are in place, a new strand has formed on each of the original strands. In this way, two new DNA molecules are formed, each identical to the original.

## Protein Synthesis

What is so important about the order of bases in the DNA molecule? DNA directs the production of substances called proteins. Proteins control most of the life processes in cells. They are also necessary for building and maintaining cells. It is the proteins that cause certain traits to be expressed in an organism.

Proteins are made up of smaller units known as amino acids. There are 20 different amino acids that can be arranged in many different combinations. The specific arrangement of amino acids determines the nature of the protein.

Recall from Chapter 1 that proteins are formed on cell parts called ribosomes. By means of intermediate molecules, DNA directs the order in which amino acids are arranged to form these proteins. Through this action, DNA controls all cell activities!

**Can you find the mutation?**

## Mutations

Occasionally, an error occurs during the process of DNA replication. This kind of change is called a **mutation.**

A mutation may cause a change in the proteins formed in a cell. Many mutations are harmful because they decrease an organism's chances for survival. In rare cases, mutations are helpful because they result in desirable traits.

Some mutations are neither harmful nor helpful. Even if they result in changes to the organism's proteins, the changes are less obvious and do not directly affect the survival of the organism.

Many mutations occur by chance. Other mutations are caused by environmental factors called mutagens. Ultraviolet radiation from the Sun and certain chemicals, such as some pesticides, can act as mutagens.

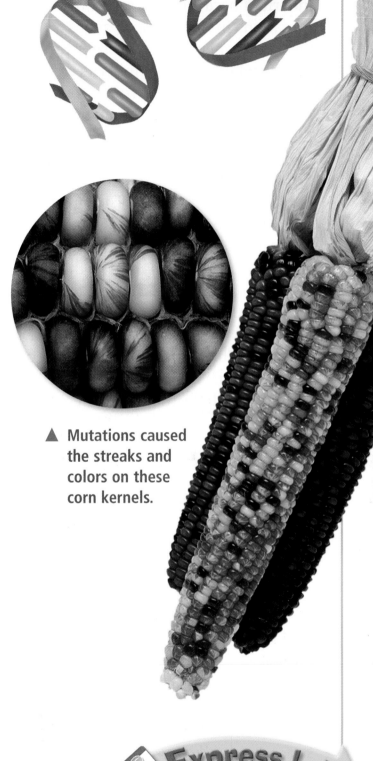

▲ **Mutations caused the streaks and colors on these corn kernels.**

**FOCUS CHECK** How does a mutation affect the traits of an organism?

**Express Lab**

**Activity Card**
*Compare Parents and Offspring*

**129**

# Genes and Health

Some human diseases are inherited because they result from mutations in one or more genes. Sickle cell anemia is a disorder that results when a person inherits a mutated gene for the production of hemoglobin. In blood, hemoglobin is the protein that carries oxygen.

In this disorder, one of the nitrogen bases in the gene for hemoglobin is changed. This error results in the production of protein that causes red blood cells to be shaped like sickles instead of the normal round shape. The sickle shape prevents the cells from working properly.

Cystic fibrosis is another inherited disorder. This is a disease that results from genes that produce a defect in proteins that control the flow of certain materials into and out of cells.

Some other inherited diseases include hemophilia and muscular dystrophy. Hemophilia is a disease in which the blood does not clot properly. Muscular dystrophy causes the muscles to break down over time.

Another type of genetic disorder occurs when chromosomes do not separate properly during reproduction. Recall that chromosomes are copied before a cell divides. The copies split apart, and one copy goes to each new cell.

Down syndrome occurs when a specific pair of chromosomes does not separate properly. The extra chromosome causes physical and mental changes in the person.

**FOCUS CHECK How does sickle cell anemia affect human health?**

## Inherited Diseases

| Disorder | Description |
|---|---|
| Cystic fibrosis | Makes mucus extra thick and sticky, clogging lungs and digestive track. |
| Hemophilia | Prevents body from producing clotting factors, resulting in uncontrolled bleeding. |
| Muscular dystrophy | Prevents body from making protein for muscle cells, resulting in muscle weakness. |
| Sickle cell anemia | Creates red blood cells shaped like sickles. Sickle cells block other cells in the bloodstream and do not carry as much oxygen. |

Sickle cell anemia produces blood cells in an abnormal sickle shape. Sickle cells block other blood cells. ▼

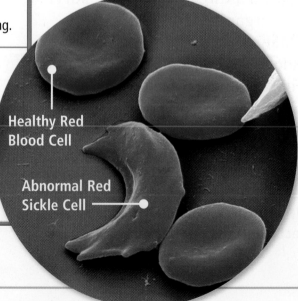

Healthy Red Blood Cell

Abnormal Red Sickle Cell

# Lesson Wrap-Up

## Visual Summary

Traits can be inherited from parents or acquired from the environment.

Genes code for an organism's inherited traits. A gene is a segment of a huge molecule called DNA.

Mutations occur when the bases in a genetic sequence change.

## Check for Understanding

### THE STORY OF YOU

- Write a story about who you are and how you became that way.

- In your story, classify your traits and behaviors as inherited, learned, or environmental. You also may compare your traits with the traits of others.

- Present your story as an illustrated booklet.

  ✓ 0507.4.2

# Review

**① MAIN IDEA** What material carries the information that determines genetic traits?

**② VOCABULARY** Write a sentence or short paragraph using the terms *genes* and *DNA*.

**③ READING SKILL: Sequence** What steps take place during DNA replication?

**④ CRITICAL THINKING: Apply** How do mutations affect an organism? Why can some mutations have no effect?

**⑤ INQUIRY SKILL: Analyze Data** What information would a scientist need to discover whether a disorder had a genetic cause, an environmental cause, or a combination of the two?

## TCAP Prep

Which of these traits or behaviors is most likely determined by genes?

**A** eye color
**B** ability to ride a bike
**C** the language you speak
**D** your favorite food

SPI 0507.4.2

## Go Digital Technology

Visit **www.eduplace.com/tnscp** to learn more about genes and heredity.

# Rosalind Franklin

## (1920–1958)

**In 1962, James Watson, Francis Crick, and Maurice Wilkins were awarded the Nobel Prize for discovering the structure of DNA.** Yet their achievement relied greatly on a woman who was not so honored. Alas, Rosalind Franklin had died four years earlier.

As a young girl, Franklin was energetic and talkative, often arguing politics with her father. She excelled in school, especially at science. She became the first woman in her family to graduate from college with a science degree.

Her most famous works are her x-ray pictures of DNA, such as the one shown here. Other scientists had tried to take pictures like this. However, Franklin recognized that DNA changed its shape in water. She carefully and precisely added just the right amount of water to her specimens. From her pictures and other data, she determined much about the shape and composition of the DNA molecule.

One of Franklin's colleagues described her with these words: ". . . Miss Franklin was distinguished by extreme clarity and perfection in everything she undertook. Her photographs are among the most beautiful of any substances ever taken."

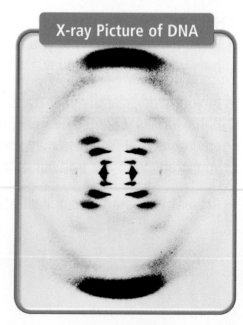

X-ray Picture of DNA

Compare Franklin's x-ray picture to the illustration of DNA on page 127. ▶

GLE 0507.T/E.1 Describe how tools, technology, and inventions help to answer questions and solve problems.

EXTEND

# Lynn Margulis
## (1938–    )

In the 1980s, scientists studying cells discovered something they did not expect. Mitochondria, the cell parts that produce energy, have their own DNA! This DNA controls only the mitochondria. It works apart from the DNA in the nucleus.

Yet the discovery did not surprise everyone. Years earlier, biologist Lynn Margulis predicted just such a finding. The prediction was part of a larger idea she proposed about cell history. It is called the endosymbiont hypothesis.

According to this hypothesis, mitochondria and chloroplasts were once small, free-living cells, much like bacteria. At some point, a larger, amoeba-like cell engulfed some of them. Yet, instead of breaking apart, the small cells stayed alive inside the larger cell. After many cycles of reproduction, they became cell parts.

The endosymbiont hypothesis explains much about mitochondria. As for Margulis, she now is recognized as an insightful and dedicated scientist.

**Animal Cell**

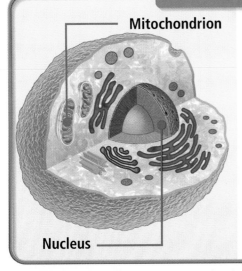

Mitochondrion

Nucleus

### Unique features of mitochondria

- Able to use oxygen
- Surrounded by a double membrane
- Divide separately from the rest of the cell
- Have their own DNA that resembles bacterial DNA

## Sharing Ideas

1. **READING CHECK** What did Franklin and Margulis show about DNA?

2. **WRITE ABOUT IT** What does Margulis's hypothesis explain about cells?

3. **TALK ABOUT IT** Which science skills did Franklin and Margulis practice?

133

**TENNESSEE STANDARDS**

**GLE 0507.Inq.1** Explore different scientific phenomena by asking questions, making logical predictions, planning investigations, and recording data.

**GLE 0507.4.1** Explain how genetic information is passed from parents to offspring during reproduction.

**Guiding Question ?**

# Why Are Some Traits Very Common?

## Why It Matters...

For a species to continue, its members must reproduce. Sometimes, new individuals are exact copies of one parent. Other times, they are similar to two parents, but not exactly like them. When the two young giraffes become adults, they may pass traits to young of their own.

## PREPARE TO INVESTIGATE

### Inquiry Skill

**Use Models** When you use models, you make an object that helps you understand a concept or a process.

### Materials

- 4 each of 3 shapes of beads or buttons, with each shape in 2 colors (12 beads total)
- chenille stems

### Science and Math Toolbox

For step 2, review **Making a Chart to Organize Data** on page H11.

# Directed Inquiry

# Chromosome Combinations

## Procedure

**1 Use Models** Model genes on chromosomes by stringing three beads on each chenille stem. Refer to the chart to find the meaning of each type of bead. Thread the ear shape gene first, then the eye color gene, and then the gene for hair color. Separate the chromosomes into two pairs to represent two parents.

**2 Record Data** In your *Science Notebook,* draw the bead shapes and colors on the chromosomes for each parent. Create a chart to organize your data.

**3 Experiment** Take one chromosome from the first parent to form a gamete chromosome. Repeat for the second parent. Draw the gamete chromosomes in the chart. Then combine them to form the chromosomes for a new cell called a zygote. Draw the chromosomes of the zygote in the chart.

## Think and Write

1. **Analyze Data** Is it possible to predict the offspring's chances of having a certain hair color, eye color, and ear shape? Why or why not?

2. **Use Models** Make a model of two parents whose traits are exactly alike and model the offspring's chromosomes. Are the traits of this offspring more predictable than those of the first offspring you modeled?

0507.4.1

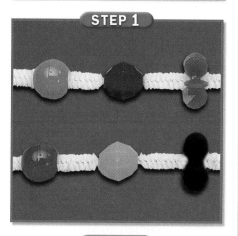

STEP 1

| Trait | A | B |
|-------|---|---|
| ear shape | Attached | Not Attached |
| eye color | Blue | Brown |
| hair color | Brown | Black |

STEP 1

STEP 3

### Guided Inquiry

**Design an Experiment** Find out what happens when you add more choices of traits. Make models with several choices for eye color, hair color, and one other trait.

# How Traits Are Passed

## VOCABULARY

adaptation
asexual reproduction
dominant
hybrid
recessive
selective breeding
sexual reproduction

## GRAPHIC ORGANIZER

**Cause and Effect** Use a chart like the one below to show the effects of selective breeding.

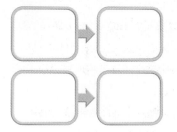

GLE 0507.4.1 Describe how genetic information is passed from parents to offspring during reproduction.

GLE 0507.4.2 Recognize that some characteristics are inherited while others result from interactions with the environment.

## Asexual Reproduction

Did you know that some kinds of living things have only one parent? In **asexual reproduction,** offspring are produced from one parent. Bacteria and many protists typically reproduce asexually.

Recall that fission and budding are the simplest types of asexual reproduction. Spore formation is another kind of asexual reproduction. Yeast, for example, may produce spores that are spread by water and wind. Each spore can grow into a new yeast organism.

When an organism reproduces asexually, an exact copy of DNA is passed from parent to offspring. Generation after generation, the offspring have the same genetic material, or DNA. Mutations are the only sources of new traits in this type of reproduction.

Plantlets are offspring that break off or are cut away from the parent plant. Each plantlet can become a separate plant without fertilization. ▼

Plantlet

New roots

**Original arm**

**Four new arms**

**Regeneration**

Starfish, or sea stars, can grow new arms to replace those that have been cut off. This regeneration is a form of asexual reproduction.

In the simplest organisms, such as bacteria, most or all reproduction is asexual. Other organisms use asexual reproduction part of the time. Many fungi and plants, for example, alternate between asexual reproduction and sexual reproduction.

Yeast also alternates. A yeast produces buds asexually. The bud breaks off from the yeast cell and begins to grow. At other times, the yeast produces male and female gametes. These cells can combine to make a new yeast cell.

Plants have several different asexual structures. Some plants produce long stems or roots that then grow plantlets, or baby plants, that break off from the parent. Other kinds of plants can grow from root cuttings or from stem fragments.

## Budding

Hydra are animals that reproduce asexually by budding. They can also reproduce using female and male gametes. ▶

Another asexual process in some animals is regeneration. For example, flatworms called *planaria* can regenerate. If a planaria is cut in half, each half will grow to produce two whole worms.

Cells divide during both asexual reproduction and regeneration. In both processes, the new cells have exactly the same DNA as the original cells. Replicating and passing on the same DNA helps ensure that traits will stay the same.

⊚ **FOCUS CHECK How many parents are needed for asexual reproduction?**

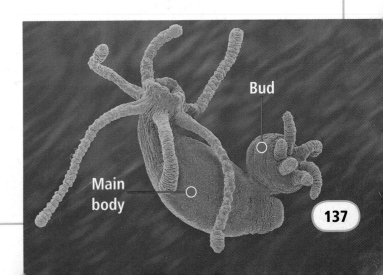

**Bud**

**Main body**

137

# Sexual Reproduction

**Sexual reproduction** occurs when a female gamete joins with a male gamete to form a new organism. In addition to yeast and algae, animals and plants also practice sexual reproduction.

A flowering plant has male and female reproductive structures in its flowers. Pollination occurs when pollen is transferred from the male part, a stamen, to the female part, a pistil. A sperm cell released by the pollen then fertilizes an egg cell.

In Lesson 1, you learned that gametes contain half the number of chromosomes as in the organism's other cells. When a sperm cell combines with an egg cell, the chromosomes become part of the same cell. The result is a cell with a complete set of chromosomes.

In this way, the offspring receives one chromosome in each pair from each parent. Each chromosome contains genes that determine the traits of the offspring. The offspring receives two genes for each trait.

Different genes may code for different forms of the same trait. For example, suppose a bee carries pollen from a red flower to a yellow flower. The offspring may receive a gene for red flower color and a gene for yellow flower color. Red and yellow are two forms of the same trait— flower color.

**1 Pollen**
Pollen contains male sex cells that have the male genes. Anthers produce pollen

**2 Pollination**
A bee or other pollinator transports male genetic material from flower to flower.

**3 Egg**
The bee brushes the pollen onto the female parts as it looks for nectar. Sperm travel from the pollen to the egg, deep in the flower.

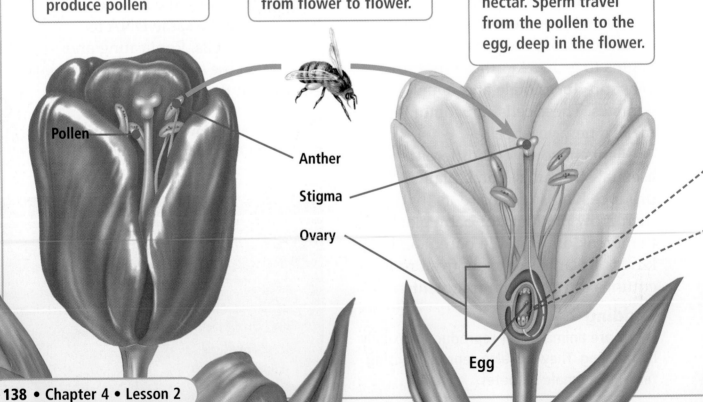

Pollen

Anther

Stigma

Ovary

Egg

The form of a trait that is expressed depends on the characteristics of the genes. Some forms of a trait are dominant and others are recessive. If an offspring receives genes for two different forms of a trait, the trait of the **dominant** gene is expressed. The **recessive** gene is not expressed.

Suppose red flowers are dominant for a particular plant. An offspring plant that receives a gene for red flowers from each parent will have red flowers. So will an offspring plant that receives a gene for red flowers from one parent and a gene for yellow flowers from the other parent. The dominant trait is expressed instead of the recessive trait. Only offspring that receive a gene for yellow flowers from each parent will have yellow flowers.

An organism that has two identical genes for a trait is said to be purebred. A purebred organism can have two dominant genes or two recessive genes. An organism that has two different genes for the same trait is called a **hybrid.**

The offspring of hybrids may express traits that are different from either parent. Think again about the red and yellow flowers. Suppose a bee carries pollen from a red flower to a red flower. Because red flowers are dominant, you might think that all of the offspring will have red flowers. If the parents are hybrids, however, they each carry a gene for yellow flowers—even though you don't see it. If an offspring happens to receive a gene for yellow flowers from each parent, it will express the recessive trait of yellow flowers.

**FOCUS CHECK** In sexual reproduction, how many cells create a new organism?

**4**

Sperm      Egg

Fertilized egg

**The fertilized egg contains DNA from both parents.**

**5** Seeds contain the embryos, or first cells, of the next generation. Their DNA comes from both parents.

**6** These flowers display the traits of their species and the dominant traits of their particular variants.

Broccoli

Cauliflower

Brussels sprouts

## Ancestral Plant?

Broccoli, cauliflower, and Brussels sprouts are just a few of the variants derived by selective breeding from an ancient cabbage plant.

## Selective Breeding

For thousands of years, humans have identified and worked to increase desirable traits in plants and animals. Long before scientists knew about chromosomes and genes, farmers and shepherds were breeding plants and animals to obtain offspring with useful traits.

The practice of breeding plants and animals for desirable traits is known as **selective breeding.** Through selective breeding, humans try to plan the arrangement of genes in offspring without actually changing the genetic material in any way.

One method of selective breeding involves combining parents with two or more different traits. This method is known as hybridization. The goal of hybridization is to produce a hybrid organism with the best traits from both parents.

For example, a plant breeder might cross a rose plant that produces large, fragrant flowers with a rose bush that does not have thorns. The desired result would be a plant that produces large, fragrant flowers and does not have thorns.

Selective breeding may produce plants and animals that survive specific environments. For example, red winter wheat is a hybrid that grows in cold weather. It allows farmers to harvest two wheat crops a year, even in cold climates.

Another method of selective breeding involves combining plants and animals with the same or similar traits. In this way, a breeder can predict that the traits of the offspring will be very similar to the traits of the parents.

This method, known as inbreeding, is in some ways opposite to hybridization. Breeders sometimes practice inbreeding to keep a breed pure. Horses and dogs, for example, are often bred pure so that offspring maintain the same traits as their parents.

One drawback of inbreeding is that it reduces the chances that an offspring will inherit new combinations of genes. This means that the genetic information among a generation is very similar.

If similar organisms are exposed to changes in their environment, such as harsh weather or disease, all may suffer. In a population where some of the organisms have a different genetic makeup, at least some may survive such conditions.

Why do you think people breed thornless roses? ▶

Today, farmers and ranchers use technology to improve crops and animals. For example, food additives can stimulate hens to lay more eggs or cows to make more milk. Some crop plants release compounds that kill insect pests. Also, computers make it easier to document selective breeding procedures and to identify patterns in the results.

⊙ **FOCUS CHECK** What is the intended result of selective breeding?

Beef cow

Dairy cow

Some cows are bred to produce beef. Others are bred to produce milk.

## Adaptations

In nature, favorable traits are not necessarily those traits that are preferred by humans. They are traits that help an organism to survive. Any trait that helps an individual to survive in its environment is called an **adaptation.**

For example, flowers of pond plants will be exposed to many water insects. Those plants that can be pollinated by water insects have an advantage over other plants. This trait makes these plants more likely to survive and reproduce in their environment.

A favorable trait in one environment may not be favorable elsewhere. The same plant that is pollinated by water insects would suffer in a dry, desert environment.

Some adaptations help organisms to find food. The shape of a pelican's beak is an adaptation that allows the bird to scoop up fish. A hummingbird's long, thin beak is adapted to feed on nectar inside flowers. A parrot's beak is short and thick, which lets it crack open seeds.

Other adaptations help organisms defend themselves. Spines or stinging rays keep predators away or wound those that get too close. Thorns, spines, or tough leaves protect plants from being eaten.

▲ Air bladders keep this seaweed floating, letting its leaves bask in the Sun.

▲ A long, deep beak helps a pelican scoop up fish.

▲ Porcupine quills are an adaptation that defends against predators.

## Different Adaptations

**Camouflage**
The walking stick is an insect that looks like a twig. It is well hidden.

**Warning coloration**
The red and yellow patterns of the poison arrow frog signal predators that it is toxic.

**Mimicry**
The king snake gets extra protection from looking like a coral snake.

**Camouflage** Many adaptations protect organisms from predators. The ability to blend into the surroundings is known as camouflage. Organisms with camouflage can hide from predators.

For example, some insects look very much like the flowers of their favorite plants. Bees typically gather honey at the times of day when shadows are deepest. Their black stripes blend into the shadows.

**Warning Coloration** While many frogs use camouflage, others have bright body colors and markings. Bright colors often indicate that an organism is poisonous. The colors warn predators to stay away. A predator that eats one poisonous frog is not likely to eat any others!

Did you know that many birds avoid eating red insects? Red insects often are poisonous.

**Mimicry** The ability to look like another species is known as mimicry. An organism might mimic another species that is more threatening to a predator. The king snake, for example, is not a venomous snake. However, it mimics the venomous coral snake, which most predators will avoid.

Sometimes two species have adaptations that work together. Butterflies, for example, are attracted to plants that have many flowers in large clusters. The butterflies can eat nectar without using too much energy flying from flower to flower. In return, the butterflies help the plants by transferring pollen from one flower to another.

**FOCUS CHECK** What is an adaptation?

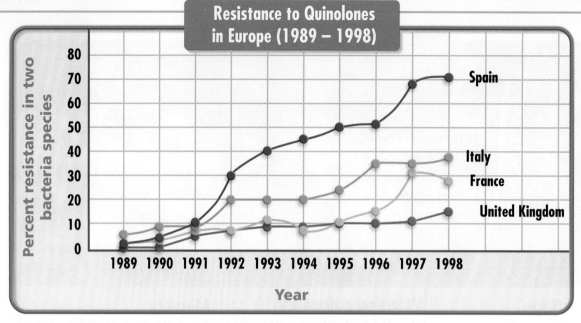

**Resistance to Quinolones in Europe (1989 – 1998)**

Percent resistance in two bacteria species vs. Year

Spain
Italy
France
United Kingdom

▲ Quinolones are a group of antibiotics. Bacteria became more resistant to them over time. The data in this graph come from different scientific studies.

## Changing Adaptations

How quickly can a new gene spread among a species? In bacteria, a gene can become common in only a few years. The reason is that bacteria exist in huge numbers and they reproduce very quickly.

The chart shows an example that involves antibiotics, which are drugs that fight bacteria. Many antibiotics are part of a group called quinolones. At first, these drugs were very effective. Yet a small number of bacteria had a gene that helped them resist quinolones. They survived while others did not, so the gene became more common.

Today, scientists continue to develop new antibiotics. But doctors use them only as a last resort. The more often a new drug is used, the quicker bacteria gain resistance to it.

Just as new genes can arise and spread, so too can genes disappear. This typically happens when the population of a species becomes very low.

In the late 1800s, for example, northern elephant seals were hunted almost to extinction. Their numbers may have fallen as low as 100 seals. Today there are 150,000 seals. Yet all have very similar genes, much more so than in other seal species. Many differences among northern seals may be lost forever.

Northern elephant seals once were hunted almost to extinction. Many of their genetic differences were lost. ▶

**Express Lab**

Activity Card
*Compare Adaptations*

# Lesson Wrap-Up

## Visual Summary

Organisms reproduce in one of two main ways: asexually from only one parent or sexually from two parents.

Through selective breeding, people develop breeds of plants and animals that have desirable traits.

Adaptations help individuals to survive in their environments.

## Check for Understanding

### NEW PLANTS

Research how plant scientists in Tennessee and elsewhere are developing new types of plants. Examples include improved farm crops, more colorful roses and other flowers, and faster-growing evergreen trees. Present your research to the class.

✓ 0507.4.1

# Review

① **MAIN IDEA** How do humans influence the traits of a species?

② **VOCABULARY** Write a sentence or short paragraph that defines and explains an adaptation.

③ **READING SKILL: Cause and Effect** What are two possible effects that changes in environment can have on a species?

④ **CRITICAL THINKING: Synthesize** Compare the benefits and drawbacks of asexual reproduction and sexual reproduction.

⑤ **INQUIRY SKILL: Use a Model** How could you create a model to show the passing down of a recessive trait through three generations?

## TCAP Prep

Which process produces offspring that have the same DNA as their parent?

A   asexual reproduction
B   sexual reproduction
C   selective breeding
D   hybrid breeding

SPI 0507.4.1

## Technology

Visit **www.eduplace.com/tnscp** to learn more about adaptations.

# Let's Dance!

**Look at those big blue feet!** What could this high-stepping bird be doing? Funny as it might look, he's trying to attract a mate!

Different species have their own ways of courting. This courting behavior is inherited. This means the blue-footed booby doesn't have to learn its unique dance. It's born with the instinct to do it. In courtship, the male tries to catch the female's eye by striking a pose with his bill in the air. Once she notices, he dances toward her, raising each foot high. If the female is attracted, she joins in the dance.

If the birds mate, their genes will pass to their offspring, giving them those remarkable blue feet and other physical traits. The offspring will also know how to dance when the time comes!

**GLE 0507.4.2** Recognize that some characteristics are inherited while others result from interactions with the environment.

EXTEND

**Peacock** The male peacock's amazing tail feathers are an inherited trait. He shakes them and dances to attract a mate.

**Prairie Chicken** The male prairie chicken inflates his orange throat sacs during his mating display.

**Sandhill Crane** To attract a mate, the male crane points his beak straight up and calls out with trumpet-like cries.

GLE 0507.4.2 Recognize that some characteristics are inherited while others result from interactions with the environment. **Math GLE 0506.5.1** Make, record, display, and interpret data and graphs that include whole numbers, decimals, and fractions. **ELA GLE 0501.3.4** Write frequently across content areas.

## Math The Mouse Maze

Four hungry mice were placed in a maze. At the end of the maze was a piece of cheese. The experiment was repeated 6 times. The results of the 6 trials are shown in the chart.

1. In this experiment, what is the range of completion times? (Note: Range is the difference between highest and lowest values.)

2. Which mouse improved with each trial? Which mouse appeared not to learn at all? Explain.

3. For each mouse, predict results of additional trials of this experiment.

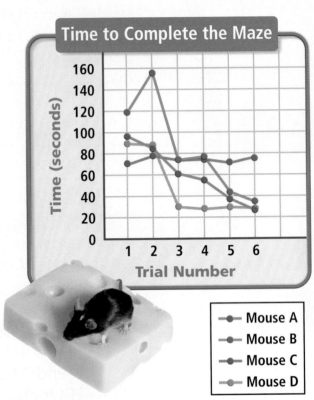

**Time to Complete the Maze**

## Narrative

Choose an animal and research its behavior. Write a story to show both its inherited and learned behaviors.

## Gregor Mendel

Gregor Mendel, a monk who lived more than 130 years ago, noticed differences among the pea plants in his garden. Some were tall, while others were short; some had smooth peas and some had wrinkled peas. Mendel cross-pollinated the plants. He took pollen from one plant and placed it on the flower of another plant.

It's easy to see the difference between wrinkled and round peas.

Mendel planted the seeds made by the cross-pollinated plants. Based on the traits of the parent plants, he predicted certain traits of the offspring. He studied thousands of pea plants to make sure he always got the same results. With so many plants in his garden over many years, Mendel had to keep very good records. His meticulous records helped him discover genetic heredity, the passing along of traits from parents to offspring through genes. Mendel's discoveries earned him the title "the father of modern genetics."

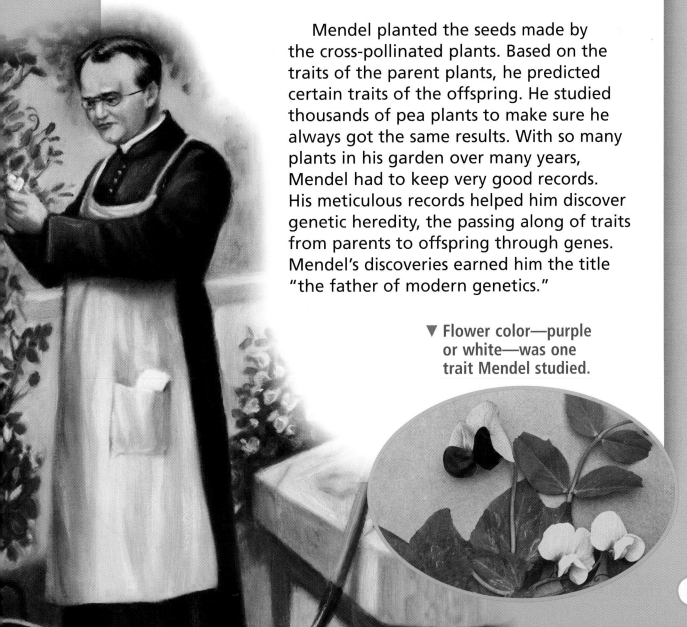

▼ Flower color—purple or white—was one trait Mendel studied.

# Review and TCAP Prep

## Vocabulary

**Complete each sentence with a term from the list.**

1. A trait developed through learning is a(n) ____.

2. A chemical sequence of DNA, or ____, determines a trait of an organism.

3. A(n) ____ is made of a phosphate, a sugar, and a base.

4. The reproductive material known as ____ appears in two strands coiled around each other.

5. A(n) ____ is a change in the arrangement of bases in a gene.

6. Bacteria multiply by ____.

7. A(n) ____ trait is expressed even if only one gene for that form of the trait is inherited.

8. A(n) ____ trait is only expressed if an organism has two genes for that form of the trait.

9. Farmers practice ____ when they mate organisms with desirable traits.

10. Any trait that helps an individual to survive in its environment is a(n) ____.

acquired trait
adaptation
asexual reproduction
chromosome
DNA
dominant
gene
heredity
hybrid
mutation
nucleotide
recessive
selective breeding
sexual reproduction

## TCAP Inquiry Skills

11. **Communicate** List three inherited or acquired traits that help you survive. Explain how each trait provides an advantage. **GLE 0507.Inq.1**

12. **Use Models** Draw a diagram that traces one person's chromosomes back through at least three generations (parents, grandparents, and great-grandparents). **GLE 0507.Inq.3**

## Map the Concept

Draw a Venn diagram like the one shown here. Write facts that apply to each category.

Asexual reproduction — Both — Sexual reproduction

**GLE 0507.4.1**

## Critical Thinking

**13. Synthesize** Explain why it is necessary in sexual reproduction for the gametes to have half the number of chromosomes found in body cells. **GLE 0507.4.1**

**14. Apply** Botanists and farmers save seeds in a seed bank. Explain the purpose of a seed bank. How can two seeds from the same plant species be different? **GLE 0507.4.1**

**15. Synthesize** Explain why asexual processes are important to organisms that reproduce from two parents. **GLE 0507.4.1**

**16. Evaluate** Give an example of genes becoming more common in a population, and an example of genes becoming less common. Why are these changes important? **GLE 0507.4.1**

 **Check for Understanding**

### Explain Traits

Suppose a younger student asks you why her hand looks different than your hand. Her hand has freckles and a scar. Write an explanation for the student. Make sure to explain the difference between where the scar came from and where the freckles came from. **0507.4.3**

### TCAP Prep

Answer the following questions.

**17** Both traits from the environment and learned behaviors are

**A** passed down through genes

**B** taught by parents to offspring

**C** always the result of human intervention

**D** acquired by individuals in each generation **SPI 0507.4.1**

**18** In sexual reproduction, genes come from

**F** either parent, but not both

**G** the father only

**H** the mother only

**J** both parents **SPI 0507.4.1**

**19** Body shape, hair and eye color, and the need for sleep are examples of

**A** inherited traits

**B** learned traits

**C** manipulated traits

**D** traits identical in every generation **SPI 0507.4.2**

**20** Which of the following traits is **not** influenced by an organism's environment?

**F** eye color

**G** height

**H** skin color

**J** favorite food **SPI 0507.4.2**

## 1 Cells

**Performance Indicator:** SPI 0507.1.1 Compare and contrast basic structures and functions of plant and animal cells.

**1** Which structure is found in plant cells but <u>not</u> in animal cells?

- **A** cell membrane
- **B** cell wall
- **C** mitochondrion
- **D** Golgi apparatus

## 2 Interdependence

**Performance Indicator:** SPI 0507.2.2 Distinguish among symbiotic, commensal, and parasitic relationships.

**2** What type of relationship is shown?

- **F** predator/prey
- **G** commensalism
- **H** parasitism
- **J** mutualism

## 3 Flow of Matter and Energy

**Performance Indicator:** SPI 0507.3.2 Compare how plants and animals obtain energy.

**3** Why are animals never the first organism in a food chain?

- **A** Animals cannot make their own food.
- **B** Food chains must begin with a decomposer.
- **C** All food chains begin with first-level consumers.
- **D** Animals don't store enough energy when they make their own food.

## 4 Heredity

**Performance Indicator:** **SPI 0507.4.2 Distinguish between inherited traits and those that can be attributed to the environment.**

4　Look at the father and son in the drawing. Which trait of the son is <u>not</u> inherited?

**F** height
**G** hair color
**H** hair length
**J** freckles

## 5 Biodiversity and Change

**Performance Indicator:** **SPI 0507.5.1 Identify physical and behavioral adaptations that enable organisms such as amphibians, reptiles, birds, fish, and mammals to survive in a particular environment.**

5　Which of the moths below is most likely to survive in its environment?

**A** Moth A
**B** Moth B
**C** Moth C
**D** Moth D

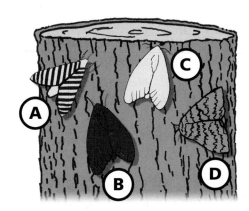

## Discover More

**My What Big Ears!** Grasslands can be hot and dry in the summer, with temperatures sometimes climbing over 38°C (100°F). Animals that live in hot places must find ways to keep cool. The jackrabbit's long ears are adapted not only for hearing, but to help cool its body.

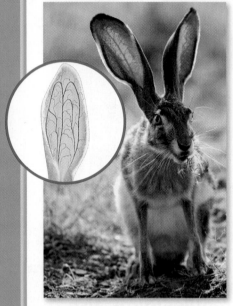

A jackrabbit's ears are about 20 cm long. The wind cools the ears' thin skin, which cools blood vessels lying closely beneath.

Other kinds of rabbits cannot survive high temperatures. They would suffer fatal heat strokes at temperatures of around 25°C (77°F) or higher.

Snowshoe hares live in cold, arctic climates. Small ears help trap body heat inside.

All organisms have adaptations to help them survive in their natural habitats. Adaptations include physical features, such as ear shape and length, as well as behaviors, such as feeding at night instead of the day. Many organisms are adapted to very specific habitats. If their habitat is destroyed, they may not survive elsewhere.

**Go Digital** Visit www.eduplace.com/tnscp to see how other adaptations help animals and plants survive.

# TENNESSEE

**Tennessee Excursions and Engineering Project**

The Stars of Tennessee . . . . . . . . . . . . . . . . . . . 156

Oceanfront Tennessee . . . . . . . . . . . . . . . . . . . 158

Making a Plateau . . . . . . . . . . . . . . . . . . . . . . 160

Build a Safe Clubhouse . . . . . . . . . . . . . . . . . . 162

**UNIT B**
**Earth Science** . . . . . . . . . . . . . . . . . . . . . . . . 163

**CHAPTER 5**
  Exploring Space . . . . . . . . . . . . . . . . . . . . . 164

**CHAPTER 6**
  Earth's Structure . . . . . . . . . . . . . . . . . . . . 198

**CHAPTER 7**
  Weather and Climate . . . . . . . . . . . . . . . . . 240

# The Stars of Tennessee

Have you ever used a map or a GPS to find your way? Maps and GPS devices help you find specific streets, places, and buildings. Before GPS technology, sailors also had to find their way across oceans. They used the stars to help them. To know and find the stars they had maps of the night sky. How did these maps help them find their way?

## Star Charts

Today, we don't use star maps to find our way, but we can still use them to find stars and constellations at night. At Fall Creek Falls State Park near Pikeville, Tennessee, groups of people use maps of the night sky to find constellations. These maps are also called star charts and star wheels. During the Tennessee Spring Star Party, people explore the night sky using star wheels.

**GLE 0507.6.2** Recognize that charts can be used to locate and
identify star patterns.

**ENGAGE**

## Following Stars

Stars seem to move through the night sky in a way similar to the way the moon and the sun move through the sky. This movement of stars follows a pattern. Stars rise and set in the same places at the same times of year. Also, some stars are visible at certain times of the night and year but not at others. A person who knows these patterns can use them to tell the time of night and the time of the year.

Using star charts, some ancient sailors could find a star or constellation and know right away how far north or south of the equator they were. Knowing how to use the star charts to tell where you were on Earth was a skill that helped them navigate from one place to another.

Star wheel

### Think and Write

❶ **Scientific Inquiry** Why did ancient sailors use the stars to find their way?

❷ **Science and Technology** Research GPS devices. How do they work?

# Oceanfront Tennessee

Tennessee's state fossil

Visualize a shallow ocean covering the southeastern and middle parts of the United States. Large marine reptiles, sharks and other fish, clams, snails, oysters, and many kinds of algae live in this ocean.

This is what western Tennessee looked like 70 million years ago. Just as in a modern ecosystem, there was a complex food web with producers and consumers. Each living thing had a specific role in this ecosystem. Scientists study fossils to learn about life in this ancient ocean.

**GLE 0507.5.2** Analyze fossils to demonstrate the connection between organisms and environments that existed in the past and those that currently exist.

**ENGAGE**

Plesiosaur fossils

Students study fossils at the Coon Creek Science Center.

# The Past and the Present

How do scientists know that water once covered western Tennessee? Scientists found many fossils in western Tennessee of animals that lived in water. From this evidence, scientists concluded that the area wasn't always as it appears now. One place where scientists found many fossils is the Coon Creek Formation. A scientist found so many fossils near Adamsville, TN, in the early 1900s that this site became a focus for fossil research.

Over the years scientists have identified more than 600 types of fossils at the Coon Creek Formation. The formation is very important for studying the time period known as the Late Cretaceous (kri TAY shuhs).

The Tennessee state fossil is *Pterotrigonia thoracica*. This fossil clam is abundant in the Coon Creek Formation. The clam lived in a shallow ocean that covered the area millions of years ago. Another fossil that can be found at Coon Creek is the plesiosaur. These swimming reptiles lived in the oceans and seas of ancient Tennessee.

## Think and Write

1. **Scientific Inquiry** Earth's continents have changed many times over millions and millions of years. Research the different continents that have existed. Will new ones form from the movement of plates?

2. **Scientific Thinking** If you found a fossil of an ancient elephant in your backyard, what might you conclude about the area in which you live?

159

Many forces formed the Cumberland Plateau. This cliff is one small part of the plateau.

# MAKING A PLATEAU

The Appalachian Mountains stretch from Canada to Alabama. To the west of these mountains is the Appalachian Plateau. A plateau (pla TOH) is a flat area that is higher than the land around it. The Appalachian Plateau is divided into two regions. They are the Allegheny Plateau to the north and the Cumberland Plateau to the south. In Tennessee, the Cumberland Plateau runs through roughly the middle of the state from north to south.

GLE 0507.7.1 Compare geologic events responsible for the earth's major geological features.

ENGAGE

# Building Mountains

How do mountains and plateaus form? Earth's surface is made of large sections called plates. The plates move very slowly. Sometimes plates move away from each other and continents may break apart. Sometimes the plates move toward each other and become joined, forming new continents.

The Appalachian Mountains formed this way. Plate movement caused Earth's crust near the boundary of the plates to fold and move upward, forming mountains. As the plates pushed against each other, the mountains grew taller. After building up this way, the Appalachian Mountains reached a height of many kilometers. During the next 350 million years, weathering and erosion wore them down.

On both sides of the mountains, the eroded materials formed different landforms. To the east of the mountains, a plain formed. To the west of the mountains, eroded material settled on the region and became sedimentary rock. The result was a plateau standing an average of 550 m (1,800 ft) higher than the surrounding land.

Over time, weathering and erosion began to wear down the plateau. Valleys, cliffs, hills, and natural arches formed. The once flat plateau wasn't so flat anymore.

**This rock shows the layers of material that helped form the Cumberland Plateau.**

## Think and Write

**1** **Scientific Inquiry** It took millions and millions of years for the Appalachian Mountains to form. Do you think there will be new mountains millions of years from now?

**2** **Scientific Thinking** The Himalayas are much taller than the Appalachian Mountains. Why do you think the Appalachians are not as tall?

# Build a Safe Clubhouse

**Identify the Problem** You want to build a clubhouse, but you live in an area where earthquakes are common.

**Think of a Solution** You need a clubhouse that will be able to withstand an earthquake. List the characteristics that a clubhouse must have so it can last through an earthquake. For example, the foundation must be strong and flexible.

**Plan and Build** Using your list of ideas, sketch and label a design for your clubhouse. Think about materials you could use. Then build a model clubhouse.

**Test and Improve** Test your model clubhouse. Improve it, if necessary. Provide sketches and explanations of what you did.

## Possible Materials

- masking tape
- paper plates
- toothpicks
- scissors
- craft sticks
- paper
- glue
- scrap cardboard
- clay
- string
- rubber bands
- straws
- 2 student desks

## Communicate

1. How did you know whether your model clubhouse design was a success?

2. Describe how your list helped you build your model clubhouse.

3. Describe one improvement that you would like to make to your design.

**GLE 0507.T/E.3** Identify appropriate materials, tools, and machines that can extend or enhance the ability to solve a specified problem.

# Earth Science

## Tennessee

**Guiding Question**

How do Earth's structure, position in the solar system, and dynamic atmosphere affect weather and landforms?

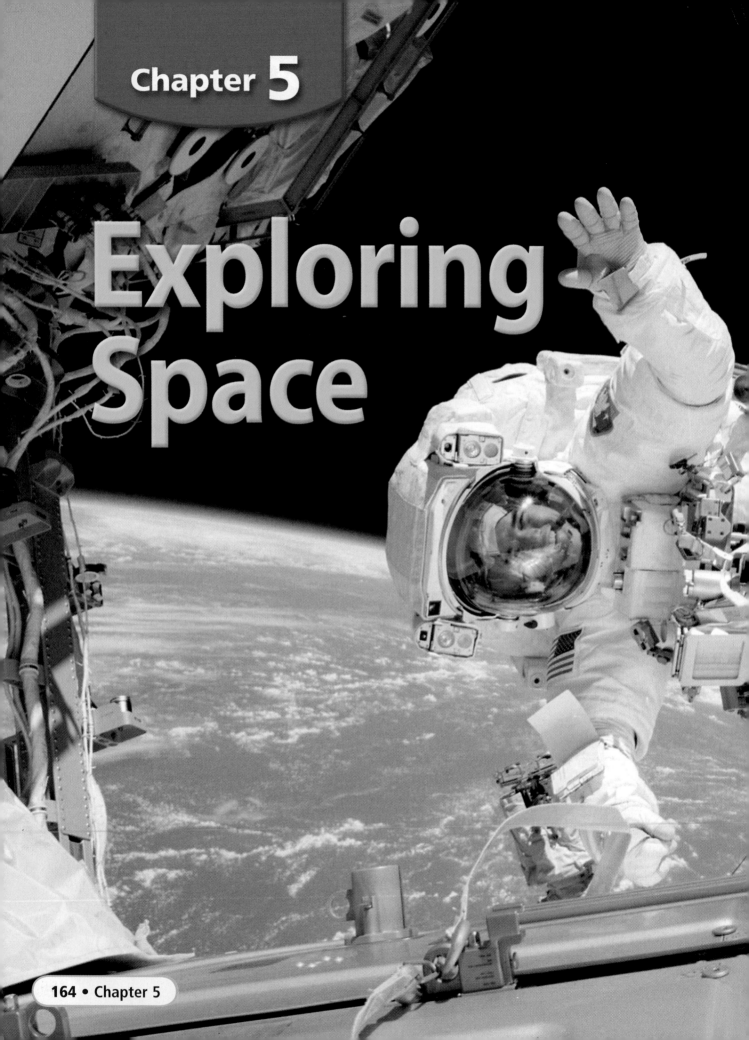

# Chapter 5

# Exploring Space

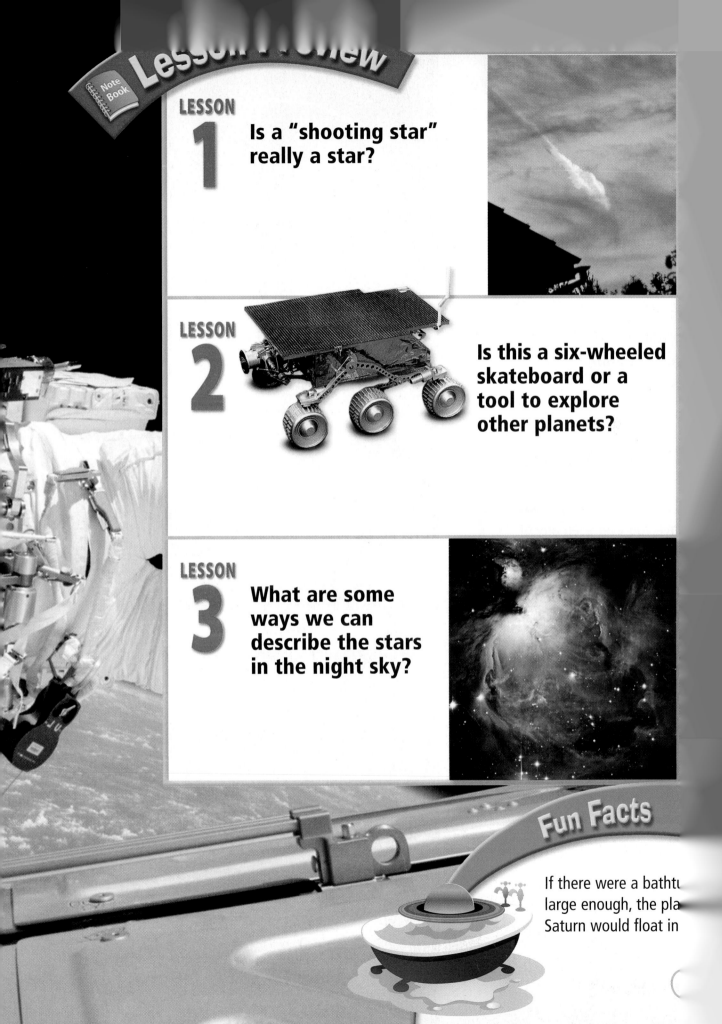

Note Book

Lesson Preview

**LESSON 1**
Is a "shooting star" really a star?

**LESSON 2**
Is this a six-wheeled skateboard or a tool to explore other planets?

**LESSON 3**
What are some ways we can describe the stars in the night sky?

Fun Facts

If there were a batht... large enough, the pla... Saturn would float in...

# Vocabulary Preview

asteroid
comet
inner planets
light-year
magnitude
meteor
meteorite
meteoroid
outer planets
solar system
star

 ## Vocabulary Strategies

Have you ever seen any of these terms before? Do you know what they mean?

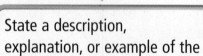

State a description, explanation, or example of the vocabulary in your own words.

Draw a picture, symbol, example, or other image that describes the term.

**Glossary** p. H18

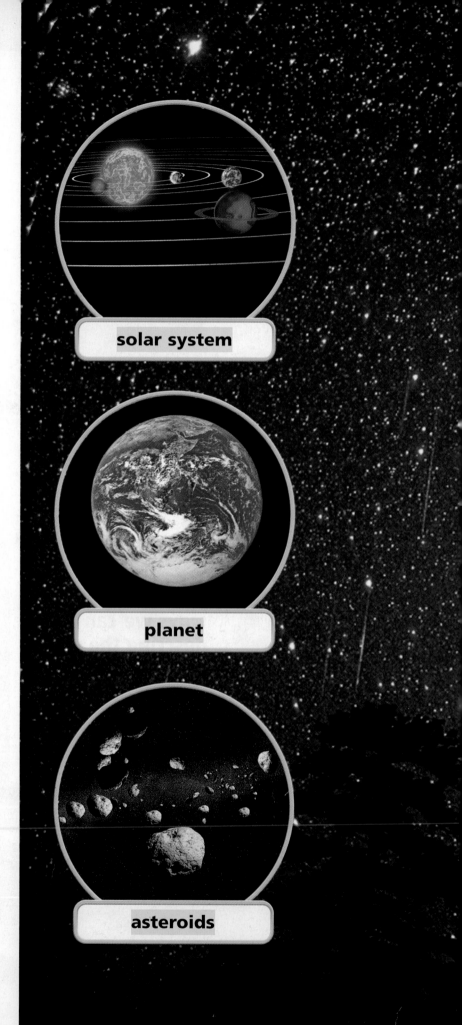

solar system

planet

asteroids

meteors

Tennessee

## Start with Your Standards

### Inquiry

**GLE 0507.Inq.5** Recognize that people may interpret the same results in different ways.

**GLE 0507.Inq.6** Compare the results of an investigation with what scientists already accept about this question.

### Technology & Engineering

**GLE 0507.T/E.4** Recognize the connection between scientific advances, new knowledge, and the availability of new tools and technologies.

### Earth and Space Science

**Standard 6—The Universe**

**GLE 0507.6.1** Compare planets based on their known characteristics.

**GLE 0507.6.2** Recognize that charts can be used to locate and identify star patterns.

## Interact with this chapter.

 www.eduplace.com/tnscp

**TENNESSEE STANDARDS**

GLE 0507.Inq.6 Compare the results of an investigation with what scientists already accept about this question.

GLE 0507.6.1 Compare planets based on their known characteristics.

Guiding Question

# What Orbits the Sun?

## Why It Matters...

Earth is only one small part of the solar system. Other planets, the Sun, and thousands of smaller bodies belong to this system, too. Yet only Earth is able to support life, at least as far as scientists can tell. Understanding Earth's position in the solar system is one key to understanding why it supports life.

## PREPARE TO INVESTIGATE

### Inquiry Skill

**Research** When you research, you use library reference materials, search the Internet, and talk to experts to learn science information.

### Materials

- large index card
- metric ruler
- 2 gummed reinforced rings
- 2 brass fasteners
- string (30 cm long)

### Science and Math Toolbox

For step 1, review **Measurements** on pages H16–H17.

# A Very Long Trip!

## Procedure

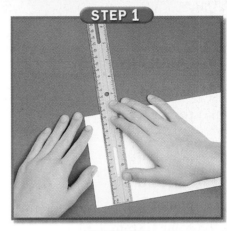
**STEP 1**

1 **Measure** Use a ruler to find the midpoint of the short side of a large index card. Draw a straight line across the center of the card.

2 **Measure** Mark two points, each 2 cm in from the edge of the card. Then measure 2 cm in from one of the points and draw a small circle. Label the circle "Sun."

3 **Use Models** Attach reinforced rings over the two marked points on the card. Carefully push the brass fasteners through the rings and the card. Spread the prongs of each fastener.

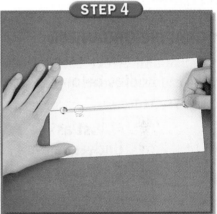
**STEP 4**

4 Tie the ends of the string to form a circle with a circumference of about 25 cm. Loop the string around the brass fasteners.

**STEP 5**

5 **Collaborate** Have a partner hold the edges of the card while you insert the tip of a pencil inside the string loop. Keeping the string tight, draw an ellipse by moving the pencil around the inside of the string. The ellipse models the orbit of a comet.

## Think and Write

1. **Observe** How does the orbit of a comet compare with the orbits of the planets?

2. **Predict** What do you think happens to a comet when it reaches the point in its orbit closest to the Sun?

✔ 0507.Inq.3

### Guided Inquiry

**Research** Find out more about comets by researching at the library or on the Internet. Use your findings to make a poster. Do the results of your investigation agree with what scientists know about comets?

# The Solar System

## The Sun and Its Neighbors

In your neighborhood, your neighbors are the people who live near you. Earth's neighborhood is the solar system. The **solar system** is the Sun and all bodies that travel, or revolve, around it. Earth is one of eight **planets**, large bodies that revolve around the Sun. The planets do not make their own light, but shine by reflecting the Sun's light.

The Sun is by far the largest and most massive part of the solar system. Its gravity holds the other parts in their orbits. Many planets, including Earth, have one or more moons. Smaller members of the solar system include dwarf planets, asteroids, comets, and meteoroids. You will learn about the difference between a planet and a dwarf planet in Lesson 2.

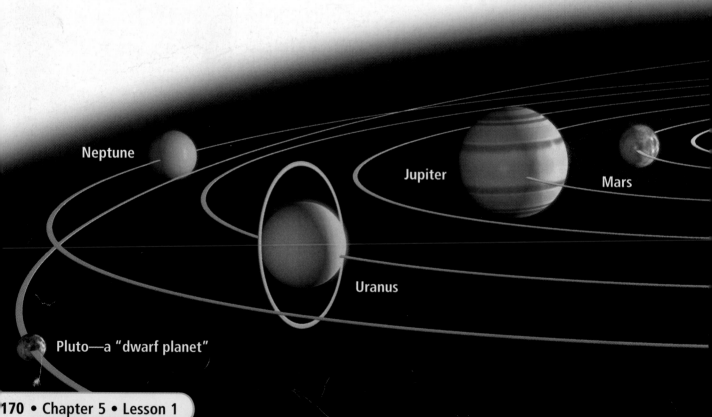

Neptune

Jupiter

Mars

Uranus

Pluto—a "dwarf planet"

Even with its thousands of parts, the solar system is a very small part of a much larger system called the Milky Way galaxy.

Scientists believe that the solar system is about 4.6 billion years old. It formed from a hot, spinning cloud of gases and dust. Over time, gravity pulled the gas and dust toward the center of the cloud, causing the cloud to collapse. As it continued to spin, the cloud flattened and its temperature rose. Eventually, great heat and pressure built up near the center of the cloud. Nuclear reactions produced a star now called the Sun.

Away from the center of the spinning cloud, temperatures were cooler. Matter in this cooler part of the cloud began to come together to form the planets and their moons.

Planets closest to the Sun formed from heavy, rocky material. Farther from the Sun, planets were able to hold onto lighter gases and form much larger planets. Moons eventually formed around all but two of the planets.

Along with the planets and their moons, other small bodies formed in the solar system. These include asteroids, comets, and meteoroids.

The paths, or orbits, of all of the bodies that travel around the Sun are shaped like slightly flattened circles called ellipses. The strong gravitational force of the Sun holds all the objects in the solar system in their orbits.

**FOCUS CHECK** **What does the illustration show about the planets and other objects in the solar system?**

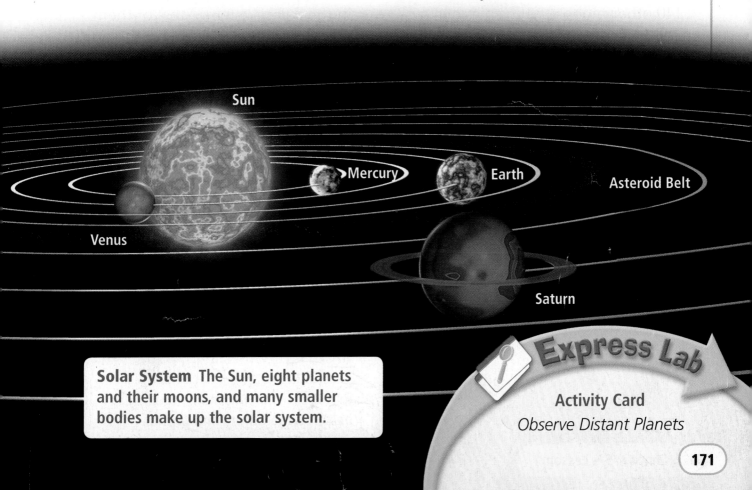

Sun

Mercury

Earth

Asteroid Belt

Venus

Saturn

**Solar System** The Sun, eight planets and their moons, and many smaller bodies make up the solar system.

**Express Lab**

Activity Card
*Observe Distant Planets*

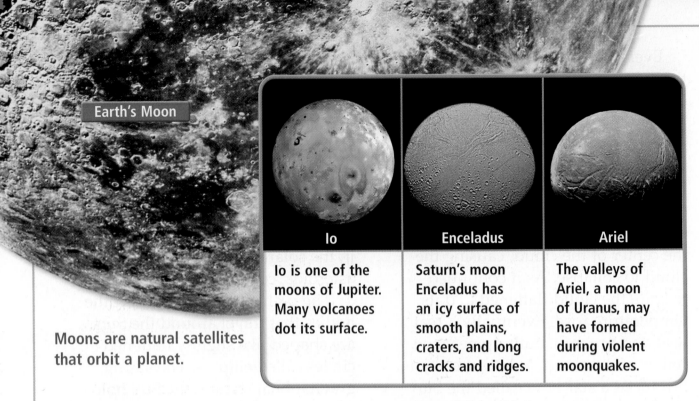

**Earth's Moon**

| Io | Enceladus | Ariel |
|---|---|---|
| Io is one of the moons of Jupiter. Many volcanoes dot its surface. | Saturn's moon Enceladus has an icy surface of smooth plains, craters, and long cracks and ridges. | The valleys of Ariel, a moon of Uranus, may have formed during violent moonquakes. |

Moons are natural satellites that orbit a planet.

## Moons

Most nights, you can see parts of the Moon—the natural satellite that orbits Earth. Did you know that astronomers have discovered about 140 other moons in the solar system? All these moons are held in their orbits by the gravitational attraction of their planets.

Unlike Earth's Moon, some moons have atmospheres surrounding them. Others show evidence that water or ice may lie deep beneath their surfaces. One moon has active volcanoes, and another has geysers!

## Asteroids

An **asteroid** is a relatively small, rocky object that orbits the Sun. Scientists estimate that millions of these chunks of rock and metal exist in the solar system. Most of them orbit in a band called the asteroid belt, located between the orbits of Mars and Jupiter.

Asteroids range in size from hundreds of kilometers in diameter to only a few meters across. Many asteroids have very peculiar shapes. Some even look like baked potatoes!

One theory about the origin of the asteroids is that Jupiter's strong pull of gravity prevented them from coming together to form a planet. Another, less likely idea is that the asteroids are remnants of several planets that collided and broke apart.

◄ Asteroids are small, rocky bodies that orbit the Sun, many in a belt between Mars and Jupiter.

# Comets

A **comet** is a small, orbiting body made of dust, ice, and frozen gases. The solid center of a comet is its nucleus. Like all objects in the solar system, comets orbit the Sun. However, most comets travel in very long, elliptical paths similar to the one shown on this page.

When a comet approaches the Sun, frozen solids in its nucleus vaporize. Gases and dust are released, producing a glowing region called a coma. Energy from the Sun causes the coma to grow. Charged particles streaming from the Sun push particles out of the coma, producing a glowing tail that can reach millions of kilometers into space.

The orbits of some comets extend to just beyond the planet Neptune. These comets make one complete trip around the Sun in fewer than 200 years. They are called short-period comets. The best known comet, Halley's comet, is a short-period comet that orbits the sun about once every 76 years. It will next be visible from Earth in the year 2061.

The orbits of other comets extend much farther from the Sun. Some scientists believe that most of these comets are found beyond Pluto. As many as a trillion comets may exist in this region. These comets can take up to 30 million years to orbit the Sun! They are called long-period comets. Hale-Bopp, a long-period comet identified in 1995, takes nearly 2,500 years to orbit the Sun.

**FOCUS CHECK** What causes the "tail" of a comet to form?

Named for its discoverer, Yuji Hyakutake, this comet was one of the brightest to approach the Sun in the 20th century. ▼

**Comet Orbit**
A comet's tail always points away from the Sun, regardless of the direction the comet is moving.

## Meteors

Have you ever seen a "shooting star" sweep across the night sky? It produces a bright, short-lived streak of light. But such streaks are not moving stars at all. They are meteors.

A **meteor** is a streak of light caused by a chunk of matter that enters Earth's atmosphere and is heated by friction with the air. These chunks of matter are called **meteoroids**. For a few moments, the meteoroids burn as they fall, appearing as streaks of light against the night sky. A few meteoroids are the size of asteroids. But most are much smaller. Many are smaller than a grain of sand.

Meteor showers occur when Earth passes through particles that were shed from the tails of comets. ▼

Meteor

Sometimes more meteors are visible in the sky than usual. These events are called meteor showers. During the meteor shower shown in the photo below, an average of 50 meteors per hour could be seen.

Meteor showers can last from a few hours to a few days. Most showers occur when Earth passes through clouds of dust left orbiting the Sun by a passing comet.

Sometimes, the falling rocks stay intact during their trip through Earth's atmosphere. When these objects strike the ground, they are called **meteorites**. Most meteorites are believed to come from the asteroid belt.

When large meteorites strike Earth's surface, they form bowl-shaped depressions called impact craters. The impact crater shown below is the Barringer Crater in Arizona. It formed sometime between 20,000 and 50,000 years ago.

⊙ **FOCUS CHECK** How is a meteorite different from a meteor?

The Barringer impact crater is over 1 km wide and almost 200 m deep.

# Lesson Wrap-Up

## Visual Summary

The solar system consists of the Sun, the planets, their moons, and many other smaller bodies that revolve around the Sun.

All but two planets in the solar system have at least one moon. Moons, comets, and asteroids are among the smaller bodies in the solar system.

Meteoroids are bits of matter that burn up when they enter Earth's atmosphere.

## Check for Understanding

### DEFEND THE PLANET

Scientists worry about what would happen to living things if a large meteorite were to strike Earth. Research some of the ways scientists have suggested solving this problem. Make a list of possible solutions. Then give at least one reason why each solution is good and bad.

✔ 0507.T/E.3

## Review

**1 MAIN IDEA** What different types of bodies make up the solar system?

**2 VOCABULARY** Write a sentence using the words *asteroid* and *comet.*

**3 READING SKILL: Cause and Effect** What causes planets to remain in their orbits?

**4 CRITICAL THINKING: Apply** Earth and its Moon formed at about the same time and from the same processes. Why do you think Earth's surface has fewer craters than the surface of the Moon?

**5 INQUIRY SKILL: Research** How could you find out more about collecting meteorites?

### TCAP Prep

Which objects cause craters to form on a planet?

**A** meteors
**B** meteorites
**C** comets
**D** moons

SPI 0507.6.1

### Go Digital Technology

Visit **www.eduplace.com/tnscp** to learn more about the solar system.

🖝 **TENNESSEE STANDARDS**

GLE 0507.Inq.1 Explore different scientific phenomena by asking questions, making logical predictions, planning investigations, and recording data.

GLE 0507.6.1 Compare planets based on their known characteristics.

Guiding Question

# What Are the Planets Like?

## Why It Matters...

By studying other planets and their moons, scientists have learned a lot about Earth and its Moon. Studying the solar system also provides clues about the stars and galaxies that lie beyond it.

## PREPARE TO INVESTIGATE

### Inquiry Skill

**Use Models** Some models are scale models. All parts of a scale model are larger or smaller than the size of the actual object being modeled, but are in exact proportions.

### Materials

- marker
- metric tape measure
- piece of string (40 m)
- wooden stakes (30 cm long)
- masking tape
- cardboard rectangles
- modeling clay

### Science and Math Toolbox

For step 1, review **Using a Tape Measure or Ruler** on page H6.

# Directed Inquiry

## Scaling the Solar System

### Procedure

**1 Measure** Work with three other students. Obtain the scale distance values from your teacher and write them in your *Science Notebook*. Using the marker and the measuring tape, mark off along the string the positions of the Sun and planets.

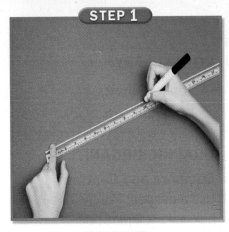

**STEP 1**

**2 Use Models** Label one of the rectangles as the Sun. Tape the sign to a stake. Gently push the stake into the ground, if outdoors. If you are indoors, make a small clay ball and push the stake into the clay.

**STEP 2**

**3 Collaborate** Work with the members in your team to label the rest of the rectangles with the planet names and tape each to a stake.

**4 Use Numbers** Have one team member hold the end of the string that represents the Sun while another student stretches the string so that it is taut. The other students in your team should place the planet stakes in their correct positions along the stretched string.

**STEP 4**

### Think and Write

1. **Analyze Data** Which group of planets—the inner planets or the outer planets—is closer together?

2. **Use Numbers** Study the distances between the first four planets from the Sun. Is there a pattern? If so, what is the pattern? Then describe distances among the outer planets.

### Guided Inquiry

**Design an Experiment**
Find the diameters of the planets on pages 179–180. Use these diameters to make a scale-size model of the Sun and each of the planets. Use a scale of 1 cm to 1,000 km.

0507.Inq.2

177

# The Planets

## The Inner Planets

The first four planets from the Sun are Mercury, Venus, Earth, and Mars. These planets are called the **inner planets** because they are closer to the Sun than the other planets in the solar system. The inner planets have certain characteristics in common. They are rocky and much smaller than most of the other planets. Yet, if you could travel to the inner planets, you would find them very different from Earth and from each other.

Mercury is the smallest of the inner planets and the one closest to the Sun. Mercury's surface temperature varies widely between its day and its night. During the planet's slow rotation, the side facing the Sun becomes extremely hot, while the side facing away becomes extremely cold.

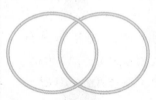

**Mercury**
Mercury's surface has many craters. Some of these may contain frozen water. ▼

Sun

**Venus** ▶
Venus has a few craters on its surface. A thick, poisonous atmosphere surrounds this planet.

The surface of Venus, the second planet from the Sun, is hidden below a thick layer of clouds made up mostly of sulfuric acid! The atmosphere itself is 96 percent carbon dioxide, creating tremendous pressure and a strong greenhouse effect.

Temperatures at the surface are hot enough to melt lead. The pressure exerted by the atmosphere is bone-crushing—about the same as that found 1 km beneath the ocean's surface on Earth.

You are familiar with conditions on Earth, the third planet from the Sun. It is the only planet known to have liquid water. Earth's atmosphere and oceans help keep its surface temperature within a range that supports life.

Mars, the red planet, is smaller than Earth, but has about the same amount of land area. Compared to other planets, Mars has been extensively observed and explored. The Mars Expedition rovers, named *Spirit* and *Opportunity*, have recently visited the surface and sent information back to Earth.

**Mars** ▲
Mars is home to the largest volcano in the solar system.

The surface of Mars shows signs of water erosion, indicating that it may once have been more like Earth. While much of its surface is flat and rocky, Mars has deep canyons and the highest volcanic mountain known in our solar system. Olympus Mons stands 24 km, or almost 80,000 ft, above the Martian surface.

**FOCUS CHECK** What are some similarities among the inner planets?

**Earth** ▲
Earth's temperature and its atmosphere make it the only planet in the solar system known to support life.

| Inner Planets | | |
|---|---|---|
| Planet | Diameter (km) | Distance from Sun (million km) |
| Mercury | 4,880 | 57.9 |
| Venus | 12,100 | 108.2 |
| Earth | 12,756 | 149.6 |
| Mars | 6,800 | 227.9 |

# The Outer Planets

The **outer planets** are Jupiter, Saturn, Uranus, and Neptune. These planets are larger than the inner planets, and their volume consists mostly of gases.

Jupiter, the fifth planet from the Sun, is one of the brightest objects in the night sky. Jupiter takes only about 10 hours to rotate once on its axis. Winds reaching speeds of 670 km/hr (400 mph) form clearly visible bands.

Jupiter is famous for its Great Red Spot. This gigantic storm system has been visible from Earth for more than 300 years.

In addition to its many moons, Jupiter also has rings. The rings are made up of small particles that may have been produced by meteor collisions with Jupiter's moons.

The planet best known for its rings is Saturn, the sixth planet from the Sun. Saturn's band of rings is 250,000 km wide, but only 1 km thick. The rings consist mostly of ice particles.

Saturn is the least dense of any planet. If you could put Saturn in water, it would float! Yet it is as massive as 95 Earths.

## Jupiter ▼
Jupiter is a giant—it is the biggest, most massive planet in the solar system. It has more than 60 moons!

| The Outer Planets and Pluto | | |
|---|---|---|
| Planet | Diameter (km) | Distance from Sun (million km) |
| Jupiter | 142,800 | 778 |
| Saturn | 120,000 | 1,427 |
| Uranus | 50,800 | 2,870 |
| Neptune | 48,600 | 4,500 |
| Pluto | 2,300 | 5,900 |

**Express Lab**

**Activity Card**
*Explore the Planets*

## Saturn ▲
Thousands of particles make up the rings that surround Saturn.

Uranus, the seventh planet from the Sun, was once called "Herschel" after the astronomer who discovered it. Like other planets, the axis of Uranus is tilted. Yet its axis is tilted so much it is nearly parallel to the plane of its orbit. Compared to other planets, Uranus is "lying" on its side.

Like Jupiter and Saturn, Uranus consists mostly of gases with a core of rock and ice. Uranus has at least 27 moons and a system of 11 rings.

Neptune, the eighth planet in the solar system, is similar in color and composition to Uranus. It has over 11 moons. Scientists predicted its existence based on observations of the motion of Uranus, but it was not discovered until 1846.

Like all gas giants, Neptune is a windy planet, but its winds are the fastest yet observed in the solar system. They reach speeds of 2,700 km/hr (1,500 mph)!

**Pluto ▶**
Pluto has ice caps at its poles and large dark spots near its equator.

## Dwarf Planets

In 2006, scientists met to form a new definition of *planet*. Because Pluto is not in a clear orbit, it was classified as a "dwarf planet." The large asteroid Ceres, and Eris, which orbits beyond Pluto, are also "dwarf planets."

Unlike the outer planets, Pluto is small, icy, and rocky. It is very cold. Pluto has one moon, called Charon.

**FOCUS CHECK  What do most of the outer planets have in common?**

**Neptune ▼**
Neptune and its largest moon, Triton, are getting closer to each other. The two probably will collide within the next 100 million years.

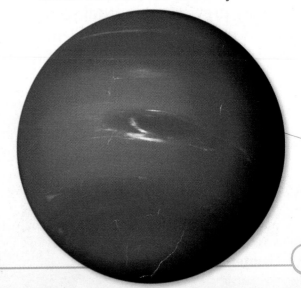

**Uranus ▲**
High concentrations of methane give Uranus a greenish color.

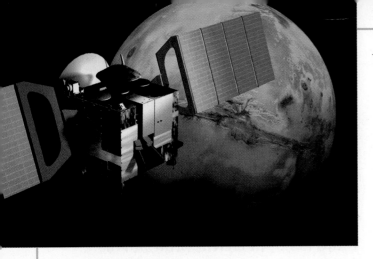

◄ The European Space Agency launched the Mars Express space probe in June of 2003.

## Exploring Space

Many early observations of the solar system were made with simple optical telescopes. With these tools, an observer looked through lenses that made objects appear larger and brighter. Such telescopes could be used only to observe nearby objects in space.

Optical telescopes are still used to explore the solar system and beyond. Today, though, many are equipped with cameras and computers that produce images and collect and process data. Other types of telescopes gather invisible radiation, such as radio or x-ray waves, to form images.

Telescopes are affected by Earth's atmosphere. Clouds and gases in the air may prevent users from seeing objects clearly in space. Thus, many telescopes are set up on mountain peaks. Others are launched into space and orbit Earth!

The space shuttle is a vehicle that takes equipment and people into space. While the shuttle orbits Earth, experiments can be carried out. After a certain time, a shuttle returns to Earth. A space station stays in space for long periods of time. It has areas in which astronauts and scientists live, sleep and conduct experiments.

A space probe is a spacecraft that carries special instruments into space. Some probes are launched into Earth's upper atmosphere. Other probes go much farther. The Mars rovers *Spirit* and *Opportunity* have explored Mars, moving across its surface and analyzing samples of rocks and dirt.

**FOCUS CHECK** **How does the space shuttle differ from a space probe?**

◄ The Mars rovers have taken many photographs and analyzed Martian rocks.

## Lesson Wrap-Up

### Visual Summary

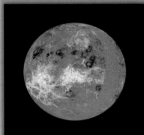

Mercury, Venus, Earth, and Mars, make up the inner planets. The inner planets are small and rocky and have few or no moons.

Jupiter, Saturn, Uranus, and Neptune are the outer planets. The outer planets are large and gaseous, and they have many moons.

Space probes can be used to explore regions of space that are too dangerous or difficult for humans to explore directly.

### Check for Understanding

**DESCRIBE THE PLANETS**

Choose five characteristics of planets, such as their distance from the sun, the number of moons they have, or their size. Make a chart with all the planets, and fill in information about the characteristics you chose. Share your chart with your classmates, and add columns with other characteristics that your classmates researched.

✔ 0507.6.1

## Review

**1 MAIN IDEA** How are the planets of the solar system grouped?

**2 VOCABULARY** Contrast space stations and space probes.

**3 READING SKILL: Compare and Contrast** Compare and contrast the characteristics of Earth with those of its two nearest neighbors.

**4 CRITICAL THINKING: Hypothesize** Why do you think the outer planets have so many moons?

**5 INQUIRY SKILLS: Use Models** Why are models useful to study the solar system?

### TCAP Prep

Which planet is the largest in the solar system and has a Great Red Spot?

**A** Mars
**B** Mercury
**C** Saturn
**D** Jupiter

SPI 0507.6.1

 **Technology**

Visit **www.eduplace.com/tnscp** to learn more about planets.

Lisa Westberg Peters studied science carefully for her book of poems about Earth. Compare her poem about meteors to the work of a non-fiction writer.

# Earth Charged in Meteor's Fiery Death

## by Lisa Westberg Peters

The earth was charged Wednesday
in connection with the fiery death
of a large meteor.

"It was a combination of gravity
and thick air," police said.
"That meteor didn't have a chance."

The meteor fell out of orbit
early Tuesday and was vaporized
as it plunged toward the earth.

"It was a fireball!"
said Jose Martinez of Sacramento.
"It lit up my whole backyard."

A hearing will be held next week.

# Meteors

**Excerpt from *Comets, Meteors, and Asteroids*, by Seymour Simon**

Meteors flash in the sky every night. They happen every day, too, but we usually can't see them in the Sun's glare.

Meteor flashes are also called falling or shooting stars. But meteors are not stars. Stars are suns far beyond our Solar System. Meteors begin as meteoroids, bits of rock or metal that orbit around the Sun. We can't see them in space because they are too small and too dark.

But sometimes meteoroids plunge into Earth's atmosphere at speeds faster than a bullet. The friction produced by rubbing against air particles makes them glow red-hot, and they are then called meteors. We see the bright flash for only a few seconds.

Meteors come much closer to the Earth than comets. Some are brighter than the brightest star and are called fireballs.

Several times each year you can see more than a dozen meteors in an hour in the same part of the night sky. This is called a meteor shower. It occurs when Earth passes through an old comet orbit and collides with some of the particles remaining from the comet's nucleus. Each year, Earth passes through the old comet path at about the same date. The Leonids, for example, are meteors from rocks left behind in the orbit of Comet Temple-Tuttle. When the Leonids appear in mid-November, they seem to come from the direction of the constellation (a group of stars) named Leo.

## Sharing Ideas

1. **READING CHECK** Why do meteors burn as they enter Earth's atmosphere?

2. **WRITE ABOUT IT** Why do meteor showers appear at certain times every year?

3. **TALK ABOUT IT** Is it reasonable to suggest that Earth causes the death of meteors, as the poem suggests?

## Lesson 3

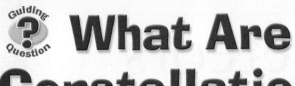

TENNESSEE STANDARDS

GLE 0507.Inq.5 Recognize that people may interpret the same results in different ways.

GLE 0507.6.2 Recognize that charts can be used to locate and identify star patterns.

**Guiding Question**

# What Are Constellations?

## Why It Matters...

Earth revolves around a star called the Sun. Without this star, Earth would be a cold, lifeless body. Reactions in the Sun's core give off energy needed by almost all the living things on Earth.

## PREPARE TO INVESTIGATE

### Inquiry Skill

**Use Numbers** You can use numbers and your math skills to understand objects, events, and ideas in science.

### Materials

- 7 long, black chenille stems
- 7 round beads that fit snugly onto the chenille stems
- piece of black poster board (about 8.5 in. x 11 in.)
- gel pen (silver, gold, or white)
- scissors
- metric ruler

### Science and Math Toolbox

For step 1, review **Using an Equation or Formula** on page H10.

# Directed Inquiry

## Star Search!

## Procedure

**1** **Use Numbers** Refer to the table on page 189. Using a scale of 1 cm equals 10 light-years, compute the scale distances in cm to each of the stars in the Big Dipper, a star group that is part of a constellation. In your *Science Notebook*, record your values in a table like the one shown.

**2** **Analyze Data** Look at the photo on page 189. Use it to mark positions for the stars of the Big Dipper on the black poster board. Connect the dots with the gel pen. Carefully use scissors to poke holes into the poster board at each star location.

**3** **Use Numbers** Cut each of the chenille stems to the correct scale length from your table. Insert each chenille stem into its correct place in the model constellation. Place a bead at the end of each chenille stem.

**4** **Observe** Observe your model from different positions.

## Think and Write

1. **Use Models** How did this scale model aid in your understanding of distances to stars in a constellation? What questions about stars does it help answer?

2. **Hypothesize** How might the star group you modeled look from a different part of the galaxy? Use your model to make a sketch that answers this question.

0507.6.2

**STEP 1**

| Star | Actual Distance (Ly) from Earth | Scale Distance (cm) |
|------|------|------|
| Alkaid | | |
| Mizar | | |
| Aloith | | |
| Megrez | | |

**STEP 3**

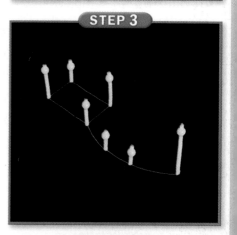

**STEP 4**

### Guided Inquiry

**Design an Experiment**
On a clear night, sit facing north and observe the sky. Sketch the brightest stars and organize them into groups. The next day, exchange sketches with a classmate. That night, try to identify your classmate's star groups.

# Constellations

## Stars Near and Far

### GRAPHIC ORGANIZER

**Main Idea and Details** Use the graphic organizer to add details that support the main idea of pages 188 to 190.

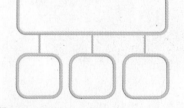

GLE 0507.6.2 Recognize that charts can be used to locate and identify star patterns.

Have you ever wondered what a star is? Why do stars twinkle, and how far are they from Earth?

A **star** is a large sphere of glowing gases. Nuclear reactions in the star's core produce energy that eventually reaches the star's atmosphere and radiates into space. The twinkle of starlight is caused by movement of particles in Earth's atmosphere.

Recall from Lesson 2 that everything in the solar system orbits a star called the Sun. The Sun is a yellow star made mostly of hydrogen and helium. Its volume is more than one million times the volume of Earth! The surface temperature of the Sun is about 5,500°C (9,932°F).

In many ways, the Sun is a typical star. Yet many stars are hotter and larger than the Sun, while others are smaller and cooler. Some are even larger and *cooler!*

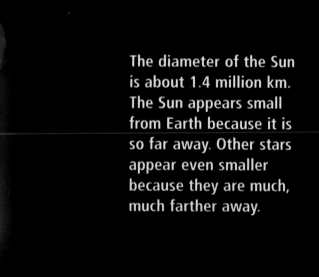

The diameter of the Sun is about 1.4 million km. The Sun appears small from Earth because it is so far away. Other stars appear even smaller because they are much, much farther away.

## Stars in the Big Dipper

| Star Name | Distance from Earth |
|---|---|
| 1 Alkaid | 108 Ly |
| 2 Mizar | 59 Ly |
| 3 Alioth | 62 Ly |
| 4 Megrez | 65 Ly |
| 5 Phecda | 75 Ly |
| 6 Merak | 62 Ly |
| 7 Dubhe | 75 Ly |

▲ The stars that form the Big Dipper are many light-years from Earth. The Big Dipper is a star group that is part of a constellation called Ursa Major.

The Sun is about 150 million km (93 million mi) from Earth. While this distance may seem very large, it is actually small compared to distances between other objects in space.

Because distances beyond the solar system are so large, astronomers often use a special unit to measure them. A **light-year,** which is abbreviated Ly, is the distance that light travels in one year—about 9.5 trillion km! For reference, the Sun is about 0.00001 Ly from Earth. The next closest star is Proxima Centauri. It is about 4.3 Ly from Earth.

For centuries, people have given names to *constellations*, or patterns of

stars. Look at the table on this page. How far from Earth are the seven stars that are part of Ursa Major?

Most of the billions of stars in the universe are very, very far from Earth. You are able to see some of these stars because they are so bright. The brightness of a star is called its **magnitude.** In general, bigger stars have greater magnitudes than smaller stars. Also, stars that are closer to Earth appear brighter than those farther away. Very hot stars appear brighter than cooler stars unless the cooler star is very large.

**FOCUS CHECK** What is a light-year?

# The Changing Night Sky

Thousands of years ago, people were able to navigate using the positions of the stars in the sky. Locating a star in the sky isn't as easy as you might think. Stars appear to move across the night sky just as the sun appears to move across the daytime sky. This is due to Earth's rotation.

In spring and summer, some constellations are visible that you cannot see in fall and winter. Which stars you can see depends on where Earth is in its journey around the sun.

The stars you see in winter are on the other side of the sun in summer.

Astronomers use star charts to locate objects in the night sky. A *star chart* is a map of stars in the night sky. On a star chart, the stars that make up a constellation are often connected by lines. Different star charts must be used at different times of the year and in different places on Earth. Many stars visible from the Southern Hemisphere cannot be seen from the Northern Hemisphere.

**FOCUS CHECK** **Why do people use star charts?**

Summer

▲ Some stars can be seen only at certain times of the year. Star patterns change with the seasons.

Winter

▲ Some stars that can be seen in winter are on the other side of the sun in summer.

**Express Lab**

**Activity Card**
*Use a Star Chart*

# Lesson Wrap-Up

## Visual Summary

Stars are enormous spheres of glowing gases. Throughout history, people have identified patterns of stars and used them in many ways.

The apparent brightness of a star depends on its size, its temperature, its real brightness, and its distance from Earth.

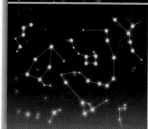

Different star patterns can be seen during different seasons. Star charts are used to locate star patterns in the night sky.

## Check for Understanding

### RESEARCH A CONSTELLATION

Choose a constellation to research. Find interesting facts about the constellation, including whether people in the past told stories about the constellation. Use a star chart to find out what constellations are near the one you chose. When is the constellation visible in your area? Include all the information you learned in a short report.

✔ 0507.6.3

## Review

❶ **MAIN IDEA** What is a star?

❷ **VOCABULARY** What three factors determine the magnitude of a star?

❸ **READING SKILL: Main Ideas/ Details** Provide details from this lesson that support the following main idea: Stars in the night sky do not all look the same.

❹ **CRITICAL THINKING: Apply** Explain why a pen pal in Australia might not understand something you write about the Big Dipper.

❺ **INQUIRY SKILL: Use Numbers** If the star Megrez stopped shining today, how long would it be before we didn't see it shining in the night sky from Earth? Use the table on page 189.

### TCAP Prep

What is the name for a star pattern that is visible in the night sky?

**A** a constellation
**B** a black hole
**C** a supernova
**D** a star chart

SPI 0507.6.3

### Technology

Visit **www.eduplace.com/tnscp** to learn more about stars.

# Out With a Bang!

What can suddenly outshine an
entire galaxy of billions of stars?
A supernova! Toward the end of their lives,
enormous stars called super-giants die in
colossal explosions that rip them apart. The
dying stars blast out hot, glowing gases
that expand and become huge nebulas.
Shown here is the Crab Nebula. It is
a remnant of a supernova that Chinese
astronomers observed in 1054. They called
it "guest star." It was so bright that for
three weeks it could be seen in broad
daylight. Then it faded away. Over 650
years later, the supernova's nebula was
discovered by telescope. Only much later
did astronomers realize that the "guest star"
of 1054 was the supernova that caused the
Crab Nebula we see today.

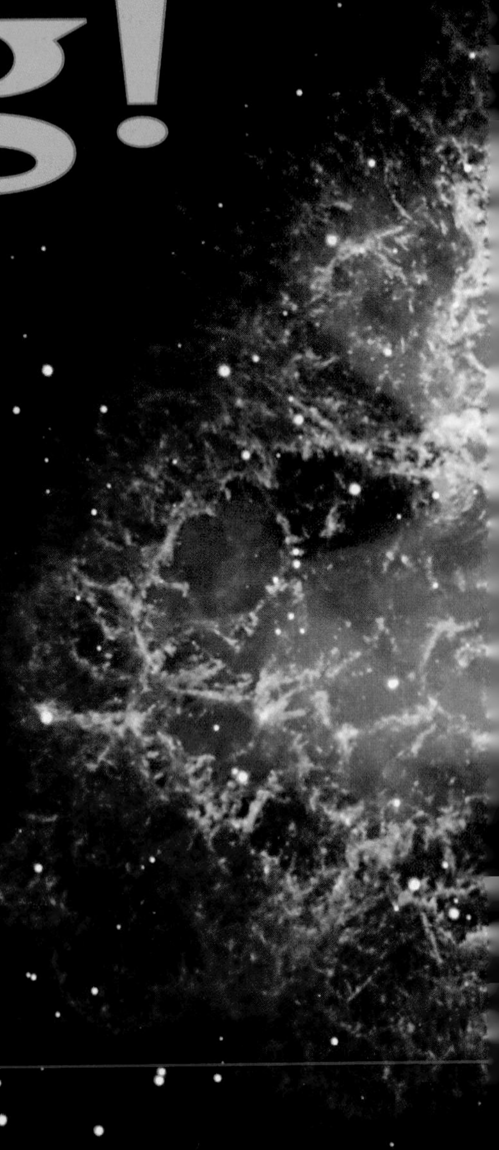

GLE 0507.T/E.4 Recognize the connection between scientific advances, new knowledge, and the availability of new tools and technologies.

EXTEND

# Planetary Nebulas

The Ring Nebula was one of the first planetary nebulas to be discovered.

Can you see why this nebula is known as the Cat's Eye Nebula?

This is the Eskimo Nebula. Can you see a head surrounded by a furry hood?

**GLE 0507.6.1** Compare planets based on their known characteristics.
**Math GLE 0506.3.4** Solve single-step linear equations and inequalities.
**ELA GLE 0501.3.2** Write in a variety of modes and genres, including narration, literary response, personal expression, description, and imaginative.

## Math Planet Circumferences

The table gives the diameter of four planets. The diameter *(d)* of a circle or a sphere is the distance across the middle, which is two times the radius. Circumference *(C)* is the distance around a circle or a sphere. You can use the formula $C = \pi d$ to find the circumference of each planet on the table. The symbol $\pi$ is the Greek letter pi. It stands for a number.

| Planet | Radius (km) |
|---|---|
| Mercury | 4,880 |
| Earth | 12,756 |
| Uranus | 50,800 |
| Jupiter | 142,800 |

1. What is the value of $\pi$? Use your math textbook or other resource to find out.

2. To the nearest kilometer, what is the diameter of each planet on the table?

3. To the nearest kilometer, what is the circumference of each planet on the table?

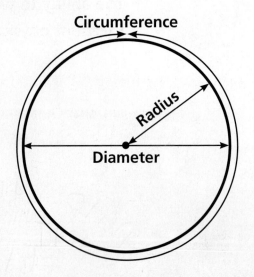

## Response to Literature

Read a fictional story about space, and tell whether or not you agree with everything you read. How does the story relate to what you have read in your textbook? Do any parts disagree with the textbook? Do any parts of what you read seem unbelievable?

## Astronaut

Astronauts work for NASA, the government agency that explores space. They pilot spacecraft, conduct scientific experiments, conduct needed repairs, and perform other tasks in space. Much of their work is done under conditions of freefall, which NASA calls microgravity.

### What It Takes!

- A degree in engineering or other scientific field
- Rigorous training in simulated spaceflight
- The ability to work in enclosed spaces
- Excellent physical condition

## Computer Systems Technician

A computer systems technician takes care of computer hardware and software. This work includes installing and maintaining networks of computers, trouble-shooting problems, and updating equipment.

### What It Takes!

- Training at a technical institute or on the job
- The ability to think logically and to solve problems
- Learning new developments and products

## Vocabulary

**Complete each sentence with a term from the list.**

1. A star's brightness is called its ____.

2. The distance light travels in one year is a(n) ____.

3. The planets closest to the Sun are called ____.

4. Saturn is one of the four ____.

5. Neptune is the outermost ____ of the solar system.

6. A(n) ____ has a frozen nucleus and can develop a glowing tail.

7. The Sun, eight planets, and thousands of other bodies make up the ____.

8. ____ are often called "shooting stars."

9. The Sun is a giant sphere of glowing gases called a(n) ____.

10. ____ are small rocky bodies found in a belt between Mars and Jupiter.

asteroids
comet
inner planets
light-year
magnitude
meteors
meteorites
meteoroids
outer planets
planet
solar system
star

## TCAP Inquiry Skills

11. **Use Models** A star chart is one kind of model of the night sky. In what ways is a star chart a good model of the night sky? How is a star chart different than the night sky? **GLE 0507.Inq.3**

12. **Use Numbers** What units would you use to express distances within the solar system? Explain your choice.

**GLE 0507.Inq.1**

## Map the Concept

Draw a Venn diagram that compares and contrasts Earth and Venus.

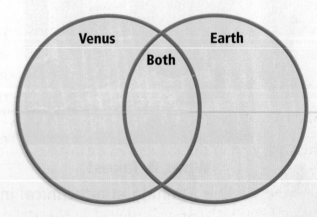

Venus   Both   Earth

**GLE 0507.6.1**

## Critical Thinking

**13. Analyze** What is another way you might divide the planets into two groups other than inner planets and outer planets? **GLE 0507.6.1**

**14. Evaluate** In a planetarium, star patterns can be projected on a domed ceiling. Do you think it is easier to learn about star patterns outdoors with a telescope or in a planetarium. Explain. **GLE 0507.Inq.3**

**15. Apply** Use what you have learned in this chapter to write a paragraph about Earth's location in the universe. **GLE 0507.6.1**

**16. Synthesize** What are some advantages of conducting experiments from a space station rather than a space shuttle? **GLE 0507.Inq.2**

**Check for Understanding**

### Use a Star Chart

Find a star chart for your location, and make a copy that you can write on. With the help of an adult, observe the stars at night. On the copy of the chart, circle the stars that you can see. What percent of the stars shown on the chart do you estimate that you could see? **0507.6.2**

## TCAP Prep

**Answer the following questions.**

**17** What is shown on a star chart?

**A** how to calculate the magnitude of stars

**B** legends about stars from past cultures

**C** constellations and their positions

**D** the location of the Milky Way **SPI 0507.6.3**

**18** Based on the table below, what can you conclude about Mercury?

| Planet | Length of Day | Lengh of Year |
|--------|---------------|---------------|
| Mercury | 1,408 hours | 88 Earth days |
| Venus | 5,832 hours | 225 Earth days |
| Earth | 24 hours | 365 Earth days |

**F** It orbits the Sun very slowly.

**G** It rotates more slowly than Earth.

**H** It rotates slower than all other planets.

**J** It is the hottest planet. **SPI 0507.6.2**

**19** Which planet is small and rocky?

**A** Jupiter

**B** Uranus

**C** Mercury

**D** Saturn **SPI 0507.6.1**

**20** How are Mercury and Mars similar?

**F** Both are inner planets.

**G** Both are outer planets.

**H** Both give off their own light.

**J** Both are gas giants. **SPI 0507.6.1**

# Chapter 6

# Earth's Structure

**LESSON 1**

Cool and crusty on the outside, hot on the inside: What is Earth's structure like?

**LESSON 2**

Shaking earthquakes and erupting volcanoes: What forces of nature cause these dramatic events to occur?

**LESSON 3**

Some mountains are tall and jagged. Others are rounded and covered in trees. How do mountains form and change?

## Fun Facts

The temperature of melted rock coming from a volcano can be as high as 1000°C (1832°F)!

# Vocabulary Preview

core

crust

dome mountains

earthquake

epicenter

fault

fault-block mountains

focus

fold mountains

★ fossil

lithosphere

magma

mantle

plate tectonics

seismic waves

★ = Tennessee Academic Vocabulary

## Vocabulary Strategies

Have you ever seen any of these terms before? Do you know what they mean?

State a description, explanation, or example of the vocabulary in your own words.

Draw a picture, symbol, example, or other image that describes the term.

**Glossary** p. H18

fault

earthquake

fossil

dome mountain

## Start with Your Standards

### Inquiry

**GLE 0507.Inq.2** Select and use appropriate tools and simple equipment to conduct an investigation.

**GLE 0507.Inq.3** Organize data into appropriate tables, graphs, drawings, or diagrams.

**GLE 0507.Inq.6** Compare the results of an investigation with what scientists already accept about this question.

### Technology & Engineering

**GLE 0507.T/E.5** Apply a creative design strategy to solve a particular problem generated by societal needs and wants.

### Earth and Space Science

**Standard 6—The Earth**

**GLE 0507.7.1** Compare geologic events responsible for the earth's major geological features.

### Interact with this chapter.

 **www.eduplace.com/tnscp**

# Lesson 1

**TENNESSEE STANDARDS**

GLE 0507.Inq.3 Organize data into appropriate tables, graphs, drawings, or diagrams.
GLE 0507.7.1 Compare geologic events responsible for the earth's major geological features.

# What Is Earth's Structure?

## Why It Matters...

Earth has a layered structure, with solid rock at the surface and partly liquid rock material below. Understanding Earth's structure can help scientists predict when a geyser or volcano will erupt, or how a river will change course over time.

## PREPARE TO INVESTIGATE

### Inquiry Skill

**Use Models** When you use models, you study, make, or operate something that stands for a real-world process or action. Models can help you to understand better or show how a process or action works.

### Materials

• modeling clay, 2 colors
• a small marble
• metric measuring tape
• aluminum foil
• plastic knife

### Science and Math Toolbox

For step 4, review **Using a Tape Measure or Ruler** on page H6.

# Directed Inquiry

# A Model World

## Procedure

**1** **Collaborate** Working with a partner, roll modeling clay into two balls of different colors. Make one the size of a golf ball and the other the size of a baseball.

STEP 1

**2** **Use Models** The smaller clay ball represents Earth's outer core. The marble represents its inner core. Push the marble into the center of the smaller clay ball and reshape the clay around it. You now have a model of Earth's two-part core.

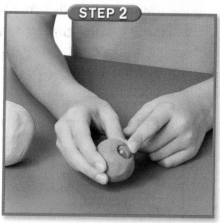

STEP 2

**3** **Observe** The larger clay ball represents Earth's mantle. Using the plastic knife, cut this clay ball in half. Reshape the clay so that this ball can be wrapped around the two-part core. You now have a model of Earth's core and mantle.

**4** **Measure** Use a measuring tape to find the distance around your model at its "equator." Cut a rectangle of foil equal to that distance in length and one-third of that distance in width. Wrap the foil around the mantle and smooth it out. This thin layer of foil represents Earth's crust.

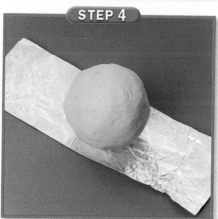

STEP 4

## Think and Write

1. **Use Models** In your *Science Notebook*, draw what your model of Earth would look like if you could slice it in half. Label the layers.

2. **Infer** How would you describe the layers that make up Earth's structure? Write about them in your *Science Notebook*.

✔ 0507.7.1

### Guided Inquiry

**Design an Experiment**
List some materials you could use to model Earth's layered structure. Describe how you would arrange them into a useful model.

# Earth's Structure

**VOCABULARY**

- core
- crust
- ★ fossil
- lithosphere
- mantle
- plate tectonics

**GRAPHIC ORGANIZER**

**Main Idea and Details**
Use a graphic organizer to track the main idea of this lesson and the many details that support it.

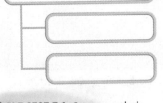

**GLE 0507.7.1** Compare geologic events responsible for the earth's major geological features.

## Hot Inside

In many parts of the world, columns of steaming hot water can be found shooting up from Earth's surface. These boiling fountains are known as geysers. The existence of geysers suggests that Earth is extremely hot inside.

Geysers form in places where water drains down a deep channel in Earth's surface. At the bottom of the channel, hot rocks heat the water into steam. When the pressure becomes great enough, the steam and hot water erupt to the surface in a sudden explosion.

Yellowstone National Park in Wyoming is well known for its numerous geysers and hot springs. Long before this region became popular, Jim Bridger explored its wonders. Bridger was a fur trader, scout, and mountain man. He told everyone he met about the many geysers and amazing sights of the region.

Visit Yellowstone today, and you too can see evidence of Earth's hot interior. But just how hot is it inside Earth?

**Jim Bridger (1804–1881) Geyser Gazer**

❝Geysers spout up 70 feet, with a terrible hissing noise, at regular intervals. In this section are the great springs, so hot that meat is readily cooked in them.❞

▲ Yellowstone National Park's hot springs, geysers, and mudpots are evidence of Earth's hot interior.

Earth's temperature increases about 25°C per km in the crust, then more gradually from the upper mantle to its center. ▶

**Temperature of Earth's Interior**

Temperature (°C): 6,000 / 5,000 / 4,000 / 3,000 / 2,000 / 1,000

Earth's Center

Depth (km): 0  1,000  2,000  3,000  4,000  5,000  6,000  7,000

Scientists cannot travel very far below Earth's surface to measure temperatures directly. By studying mines and holes drilled in the crust, scientists know that the temperature increases about 2 to 3°C for every 0.1 km (300 ft) below the surface. However, the deepest drill holes reach less than 15 km (9 mi) below the surface. So scientists depend on other, less direct evidence.

Scientists study geysers and volcanic activity to learn what Earth is like inside. They also conduct experiments on surface rocks and minerals under conditions of high pressure and temperature.

More information about Earth's interior can be gained by observing seismic waves. These waves are vibrations that travel through the solid Earth during earthquakes. Seismic waves change as they travel deeper. They also change as they move through different kinds of materials at different temperatures.

**FOCUS CHECK** What evidence shows that Earth is hot inside?

## Layers of the Earth

**Crust**
Earth's thin outermost layer is solid rock. It is about five times thicker under the continents than it is under the oceans.

**Mantle**
This thick layer is between the crust and the outer core. The solid upper mantle combines with the crust to form the lithosphere.

**Outer Core**
Formed mostly of molten metal, this is Earth's only liquid layer.

**Inner Core**
Pressure keeps this super-hot metallic region in a solid state.

## Earth's Layers

Earth has a layered structure. Most of these layers are made up of solid or partly melted rock. The innermost layers are mostly a mixture of metals.

Earth's layers vary in thickness. The **crust**, the uppermost layer, is much thinner than the other layers. The crust is nearly all solid rock. Under the continents, the crust is mostly granite and other light rocks.

Below the oceans, the crust is mostly made of basalt—a dark, dense rock.

The crust is by far the thinnest of Earth's layers. Under the continents, the average thickness of the crust is about 40 km (24 mi), but it may be as much as 70 km (42 mi) in mountainous regions. The crust is even thinner under the oceans. The ocean-floor crust has a thickness of about 7 km (4 mi).

As discussed earlier, temperature increases as you go deeper into the Earth. So, the deeper that rocks are located, the hotter they are.

The layer just below Earth's crust is the **mantle**. The mantle is about 2,900 km (1,800 mi) thick and makes up more than two-thirds of Earth's mass. At the boundary where the upper mantle meets the crust, the mantle rock is solid. This solid upper mantle and crust combine to form a rigid shell called the **lithosphere**.

Below the lithosphere, much of the rock material in the mantle is partially melted. This material can flow very slowly, like plastic that has been heated almost to its melting point. The solid lithosphere can be thought of as "floating" on this thick lower mantle.

The innermost of Earth's layers is the **core**, which extends to the center of the Earth. The core is divided into two regions, or layers—the outer core and the inner core. The outer core is about 2,200 km (1,400 mi) thick, and is the only layer that is in a liquid state. It is made up mostly of molten iron and nickel, with some sulfur and oxygen also present.

The inner core, about 1,200 km (720 mi) thick, is even hotter than the outer core. It is probably made up of iron and nickel as well. However, the extremely high pressure so deep inside Earth keeps this metal from melting.

Many scientists believe that the presence of molten iron and nickel in Earth's core explains why Earth is surrounded by a magnetic field. According to one theory, convection currents move slowly throughout the liquid outer core. Electric currents are produced as Earth rotates, setting up Earth's magnetic field.

A hard-boiled egg is often used to model Earth's structure. The hard, thin shell of the egg is the crust. The egg white is the mantle, and the yolk is the core. Others compare Earth to a peach or similar fruit with a thin skin and a pit in the center.

**FOCUS CHECK** From the surface inward, list the layers of Earth.

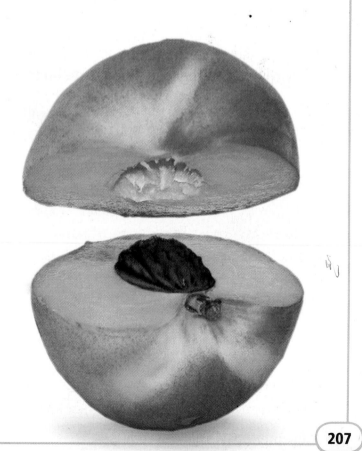

When a peach is used as a model of Earth, what does the peach pit represent? ▶

## Moving Plates

Have you ever wondered if Earth's surface always looked as it does today? Alfred Wegener wondered. Wegener was a German meteorologist and geologist. In 1915, he suggested that the continents were moving very slowly across Earth's surface.

Known as the theory of continental drift, Wegener's ideas were based on evidence that included fossils and rock formations. However, Wegener could not explain how the continents moved through the solid crust of the sea floor. Nor could he explain the forces that moved them. So, most scientists rejected his theory.

In the 1950s, scientists discovered that molten rock from the mantle was rising to Earth's surface in the ocean basins. As this rock cooled and hardened, it was being added to Earth's crust.

This discovery led scientists to suggest that the lithosphere is not one solid shell of rock. In fact, they now believe that the lithosphere is broken up into giant slabs of rock called plates. These plates seem to "float" on top of the mantle, much like giant ships floating on a sea of thick molten rock.

The idea of giant plates of rock moving slowly across Earth's surface is called **plate tectonics**. As you might expect, the plates move very slowly. Their average speed is about 10 cm (4 in.) a year. However, over millions of years, plates can move thousands of kilometers.

There are two kinds of plates. Oceanic plates consist almost entirely of dense ocean-floor material. Continental plates are made up of lighter continental rock "riding" on top of denser rock.

This map shows Earth's major plates. The plates' movement causes many changes to the land along plate boundaries. ▼

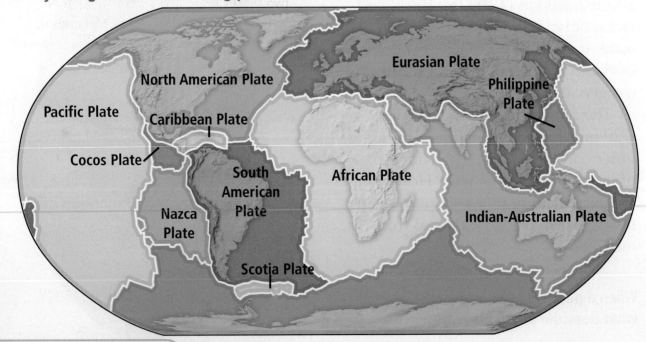

Plates interact at their edges, or plate boundaries. The pictures show the interaction that takes place at each type of boundary.

At converging boundaries, two plates converge, or move toward each other. Eventually they collide. When plates collide, one may ride up over the other. The upper plate forces the edge of the lower plate under the surface. This is called subduction.

Subduction usually occurs when a continental plate and an oceanic plate converge. The dense rock of the oceanic plate slides under the lighter rock of the continental plate.

At diverging boundaries, two plates move away, or diverge, from each other. Molten rock rises up in the gap between the plates, forming new crust. This usually happens in the middle of the ocean floor, so it is called sea-floor spreading.

Plates also may slide past each other in opposite directions. This occurs at sliding boundaries.

Whether converging, diverging, or sliding, Earth's plates never stop moving and changing. New rock is added to Earth's crust in some places, while old rock is "lost" to the mantle in other places.

The moving, separating, and merging of the continents has been happening for billions of years. As you will discover, such movements cause many constructive and destructive changes to Earth.

**FOCUS CHECK** Describe three types of plate boundaries.

## Types of Plate Boundaries

**Converging Boundaries**
Two plates move toward each other. One plate may move under the other in a process called subduction.

**Diverging Boundaries**
Two plates move away from each other. Molten rock rises to fill the gap, creating new crust.

**Sliding Boundaries**
Two plates slide past each other, moving in opposite directions.

◀ A fossil of a tropical fern like the one shown below was found in this snowy place. Since the fossil formed, the region may have moved 3,200 km on a section of a continental plate.

## Evidence for Moving Plates

Scientists conclude that Earth's plates have been moving for at least two billion years. Their evidence comes from rocks at Earth's surface. These rocks have been eroded and deposited since the planet formed.

Layers of sedimentary rocks provide clues to changes that were taking place at the time the layers were forming. Layers can show the mineral content of the rocks and how the sediment was deposited. The layers may also contain fossils.

A **fossil** is the physical remains or trace of a plant or animal that lived long ago. Fossils are usually found in layers of sedimentary rock. By studying fossils in rock layers, scientists infer how plates moved.

For example, fossils of similar species were buried on opposite sides of an ocean along the edges of different continents. Scientists infer that the fossils come from a period when the continents were joined. Over time, the continents separated, moving the fossils with them.

Some fossils seem to be very far from where they were deposited. Fossils of tropical plants and animals have been found in polar regions. Fossils of salt-water fish have been found far from oceans. Scientists believe that moving tectonic plates carried these fossils to new locations.

**FOCUS CHECK** How do fossils provide evidence for moving plates?

## Express Lab

**Activity Card**
*Make an Earth Model*

## Lesson Wrap-Up

### Visual Summary

Earth has a layered structure consisting of the crust, mantle, outer core, and inner core.

The crust and upper mantle make up the rigid lithosphere, which is broken into large sections called plates.

Plates interact in three ways at their boundaries: they may converge, diverge, or slide past one another.

Fossils and other material in layers of rock provide evidence of Earth's moving plates.

### ✓ Check for Understanding

**PLATE BOUNDARY MODEL**
Build a working model of each type of plate boundary discussed in this lesson. Use blocks of clay, construction paper, or other available materials. Use your model to show how Earth changes along plate boundaries.

🖊 0507.7.1

## Review

❶ **MAIN IDEA** How could you use a hard-boiled egg to model the layers of Earth?

❷ **VOCABULARY** What parts of Earth's structure combine to form the lithosphere?

❸ **READING SKILL: Main Idea and Details** What evidence supports the theory that the lithosphere is divided into moving tectonic plates?

❹ **CRITICAL THINKING: Applying** At a converging boundary, why do ocean plates usually subduct beneath continental plates?

❺ **INQUIRY SKILL: Use Models** Describe how you would use small rocks, pieces of cardboard, and a tub of water to model Earth's lithosphere.

### TCAP TCAP Prep

Where on Earth is new crust formed?

**A** in the outer core
**B** at converging boundaries
**C** at diverging boundaries
**D** where fossils form

SPI 0507.7.1

### Go Digital Technology

Visit **www.eduplace.com/tnscp** to learn more about Earth's structure.

**TENNESSEE STANDARDS**

GLE 0507.Inq.6 Compare the results of an investigation with what scientists already accept about this question.

GLE 0507.7.1 Compare geologic events responsible for the earth's major geological features.

**Guiding Question**

# What Are Earthquakes and Volcanoes?

## Why It Matters...

When a fruit pie bakes in an oven, juices and steam seep up through cracks in the crust. That is similar to how a volcano forms.

Volcanic eruptions and earthquakes can be violent events. By learning more about them, people may be able to avoid some of the dangers they pose.

## PREPARE TO INVESTIGATE

### Inquiry Skill

**Analyze Data** When you analyze data, you look for patterns in information you collect. Those patterns can lead you to draw conclusions, make predictions, and state generalizations.

### Materials

- world atlas
- blank world map
- red pencil
- green pencil

◄ A volcanologist is a scientist who studies volcanoes.

# Directed Inquiry

# Picking Out a Pattern

## Procedure

**1** **Compare** Read and compare the lists of earthquake and volcano locations below. What similarities do you find?

| Earthquakes | Year |
|---|---|
| Banda Sea, East Indonesia | 1938 |
| Concepción, Chile | 1751 |
| Esmeraldas (offshore), Ecuador | 1906 |
| Kamchatka Peninsula, Russia | 1952 |
| Kobe, Japan | 1995 |
| Prince William Sound, Alaska | 1964 |
| San Francisco, California | 1906 |
| Tangshan, China | 1976 |

| Volcanoes | Year |
|---|---|
| Mt. Pinatubo, Philippines | 1991 |
| Mt. St. Helens, Washington | 1980 |
| Krakatau, Indonesia | 1883 |
| Mt. Fuji, Japan | 1707 |
| Arenal, Costa Rica | 1968 |
| Momotombo, Nicaragua | 1609 |
| Mt. Hood, Oregon | 1865 |
| Tiatia (Kurile Islands), Russia | 1973 |

STEP 2

STEP 3

**2** **Use Models** Use an atlas to find the locations of the earthquakes and volcanoes.

**3** **Record Data** Mark each location on the blank world map. Draw a red triangle for a volcano. Draw a green circle for an earthquake. Check your work.

## Think and Write

1. **Analyze Data** In your *Science Notebook*, draw conclusions about the pattern you see.

2. **Predict** Using what you know about Earth's structure, predict the relationship between the planet's plates and the places where most volcanoes and earthquakes occur.

**Guided Inquiry**

**Research** Use the Internet or other reference sources to research a recent major earthquake or volcanic eruption. Where did it take place? What damage did it cause? Report your findings.

✔ 0507.7.1

213

# Earthquakes and Volcanoes

## At the Faults

As you have learned, Earth's crust moves very slowly. Typically, this motion can hardly be felt. But at times, it can cause sudden and unexpected changes to Earth's surface. Sometimes these changes are quite destructive.

Most major surface changes occur at or near plate boundaries. Recall that plates may push together (converge), move apart (diverge), or slide past each other at plate boundaries.

**Faults** are cracks in Earth's crust along which movement takes place. At a fault, rocks often bend and fold. Sometimes, they lock together and jam along the fault. Over many years, stress builds up on the rocks as the plates strain against each other. Finally, the rocks break. The plates shudder and jolt into a new position. This sudden movement causes Earth's crust to shake.

The San Andreas fault extends almost the full length of California. ▽

The wavy lines from a seismograph indicate the strength of seismic waves. ▽

As the crust shakes, it sends out shock waves of energy known as **seismic waves**. A seismograph has sensors that detect and measure vibrations of Earth's crust. The seismograph produces a record of seismic waves called a seismogram.

The movement of rocks along a fault is called faulting. During faulting, the rocks crack or split into blocks. The blocks then continue to move in relation to each other, sometimes leading to further faulting.

The drawings show the three main types of faults. Each is caused by a different type of force applied in the region where movement takes place.

At diverging boundaries, the force stretches rock. Eventually the rock breaks and one block moves down along a sloping crack. Mid-ocean ridges are typical locations for these types of faults.

Other faults occur at converging boundaries. Here, the force squeezes rock. When the rock breaks, one block moves up along a sloping crack while the other moves down. Often this occurs in regions of subduction, where one plate plunges below the other.

The third type of fault occurs in regions where blocks move horizontally past each other. These faults are common at sliding boundaries, such as the San Andreas Fault in California.

**FOCUS CHECK** What happens when stress builds up along a fault?

## Different Kinds of Faults

**Fault at Diverging Boundary**
As sections of the crust move apart, rocks are stretched until they snap, causing one block to move down along a sloping crack.

**Fault at Converging Boundary**
Rocks are compressed as they come together, causing one block to move up along a sloping crack as the other moves down.

**Fault at Sliding Boundary**
Rocks grind against each other as they move horizontally past each other in opposite directions. Pressure builds up along the fault until the rocks break.

▲ The city of Taipei in Taiwan suffered a devastating earthquake on September 21, 1999.

## Earthquakes

An **earthquake** is a violent shaking of Earth's crust. The release of built-up energy along a fault is what makes Earth shake, or quake. The energy released depends on how much rock breaks and how far the blocks of rock shift.

With the records produced by seismographs, scientists can measure an earthquake's energy. This measurement expresses its size, or magnitude, using a scale called the Richter scale. For example, an earthquake with a magnitude of less than 3.5 may not even be felt, although it is recorded by the seismograph. An earthquake measuring 7.5 is a major earthquake.

The surface effects, or intensity, of an earthquake vary from place to place. Intensity is measured by what can be seen and felt on the surface.

What people see and feel often depends on how far they are from the earthquake's focus. The **focus** of an earthquake is the point underground where the faulting occurs. Most focus points are less than 72 km (45 mi) below Earth's surface.

The point on the surface directly above the focus is an earthquake's **epicenter**. That is where the intensity is strongest. Why? The epicenter is the closest surface point to the focus, where seismic waves are strongest.

The shaking is caused by the energy of the seismic waves. Long after the initial earthquake occurs, continued seismic wave activity can cause miniquakes, or aftershocks.

### Seismic Waves

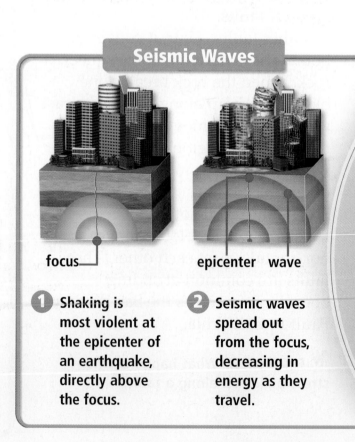

focus

epicenter   wave

**1** Shaking is most violent at the epicenter of an earthquake, directly above the focus.

**2** Seismic waves spread out from the focus, decreasing in energy as they travel.

There are two general types of seismic waves—body waves and surface waves. Waves that travel through Earth's interior are called body waves. The deeper they extend, the faster they travel.

Body waves called *P waves* can travel through Earth's interior in less than an hour. They can pass through solids and liquids. As P waves pass into and out of the liquid outer core, they change direction. They return to Earth's surface, where they cause back-and-forth motions of rock.

Body waves called *S waves* travel slightly slower than P waves. When S waves reach the surface, they cause it to move up and down. However, S waves can travel only through solids. So, S waves that pass from the mantle into the liquid outer core lose their energy and do not return to the surface.

Surface waves, or *L waves*, travel along Earth's surface. These waves travel more slowly than body waves. They also travel only so far from the epicenter. However, surface waves cause the most damage, because they make the ground swell and roll like ocean waves.

The damage caused by surface waves can be extensive. Buildings fall down and roads heave up. Bridges collapse. Glass breaks. Rivers change course or flood their banks. Trees topple and cliffs crumble.

Out at sea, massive waves are set in motion. These waves, often 30 m (90 ft) high, can move very quickly. They may travel 500 km (300 mi) in one hour! Such waves can cause great amounts of damage when they crash onto the shore.

**⊙ FOCUS CHECK** Why do surface waves cause great damage?

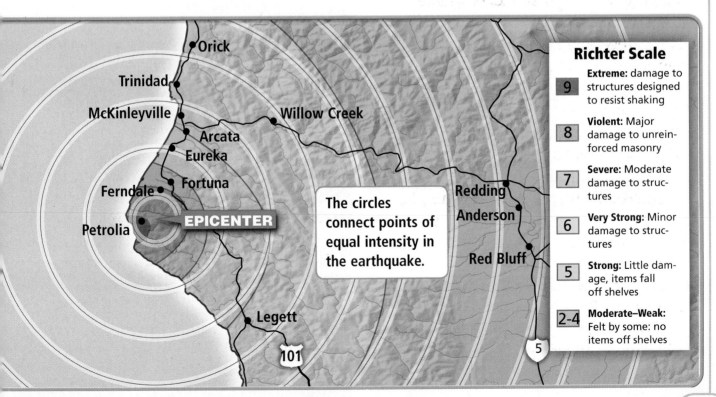

The circles connect points of equal intensity in the earthquake.

**Richter Scale**

9 — **Extreme:** damage to structures designed to resist shaking

8 — **Violent:** Major damage to unreinforced masonry

7 — **Severe:** Moderate damage to structures

6 — **Very Strong:** Minor damage to structures

5 — **Strong:** Little damage, items fall off shelves

2–4 — **Moderate–Weak:** Felt by some: no items off shelves

# Volcanoes

A volcano is an opening in Earth's surface through which melted rock, hot gases, rock fragments, and ash burst forth, or erupt. A violent eruption can release rivers of red-hot molten rock, hissing jets of poisonous gas, curling clouds of thick gray ash, and explosions of scorched rock.

Volcanoes are sometimes referred to as mountains of fire. In fact, the word *volcano* comes from the ancient Roman god of fire, Vulcan.

How do such mountains of fire form? Volcanoes come from Earth's hot interior. Most volcanoes start 37 to 100 miles below the surface. At these depths, rock can become so hot it melts. Melted rock below Earth's surface is called **magma**.

When rock melts, it releases gases. These gases mix with the magma, making it lighter than the solid rock around it. Slowly, the gas-filled magma rises toward the surface. As it rises, it melts rock around it, gradually forming a large chamber. This chamber may be only a few kilometers below the surface.

Under pressure from the weight of surrounding rock, the magma forces a channel into nearby cracked rock or melts the rock above it. Near the surface, gas and magma burst through a central opening, or vent. The erupting material cools and hardens on the surface. It builds up a volcanic mountain, or volcano.

After an eruption, a volcano usually collapses into a bowl-shaped mouth called a crater. At the bottom of the crater lies the central vent. Many volcanoes erupt many times. In such cases, volcanic material may remain below the surface or push out through side vents.

## Lava Flows

Volcanoes have been called mountains of fire. ▼

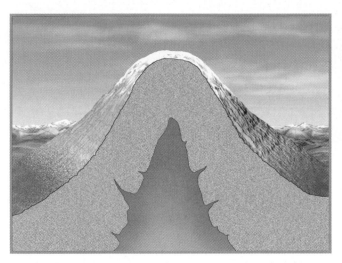

**1** Hot, gas-filled magma rises, melting rock along the way, until it forms a chamber near the surface.

**2** Pressure builds until the gas and magma force open a channel leading to the surface. Volcanic material moves through this channel and erupts through the vent.

Three main types of volcanic material are ejected during an eruption. The main one, magma, is called lava once it reaches the surface. It may be fast-flowing and liquid-like or thick and slow-flowing.

As it comes from a volcano, flowing lava may be hotter than 1,000°C (1,830°F). As it cools, lava hardens into formations such as boulders, domes, cones, tubes, and smooth or jagged sheets.

Rock fragments may form when gas in sticky magma cannot escape. Pressure builds up until the gas blasts the magma apart.

The fragments erupt into dust, ash, and large chunks called bombs. Small bombs, called cinders, may be no larger than a baseball. The largest bombs can be more than 1 m (3 ft) wide and weigh 100 tons!

Gases are also released during a volcanic eruption. Mostly steam, volcanic gases often contain poisonous chemicals. These gases mix with ash to form a deadly black smoke.

There are different classes of volcanoes and volcanic cones. Shield volcanoes form when a lot of lava flows smoothly from a vent and spreads out to cover a wide area. This action creates a broad, low, dome-shaped volcano.

Cinder cones form when mostly rock fragments erupt and are deposited around the vent. This creates a cone-shaped volcano with steep sides.

Composite volcanoes are also cone shaped. The sides of these volcanoes are steeper than those of a shield cone, but not as steep as a cinder cone.

**FOCUS CHECK** What causes magma to rise to the surface?

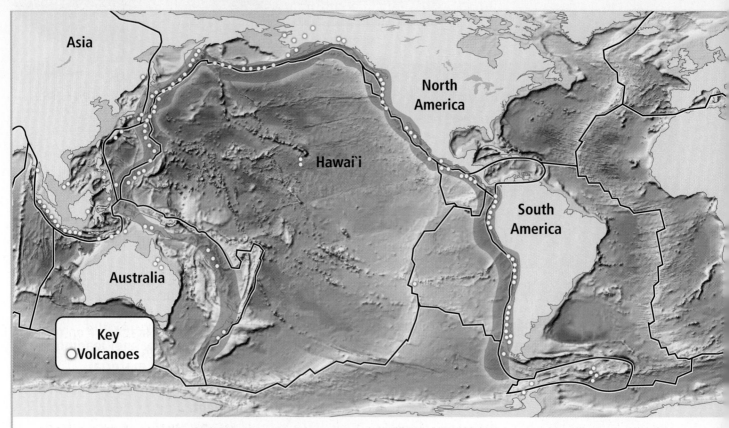

▲ A large number of volcanoes and earthquakes strike along the edge of the Pacific Ocean. This explains why this zone is called the Ring of Fire.

## Ring of Fire

Many earthquakes and volcanoes occur in a zone that borders the Pacific Ocean. For that reason, this zone has been named the Ring of Fire.

The Ring of Fire outlines Earth's subduction zones, places where one of Earth's plates is forced under another. The Pacific Plate converges with several continental plates to form the Ring of Fire.

Faulting during subduction causes earthquakes and can also lead to volcanic activity. As the subducting plate sinks into the mantle, it melts to form magma. The magma may later rise to the surface as a line of volcanoes.

On the ocean floor, a deep, narrow valley called an ocean trench may form along a subduction zone. Resulting volcanoes often parallel the trench, usually in an arc.

Faulting at diverging boundaries also causes earthquakes and creates volcanoes. Diverging boundaries are usually located near the middle of ocean basins. At these boundaries, magma rises to the surface between separating plates, forming volcanic mountain ranges known as ocean ridges. Faulting at the ridges leads to earthquakes.

**FOCUS CHECK** Why is the Pacific Ocean outlined by a region of earthquakes and active volcanoes?

# Lesson Wrap-Up

## Visual Summary

An earthquake is a violent shaking of Earth's crust caused by faulting, which shifts rock and sends out seismic waves.

Volcanoes form when gas-filled magma rises through Earth's interior. This forces volcanic materials to burst through a vent.

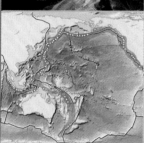

Many volcanoes and earthquakes occur in a subduction zone around the Pacific Ocean called the Ring of Fire.

## Check for Understanding

### CONSTRUCTIVE AND DESTRUCTIVE

- An earthquake or volcano can act as a constructive force by building up the land. Or it can act as a destructive force.
- Research a recent earthquake or volcanic eruption and classify the changes it caused.
- Report your findings. Include a model to show and explain the changes to Earth's surface.

✓ 0507.7.1

## Review

❶ **MAIN IDEA** Why do earthquakes and volcanoes usually occur at plate boundaries?

❷ **VOCABULARY** Define *epicenter* and *focus* and describe their relationship.

❸ **READING SKILL: Cause and Effect** Explain why volcanoes are common in the Ring of Fire.

❹ **CRITICAL THINKING: Analyze** How would Earth be different if its crust did not move and it lacked tectonic plates?

❺ **INQUIRY SKILL: Analyze Data** Research at least five recent earthquakes or volcanic eruptions. Add them to the list on page 213. Do the additional data support the conclusions that this lesson presents about earthquakes and volcanoes?

### TCAP Prep

Which can cause an earthquake?

**A** volcanic eruptions
**B** plate movement
**C** P waves
**D** S waves

SPI 0507.7.1

### Technology

Go Digital

Visit **www.eduplace.com/tnscp** to learn more about the most famous volcanic eruptions in recorded history.

# Look Out! It's an Earthquake!

**Can earthquakes be stopped?**
No, they cannot. But as three Tennessee students
will learn, new technology helps reduce damage when
earthquakes strike.

## Characters

**Narrator**
**Science Students:**
>   Marcy
>   Sam
>   Paulo

**Dr. Fine:**
a structural engineer

**Dr. Ash:**
an earthquake researcher

GLE 0507.T/E.5 Apply a creative design strategy to solve a particular problem generated by societal needs and wants..

EXTEND

**Marcy** (*reading from a book*): An earthquake is a violent shaking of Earth's crust.

**Sam:** I wonder what that feels like.

**Paulo:** We may never know. Strong earthquakes are very rare in Tennessee.

*Scene changes to the inside of a skyscraper.*

**Marcy:** Hey, what happened?

**Narrator:** Welcome to San Francisco, California.

**Sam:** Who are you?

**Narrator:** I am the Narrator, and your guide to earthquakes.

**Paulo** (*looking around*): We must be 30 floors off the ground. I am not sure I want to be here during an earthquake.

**Narrator:** Actually, this tower is very safe. See for yourself.

*Sound effect: deep, rumbling noises. The room sways slightly for a few seconds. The students lose their balance but do not fall down.*

**Marcy:** Wow! Was that an earthquake?

**Narrator:** Indeed.

**Sam:** The room moved back and forth, but I don't think the walls or floors were damaged.

**Dr. Fine** (*entering*): As according to plan! I am Dr. Fine, a structural engineer. I designed this tower to stand up to earthquakes.

**Paulo:** How did you do that?

**Dr. Fine:** The tower rests on a stack of wide, flat plates. When an earthquake strikes, the bottom plates slide back and forth under the top plates.

**Marcy:** So the tower shakes much less than it would otherwise?

**Dr. Fine:** Yes. And the shaking is more side-to-side than up and down.

**Narrator:** Other buildings rest on supports that act like giant cushions. These supports soften the effects of earthquakes.

**Sam** (*pointing out the window*): Look at that pyramid-shaped building. Does its shape help it stand up to earthquakes?

**Dr. Fine:** Oh yes, a pyramid is a very stable shape.

**Paulo:** I am glad to see that San Francisco is prepared for earthquakes.

**Sam:** So why do earthquakes strike here so often?

*Scene changes to an earthquake research station near Parkfield, California.*

223

**Marcy:** Look at that long ditch in the ground!

**Narrator:** That ditch was formed by the San Andreas Fault, which lies just below us. The fault runs almost the entire length of California.

**Sam:** So this is the cause of all the trouble.

**Dr. Ash** *(entering):* My goodness, more visitors. Welcome to Parkfield, the best place in the world for studying earthquakes.

**Paulo:** I bet those laser lights are helping you.

**Dr. Ash:** Yes. We use them to measure changes in the ground's position. We also study data from satellites in orbit above Earth.

**Sam:** Do you dig into the ground, too?

**Dr. Ash:** Indeed we do! Over there is SAFOD—the San Andreas Fault Observatory at Depth.

**Marcy:** It looks like an oil well.

**Dr. Ash:** You may compare it to an oil well, but its purpose is very different. We drill deep holes to place instruments underground. We also collect rock samples.

Land over the
San Andreas Fault

**Narrator** *(to all):* So why is it important to study earthquakes?

**Sam:** Earthquakes come from forces deep inside Earth. We cannot stop them.

**Marcy:** But we can learn to live with earthquakes.

**Paulo:** Yes, technology can help buildings stand up to them.

**Dr. Fine** *(entering):* Today, we cannot predict just when or where an earthquake will strike.

**Dr. Ash:** Yet we are learning more every day. In the future, our predictions could be more precise and useful.

*Sound effects: deep rumbling noise. All sway slightly.*

**Narrator:** From Parkfield, California, we now return you to your science classroom.

**Sam:** Hey, isn't there more to learn about earthquakes?

**Marcy:** Of course there is.

**Paulo:** You can research earthquakes at the library or online.

To build the San Andreas Fault Observatory at Depth (SAFOD), scientists dig deep into the fault.

## Sharing Ideas

1. **READING CHECK** How are scientists studying earthquakes in Parkfield, California?

2. **WRITE ABOUT IT** How can buildings be designed to stand up to earthquakes?

3. **TALK ABOUT IT** What questions do you have about earthquakes?

**TENNESSEE STANDARDS**

GLE 0507.Inq.2  Select and use appropriate tools and simple equipment to conduct an investigation.

GLE 0507.7.1  Compare geologic events responsible for the earth's major geological features.

# ? How Do Mountains Form?

*Guiding Question*

## Why It Matters...

Have you ever wondered why mountains often form along a coastline? Or why those mountains look like wrinkled land?

Understanding how mountains form allows people to understand what Earth's surface was like in the past. It also helps them predict future changes in Earth's surface.

## PREPARE TO INVESTIGATE

### Inquiry Skill

**Observe**  When you observe, you use your senses to accurately describe things, making sure to distinguish between facts and opinions or guesses.

### Materials

- shoebox lid
- scissors
- wax paper
- moist sand
- measuring cup
- goggles

### Science and Math Toolbox

For step 2, review **Measurements** on pages H16–H17.

# Directed Inquiry

# Make a Mountain!

## Procedure

**Safety:** Be careful when using scissors. Wear goggles for this investigation.

1. **Collaborate** Work with a partner. Place a shoebox lid upside down on a flat surface. Then carefully cut a narrow slit along one end of the lid where it bends up.

STEP 1

2. **Measure** Line the top of the lid with wax paper. It should be the width of the slit and about 2.5 cm (1 in.) longer than the lid.

3. **Use Models** Place the wax paper in the lid. Pull one end of the paper about 2.5 cm (1 in.) through the slit. Spread half of the sand at the end of the lid near the slit.

STEP 3

4. **Use Models** Spread the other half near the center of the lid. Each pile of sand represents the crust on one of Earth's plates. Draw the model setup in your *Science Notebook*.

5. **Use Models** Slowly pull the wax paper through the slit to model the movement of one of Earth's plates.

## Think and Write

1. **Observe** In your *Science Notebook*, draw what happened to the sand as accurately as you can.

2. **Compare** How does what happened to the sand compare to what happens to rocks in the crust when two plates collide?

### Guided Inquiry

**Design an Experiment** Select materials to model what happens along a diverging boundary.

0507.7.1

# Mountain Formation

GLE 0507.7.1 Compare geologic events responsible for the earth's major geological features.

**GRAPHIC ORGANIZER**

**Categorize/Classify** Use a chart to list the types of mountains and the forces that build them.

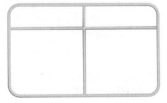

## Folding and Faulting Forces

Awesome! That is what you might think as you look down from a high mountain peak or gaze at mountains along a horizon. Indeed, mountains are awe-inspiring. Not only are they Earth's highest surface features, but they are some of its most beautiful. From the Alps in Central Europe to the Rockies in North America, mountains make up the backdrop to many of the world's scenic spots.

Grand in scale and great in mass, mountains may seem permanent. However, like Earth's other surface features, they are continually being made and destroyed.

Most mountains form at or near plate boundaries. In fact, most of the largest mountain ranges form where two plates collide and force layers of rock into folds. These are known as **fold mountains.** The Andes shown below are examples.

**Folding**
Folding often occurs at the edge of a continent and results in long, narrow mountain ranges, such as the Andes along South America's west coast.

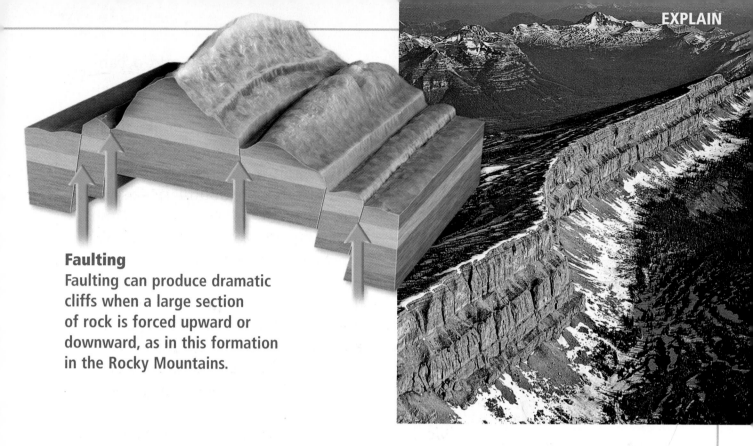

**Faulting**
Faulting can produce dramatic cliffs when a large section of rock is forced upward or downward, as in this formation in the Rocky Mountains.

Fold mountains often form where an oceanic plate collides with a continental plate. Sediment from the ocean floor becomes attached to the edge of the continent. The sediment and continental rock crumple together, creating rolling folds. As the layers of rock wrinkle, they may also crack. This creates faults, or fractures, in the crust.

Erosion softens the folds over time. For that reason, some of the oldest fold mountains, like Arkansas's Ouachita Mountains, have rounded peaks. These mountains formed before dinosaurs lived!

**Fault-block mountains** may form wherever faulting occurs. They may even occur at faults within fold mountains. You know that during faulting, rocks break into blocks at a fault. The blocks may move in several ways along one or more faults to make mountains.

Most fault-block mountains appear to form at converging or diverging boundaries. However, mountain-building activity also occurs at sliding faults. The mountains may split and slip sideways like a stack of magazines falling to one side. The new range may then shift along the sliding fault. This is what has happened to some mountain ranges bordering Death Valley in California.

As with fold mountains, erosion helps shape fault-block mountains. Many of the large isolated mountains in the Southwest are fault-block mountains. They are separated by wide plains filled with eroded material from those mountains.

**FOCUS CHECK** Which type of mountain is usually formed at converging boundaries?

229

## Volcanic Forces

Sometimes volcanic activity can form mountains. This type of mountain usually forms at plate boundaries.

Volcanic activity may happen at certain types of converging boundaries, when the edge of one plate sinks beneath another and melts into magma. The magma may rise and burst through the crust, which is called an eruption. As the magma cools into solid rock, it typically forms a volcanic mountain.

This process may even happen within mountains formed by other processes. Many of the mountains in the Andes chain in South America are volcanoes. Ancient volcanoes helped form the Appalachian Mountains.

Volcanic mountains also form at other types of boundaries. At diverging boundaries, magma rises up in the gap between the two plates. It then cools on the surface into ridges of new plate material.

As you read earlier, mid-ocean ridges form on the ocean floor at diverging boundaries. These underwater mountains make up the world's longest mountain chain.

Volcanic mountains can form away from plate boundaries as well. Areas called "hot spots" sometimes appear in the middle of plates. At a hot spot, magma from the mantle reaches unusually high into the crust. The volcanic mountains of Hawaii formed as the Pacific Plate moved over a hot spot.

Dome mountains also may form over hot spots. A **dome mountain** forms when magma rises up from the mantle, but does not break through the surface. Instead, the magma pushes up the rocks above it. This forms a dome-shaped mound, or dome mountain.

hardened magma

**Dome**
Dome mountains form when volcanic material bulges upward under the crust, hardening as it cools. A number of dome mountains lie to the east of the Rocky Mountain range.

## Erosion Mountains

Weathering and erosion are destructive forces that continually shape Earth's landforms. Although all mountains are affected by these forces, a few mountains were formed entirely by them. They are called erosion mountains.

The Catskills in New York State are one example. The Catskills were once a plateau, or raised area of flat land. Mountains began forming during the last ice age, when glaciers carved the plateau into peaks and valleys. Later, rushing streams further sculpted the land. Today, the Catskills include 98 peaks that are more than 900 meters (3,000 feet) high.

Erosion has shaped other kinds of mountains after they formed originally. The results often are irregular peaks and valleys. The Black Hills dome mountain, for example, has been eroded into the shape you find it today.

**The forces of glaciers, rivers, and gravity all helped shape the gentle, rolling hills of the Catskills. ▼**

▲ At the Delaware Water Gap, erosion has exposed the tilted rock layers of Mount Minsi, Pennsylvania.

The Sierra Nevada, a mountain range in California, was also shaped by erosion. Glaciers shaped some of the peaks and carved out bowls, now filled with small lakes. Glaciers also widened V-shaped mountain valleys into the U-shaped valleys now seen in parts of the Sierras.

**FOCUS CHECK How are dome mountains different from most other mountains?**

Express Lab

**Activity Card**
*Make a Mountain Type*

▲ The mountains of the eastern United States are the result of many constructive and destructive processes.

## Appalachian Mountains

Study a physical map of North America. It will show a vast system of mountains running north and south across eastern Canada and the eastern United States. These are the Appalachians, one of Earth's oldest mountain ranges.

The Blue Ridge Mountains form the section of the Appalachians that cover the eastern edge of Tennessee. These mountains get their name from their soft blue color when they are viewed from a distance.

The Appalachians first formed as fold mountains about 680 million years ago. The tectonic plates holding North America, Europe, and Africa all collided. Later, these plates separated. The original mountain range also separated. Part of it is on each of those tectonic plates today. The Scottish Highlands are in Scotland in Europe. The Anti-Atlas Mountains are in Morocco in northwestern Africa.

Over millions of years, both constructive and destructive forces helped to shape Tennessee's mountains. Streams flowed into rivers, and they carved out valleys from the rock. Water, wind, and gravity helped weather and erode the mountains' peaks. These forces formed the rounded and flattened mountain peaks you can see today.

As soil built up, moderate rainfall and warm summers helped support vast forests. Most of Tennessee's mountains are covered in trees. Clingmans Dome, the highest point in Tennessee, is no exception. Taller mountain ranges, such as the Rocky Mountains in western North America, have peaks that are bare.

**FOCUS CHECK** How was Clingmans Dome formed?

# Lesson Wrap-Up

## Visual Summary

Mountain formation is a constructive process. Fold mountains form when a plate folds as two plates push against one another.

Fault-block mountains form when the crust breaks into chunks, and the chunks are pushed upward.

Dome mountains form when magma pushes upward and hardens under the crust.

## Check for Understanding

### EARTH'S SURFACE FEATURES

Make a chart that shows how folding and faulting affect Earth's surface features.

✓ 0507.7.2

## Review

**1 MAIN IDEA** Name and describe the four types, or classes, of mountains.

**2 VOCABULARY** How does a dome mountain form?

**3 READING SKILL: Categorize/ Classify** Which two types of mountains are formed by volcanic activity?

**4 CRITICAL THINKING: Synthesize** What might you conclude if you notice sections of warped and wrinkled rock layers on the side of a mountain?

**5 INQUIRY SKILL: Observe** If someone described a dome mountain as "beautiful," would that be an accurate scientific observation? Why or why not?

### TCAP Prep

Which geological feature forms over time when Earth's crust cracks and the pieces move upward?

**A** volcanoes
**B** valleys and ridges
**C** fold mountains
**D** fault-block mountains

SPI 0507.7.1

 **Technology**

Visit **www.eduplace.com/tnscp** to learn more about mountain formation.

233

# SLEEPING GIANT ERUPTS!

**Talk about waking up on the wrong side of the bed!** Snow-capped Mount St. Helens slept for a hundred years. Then on May 18, 1980, the volcano blew its top! It was one of the most destructive explosions in recorded history.

The sideways blast covered 150 square miles and blew down enough trees to build 300,000 homes. Ash from the volcano piled 600 feet deep. It even blocked nearby rivers!

Before the eruption, the height of the mountain was 9,677 feet. Afterward, it was 1,314 feet shorter! Recently, the volcano has shown signs of new activity. Scientists are monitoring it closely to determine if another major eruption will occur.

In 1980, plumes of ash reached a height of 80,000 ▶ feet, blocking air traffic. In three days, the ash traveled all the way across the United States.

**GLE 0507.7.1** Compare geologic events responsible for the earth's major geological features.

EXTEND

## The View from Inside
This picture is taken from inside the blown-out top of Mount St. Helens. Here you can see the inner walls of the volcano's cone. ▼

**Steam plume**

**Danger Mounting** This rising, steaming lump is called a lava dome. As magma pushes up from underneath, it rises higher and higher—until the next big eruption. When will it be?

235

GLE 0507.7.1 Compare geologic events responsible for the earth's major geological features. **Math GLE 0506.1.1** Use mathematical language, symbols, and definitions while developing mathematical reasoning. **ELA GLE 0501.3.2** Write in a variety of modes and genres.

## Math
## Earthquake Totals

In the bar graph, orange bars show yearly totals for earthquakes of at least moderate strength. They measured 5.0 or higher on the Richter Scale. The red sections of the bars show severe earthquakes that measured greater than 6.0.

1. About how many severe earthquakes struck worldwide from 2000 to 2005?

2. Does the graph show in which year earthquakes caused the most damage? Explain.

3. For the earthquakes of at least moderate strength, is the fraction of severe earthquakes closer to $\frac{1}{10}$, $\frac{1}{5}$, or $\frac{1}{4}$? How can you tell quickly?

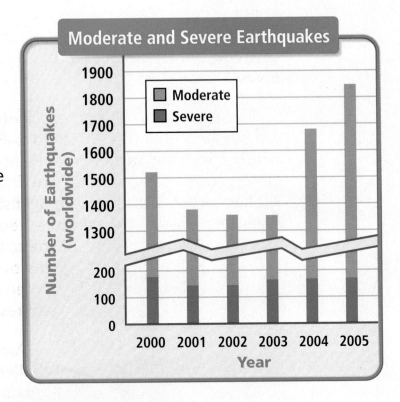

**Moderate and Severe Earthquakes**

Number of Earthquakes (worldwide)

- ☐ Moderate
- ☐ Severe

1900 1800 1700 1600 1500 1400 1300 200 100 0

2000 2001 2002 2003 2004 2005

Year

**Narrative**

Research a powerful earthquake, such as the one that struck near San Francisco in 1989. Write a story in which characters live through the earthquake.

## Peter Malin

If you were studying earthquakes, how would you want to measure them? Scientist Peter Malin wants to place seismographs and other tools as close to an earthquake's focus as possible—several kilometers below the surface!

Professor Malin and other scientists are working on a project called SAFOD, which stands for San Andreas Fault Observatory at Depth. They are drilling down 3.2 kilometers into the fault. By installing tools to measure pressure, temperature, rock strain, and other data, the scientists hope to discover just what happens when an earthquake strikes.

Part of Malin's challenge is to build instruments that can work deep underground. At a depth of 2 kilometers, temperatures are high enough to boil water. The air pressure is three times greater than on the surface.

◄ The task of building the observatory is much like drilling for oil.

## Vocabulary

**Complete each sentence with a term from the list.**

1. The outermost layer of Earth is called the _____.

2. The solid upper mantle and the crust compose the _____.

3. The point underground where faulting occurs is the _____ of an earthquake.

4. The layer of Earth between the crust and the outer core is called the _____.

5. Shock waves of energy released in an earthquake are called _____.

6. The release of energy along a fault causes a(n) _____.

7. Earth's innermost layer is the _____.

8. Molten rock, or _____, that flows to Earth's surface is called lava.

9. A crack in the crust along which rocks move is called a(n) _____.

10. When magma pushes up from beneath Earth's crust it forms _____.

core
crust
dome mountains
earthquake
epicenter
fault
fault-block
   mountains
focus
fold mountains
★ fossil
lithosphere
magma
mantle
plate tectonics
seismic waves

## TCAP Inquiry Skills

11. **Use Models** Fran uses a sheet of bread dough to model tectonic plates. Why might she slice the sheet into two pieces? **GLE 0507.7.1**

12. **Analyze Data** A scientist announces that an earthquake of magnitude 2.1 on the Richter scale has struck central Tennessee. Describe its effects. **GLE 0507.7.1**

13. **Infer** Describe three ways that scientists infer the temperature of Earth's interior. **GLE 0507.Inq.4**

## Map the Concept

Fill in the concept map to show the layers of Earth.

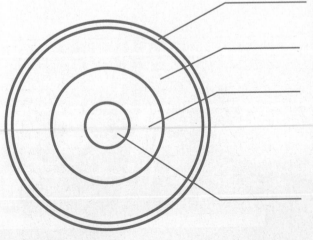

**GLE 0507.Inq.3**

## Critical Thinking

**14. Apply** Mt. Everest and the Himalayas lie on the northern border of India, which is also a plate boundary. Use the theory of plate tectonics to explain why Mt. Everest is increasing in height. What types of mountains are the Himalayas? **GLE 0507.7.1**

**15. Synthesize** Why can volcanoes be both a constructive and a destructive force? **GLE 0507.7.1**

**16. Evalute** Why do fault-block and fold mountains form at converging and diverging boundaries, but not typically at sliding boundaries? **GLE 0507.7.1**

## Check for Understanding

**Earth's Surface Features**

Make a chart that compares how volcanoes, earthquakes, faulting, and plate movements affect Earth's surface features.

✔ **0507.7.2**

## TCAP Prep

Answer the following questions.

**17** Where is a volcano <u>most</u> <u>likely</u> to form?

   **A** northern Tennessee
   **B** the rim of the Pacific Ocean
   **C** Florida
   **D** the Himalayas    **SPI 0507.7.1**

**18** Which of the following can cause a new ocean to form between continents?

   **F** faulting
   **G** volcanoes
   **H** earthquakes
   **J** plate movements    **SPI 0507.7.1**

**19** Over many years, erosion changes a mountain range by making the peaks

   **A** more jagged
   **B** taller
   **C** shift to the east or west
   **D** shorter and rounder    **SPI 0507.7.1**

**20** The constructive forces that build mountains are best explained by

   **F** the theory of plate tectonics
   **G** weathering and erosion
   **H** the water cycle
   **J** deposition from rivers    **SPI 0507.7.1**

# Chapter 7

# Weather and Climate

## Lesson Preview

**LESSON 1**

Winter—or summer—wonderland? Why is the Arctic always cold?

**LESSON 2**

How does hi-tech equipment in space help you decide what clothes you should wear?

### Fun Facts

The temperature can be as much as 7°C (13°F) cooler at the top of Lookout Mountain than at the bottom.

# Vocabulary Preview

air mass
atmosphere
climate
El Niño
front
mesosphere
ocean currents
stratosphere
thermosphere
troposphere

 **Vocabulary Strategies**

Have you ever seen any of these terms before? Do you know what they mean?

State a description, explanation, or example of the vocabulary in your own words.

Draw a picture, symbol, example, or other image that describes the term.

**Glossary** p. H18

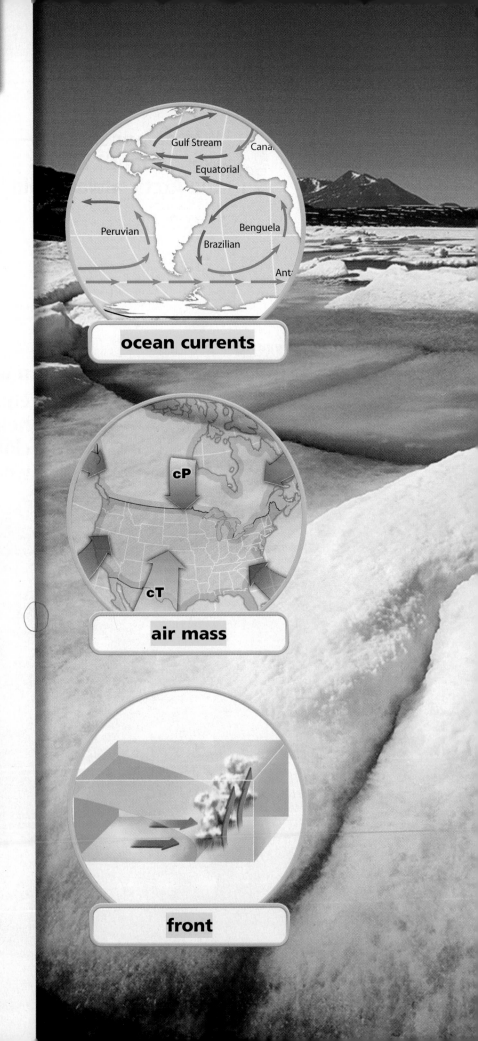

**ocean currents**

**air mass**

**front**

242 • Chapter 7

climate

## Start with Your Standards

### Inquiry

**GLE 0507.Inq.1** Explore different scientific phenomena by asking questions, making logical predictions, planning investigations, and recording data.

**GLE 0507.Inq.6** Compare the results of an investigation with what scientists already accept about this question.

### Life Science

**Standard 2—Interdependence**

**GLE 0507.2.3** Establish the connections between human activities and natural disasters and their impact on the environment.

### Earth and Space Science

**Standard 8—The Atmosphere**

**GLE 0507.8.1** Analyze and predict how major landforms and bodies of water affect atmospheric conditions.

## Interact with this chapter.

 www.eduplace.com/tnscp

**Lesson 1**

**TENNESSEE STANDARDS**

GLE 0507.Inq.6 Compare the results of an investigation with what scientists already accept about this question.
GLE 0507.8.1 Analyze and predict how major landforms and bodies of water affect atmospheric conditions.

Guiding Question

# What Factors Affect Climate?

## Why It Matters...

All organisms, including humans, are affected by the climate of the part of the world they live in. Understanding the factors that affect climate helps people predict and prepare for changes in weather.

## PREPARE TO INVESTIGATE

### Inquiry Skill

**Compare** When you compare, you describe how two or more objects or events are the same and how they are different.

### Materials

- graph paper, 2 sheets
- meter stick
- protractor
- large flashlight

---

**Science and Math Toolbox**

For step 5, review **Measurements** on pages H16–H17.

---

# Directed Inquiry

## Lighten Up!
### Procedure

**Safety:** Do not shine the light into anyone's eyes, including your own.

**①** **Collaborate** Work with a partner. Place a sheet of graph paper on the floor in your work area.

STEP 2

**②** **Measure** Hold the flashlight 1/2 meter above the graph paper and pointed directly at it. When the room has been darkened, shine the flashlight directly onto the center of the graph paper at an angle of 90 degrees.

**③** **Record Data** While you hold the light steady, have your partner carefully trace the lighted area of the graph paper. Label the drawing. Pick up the graph paper and replace it with a clean piece.

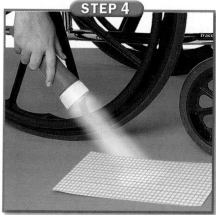

STEP 4

**④** Now tilt the flashlight at an angle of 45 degrees to the graph paper. Use a protractor to help you determine the angle. Repeat steps 2 and 3.

**⑤** **Use Numbers** Count the squares inside each shape traced in the sheets of graph paper to find the areas of the two shapes. Record the areas in your *Science Notebook*.

## Think and Write

1. **Compare** What differences did you notice between the two lighted areas? How do the two areas compare?

2. How might the difference in the lighted areas explain why Earth's surface is not evenly heated by the Sun?

✔ 0507.Inq.3

### Guided Inquiry

**Design an Experiment**
Design an experiment to show how striking a curved surface, such as a large ball, affects the angle of the Sun's rays. Predict what will happen, then test your prediction.

# Climate

## GRAPHIC ORGANIZER

**Cause and Effect** Copy and complete the table to show the factors that affect climate.

GLE 0507.8.1 Analyze and predict how major landforms and bodies of water affect atmospheric conditions.

Uneven heating of Earth's surface affects the climate of an area.

## Uneven Heating

In summer, would you wear a bathing suit at the North Pole? Would you wear a down jacket in Egypt? No, you would not. The North Pole would be too cold and Egypt too hot. Why? Earth's shape and the tilt of its axis cause the Sun's rays to strike different parts of Earth's surface at different angles. So, energy from the Sun heats the surface unevenly.

Egypt is located near the equator, where the Sun's rays strike the surface at an angle near 90 degrees. This causes these areas to be warm year round. Near the poles, the rays strike the surface at angles much less than 90 degrees, resulting in much cooler temperatures. What kinds of temperatures might you expect to find in areas between these two regions?

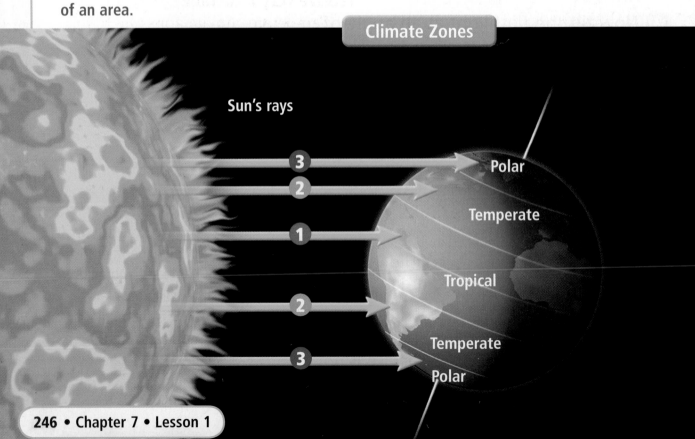

**Climate Zones**

Sun's rays

3
2
1

Polar
Temperate
Tropical
Temperate

2

3

Polar

**1** **Tropical climates** are very warm and often very rainy.

**2** **Temperate climates** have warm summers and cool to very cold winters.

**3** **Polar climates** have cold temperatures year round, even during summer months.

## Major Climate Zones

**Climate** is the normal pattern of weather in an area over many years. Uneven heating of Earth's surface by the Sun creates three major climate zones: tropical, temperate, and polar.

The major difference among the climate zones is their yearly average temperature and amount of precipitation. Precipitation, as you might already know, is any type of water—rain, snow, sleet, or hail—that falls from clouds.

Tropical climates occur at the equator and in areas just north and south of it. The temperatures in these climates are very warm year round. The coldest month in this type of climate is often no cooler than 15°C (59°F). Tropical climates can receive up to 250 cm (100 in.) of rain per year. However, some tropical areas receive very little rain.

Temperate climate zones lie to the north and south of the tropics. Some temperate climates have mild winters and mild summers. Others have very warm summers and very cold winters. In temperate climates, much of the precipitation in summer is rain. In winter, it is snow.

Places close to Earth's North Pole and South Pole have polar climates. Temperatures in these areas are very cold year round. Most of the precipitation falls as snow.

Study the figure on page 246. In which climate zone do you live?

**FOCUS CHECK** How does uneven heating by the Sun affect climate on Earth?

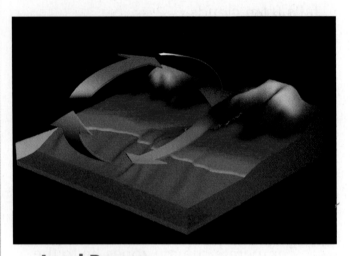

## Sea Breeze
A sea breeze flows from the water toward the land. ▲

## Land Breeze
A land breeze flows from the land toward the water. ▲

## Land and Sea Breezes

If you've ever been to the shore, you may have noticed that land and water heat up and cool down at different rates. The unequal heating of the two different surface types causes local winds known as land breezes and sea breezes.

During the day, land heats faster than water. As warm air rises over the land, cool air moves in from the water to take its place. This creates a sea breeze.

At night, air moves in the opposite way. Land cools faster than water, so the air over the water is warmer. Warm air rises over the water, and cool air moves from land to water. This creates a land breeze.

**2** **Condensation** The mountains force the warm, moist air to rise into cooler parts of the atmosphere, causing the water vapor to condense.

**1** **Evaporation** The Sun provides the energy for liquid water to become water vapor, an invisible gas.

# Mountain Effect

Why are some places rainier than others? Mountains near oceans hold part of the answer. These mountains affect the water cycle—the movement of water between Earth's atmosphere and land.

Recall that most of Earth's water is in oceans. When water evaporates from oceans, it becomes water vapor in the air. The warm, moist air rises and moves over land.

Air that meets mountains is forced higher, where temperatures are colder. Cold air can hold less water vapor than warm air. So, the water condenses into tiny water droplets.

The droplets form clouds that can drop rain or snow along one side of the mountain. This side, which faces the wind, is called the windward side of a mountain. Some of the wettest places on Earth are on the windward sides of mountains.

When the air finally crosses to the other side of the mountain, it usually has very little moisture left. Dry winds sweep down this side of the mountain, which is called the leeward side. These dry areas on the leeward slopes are called rain shadows. Desert climates are common in rain shadows.

**FOCUS CHECK** Describe the difference in precipitation on the leeward side and windward side of a mountain.

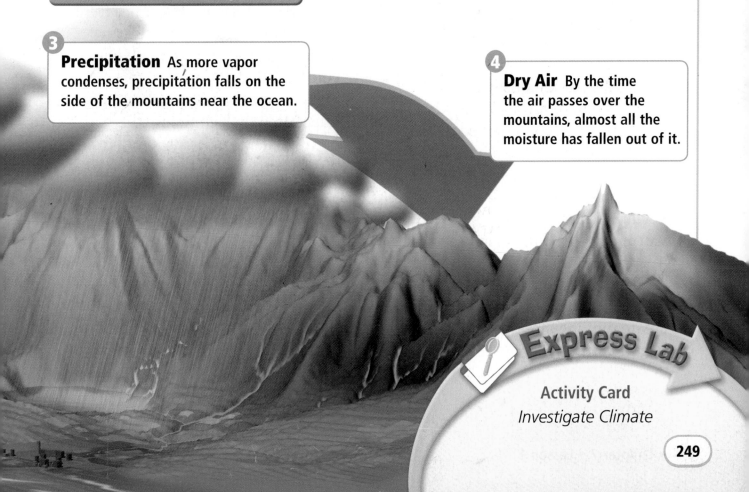

**Mountain Effect Precipitation**

**3 Precipitation** As more vapor condenses, precipitation falls on the side of the mountains near the ocean.

**4 Dry Air** By the time the air passes over the mountains, almost all the moisture has fallen out of it.

**Express Lab**

Activity Card
*Investigate Climate*

Cold Current
Warm Current

North Pacific
California
Equatorial
Peruvian
Labrador
Gulf Stream
Equatorial
Brazilian
Benguela
Antarctic
Canary
Equatorial
West Australian
Equatorial
East Australian

Ocean currents move water and energy from place to place.

## Oceans and Climate

As the map above shows, about 70 percent of Earth's surface is covered by water. Most of this is ocean water. Ocean waters absorb huge amounts of energy from the Sun.

Recall that regions near the equator absorb more energy than those near the poles. So, ocean waters are warmest near the equator and coldest near the poles.

Air just above warm ocean water is warmed by the water below. The warm air rises and cooler air moves in to take its place. This exchange of air near Earth's surface creates winds. Winds blowing across the ocean create moving streams of water called **ocean currents.**

The currents shown on the map above are surface currents. As you can see, some currents are warm and others are cold. Warm currents move warm ocean water toward polar regions. Cold currents move cold ocean water toward the equator. These currents have a moderating effect on world climates.

Like many patterns in nature, the pattern of ocean currents can change from time to time. **El Niño** is a name given to a periodic change in direction of warm ocean currents across the Pacific Ocean. El Niño events occur every five to seven years, and can cause temporary changes in climate around the globe.

**FOCUS CHECK** **How do ocean currents affect climate?**

# Lesson Wrap-Up

## Visual Summary

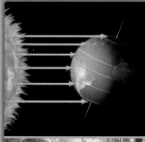

Uneven heating by the Sun causes some parts of Earth to be warmer than others.

Climate is the normal pattern of weather in an area over many years.

Bodies of water, mountains, and ocean currents can affect climate.

## ✔ Check for Understanding

### CLIMATE FACTORS

Research various land maps. Record information about the climate of different areas around the world. Examine the maps, and use them to demonstrate how various factors affect the climate in those areas.

✔ 0507.8.4

## Review

**1 MAIN IDEA** What are some factors that affect climate?

**2 VOCABULARY** What are ocean currents? What sets them in motion?

**3 READING SKILL: Cause and Effect** Describe two ways in which bodies of water can affect climate. Use these words in your answer: *land breeze, sea breeze,* and *ocean currents.*

**4 CRITICAL THINKING: Synthesize** Study the illustrations on pages 246 and 250. What kind of climate do you think Miami, Florida, has? Explain.

**5 INQUIRY SKILL: Cause and Effect** What factors help to account for the differences among tropical, temperate, and polar climates?

## TCAP Prep

Ocean currents affect climate because they

**A** are always cold

**B** are always warm

**C** move water and energy from one place to another

**D** cause winds to move air from one place to another

## Go Digital Technology

Visit **www.eduplace.com/tnscp** to learn more about climate.

# EXTREME Science

# Twister!

**It can rumble like an avalanche.** It can uproot trees and lift houses. It can destroy towns and cities. Few things can withstand its fury. It's the mightiest wind on Earth—the tornado!

Tornadoes are concentrated, twisting columns of air. Tornadoes contain the fastest winds on Earth. The most powerful reach over 300 miles per hour!

In April 1974, the United States had the biggest tornado outbreak in its history. A total of 148 tornadoes hit 13 states. Called the Super Outbreak, this storm system produced 30 devastating F4 and six incredible F5 tornadoes.

GLE 0507.2.3 Establish the connections between human activities and natural disasters and their impact on the environment.

EXTEND

**Wedge** The most powerful tornadoes often have a wedge shape. The largest wedges can span a mile or two.

**Rope** Many tornadoes end their lives in what is called the rope stage. Although it looks thin and strung out, the winds of a roped-out tornado can still do great damage.

| Fujita Scale | | |
|---|---|---|
| F0 | 40–72 mph | light |
| F1 | 73–112 mph | moderate |
| F2 | 113–157 mph | considerable |
| F3 | 158–206 mph | severe |
| F4 | 207–260 mph | devastating |
| F5 | 261–318 mph | incredible |

The Fujita scale is a way to classify tornadoes based on wind damage.

 TENNESSEE STANDARDS

**GLE 0507.Inq.1** Explore different scientific phenomena by asking questions, making logical predictions, planning investigations, and recording data.
**GLE 0507.8.1** Analyze and predict how major landforms and bodies of water affect atmospheric conditions.

Guiding Question

# How Are Weather Forecasts Made?

## Why It Matters...

Who depends on the weather forecast? Farmers need to know the weather before plowing fields or harvesting crops. Airplane pilots need to plan the best routes. And many businesses, from outdoor restaurants to baseball teams, make plans based on the weather.

Sometimes everyone depends on the forecast. When a severe storm approaches, the correct forecast can save people's lives.

## PREPARE TO INVESTIGATE

### Inquiry Skill

**Collaborate** When you collaborate, you work with others to conduct experiments, exchange information, and draw conclusions.

### Materials

- 2 round uninflated balloons
- scissors
- small baby food jar
- 2 thick rubber bands
- toothpick
- transparent tape
- large wide-mouth jar

# Directed Inquiry

## The Pressure's On!

## Procedure

**Safety:** Be careful when using scissors.

STEP 1

1. **Collaborate** Work with a partner. Cut the top off of two balloons. Then, cut one of the balloons 1/3 of the way down.

2. Stretch the smaller balloon over the mouth of the smaller jar until it is tight. Secure it with a rubber band. Tape a toothpick on the balloon over the center of the mouth of the jar. Leaving the toothpick hanging over the lip of the jar.

STEP 2

3. Carefully place the small jar inside the larger jar. Stretch the larger balloon tightly over the mouth of the large jar. Secure it with a rubber band.

4. **Experiment** While one partner holds the large jar, the other partner should push down on the balloon to increase the air pressure inside the large jar.

STEP 3

5. **Observe** In your *Science Notebook*, record what happens to the toothpick when the balloon is stretched downward.

6. **Experiment** Repeat step 4, this time pulling up on the balloon. Record what happens to the toothpick.

## Think and Write

1. **Infer** How does pulling up on the balloon affect the air pressure inside the jar?

2. **Hypothesize** What does your model show about how changes in air pressure can be observed?

✓ 0507.Inq.3

### Guided Inquiry

**Design an Experiment** How could you modify this experiment to detect actual changes in atmospheric air pressure? Compare your observations with air pressures listed in the newspaper.

# Earth's Atmosphere

**VOCABULARY**

air mass
atmosphere
front
mesosphere
stratosphere
thermosphere
troposphere

**GRAPHIC ORGANIZER**

**Draw Conclusions**
Select one of the air masses described in the lesson. Draw a conclusion about the kind of weather it might produce.

**GLE 0507.8.1** Analyze and predict how major landforms and bodies of water affect atmospheric conditions.

**GLE 0507.Inq.2** Select and use appropriate tools and simple equipment to conduct an investigation.

## Composition of Earth's Atmosphere

Earth's **atmosphere** is a mixture of gases that surrounds the planet. This ocean of air is made mostly of nitrogen and oxygen. Other gases are present in very small amounts. As you can see from the graph below, argon makes up about 0.93 percent of dry air. Carbon dioxide makes up about 0.03 percent of dry air. Neon and helium each make up a tiny percentage of our atmosphere.

The amount of any one gas in the atmosphere can vary. In dry air, for example, there is little or no water vapor. In the moist air over an ocean, water vapor can make up four percent of the air.

Carbon dioxide is another gas that is present in the atmosphere in varying amounts. You might already know that the amount of this gas in the atmosphere increases when fossil fuels are burned.

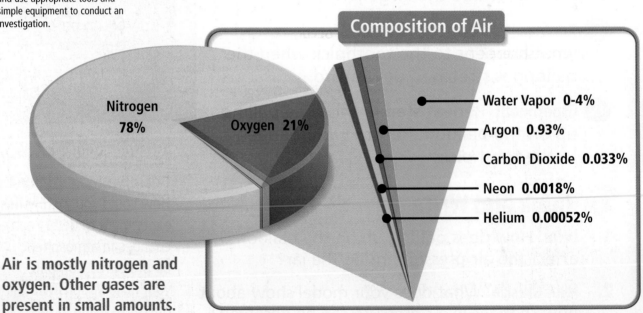

**Composition of Air**

- Nitrogen 78%
- Oxygen 21%
- Water Vapor 0-4%
- Argon 0.93%
- Carbon Dioxide 0.033%
- Neon 0.0018%
- Helium 0.00052%

Air is mostly nitrogen and oxygen. Other gases are present in small amounts.

## Structure of the Atmosphere

Earth's atmosphere can be divided into four main layers. The layer closest to Earth, where almost all weather occurs, is the **troposphere.** Although it is the thinnest layer, the troposphere contains about 75 percent of the gases that make up the atmosphere.

Temperature and air pressure decrease with distance from Earth's surface. Air pressure, which is an important element of weather, is caused by the weight of the gases in the atmosphere. Air pressure affects the water cycle which, in turn, affects the weather.

The **stratosphere** lies above the troposphere. Air in this layer is much colder and drier than air in the troposphere. The stratosphere contains most of our planet's ozone, a form of oxygen. Ozone absorbs certain types of harmful radiation from the Sun.

The **mesosphere** lies above the stratosphere. The top of the mesosphere is the coldest part of Earth's atmosphere.

The very thin air of the **thermosphere** is the first part of the atmosphere struck by sunlight. Temperatures in the thermosphere can reach 1,700°C.

**FOCUS CHECK** Why does most weather occur in the troposphere?

Earth's atmosphere is a mixture of gases that form four main layers.

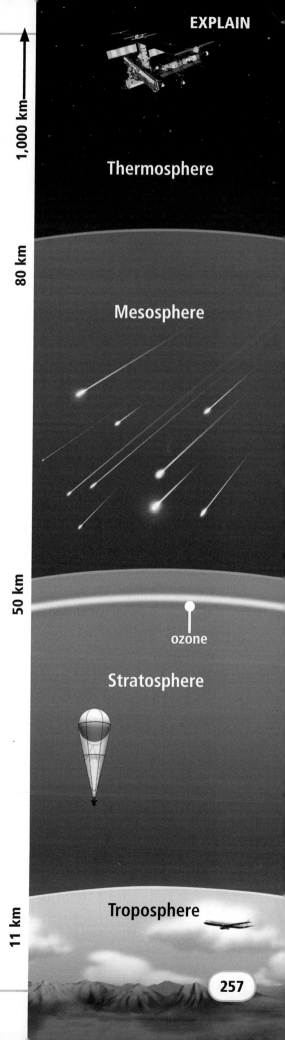

Thermosphere

1,000 km

80 km

Mesosphere

Mesosphere

50 km

ozone

Stratosphere

11 km

Troposphere

257

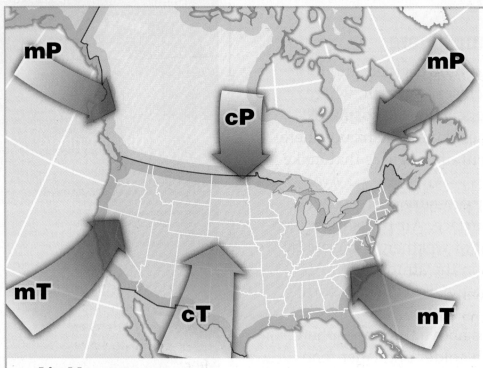

◀ Different air masses bring air of different temperatures and water content to North America.

**Key**

| | |
|---|---|
| mP | maritime polar |
| cP | continental polar |
| mT | maritime tropical |
| cT | continental tropical |

## Air Masses

In the troposphere, where almost all weather occurs, large volumes of air called air masses are always moving. An **air mass** is a body of air that has about the same temperature and moisture throughout.

The temperature and moisture properties of an air mass depend on where it develops. Polar air masses form at middle to high latitudes and are generally cold. Tropical air masses form at low latitudes and tend to be warm. Continental air masses form over land and are generally dry. Maritime air masses form over water and are moist.

The map above shows the types of air masses that affect most of North America. Notice that pairs of letters are used to identify the different air masses. Taken together, each pair identifies the moisture and temperature properties of the air mass.

Find the mP and mT air masses on the map. These moist air masses are responsible for fog and drizzle in coastal regions. They also bring moisture to the center of the country.

Now locate and cP and cT air masses. These air masses, which form over land, contain little moisture. When such air masses move into an area, they generally bring fair weather.

You know that as air masses go over mountain ranges, they lose a lot of their moisture. This can cause a moist air mass to become dry.

Now look at the map to find the type of air mass responsible for much of the weather in your area. What are its properties? Is it humid or dry? Warm or cold? Does this agree with the type of weather your area experiences?

# Fronts

When two air masses meet, a front forms. A weather **front** is the boundary between two air masses with different properties. The approach of a front is usually marked by a change in the weather. Such changes occur because cold air is denser than warm air.

A warm front forms when a warm air mass moves into an area of colder air. The warm air slides up and over the colder air, forming a gently sloping front. A warm front generally brings a large area of clouds and precipitation. On a weather map, a warm front is shown by a red line with red half circles along one side.

A cold front forms when cold air pushes its way into a warmer air mass. The dense cold air forces warmer air to rapidly rise high into the atmosphere. Clouds, heavy rain, and thunderstorms are produced along cold fronts. On a weather map, a cold front is shown by a blue line with blue triangles.

Sometimes when two air masses meet, neither mass moves forward. This type of front is called a stationary front. On a weather map, a stationary front is shown by a line with both red half circles and blue triangles.

🎯**FOCUS CHECK** How do air masses affect weather?

## Warm Front

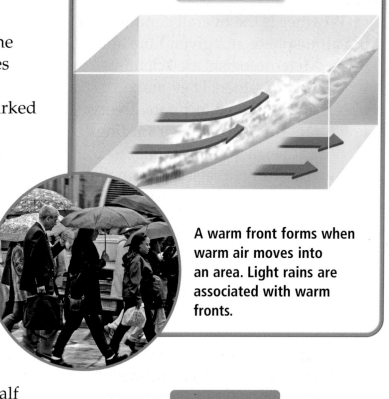

A warm front forms when warm air moves into an area. Light rains are associated with warm fronts.

## Cold Front

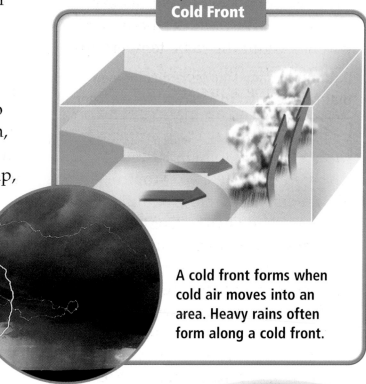

A cold front forms when cold air moves into an area. Heavy rains often form along a cold front.

**Express Lab**

Activity Card
*Compare Regions*

# Observing Weather

Weather is the overall condition of the atmosphere at a given time and place. Meteorologists are scientists who study weather. They make observations and collect data. Every few hours they record their findings on a weather map like the one below. By studying a series of maps, meteorologists are able to forecast future weather conditions.

Like all maps, weather maps use symbols. A key is provided to help understand the map. Study the map and look for the symbols for fronts as described on page 259. Identify and locate the warm fronts and cold fronts. Symbols are also used to indicate certain conditions, such as cloud cover, type of precipitation, and the occurrence of thunderstorms.

Notice that colors are used to represent air temperatures. In the United States, temperature is usually reported in degrees Fahrenheit.

Weather maps also identify areas of high and low air pressure. In a high-pressure system, indicated by an H, air sinks to the surface and moves away from the center. High-pressure systems usually have clear weather.

In a low-pressure system, shown by an L, air at the center of the system rises. Air around the system moves in towards the center to take the place of the rising air. Cloudy and rainy weather is usually present in a low-pressure system.

Most weather systems move from west to east across the United States. Look at the map below. What kind of weather might you expect in Tennessee in a few days?

**Data from many sources are combined on maps that can be used to forecast the weather.** ▼

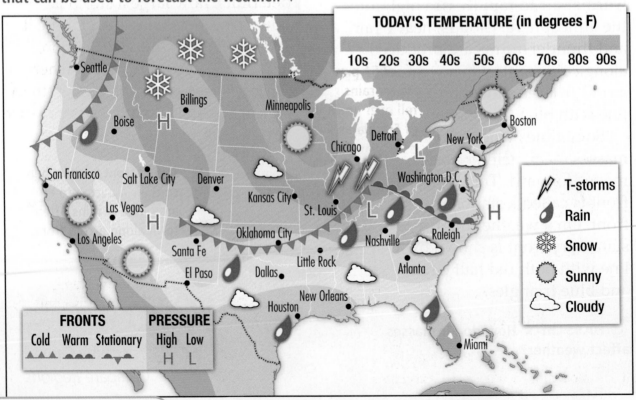

TODAY'S TEMPERATURE (in degrees F)

10s 20s 30s 40s 50s 60s 70s 80s 90s

T-storms
Rain
Snow
Sunny
Cloudy

FRONTS | PRESSURE
Cold Warm Stationary | High Low
H L

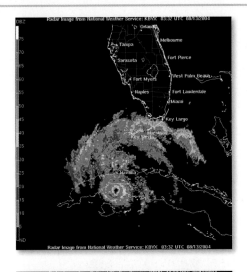

**1** 3:32 A.M. Hurricane Charley first struck Florida in the early morning.

**2** 11:53 A.M. Hurricane Charley continued to move up the western coast.

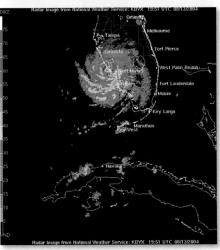

**3** 7:51 p.m. Heavy rains fell over much of Florida as the storm moved across the state.

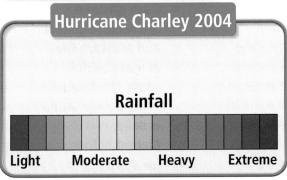

Hurricane Charley 2004

Rainfall

Light　　Moderate　　Heavy　　Extreme

# Radar

A useful tool for observing and forecasting weather is radar. A weather radar transmitter sends out radio signals. When these signals hit rain, snow, or other forms of precipitation, the signals bounce back to the transmitter and are recorded.

These radar signals can be used to create an image of a storm. You may have seen radar images, which look like fuzzy patches, used in weather reports on television.

Study the three images to the left. They are some of the early radar images of Hurricane Charley, which struck Florida in 2004. Note the different colors in the images. The colors indicate the strength of the rain brought by the hurricane. Where is the rainfall light? Where in the storm system is the rainfall the heaviest?

Radar can also be used to determine how large a storm is, how fast it is moving, and where it is headed. With this information, forecasters can warn people when severe storms are approaching. In the case of large, destructive storms, such as hurricanes, early warnings can save lives and property.

Look again at the radar images on this page. In what direction did Charley move as it passed over Florida?

**FOCUS CHECK** What are two types of weather data that can be observed with radar?

261

# Other Weather Instruments

Weather satellites are another important tool used in observing and forecasting weather. Satellites orbit high above Earth and use instruments to gather data from the upper atmosphere.

Information from these instruments can be used to determine temperatures and wind speeds on Earth. Using satellites, weather forecasters can monitor the motion of clouds and track hurricanes and other large storms.

In addition to maps, radar, and satellites, other tools are used to measure weather conditions. As you probably already know, thermometers measure temperature. Look at the other instruments described below. Which one seems the most interesting to you?

**Weather vanes** are used to indicate the direction from which wind is blowing. ▲

**FOCUS CHECK** Why are weather satellites an important tool for weather forecasters?

**Thermometers** are used to measure temperature. They may report degrees Fahrenheit (°F), degrees Celsius (°C), or both. ▲

**Anemometers** measure wind speed. Some also indicate the direction of the wind. ▲

**Barometers** measure air pressure. In the United States, air pressure is usually reported in inches of mercury. ▲

**Rain gauges** are used to collect and measure the amount of rain, snow, sleet, or hail. If the precipitation is solid, it is melted before it is measured. ▲

# Lesson Wrap-Up

## Visual Summary

The atmosphere is a blanket of air that surrounds Earth.

Large bodies of air, called air masses, form in the layer of the atmosphere closest to Earth. These air masses meet to form fronts, along which weather changes occur.

Different kinds of instruments can be used to make observations about the weather.

## Check for Understanding

### VARYING CLIMATES

Research the climates of an inland city and a coastal city that are located at similar latitudes. Compare these climates, and demonstrate how the ocean impacts weather and climate.

✔ 0507.8.1

## Review

**①  MAIN IDEA** What is an air mass, and what determines its properties?

**②  VOCABULARY** How are cold fronts and warm fronts similar and different?

**③  READING SKILL: Draw Conclusions** Suppose your area is experiencing thunderstorms. What kinds of changes in the atmosphere led to the formation of the storms?

**④  CRITICAL THINKING: Apply** How might radar images help to reduce damage from an approaching storm?

**⑤  INQUIRY SKILL: Collaborate** How might sharing data gathered in different regions allow scientists to better predict the weather?

### TCAP TCAP Prep

How do mountains affect air masses?

**A** They make them wetter.
**B** They make them colder.
**C** They make them drier.
**D** They make them tropical.

SPI 0507.8.2

### Go Digital Technology

Visit **www.eduplace.com/tnscp** to learn more about weather.

# Drought in Tennessee

Most places in Tennessee have more than 100 days every year when some precipitation falls. Sometimes it doesn't rain or snow as much as it usually does. A *drought* is a long period of time with below-normal precipitation. Droughts can last for several months or even several years!

Droughts are caused by changes in weather patterns. When an area gets much less rain than it usually does, it may be considered a drought. Some places, such as deserts, do not get much rain each year. If it doesn't rain in a desert for several months, it would not be considered a drought.

Droughts can cause serious problems for living things. Precipitation provides water that plants and animals need to survive. Rivers and lakes can begin to dry up, and forest fires are more likely to start during a drought.

A drought affects people in many ways. When there isn't enough water, crops can die. People may have to conserve as much water as possible. Sometimes communities will put restrictions on how and when people can use water. People may be told not to wash their cars or water their lawns.

Farmers can provide information about how droughts have affected their crops. This corn has wilted because of a drought. ▶

GLE 0507.2.3 Establish the connections between human activities and natural disasters and their impact on the environment.

EXTEND

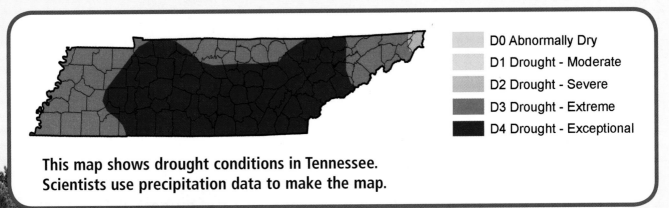

D0 Abnormally Dry
D1 Drought - Moderate
D2 Drought - Severe
D3 Drought - Extreme
D4 Drought - Exceptional

This map shows drought conditions in Tennessee. Scientists use precipitation data to make the map.

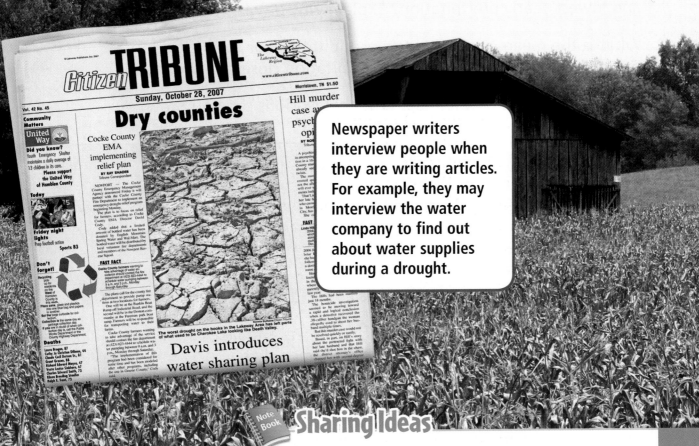

Newspaper writers interview people when they are writing articles. For example, they may interview the water company to find out about water supplies during a drought.

## Sharing Ideas

1. **READING CHECK** What is a drought, and what causes it?

2. **WRITE ABOUT IT** Describe ways that droughts affect people and other animals.

3. **TALK ABOUT IT** Look at the map of drought conditions in Tennessee. Does the map show that mountains affect drought conditions? Discuss.

 **GLE 0507.8.1** Analyze and predict how major landforms and bodies of water affect atmospheric conditions. **Math GLE 0506.5.2** Describe the shape and important features of a set of data using the measures of central tendency. **ELA GLE 0501.3.3** Know and apply the steps of the writing process: prewriting, drafting, revising, editing, evaluating, and publishing.

# Math Yearly Precipitation

1. Choose a city from the chart and find its average yearly precipitation. Does that value equal the average of the highest and lowest yearly precipitation? Explain why or why not.

2. What is the mean value of yearly precipitation for the 7 cities on the chart? In which city is yearly precipitation closest to the mean?

3. Locate the 7 cities on the map. What conclusions can you draw about precipitation in Tennessee?

| City | Lowest | Average | Highest |
|---|---|---|---|
| **Yearly Precipitation 1957–2007 (cm)** | | | |
| Memphis | 88 | 132 | 195 |
| Mobile | 108 | 166 | 220 |
| Miami | 72 | 121 | 180 |
| Atlanta | 91 | 139 | 208 |
| Vicksburg | 108 | 146 | 189 |
| Charleston | 70 | 116 | 186 |
| Raleigh | 79 | 117 | 149 |

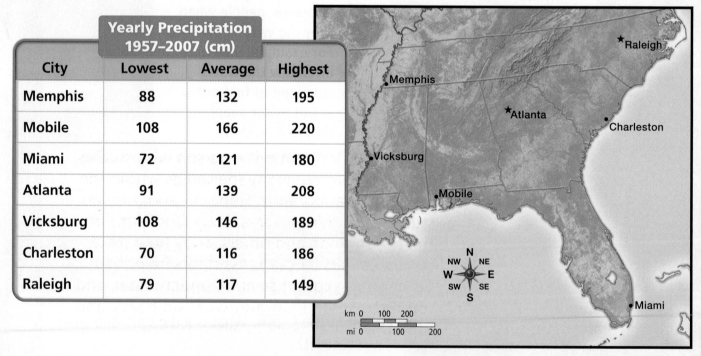

 **Informational**

Choose a large city and research its climate. Write a report about the city's climate and how it is affected by nearby landforms and bodies of water.

## Meteorologist

A meteorologist is a person who studies weather. Some meteorologists make weather forecasts, or predictions of upcoming weather. You have probably seen a meteorologist on the news. Many meteorologists don't work for television stations, though. They work for agencies such as the National Weather Service. Meteorologists collect data about the weather from satellites, weather balloons, and weather stations. Then they look for patterns and use computer models to analyze the data and make forecasts.

**What It Takes!**

- A college degree
- An ability to analyze data
- Good communication skills

## Oceanographer's Assistant

An oceanographer is a person who studies oceans. There are many specialties within the field of oceanography. Some oceanographers study living things, some study landforms on the ocean floor, and others study how water circulates in the ocean. Assistants help them gather data, collect samples under water, and run tests. Sometimes they work on boats, and sometimes they work in laboratories.

**What It Takes!**

- High school diploma and special training
- On the job experience
- Ability to pay attention to detail

## Vocabulary

**Complete each sentence with a term from the list.**

1. The range of normal weather conditions in an area over a long period of time is _____.

2. A large body of air that has similar properties of temperature and moisture is a(n) _____.

3. When two air masses with different properties meet a(n) _____ forms.

4. Movements of large volumes of ocean water are called _____.

5. The mixture of gases that surrounds the planet is Earth's _____.

6. The layer of Earth's atmosphere where most weather takes place is the _____.

7. The coldest layer of the atmosphere is the _____.

8. The hottest layer of the atmosphere is the _____.

9. A layer of ozone in the _____ protects Earth's surface from dangerous radiation.

10. Warm ocean currents change direction in the Pacific Ocean during an event called _____.

air mass ✗
atmosphere ⟍
climate ✓
El Niño ⟋
front ✓
mesosphere
ocean currents ✓
stratosphere ✗
thermosphere
troposphere ✓

## TCAP Inquiry Skills

11. **Compare** Use maps and information from this chapter to compare the climate of Florida with the climate of Ohio. What effect do bodies of water have on the climates of these two states?

    **GLE 0507.8.1**

12. **Predict** Suppose you live on the leeward side of a mountain. There is a moist air mass heading toward the windward side of the mountain. Predict if you will need an umbrella that day.

    **GLE 0507.8.1**

## Map the Concept

In the boxes, describe the features of a maritime tropical air mass at each location indicated in the box above it.

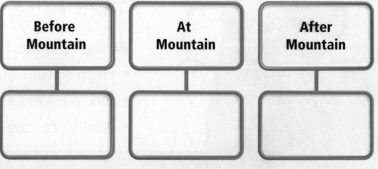

| Before Mountain | At Mountain | After Mountain |
|---|---|---|
|  |  |  |

**GLE 0507.8.1**

## Critical Thinking

**13. Synthesize** Look at the photo on page 89. What kind of climate does this area have? Infer what might cause the area to have this kind of climate.

GLE 0507.8.1

**14. Apply** Where would you expect to find hot, dry climates in the United States? Explain your answer. GLE 0507.8.1

**15. Analyze** The amounts of water vapor in the atmosphere can change from time to time. Why do you think this is so?

GLE 0507.8.1

**16. Evaluate** Would you expect weather forecasts made weeks in advance to be more or less accurate than short-term forecasts? Explain. GLE 0507.Inq.1

## Check for Understanding

Use the Internet to study the current radar for eastern Tennessee. Predict the weather for the next few hours based on the radar. Explain your prediction. Compare your prediction to the actual weather that place experiences.

✔ 0507.8.2

## TCAP Prep

Answer the following questions.

**17** Which side of a mountain is most often more dry?

**A** the windward side

**B** the maritime side

**C** the continental side

**D** the leeward side    SPI 0507.8.2

**18** A land breeze is a local wind that blows _____.

**F** only over land

**G** only over water

**H** from land toward water

**J** from water toward land    SPI 0507.8.1

**19** Which of the following can cause an air mass to become less moist?

**A** oceans

**B** rivers

**C** mountains

**D** valleys    SPI 0507.8.2

**20** A(n) ____ forms when warm air moves into an area of cooler air.

**F** warm front

**G** cold front

**H** polar air mass

**J** maritime air mass    SPI 0507.8.1

## 6 The Universe

**Performance Indicator:** SPI 0507.6.2 Select information from a complex data representation to draw conclusions about the planets.

**1** Based on the data in the table, which conclusion can you draw?

### Planet Data

| Planet | Length of Day (hours) | Length of Year (Earth years) | Distance from sun (kilometers) |
|---|---|---|---|
| Mercury | 1408 | 0.2 | 57,909,000 |
| Venus | 5832 | 0.6 | 108,209,000 |
| Earth | 24 | 1.0 | 149,598,000 |
| Mars | 25 | 1.9 | 227,937,000 |
| Jupiter | 10 | 11.9 | 778,412,000 |
| Saturn | 11 | 29.4 | 1,426,725,000 |
| Uranus | 0.7 | 84.0 | 2,870,972,000 |
| Neptune | 16 | 164.8 | 4,498,253,000 |

**A** The farther a planet is from the Sun, the longer it takes to orbit.

**B** The farther a planet is from the Sun, the longer it takes to rotate.

**C** All of the inner planets have days that are many times longer than days on the outer planets.

**D** All of the inner planets are much warmer than the outer planets.

## 6 The Universe

**Performance Indicator:** SPI 0507.6.3 Identify methods and tools for identifying star patterns.

**2** Which tool is easiest to use to find out if the constellation Orion is visible during summer in Tennessee?

**F** a planetarium

**G** a contour map

**H** a calendar with the moon phases

**J** a star chart for the Northern Hemisphere

## 7 The Earth

**Performance Indicator:** SPI 0507.7.1 Describe internal forces such as volcanoes, earthquakes, faulting, and plate movements that are responsible for the earth's major geological features such as mountains, valleys, etc.

**3** Look at the map of the tectonic plates. Which location is most likely to have a volcano?

A Location 1
B Location 2
C Location 3
D Location 4

## 8 The Atmosphere

**Performance Indicator:** SPI 0507.8.1 Describe the effects of the oceans on weather and climate.

**4** The arrow on the map shows where an air mass is moving. Which is the best description for the air mass?

F warm and moist
G warm and dry
H cold and moist
J cold and dry

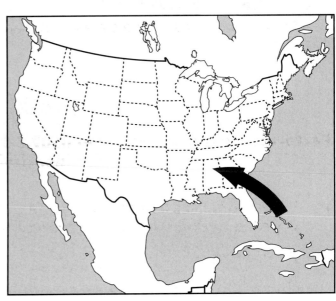

## Discover More

**Volcanoes Up Close** Some volcanoes form along a fault, which is a boundary between two tectonic plates. Other volcanoes form over "hot spots," places where thin columns of magma rise from the mantle. A hot spot tends to stay in place while the tectonic plate above it keeps moving.

According to one theory, a volcano that forms over a hot spot becomes extinct when the tectonic plate moves past the hot spot. The Hawaiian Islands likely formed in this way.

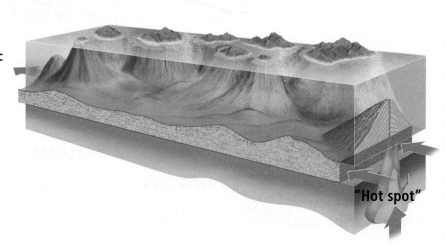

"Hot spot"

Scientists are debating why volcanoes at faults become extinct. Such volcanoes may not be hot enough to keep rocks melted. Or paths from the magma chamber to the outside may become plugged.

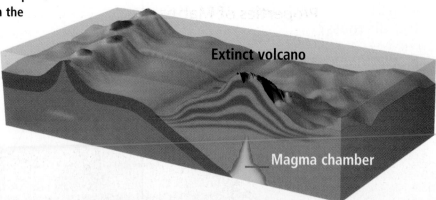

Extinct volcano

Magma chamber

 Visit **www.eduplace.com/tnscp** to see how volcanoes change.

# TENNESSEE

## Tennessee Excursions and Engineering Project

Bristol Motor Speedway and
  Bristol Dragway. . . . . . . . . . . . . . . . . . . . . .274

Dollywood Craft Preservation School . . . . . . .276

iGNiS Glass Studio. . . . . . . . . . . . . . . . . . . .278

Build a Solar Oven . . . . . . . . . . . . . . . . . . . .280

## UNIT C
## Physical Science. . . . . . . . . . . . . . . . . . . . .281

**CHAPTER 8**
  Properties of Matter. . . . . . . . . . . . . . . . . .282

**CHAPTER 9**
  Energy . . . . . . . . . . . . . . . . . . . . . . . . . . . .320

**CHAPTER 10**
  Forces, Motion, and Work . . . . . . . . . . . . .348

Bristol, TN

# Bristol Motor Speedway and Bristol Dragway

Zoom! Cars in Bristol, Tennessee, go fast. Since 1961, cars have been racing at the Bristol Motor Speedway. Because the oval track is just under 1 km (0.62 mi) long, race fans call Bristol "The World's Fastest Half Mile." In 1965, Bristol Dragway opened to give drag racers a place to start their engines. The top speed ever reached on Bristol Dragway is more than 530 km/h (329 mi/h).

Even though Bristol Motor Speedway and Bristol Dragway are both race tracks, the two have many differences. Races held on the speedway's oval track last for 150 to 500 laps. A race held on the straight dragway lasts only one length of the track.

GLE 0507.11.1 Design an investigation, collect data and draw conclusions about the relationship among mass, force, and distance traveled.

ENGAGE

# Forces Affect Race Cars

Engineers must consider many forces when designing race cars. Weight is one force. Because lighter cars are able to travel faster, weight minimums give each car a fair chance of winning. The rules of the National Association of Stock Car Auto Racing (NASCAR) state that an empty stock car must be over 1,550 kg (about 3,400 lb). A dragster must be over 1,080 kg (about 2,400 lb).

Friction is another force that affects all race cars. Look at the tires in the pictures. The tires on the stock car are different from the tires on the dragster. Stock-car tires are made of more-durable rubber to enable the driver to better steer the car, even at high speeds. A dragster doesn't need to go through turns, but it does need to accelerate quickly. Its tires are designed to increase friction to allow the car to rapidly accelerate away from the starting line.

**Tires for NASCAR cars usually last less than 100 km.**

## Think and Write

**1** **Scientific Thinking** How does the weight of a car affect its top speed?

**2** **Science and Technology** Use reference sources to research new technologies in race-car design and materials. Make a model to present your findings to the class.

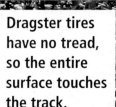

**Dragster tires have no tread, so the entire surface touches the track.**

275

# Dollywood
## Craft Preservation School

**C**an you imagine life without computers? How about televisions and electric lights? Each of these technologies has changed life. While technology changes how people live, it may also result in forgetting the old ways of doing things. The Dollywood Craft Preservation School in Pigeon Forge is dedicated to preserving knowledge about the old ways of doing things.

**GLE 0507.10.2** Conduct experiments on the transfer of heat energy through conduction, convection, and radiation.

**ENGAGE**

## The Flow of Heat

The Blacksmith Shop is one of Dollywood's most popular attractions. Blacksmiths don't just make horseshoes. These craftspersons often make art or decorations for the home. Wind chimes, gates, and umbrella stands can be made out of iron.

A blacksmith's most important tool is called a forge. The forge holds the fire needed to heat iron so that it can be shaped. The iron the blacksmith will work is placed into the forge where the flames heat it up by conduction. The flame actually touches the metal. The air above the forge is heated by convection. Once the iron is red-hot, the blacksmith can use tools like a hammer and an anvil to shape the iron into an object. While the iron is glowing, heat is being transferred by radiation. As the blacksmith works on the iron, it begins to cool down. Heat flows from the glowing metal to the cooler surroundings, the metal starts to lose its glow. The blacksmith may need to reheat the iron to complete his work on it. When the blacksmith is done, the iron object is placed in a tub of water to quickly cool it.

### Think and Write

1. **Scientific Thinking** Why do blacksmiths need to place iron objects back in the forge as they work on them?

2. **Science and Technology** What problems would you need to consider when designing a forge to heat iron to its melting point (1,538°C, about 2,800°F)

Heat is needed to shape iron objects.

# iGNiS
## Glass Studio

**H**ave you ever seen a glass vase being made? How about a glass candlestick? You can see both at the iGNiS Glass Studio in Chattanooga, Tennessee. Artists make many different types of glass objects in the studio. Owner Chris Mosey studied fine arts at the Appalachian Center for Crafts at Tennessee Technological University. There he learned how to blow and shape glass.

These bowls were made by artists at iGNiS Glass Studio.

**GLE 0507.9.3** Investigate factors that affect the rate at which various materials freeze, melt, or evaporate.

ENGAGE

One artist blows air into the ball of glass to enlarge it, while the other artist shapes it.

## Glassblowing Is an Art

Visitors can watch Mosey and other artists blow and shape glass. The artists usually work in pairs. One person uses a blowpipe to blow air into the glass to make a bubble. Then the artists use tools like metal tongs and wooden paddles to shape and sculpt the glass. Large tweezers can be used to pull the glass into its final shape or to add small details.

Glassblowers use three types of ovens to heat glass. In each oven, heat energy is transferred to the glass by convection. In the first oven, glass is heated until it is molten, usually at 1,100°C (about 2,000°F), in a container called a crucible. Crucibles are made of materials that can withstand high temperatures. The glassblower uses a second oven, at a slightly lower temperature, to reheat the glass while working on it. The third oven slowly cools the finished object. The cooling process can take several days. Faster cooling could cause the glass to crack.

Some of the pieces glassblowers make are usable, like glasses and bowls, while others are just decorative. But, whatever the purpose is, each and every piece is made by hand.

### Think and Write

1 **Scientific Thinking** How is heat energy transferred in an oven to melt glass?

2 **Scientific Inquiry** Glassblowers must heat glass before they can shape it. They use high-temperature ovens. Name some other ways that they could heat glass.

279

# Build a Solar Oven

**Identify the Problem** You are going on a class trip next week to study wildlife near a lake. You will need a way to warm up your lunch without lighting a fire.

**Think of a Solution** A solar oven could warm your food using energy from the Sun. List the characteristics that such an oven must have in order to warm your lunch. For example, it must focus the Sun's energy to increase the temperature in the oven.

**Plan and Build** Using your list of ideas, sketch and label a design for the oven. Think about materials you could use. Then build it.

**Test and Improve** Test your oven and, if necessary, improve it. Provide sketches and explanations of what you did.

## Communicate

1. How did you know whether your design for a solar oven was a success or not?

2. Describe how your list helped you build your solar oven.

3. Describe one improvement that you would like to make to your design.

## Possible Materials

- masking tape
- aluminum foil
- black construction paper
- scissors
- craft sticks
- wax paper
- glue
- cardboard box
- clear wrap
- string
- newspaper

**GLE 0507.T/E.5** Apply a creative design strategy to solve a particular problem generated by societal needs and wants.

# Physical Science

 **Guiding Question**

What relationships exist between matter and energy that can cause physical and chemical changes in matter?

# Chapter 8

# Properties of Matter

**LESSON 1**

A flower's petals are bright and smooth. A tree trunk is dark and rough. What words describe matter?

This statue is made of matter that resists changes. When the statue was carved, was a new kind of matter formed?

**LESSON 3**

The Great Smoky Mountains are known for foggy weather. Where does the water in the air come from?

**Fun Facts**

When heated, mercury expands much more than many substances. That's why it is used in some thermometers.

283

# Vocabulary Preview

atom
boiling point
★ chemical
   property
condensation
conductivity
density
deposition
evaporation
matter
melting

melting point
molecule
physical
   property
solubility
★ states of
   matter
sublimation
thermal
   expansion
vaporization

★ = Tennessee Academic Vocabulary

 **Vocabulary Strategies**

Have you ever seen any of these terms before? Do you know what they mean?

State a description, explanation, or example of the vocabulary in your own words.

Draw a picture, symbol, example, or other image that describes the term.

**Glossary** p. H18

**molecule**

**boiling point**

**condensation**

state of matter

# Start with Your Standards

## Inquiry

**GLE 0507.Inq.1** Explore different scientific phenomena by asking questions, making logical predictions, planning investigations, and recording data.

**GLE 0507.Inq.3** Organize data into appropriate tables, graphs, drawings, or diagrams.

**GLE 0507.Inq.4** Identify and interpret simple patterns of evidence to communicate the findings of multiple investigations.

**GLE 0507.Inq.5** Recognize that people may interpret the same results in different ways.

## Physical Science

### Matter

**GLE 0507.9.1** Observe and measure the simple chemical properties of common substances.

**GLE 0507.9.2** Design and conduct an experiment to demonstrate how various types of matter freeze, melt, or evaporate.

**GLE 0507.9.3** Investigate factors that affect the rate at which various materials freeze, melt, or evaporate.

**Interact with this chapter.**

 www.eduplace.com/tnscp

# Lesson 1

**TENNESSEE STANDARDS**

GLE 0507.Inq.3 Organize data into appropriate tables, graphs, drawings, or diagrams.

GLE 0507.Inq.5 Recognize that people may interpret the same results in different ways.

# What Makes Up Matter?

## Why It Matters...

Matter is everywhere. The air you breathe, the water you drink, and the clothes you wear are made of it. Matter can be hard or soft, rough or smooth, and any color of the rainbow, or no color at all.

What makes up matter? Looking very closely at matter is a good way to begin answering this question.

## PREPARE TO INVESTIGATE

## Inquiry Skill

**Observe** When you observe, you gather information about the environment using your five senses: seeing, hearing, smelling, touching, and tasting.

### Materials

- sugar cube
- granulated sugar
- powdered sugar
- plastic spoon
- black construction paper
- hand lens

# Directed Inquiry

# Compare Matter

## Procedure

1. **Collaborate** Work with a partner. In your *Science Notebook*, make a chart like the one shown.

2. Place a sugar cube, a spoonful of granulated sugar, and a spoonful of powdered sugar on a sheet of black paper. Label each sugar sample.
**Safety:** Do not taste the sugar samples.

3. **Observe** Look at the color and texture of each sugar sample. Break off a small piece of the sugar cube and rub it between your fingers. Now rub a small amount of each of the other two samples between your fingers. Note how hard or soft each sample feels. Record your observations in your chart.

4. **Observe** Use a hand lens to observe each sugar sample. Record your observations.

## Think and Write

1. **Compare** What differences did you observe when you looked at the sugar samples without a hand lens? With a hand lens? How were the samples alike?

2. **Infer** Which do you think contains more small pieces, or particles, of sugar—the spoonful of granulated sugar or the spoonful of powdered sugar? Explain.

**STEP 1**

| Method of Observation | Sugar Cube | Granulated Sugar | Powdered Sugar |
|---|---|---|---|
| Touch | | | |
| Sight | | | |
| Sight (with hand lens) | | | |

**STEP 2**

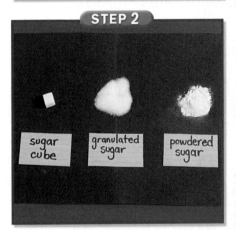

**STEP 4**

### Guided Inquiry

**Design an Experiment**
Use a microscope or hand lens to study other examples of matter. Try soil samples, pond water, or scraps of paper. Sketch what you observe. Compare results with your classmates.

✔ 0507.Inq.4

287

# Matter Everywhere

## Observing Matter

Look around you. What do you see? Perhaps you see desks, walls, and other people. Other senses may tell you that a cool breeze is blowing, or that tasty food is cooking nearby.

Things you see, feel, smell, or taste are examples of matter. **Matter** is anything that has mass and takes up space. It is the "stuff" that makes up the world around you!

Matter has many different properties, such as size, shape, texture, and odor. Some properties can be observed only by using a microscope or a hand lens. Such tools, for example, would help you see the cube-shaped crystals of a grain of salt.

### A Closer Look

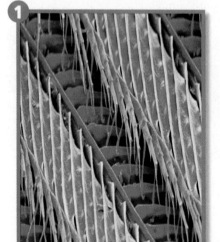

Scientists use microscopes to magnify objects to observe the properties of matter. Look at the magnified objects. What do you think each one is? (The answers are at the bottom of the next page.)

Notice how differently matter appears when it is magnified, or enlarged. That is because every object in your world is made of smaller parts. In fact, those smaller parts are made of parts that are smaller still.

So what is matter made of? Scientists have identified about 100 different elements, which are the building blocks of matter. The smallest particle of an element that has the properties of that element is called an **atom** (AT uhm).

All objects that you can see are made of a very large number of atoms. One grain of sand holds more atoms than there are people on Earth!

Most matter is made up of atoms that have combined with other atoms to make a molecule. A **molecule** (MAHL ih kyool) is a particle of matter that is made up of two or more atoms joined together. The smallest particle of water is a molecule made up of three atoms.

How small are atoms and molecules? They are too small to be seen with all but the most powerful microscopes! Even the photographs below are not magnified enough to show individual atoms.

Yet while atoms and molecules are small, they still have the properties of matter. They take up space and have mass. The mass of any object you choose—a ball, a pencil, a glass of water—is equal to the mass of the huge number of atoms inside it!

**FOCUS CHECK** What are examples of matter?

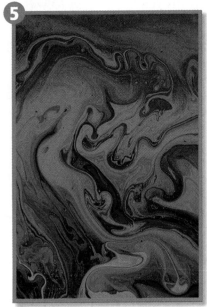

1. feather; 2. moth's eye; 3. salt; 4. nylon fibers; 5. bubble; 6. dentist's drill

## Three States of Matter

Whoosh! Look at that geyser! A rush of steam bursts into the air on a winter day. You can see three different forms, or states, of water in this scene—or can you? The **states of matter** are three forms that matter usually takes: solid, liquid, and gas. The ice on the ground is a solid. The water in the pool and the mist above it are liquids. You cannot see water as a gas. Water vapor is invisible.

The three states of water—ice, liquid water, and water vapor—look very different. They also have very different properties. However, ice, liquid water, and water vapor are alike in one important way. They all are forms of the same substance: water. In each state of matter, water molecules remain the same. They always are made up of the same combination of three atoms.

What causes solids, liquids, and gases to have different properties? The particles of matter in different states are arranged differently. Look at the diagrams to find out how the particles are arranged in the different states.

**FOCUS CHECK** How are ice, water, and water vapor alike?

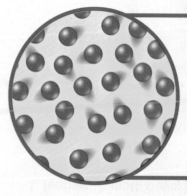

**Liquid Water**
The molecules in a liquid slide past each other but stay close together. They do not form a regular pattern.

## Water Vapor

Water vapor is a gas. The molecules of a gas are not arranged in any pattern. They move rapidly and do not stay close together.

## Ice

Ice is a solid. The molecules of a solid are packed together in a regular pattern. They vibrate back and forth in place.

**Express Lab**

**Activity Card**
*Investigate Scents*

291

# Properties of Solids, Liquids, and Gases

How can you tell that water is inside this tea kettle? The steam gives a clue.

When water in the kettle is heated to 100° C, it changes from the liquid state to water vapor, the gas state. When the water vapor cools in the air, some of it changes back into liquid droplets. This forms steam.

State of matter is an example of a physical property. A **physical property** is a characteristic of matter that can be observed by the senses without changing matter into something new. Size, shape, color, odor, and texture are examples of physical properties.

The table below compares the physical properties of solids, liquids, and gases. A solid keeps its shape. A liquid takes the shape of its container. For example, water will change shape depending on the shape of the glass it is in. A gas spreads apart or can be squeezed together to fit into a given space. In a room, a gas will dissipate, or spread out in all directions.

**FOCUS CHECK** What is a physical property?

## States of Matter

| State of Matter | Shape | Size |
|---|---|---|
| Solid | Definite shape | Fixed size |
| Liquid | No definite shape | Fixed size |
| Gas | No definite shape | No fixed size |

The clear space above the spout is water vapor, a gas. The cloud above the space is not a gas. It is water droplets mixed in air.

## Lesson Wrap-Up

### Visual Summary

All matter has mass and takes up space. Matter is made up of atoms and molecules.

Three states of matter are solid, liquid, and gas. Solids and liquids have a definite size. Gases do not.

Some physical properties of matter are its state, size, shape, color, odor, and texture.

### Check for Understanding

**MAGNIFICATION REVIEW**
Throughout history, what tools have helped scientists improve how they see small objects? What new tools might help them magnify objects in the future? Research these questions. Present your findings in a report.

0507.T/E.1

## Review

**1 MAIN IDEA** Explain why the color blue and the number 12 are not considered matter.

**2 VOCABULARY** What is the difference between an atom and a molecule?

**3 READING SKILL: Main Idea and Details** List two details that support the idea that matter has properties that can be observed.

**4 CRITICAL THINKING: Apply** Explain why people use solids and not liquids or gases to build houses.

**5 INQUIRY SKILL: Observe** Choose one of the six magnified objects on pages 288 and 289. What properties of the object do you observe?

### TCAP Prep

Water vapor, liquid water, and ice are examples of

**A** one substance
**B** two substances
**C** three substances
**D** invisible substances

SPI 0507.9.1

### Technology

Visit **www.eduplace.com/tnscp** to learn more about states of matter.

**TENNESSEE STANDARDS**

GLE 0507.Inq.1 Explore different scientific phenomena by asking questions, making logical predictions, planning investigations, and recording data.

GLE 0507.Inq.4 Identify and interpret simple patterns of evidence to communicate the findings of multiple investigations.

**Guiding Question**

# What Are Physical and Chemical Properties?

## Why It Matters...

Different materials each have their own unique physical and chemical properties. Different paints, for example, have different colors. The properties of a material determine ways it can be used. Discovering new properties of a material can lead to new uses and advances in technology.

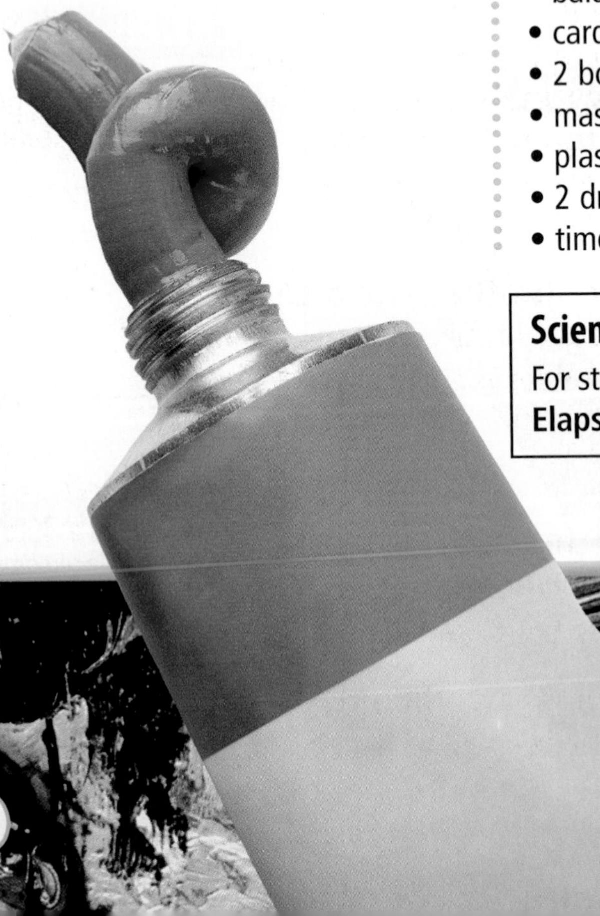

## PREPARE TO INVESTIGATE

### Inquiry Skill

**Use Numbers** When you use numbers, you use numerical data, mathematical skills, and language to describe and compare objects and events.

### Materials

- two 250-mL beakers
- vegetable oil
- water
- balance
- cardboard
- 2 books
- masking tape
- plastic wrap
- 2 droppers
- timer, or stopwatch

### Science and Math Toolbox

For step 4, review **Measuring Elapsed Time** on pages H14–H15.

# Directed Inquiry

## Oil and Water

### Procedure

**1** **Collaborate** Work with a partner. Using the balance, find the mass of an empty 250-mL beaker. Then add 100 mL of vegetable oil to the beaker. Find the mass of the beaker and oil. Subtract to find the mass of the oil. Record the results in your *Science Notebook*.

STEP 1

**2** **Use Numbers** Repeat step 1 with the other beaker and 100 mL of water. Compare the masses of the two liquids. Then subtract to find the difference.

**3** **Collaborate** Cover the cardboard with plastic wrap. Lean the piece of cardboard against a stack of books to make a ramp. Tape the ramp to the books. Place strips of tape near the top and bottom of the ramp. They are "start" and "finish" lines.

STEP 2

**4** **Observe** One partner will start the timer while the other adds five drops of oil to the starting line. Time how long it takes for the oil to travel down the ramp. Record your observations. Repeat with water on the right side of the ramp.

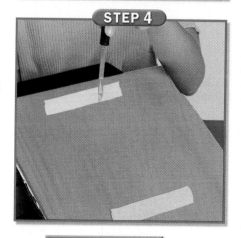
STEP 4

**5** **Observe** Pour the water into the oil and stir the mixture. Observe the mixture for about a minute. Record your observations.

### Think and Write

1. **Use Numbers** Calculate the density (*D*) of oil by dividing its mass by its volume ($D = M/V$). Then calculate the density of water.

2. **Apply** What happens when two liquids of different densities are mixed together?

### Guided Inquiry

**Design an Experiment**
Viscosity is a measure of how much a fluid resists flowing. Does a liquid's density affect its viscosity? Design an experiment to test your answer.

# Properties

## GRAPHIC ORGANIZER

**Main Idea and Details**
As you read, write down details that describe different physical properties of matter.

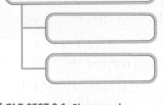

GLE 0507.9.1 Observe and measure the simple chemical properties of common substances.

## Using Your Senses

Every object or material you can think of is some form of matter. And every sample of matter has properties that can be used to describe it. You can use your senses to observe certain properties. For example, you might describe an ice cube as cold, colorless, odorless, and cube-shaped. A puff of smoke from a wood fire might be gray and shapeless, with a distinct odor.

Properties can also be used to help identify pure substances—elements and compounds—and to tell one kind of matter from another. The chart on the next page compares some properties of water and glass.

You study, compare, and apply the properties of matter all the time! When you want to write a letter, you choose a piece of paper. Paper's properties are ideal for writing. When you want to play baseball, you choose a bat made of wood or metal, not paper. What other choices of matter do you make?

**Water Bottle**
The plastic is dark, lightweight, and flexible. Unlike glass, it won't break when you drop it. ▶

**Shoes**
Tough, sturdy, spikes dig into the ground. The shoe is softer inside, where the foot fits. ▼

## Some Properties of Materials

| Property | Water | Glass |
| --- | --- | --- |
| Color | colorless and clear | colorless and clear |
| State | liquid at room temperature | solid at room temperature |
| Melting point | 0°C | greater than 1,000°C |
| Conductivity | conducts electricity | does not conduct electricity |
| Reactivity with sodium hydroxide | dissolves in sodium hydroxide to form ions | reacts with sodium hydroxide, which etches the glass |

Two kinds of properties can be used to describe and classify matter—physical properties and chemical properties. Think about a sheet of paper and a sheet of aluminum foil. Both are thin, flat, and flexible, which are physical properties. Also note that paper will burn and aluminum foil will not. These are chemical properties.

A physical property can be measured or detected by the senses. Some physical properties include state, size, color, and odor. Many physical properties, such as length, volume, and mass, can be measured. In fact, matter is often defined as anything that has mass and volume.

A **chemical property** is the ability or tendency of a material to change its chemical makeup. Materials are made of smaller particles—atoms and molecules. When the arrangement of atoms or molecules changes, a new material is formed. The new material has a different identity and different properties from the original material.

You can discover a material's chemical properties by observing how it changes under different conditions. For example, when a piece of paper is held in a flame, the paper will burn. Burning is a chemical change in which matter combines with oxygen. Burning paper produces new matter that is very different from the paper and the oxygen.

**FOCUS CHECK** Compare the properties of two examples of matter.

**Glove and Baseball**
A glove is shaped like the hand that fits inside it. It is ideal for catching the hard, tough baseball. ▼

**Basketball**
Air inside the basketball keeps it round and bouncy. Compare its size and shape to the baseball. ▶

## Mass, Volume, and Density

Mass is a measure of the amount of matter in an object or a material. It can be measured in grams (g) or kilograms (kg). A large object contains more matter than a smaller object made of the same material. So, the larger sample has a greater mass.

Volume is the amount of space a sample of matter takes up. The volume of a solid can be measured in cubic centimeters (cm³). Liquid volumes are measured in liters (L) or milliliters (mL). One cubic centimeter is equal to one milliliter.

You can find the volume of a rectangular solid by multiplying its length, width, and height. To find the volume of an odd-shaped solid, sink it in water in a beaker or graduated cylinder. The object's volume equals the increase in the water level.

The **density** of a material is its mass per unit volume. To find the density of a sample, measure its mass and its volume, then divide. For example, a 10-mL sample with a mass of 13 g has a density of 1.3 grams per milliliter (g/mL).

All samples of a pure substance kept under the same conditions have the same density. A drop of pure water and a tub-load of pure water both have density of 1 g/mL. This is the density of pure water in the liquid state. Liquids with other densities are not pure water.

Remember that density is not the same as mass. For example, lead is much denser than aluminum. If a block of lead and a block of aluminum each have a mass of 10 g, what can you conclude about them?

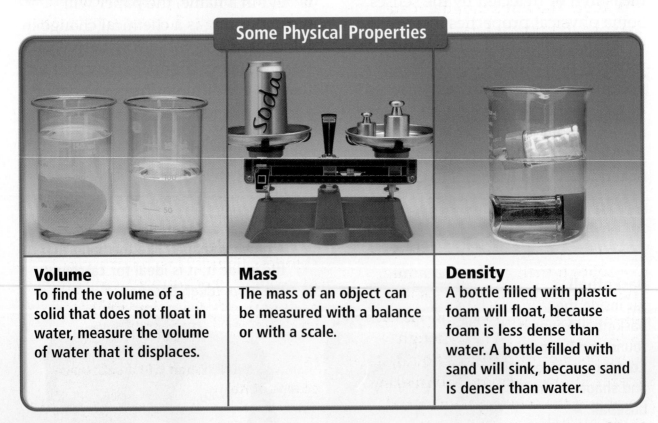

## Some Physical Properties

**Volume**
To find the volume of a solid that does not float in water, measure the volume of water that it displaces.

**Mass**
The mass of an object can be measured with a balance or with a scale.

**Density**
A bottle filled with plastic foam will float, because foam is less dense than water. A bottle filled with sand will sink, because sand is denser than water.

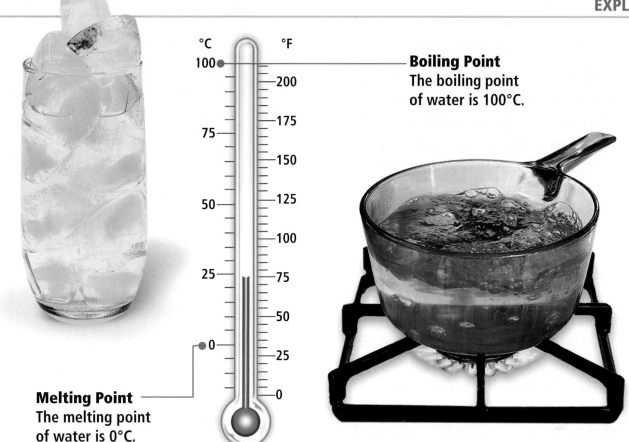

**Boiling Point**
The boiling point of water is 100°C.

**Melting Point**
The melting point of water is 0°C.

## Melting and Boiling Points

Another physical property is state of matter. The three familiar states are solid, liquid, and gas.

Solids are rigid. They have a definite shape and volume. Liquids can flow. They take on the shape of their container, but keep the same volume. Gases have no definite shape or volume. They can expand or contract to fill any container. They typically are much less dense than solids and liquids.

When enough energy is added to a solid, it melts to form a liquid. The temperature at which a solid substance changes to a liquid is called its **melting point**. When enough energy is removed from a liquid, it freezes to form a solid. The freezing point and the melting point for a given substance are the same.

Like density, the melting point is the same for all samples of any given substance. So, this property can be used to identify different substances. For example, the melting point of water is 0°C (32°F). The melting point of gold is about 1,060°C (1,940°F).

When enough energy is added to a liquid, it changes rapidly into a gas. The temperature at which this happens is called the **boiling point**.

Boiling point can also be used to identify a substance. For example, both water and rubbing alcohol are colorless liquids. The boiling point of water is 100°C (212°F), while the boiling point of rubbing alcohol is 82°C (180°F).

**FOCUS CHECK** When will a substance change state?

# Solubility and Conductivity

Stir sugar in water, and you can observe the sugar dissolve in the water, that is, mix evenly with it. The mixture that results is called a solution. You will learn more about solutions later in this chapter.

The measure of how much of one substance can dissolve in another is called **solubility**. Solubility is another physical property of matter. Some substances, like salt and sugar, are very soluble in water. Other substances, like oil and sand, are not. And while salt is soluble in water, it is not soluble in alcohol. You could use this property to tell the difference between samples of salt and sugar.

Another physical property of matter is conductivity. The **conductivity** of a material is its ability to carry energy. Electrical conductivity refers to carrying electricity. Thermal conductivity refers to carrying heat.

Most metals are good conductors of both electricity and heat. For example, copper is used both in cookware and in electrical wires.

Materials that have a low conductivity, such as rubber and plastic, are used to insulate conductors. In an electric cord, insulation around a metal wire prevents both electricity and heat from escaping.

You should never use a current-carrying electrical cord that has frayed insulation. You might get an electrical shock, or heat from the cord could start a fire!

**FOCUS CHECK** Describe the solubility of sugar in water.

**Solubility**

▲ Oil and sand will not dissolve in water, so they form separate layers when mixed with water.

▲ Powdered drink mix will dissolve in water, so the two form a colored solution when mixed.

wire

insulation

◄ Metal wires have a higher electrical conductivity than plastic insulation.

◀ Like physical properties, the chemical properties of matter affect how matter is used. Wood can be burned as fuel. The ashes of these burnt logs cannot be used as fuel.

Both the logs and the boards that are cut from them will burn. They are both made of wood. They differ only in their physical properties. ▶

## Chemical Properties

Compare the burnt log to the cut log. The logs differ in size, shape, and texture, which you have learned are physical properties. Would you be able to burn the burnt log again? Probably not. In this way, the burnt log differs from a cut log, as well as from boards that are cut from the log.

The ability to burn is a property of matter called a chemical property. A chemical property is a characteristic of matter that can be observed only when matter is changed into a new kind of matter. After burning, wood becomes ash. Ash is made of a different kind of matter than wood.

If you leave an iron nail outside in the rain, it will get rusty. The ability to rust is another example of a chemical property.

**FOCUS CHECK How is a chemical property different than a physical property?**

**Express Lab**

**Activity Card**
*Observe Chemical Reactions*

301

Cooking an egg causes new kinds of matter to form.

## Describing Chemical Properties

Look at the egg sizzling in the frying pan. How does cooking change the properties of an egg? You couldn't use the cooked egg to make cookie dough. Heat has changed the raw egg into something different. The ability of matter to change into a new kind of matter when heated is a chemical property.

Has the frying pan changed? After heating, the frying pan is still the same kind of matter, only warmer. The frying pan has had only a physical change, not a chemical change.

Chemical properties are often related to how matter reacts with air, heat, and water. Cooking describes how some kinds of matter undergo a chemical change when heated.

Other chemical properties include the ability to burn, rust, explode, and tarnish. You can observe these properties only when you try to change matter. An iron nail will rust if it gets wet. However a nail will not burn. A toothpick will not rust, but it will burn easily.

You can use chemical properties to classify matter in the same way you use physical properties to classify matter. The ability to burn is a chemical property of wood, but is not a chemical property of silver. The ability to tarnish is a chemical property of silver, but is not a chemical property of wood.

**FOCUS CHECK** **Give an example of a chemical property.**

# Lesson Wrap-Up

## Visual Summary

A physical property is a characteristic that can be measured or detected by the senses.

To find the volume of an object with an irregular shape, sink it in water.

Melting point is the temperature at which a solid changes to a liquid. Boiling point is the temperature at which a liquid changes to a gas.

## Check for Understanding

### SHINING PENNIES

Obtain three dishes, and place a dull, brown penny in each. In one dish, pour enough white vinegar to cover the penny. In another, pour lemon juice. In a third, add water. Watch closely for several minutes. What do you observe? Rinse the pennies with water, and dry them with a soft cloth. What happened? Why?

✔ 0507.9.1

## Review

❶ **MAIN IDEA** What is the difference between physical and chemical properties?

❷ **VOCABULARY** How is the density of a substance related to its mass and its volume?

❸ **READING SKILL: Main Idea and Details** What can you conclude about two liquid samples that have different boiling points?

❹ **CRITICAL THINKING: Apply** Don't swim outdoors during a thunderstorm! A lightning strike could send an electric charge through the water to your body. Which physical property of water explains this safety tip?

❺ **INQUIRY SKILL: Use Numbers** What is the volume, in milliliters, of a rectangular solid that has a length of 3 cm, a width of 2 cm, and a height of 2 cm?

### TCAP Prep

Which of the following is a chemical property of matter?

**A** conductivity
**B** density
**C** reactivity
**D** solubility

SPI 0507.9.1

## Go Digital Technology

Visit **www.eduplace.com/tnscp** to learn more about using properties to identify substances.

303

# Vanishing Bottles

**Why do these bottles fall apart in only a few months?** The answer is that they were designed to do just that!

These bottles are made of biodegradable plastic. *Biodegradable* means that a substance can be broken down by processes in nature, such as the growth of bacteria, molds, and other microorganisms. These tiny living things are able to use biodegradable plastic for food. The waste products are a kind of mush or powder.

Most plastics are not biodegradable. They resist chemical reactions with water, air, and even strong acids. They stay intact for hundreds, perhaps thousands of years.

Biodegradable plastics may help save space in landfills and trash dumps. Sending plastics to a recycling plant does this, too!

**Day 1**

**GLE 0507.T/E.1** Describe how tools, technology, and inventions help to answer questions and solve problems.

**EXTEND**

Most plastic is not biodegradable. If a Pharaoh had drunk from an ordinary plastic bottle, that bottle might last as long as the stone pyramids — thousands of years!

# Going, going, gone!

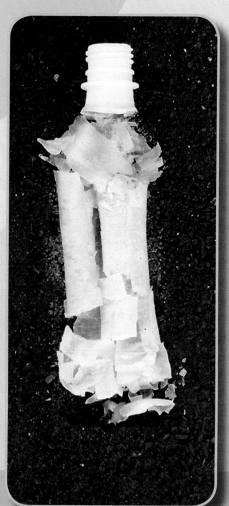

**Day 30**

**Day 50**

**Day 64**

**TENNESSEE STANDARDS**

**GLE 0507.Inq.1** Explore different scientific phenomena by asking questions, making logical predictions, planning investigations, and recording data.

**GLE 0507.9.2** Design and conduct an experiment to demonstrate how various types of matter freeze, melt, or evaporate.

**Guiding Question**

# How Does Matter Change State?

## Why It Matters...

The teakettle is on the stove. As liquid water in the kettle heats up, changes of state begin to take place. Soon steam comes out of the spout.

Water in the gas state is invisible. But when it hits the cool air, it changes to a "cloud" of tiny droplets of water you can see. The water has changed from a liquid to a gas and back to a liquid—just like that! Changes of state are part of everyday life.

## PREPARE TO INVESTIGATE

### Inquiry Skill

**Observe** You can find out more about a substance by using your senses to make careful observations of its properties.

### Materials

- clear plastic cup
- warm water
- paper towel
- food coloring
- ice cube
- plastic wrap

# Directed Inquiry

## Making Rain

### Procedure

STEP 1

1. **Observe** Fill a clear plastic cup one-half full of warm water from the tap. Place the cup on a paper towel. Add 2 drops of food coloring. Observe the properties of the water. Record your observations in your *Science Notebook*.

2. **Observe** Get an ice cube from the freezer. Record your observations of the ice cube's properties.

STEP 2

3. **Predict** Cover the plastic cup tightly with plastic wrap. Place the ice cube on top of the plastic wrap. Predict what will happen. Then watch what happens and record your observations.

### Think and Write

STEP 3

1. **Hypothesize** What substance collected underneath the plastic wrap? Where do you think the substance came from? Draw a diagram to explain your idea.

2. **Infer** What kind of change took place on top of the plastic wrap? What kind of change took place beneath the plastic wrap?

3. **Experiment** Design an experiment to test your hypothesis. How could you prove where the substance came from?

**Guided Inquiry**

**Design an Experiment**
Use what you know about ice and liquid water to design an experiment to show that mass is conserved when ice melts.

0507.Inq.2

# Changes of State

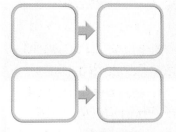
## Melting and Freezing

In many places, spring brings warmer temperatures. Snow and ice begin changing state from solids to liquids. A change of state is a physical change. The substance involved keeps its identity, and matter is always conserved.

When energy is added to a solid, its temperature will rise to a certain point. The solid starts **melting**, or changing from a solid to a liquid, at its melting point. The melting point is different for different types of matter.

The process is reversed when energy is removed from a liquid. If the temperature drops to the freezing point, the liquid freezes, or changes from a liquid to a solid. The temperature stays the same while the liquid freezes. A subtance's melting point and freezing point are the same.

A change of state takes place when snow and ice begin melting in the spring.

# Vaporizing and Condensing

Watch a drop of water on a hot frying pan. It sizzles, pops, and disappears. The change of state is caused by a rapid increase in temperature.

Adding energy to a substance makes its particles speed up, raising the temperature. At some point, the particles have so much energy that they break the forces that keep them in the liquid state. The water vaporizes. **Vaporization** is the change of state from a liquid to a gas.

Rapid vaporization is called boiling. The boiling point of a substance is the temperature at which rapid vaporization occurs. Boiling points can be slightly different from place to place because of air pressure. The boiling point for water at sea level is 100°C (212°F).

Slow or gradual vaporization is called **evaporation**. Evaporation takes place at the surface of a liquid. The higher the temperature of the surroundings, the faster evaporation takes place.

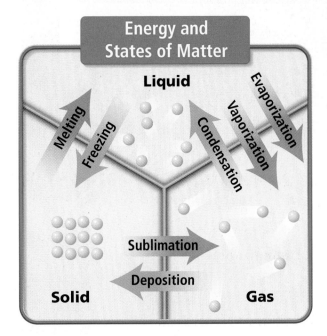

**Energy and States of Matter**

Liquid

Melting • Freezing • Condensation • Vaporization • Evaporation

Sublimation

Deposition

Solid          Gas

Changes in energy can cause changes in state.

When energy is removed from a gas, it will undergo **condensation**, a change of state from a gas to a liquid. You can observe condensation on a hot day when you make a pitcher of ice-cold lemonade. The pitcher will begin to "sweat," as water droplets form on the outside of the glass. The droplets come from water vapor in the air condensing on the cold glass.

You can also observe condensation on a freezing cold day. The air you breathe out contains water vapor, which condenses when it loses energy to the cold air.

**⊙ FOCUS CHECK** How does temperature affect the motion of particles that make up a substance?

The cold bottle removes energy from water vapor in the air that touches it. The water vapor condenses into liquid droplets on the outside of the bottle.

## Skipping a Step

Different kinds of matter will change states at different temperatures and at different rates. Each change depends on the particles that make up matter and the forces among the particles.

Sometimes, matter can skip the liquid state! When conditions are right, adding energy to a solid will change it directly to a gas. The process of changing from a solid to a gas is called **sublimation**.

Sublimation explains why dry ice is "dry." Dry ice is solid carbon dioxide. It doesn't melt into a liquid.

**Sublimation ▶**
In sublimation, a solid changes directly to a gas without passing through the liquid state.

Instead, it sublimates into carbon dioxide gas. People use dry ice instead of ordinary ice when they want to keep something cold, but not wet.

The opposite of sublimation is deposition. **Deposition** is the change of state from gas to solid. When energy is removed from a gas, its particles slow down. Under certain conditions, the gas can change directly into a solid.

Frost is a common example of deposition. Frost forms on grass, cars, and window panes when the temperature of these surfaces is below 0°C, the freezing point of water. When water vapor in the air touches these surfaces, it changes directly from a gas to tiny crystals of ice.

# Freezing, Melting, and Evaporation Rates

When it's really hot outside, your ice cream melts faster than when the temperature is mild. If you ate ice cream outside on a day when the temperature was 0°C or lower, the ice cream might not melt at all! The more extreme a temperature is, the more quickly substances will freeze, melt, or evaporate. When it is 0°C outside, a lake will freeze, but if the temperature is −30°C the lake will freeze much more quickly. The same is true for ice on a hot day. Ice will melt at 10°C, but it will melt much more quickly at 35°C.

The surface area, or area that is exposed, of a substance will also affect the rate of freezing, melting, and evaporating. One large block of ice will melt more slowly than many smaller blocks of ice with the same mass. The large block has much less area exposed than the many smaller blocks. Perhaps you've seen snow sculptures that last much longer than the snow on the ground around them. Compared to the snow on the ground, much less snow is exposed in the sculpture. The sculpture melts more slowly.

**FOCUS CHECK** What are two factors that can affect how quickly a substance freezes, melts, or evaporates?

This ice cube is outside in the sunlight. It is melting quickly. ▼

This ice cube is in the kitchen of an air conditioned home. It is melting more slowly than the one that is outside. ▼

Express Lab

**Activity Card**
*Observe Condensation*

## Expansion and Contraction

For most substances, a sample of solid matter will expand, or increase in size, when it is heated. The increase in size of a substance due to a change in temperature is called **thermal expansion**.

Remember that the particles of solids are constantly vibrating in place. When the temperature of a solid rises, its particles vibrate more rapidly and move farther apart. As a result, the entire sample expands. It's like the difference between small and large jumps: when you jump higher, you take up more space.

When a solid sample is cooled, the opposite happens. The particles vibrate more slowly. The sample contracts, or decreases in size. When a solid undergoes thermal contraction due to cooling, it takes up less space.

The molecules of water in ice take up more space than in a liquid. So, water expands when it freezes.

Thermal expansion and contraction can strain bridges. Engineers make bridges safer by adding expansion joints. These are spaces between metal parts that allow the bridge to change length without weakening or breaking.

Not all substances get smaller when they get colder. Water expands when it freezes because the molecules in ice crystals are spread farther apart than the molecules in liquid water.

Expansion of water explains why ice floats. Because a given mass of ice has a greater volume than an equal mass of liquid water, the solid ice is less dense than the liquid water.

Although heating or cooling may change the volume of matter, the mass will stay the same. One gram of any substance—solid, liquid, or gas—remains one gram at any temperature.

**FOCUS CHECK** Why does water expand when it freezes?

◀ Engineers add expansion joints to bridges to ease the strain of expansion and contraction.

## Lesson Wrap-Up

### Visual Summary

Adding energy to a liquid results in evaporation. Removing energy from a liquid results in freezing.

Removing energy from a gas can result in condensation.

Adding energy to a solid results in melting or, in some cases, sublimation.

Solids expand when they are heated and contract when they are cooled.

### Check for Understanding

**INVESTIGATE EVAPORATION**

Have an adult help you gather three bowls. Fill one with ice water and one with warm water. Leave the third bowl empty. Stretch a piece of plastic wrap over the top of each bowl. Use a dropper to place five drops of rubbing alcohol on each piece of plastic wrap. Record the amount of time it takes each drop to evaporate. Summarize your results.

0507.9.2
0507.9.3

## Review

**1 MAIN IDEA** Name three changes of state that can take place when energy is removed from a substance.

**2 VOCABULARY** Describe the processes of vaporization and condensation. How are the processes related?

**3 READING SKILL: Cause and Effect** When will a liquid evaporate, and when will it boil? Compare the two changes.

**4 CRITICAL THINKING: Apply** A scientist removes energy from a sample of gas. The matter that results has definite shape and definite volume. What change of state took place?

**5 INQUIRY SKILL: Observe** A solid has undergone a physical change. What observations can you make to determine which change of state took place?

### TCAP Prep

At which temperature will an ice cube melt fastest?

A   0°C
B   10°C
C   32°C
D   −10°C

SPI 0507.9.3

### Technology

Visit **www.eduplace.com/tnscp** to learn more about changes of state.

# Cooling Off

Have you ever heard someone call a refrigerator an *icebox?* One hundred years ago, people kept their food in a wooden cabinet. The cabinet had a large block of ice inside that kept the food cool. It was a box of ice, or an icebox. But because the ice would melt, the icebox could not freeze food.

Today, a refrigerator can keep food cool or even frozen. It does this by removing thermal energy from the food. Because thermal energy is removed, the particles of the food slow down, or even freeze.

Ice was once very valuable. People cut blocks of ice from frozen lakes and stored them for the summertime. Some of the ice was shipped to warm places.

GLE 0507.T/E.2 Recognize that new tools, technology, and inventions are always being developed.

EXTEND

# A Modern Refrigerator

**1** Refrigerators use changes of state to cool food. A compressor squeezes a gas called a coolant until it changes to a liquid.

**2** The liquid coolant moves into a new container where it begins to evaporate. As it evaporates it takes in thermal energy from its surroundings.

**3** The cooling gas moves through tubes inside the refrigerator, keeping the food cold.

## Sharing Ideas

1. **READING CHECK** Describe how a refrigerator keeps food cold.

2. **WRITE ABOUT IT** Compare a refrigerator to an old-fashioned icebox.

3. **TALK ABOUT IT** How do you think refrigerators have changed the kinds of foods people eat?

315

**GLE 0507.9.2** Design and conduct an experiment to demonstrate how various types of matter freeze, melt, or evaporate. **Math GLE 0506.5.1** Make, record, display and interpret data and graphs that include whole numbers, decimals, and fractions. **ELA GLE 0501.8.2** Experience various literary genres, including fiction and nonfiction, poetry, drama, chapter books, biography/autobiography, short stories, folk tales, myths, and science fiction.

## Math Melting Point

Different types of substances have different melting and boiling points. A substance becomes a liquid at its melting point. At its boiling point, a substance becomes a gas. Make a bar graph using the data in the table. Use the information to answer the questions about melting and boiling points.

| Substance | Melting point | Boiling point |
|-----------|---------------|---------------|
| Water | 0°C | 100°C |
| Table Salt | 801°C | 1465°C |
| Aluminum | 660°C | 2519°C |

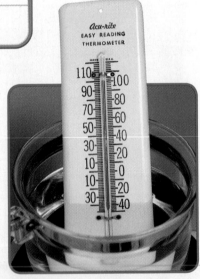

1. How much higher is the boiling point of aluminum than the boiling point of table salt?

2. In which range of temperatures would table salt be a gas and aluminum be a liquid?

3. Which substance has the greatest range of temperatures at which it is a liquid?

 **Writing** **Response to Literature**

Find a story or a poem that talks about the different states of matter. This could be a poem about snow, or a book about how to make a grilled cheese sandwich. When you have finished reading, write a report about it. Present your report to the rest of the class.

## Chavonda Jacobs-Young

How is wood changed into paper? Paper makers use many different processes. All involve both physical and chemical changes to wood. Typically, wood chips, water, and chemicals are mixed and heated. This forms a soft fibrous mixture called pulp. The pulp is stretched, pressed, and rolled into paper sheets.

To learn more, you could read one of the many books about paper making. Some quote Dr. Chavonda Jacobs-Young. She is an expert in wood and paper science. She has researched new steps for improving the paper-making process.

At a paper mill, wood is changed physically and chemically. The end result is a huge roll of paper.

## Vocabulary

**Complete each sentence with a term from the list.**

1. Size, shape, color, or texture is an example of a(n) _____.

2. The _____ are three forms that matter usually takes: solid, liquid, and gas.

3. A puddle of water slowly turns to a gas in a process called _____.

4. A particle of matter made up of two or more atoms joined together is called a(n) _____.

5. When a gas turns to a liquid, it is called _____.

6. The _____ of water is 0°C, which is also its freezing point.

7. The smallest particle of matter that has the properties of that matter is a(n) _____.

8. A characteristic of matter that can be observed only when matter is changed into a new kind of matter is called a(n) _____.

9. A balloon gets larger when it is heated due to _____.

10. Anything that has mass and takes up space is _____.

atom
boiling point
★ chemical property
condensation
conductivity
density
deposition
evaporation
matter
melting
melting point
molecule
physical property
solubility
★ states of matter
sublimation
thermal expansion
vaporization

## TCAP Inquiry Skills

11. **Predict** A pot of water is being heated on a stove. Will the physical properties of the water change? Will its chemical properties change? Explain.
GLE 0507.Inq.1

12. **Measure** A toy house is made of many small parts that snap together or apart. You have a balance, but the house won't fit on it. How could you use the balance to measure the mass of the house?
GLE 0507.Inq.2

13. **Observe** Can you use a light microscope from your school to observe atoms and molecules? Explain.
GLE 0507.Inq.2

## Map the Concept

Use terms from the list to complete the concept map.

Solid          Liquid
States of Matter          Gas

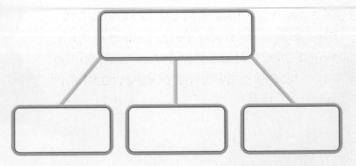

GLE 0507.9.2

## Critical Thinking

**14. Evaluate** An unknown substance has a volume of 25 mL. It is placed into a different container and its volume changes to 50 mL. What can you conclude about the state of matter of this substance? Explain.

GLE 0507.9.2

**15. Synthesize** James has two small pools in his backyard. They both hold the same amount of water. One pool is deep and round. The other pool is shallow and square. Explain why James will have to add water to one of the pools more often than the other pool.

GLE 0507.9.3

**16. Analyze** Choose a food that you enjoy, and list some of its physical and chemical properties. Describe how its properties change when it is cooked.

GLE 0507.9.1

 **Check for Understanding**

### Freezing Points of Liquids

In four paper cups, make salt water by adding salt to water. Each cup should have a different amount of salt. Also gather some common edible household liquids such as vegetable oil, maple syrup, vinegar, and soda. Fill an ice cube tray with the salt water and other liquids. Place a different liquid in each compartment. Which liquids freeze when the tray is placed in the freezer? What conclusion can you draw?

0507.9.2

## TCAP TCAP Prep

Answer the following questions.

**17** Which tool would best help you observe the small parts of an object?

**A** telescope

**B** hand lens

**C** balance

**D** graduated cylinder    SPI 0507.Inq.1

**18** Which is an example of water changing its state of matter?

**F** mixing water and cooking oil

**G** wood burning

**H** building a snowman

**J** steam rising from a kettle    SPI 0507.9.1

**19** Which is a chemical property of an iron nail?

**A** It stays straight when hammered.

**B** It bends easily when hammered.

**C** It burns easily.

**D** It rusts easily.    SPI 0507.9.1

**20** How do water molecules in ice change when the ice melts?

**F** The number of atoms increases.

**G** Their chemical properties change.

**H** Their arrangement changes.

**J** Their mass increases.    SPI 0507.9.2

# Chapter 9

# Energy

**LESSON 1**

**What kind of energy comes from a swinging wrecking ball?**

**LESSON 2**

**How does energy from the Sun reach Earth?**

## Fun Facts

Sand heats about five times more quickly than water does.

# Vocabulary Preview

- ★ **conduction**
- ★ **conductor**
- ★ **convection**
-   **energy**
-   **heat**
- ★ **insulator**
- ★ **kinetic energy**
- ★ **potential energy**
- ★ **radiation**
-   **temperature**
-   **thermal energy**

★ = Tennessee Academic Vocabulary

 **Vocabulary Strategies**

Have you ever seen any of these terms before? Do you know what they mean?

State a description, explanation, or example of the vocabulary in your own words.

Draw a picture, symbol, example, or other image that describes the term.

**Glossary** p. H18

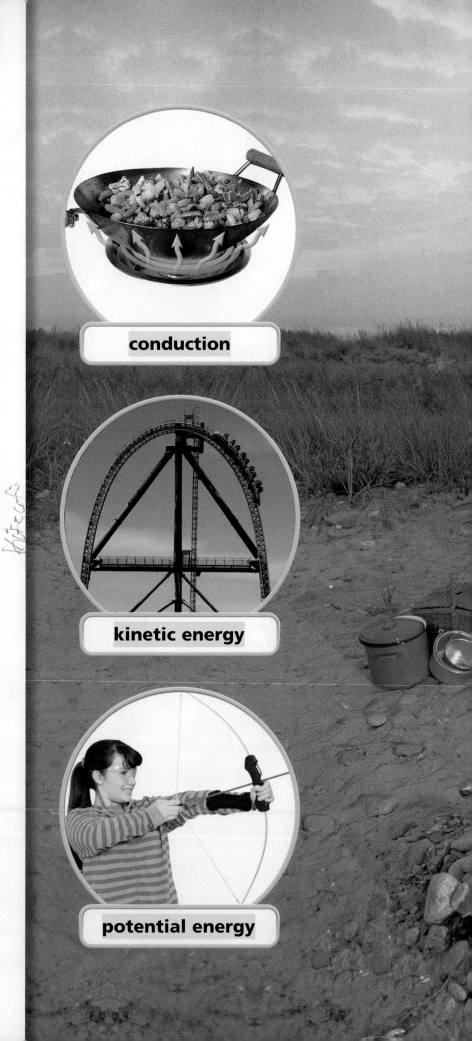

conduction

kinetic energy

potential energy

radiation

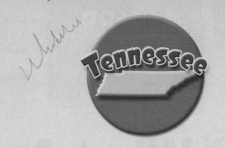

# Start with Your Standards

## Inquiry

**GLE 0507.Inq.1** Explore different scientific phenomena by asking questions, making logical predictions, planning investigations, and recording data.

**GLE 0507.Inq.3** Organize data into appropriate tables, graphs, drawings, or diagrams.

## Technology & Engineering

**GLE 0507.T/E.1** Describe how tools, technology, and inventions help to answer questions and solve problems.

## Physical Science

### Standard 10—Energy

**GLE 0507.10.1** Design an experiment to illustrate the difference between potential and kinetic energy.

**GLE 0507.10.2** Conduct experiments on the transfer of heat energy through conduction, convection, and radiation.

**Interact with this chapter.**

**www.eduplace.com/tnscp**

**TENNESSEE STANDARDS**

GLE 0507.Inq.3 Organize data into appropriate tables, graphs, drawings, or diagrams.

GLE 0507.10.1 Design an experiment to illustrate the difference between potential and kinetic energy.

# What Are Kinetic and Potential Energy?

## Why It Matters...

Drop a ball in water. Waves will ripple away from the place where it strikes, forming wider and wider circles. Why does this happen? Some of the energy of the falling ball is transferred to the water, making waves.

Changes in energy take place all the time. If you understand them, you can put them to good use.

## PREPARE TO INVESTIGATE

### Inquiry Skill

**Predict** When you predict, you use observations, patterns, data, or cause-and-effect relationships to anticipate results.

### Materials

• tape
• 1.5 m of clear plastic tubing
• marble

### Science and Math Toolbox

For step 1, review **Making a Chart to Organize Data** on page H11.

# Directed Inquiry

# Rollerball

## Procedure

**1** **Collaborate** Work with a partner to create a roller coaster for the marble. Tape one end of the tubing to the edge of your desk. This will be the start of the track. In your *Science Notebook,* create a chart like the one shown.

**2** **Experiment** Tape the other end of the tubing to the seat of a chair that is lower than the desk. Let the tubing drape between the desk and the chair so that it just touches the floor.

**3** **Observe** Drop the marble into the top of the tubing. Observe how the marble travels. Use a chart to record your observations of the marble's changes in speed.

**4** **Use Variables** Tape the tubing that was on the chair to another desk of the same height as the first desk. Drop the marble through the tube. Record your observations of the marble's movement.

**5** **Predict** Hold the end of the tube higher than the desk. Predict how far the marble will run through the tubing. Test your prediction.

## Think and Write

1. **Infer** How did the height at the end of the track affect the speed of the marble through the tubing?

2. **Hypothesize** Was your prediction in step 5 correct? Propose an explanation of the results.

0507.10.1

STEP 1

| Height at Start | | |
|---|---|---|
| Height at End | | |
| Observations | | |

STEP 2

STEP 3

### Guided Inquiry

**Design an Experiment**
Will twists and turns in the tubing change the height a marble can travel? Experiment with different arrangements. Choose a graph or chart to report data from the experiment.

## GRAPHIC ORGANIZER

**Classify** What are some examples of potential energy and what are some types of kinetic energy?

**GLE 0507.10.1** Design an experiment to illustrate the difference between potential and kinetic energy.

# Energy

## Forms of Energy

Energy is a familiar part of your everyday life. A burning lump of coal, a falling rock, and a spinning fan all have energy. What do these examples have in common? Each describes an object that is changing. Each is an example of energy's effect on matter.

Just what is energy? **Energy** is the ability to do work. Energy and work are measured by the same unit, the joule.

Energy comes in many different forms. When coal is burned, for example, chemical energy stored in the coal is converted to light that you can see and heat that you can feel. The motor of a fan changes electrical energy into energy of the spinning blades. A falling rock has energy because it is moving.

Even objects at rest have energy. Remember that matter is made up of particles that are constantly in motion. Thermal energy is the random motion of these particles, which you can feel as heat. When energy is changed from one form to another, some of it is almost always changed into thermal energy.

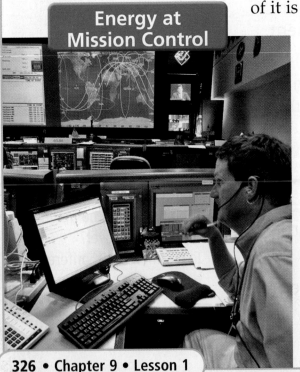

**Energy at Mission Control**

◄ Electrical energy powers the computers. Radio waves, a form of electromagnetic energy, enable controllers to talk to the astronauts.

Visible light is one type of electromagnetic energy. So are microwaves, radio waves, and x-rays.

When the electromagnetic energy in sunlight reaches Earth, some of it is absorbed and changed into thermal energy. Plants also use the energy in sunlight to produce food, which they store as chemical energy.

Matter contains chemical energy, which can be released during a chemical reaction. Chemical energy in coal is released when the coal burns. Chemical energy in a battery is used to power devices such as flashlights.

Electricity is the movement of charged particles. People use electricity to power toasters, streetlights, televisions, computers, and many other things. In each, electrical energy is changed into thermal energy, electromagnetic energy, or mechanical energy.

The energy that an object has because of its motion or its position is called mechanical energy. For example, an acorn hanging from a tree has mechanical energy because of its position above the ground. When it falls, it has mechanical energy because it is in motion.

A vibrating object has mechanical energy that may be changed to sound energy. Wind is the mechanical energy of moving air. The moving parts of a machine have mechanical energy, too.

**FOCUS CHECK** **A large rock on the edge of a cliff has what form of energy?**

**Energy at the Launch**

Chemical energy in the rocket fuel is changed to the mechanical energy of the moving rocket, as well as thermal energy and electromagnetic energy. ▶

## Potential Energy and Kinetic Energy

Recall that energy is the ability to do work. Energy can be transferred from one object to another, and it can change form. How do these ideas relate to one another?

Work involves applying a force to matter over a distance. Any time that work is done, energy is either transferred from one object to another or changed from one form to another.

Think of a bowling ball rolling down a lane. Work was done to set the ball in motion. Work is done on the pin when mechanical energy from the ball is transferred to the pin.

When chemicals react in a battery, electrons move through a wire or other conductor. Chemical energy is transformed to electrical energy when work is done on the electrons.

From these examples, you can see that motion and matter are an important part of understanding energy. In fact, energy can be described by the way it relates to the motion of matter.

Any object that is in motion has **kinetic energy**. Kinetic energy is the energy of a moving object. A moving bowling ball has kinetic energy. So do the moving electrons in an electric current.

**Potential energy** is energy that is stored in an object. Chemical bonds in a bowler's muscles store potential energy that the bowler uses to swing the ball. The chemicals in a battery store potential energy that is used to create an electric current.

The archer in the picture used energy to pull the bowstring and bend the bow. While she holds the bowstring and takes aim, that energy is stored in the bent bow. Because of its position and the condition of the bow, the arrow has potential energy.

◀ A pulled bow has potential energy. When the bow is released, the energy is changed to the kinetic energy of a moving bow and arrow.

As soon as she releases the bowstring, the bow will return to its original shape. The potential energy stored in the bow will be transformed into kinetic energy of the moving bowstring. Some of that kinetic energy will be transferred to the arrow and send it flying forward.

The archer was able to store energy in the bow by changing the bow's shape. Potential energy can also be stored in an object by changing the object's height.

If you lift a box from the floor and set it on a table, you are applying a force to raise the box against the force of gravity. So, you do work on the box. As it rests on the table, the box has potential energy due to its height. Push the box off the table, and that potential energy would be converted to kinetic energy as the box falls.

Energy is either potential or kinetic. The charts provide examples.

**FOCUS CHECK** **Give two examples of energy changing from potential energy to kinetic energy.**

| Potential Energy | |
|---|---|
| **Potential Energy** | **Example** |
| Chemical | battery |
| Elastic | compressed spring |
| Mechanical | rock on a ledge |

| Kinetic Energy | |
|---|---|
| **Kinetic Energy** | **Example** |
| Sound | vibrating object |
| Thermal | hot cocoa |
| Mechanical | falling rock |
| Electrical | electrons in an electrical current |

Some of the kinetic energy of the moving boat is transferred to the water, making waves. ▼

**Express Lab**

**Activity Card**
*Store and Release Energy*

329

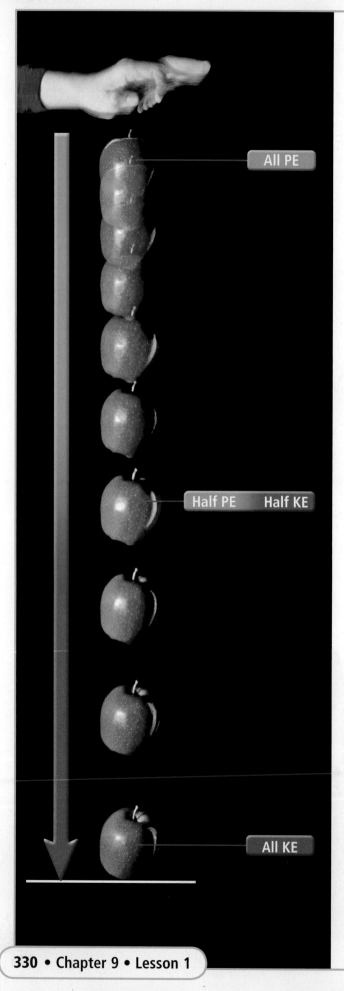

All PE

Half PE    Half KE

All KE

## Calculating Mechanical Energy

When an object that has potential mechanical energy starts moving, some of its potential energy is transformed into kinetic mechanical energy. As the object's kinetic energy increases, its potential energy decreases. Another way of saying this is that the mechanical energy (ME) of an object equals the sum of its potential energy (PE) and its kinetic energy (KE).

$$ME = PE + KE$$

Look at the falling apple. As the apple is held by its stem, all of its mechanical energy is stored as potential energy, due to its height above the ground. The apple is not in motion, so it has no kinetic energy.

As the apple is released and starts to fall, it loses potential energy and gains kinetic energy. The farther the apple falls, the greater its kinetic energy and the less its potential energy. The total mechanical energy remains the same.

The instant before the apple hits the floor, all of its mechanical energy is in the form of kinetic energy. It has no more potential energy relative to the ground.

**◎ FOCUS CHECK How does the mechanical energy of an object change as it falls?**

◀ In this time-lapse photograph, the energy of the falling apple is changed from potential to kinetic.

# Lesson Wrap-Up

## Visual Summary

Energy has many different forms. It can be changed from one form to another, but not created or destroyed.

Potential energy is energy stored in an object. Kinetic energy is the energy of motion.

Mechanical energy of a falling object is the sum of its potential energy and kinetic energy.

## Check for Understanding

### ENERGY ORGANIZER

Copy the two tables from page 329 onto a sheet of paper. Do not fill in the example column in either table. Look around the school for different examples of each type of energy. List them in the examples column.

✓ 0507.10.2

## Review

**1 MAIN IDEA** What is the difference between potential energy and kinetic energy?

**2 VOCABULARY** Explain how potential energy and kinetic energy relate to mechanical energy.

**3 READING SKILL: Classify** Describe the changes in energy when an apple falls.

**4 CRITICAL THINKING: Evaluate** When are an object's potential energy and kinetic energy equal? Give an example.

**5 INQUIRY SKILL: Predict** How do you think an object's speed affects its kinetic energy? Do you think mass affects kinetic energy? How might you test your answers?

### TCAP Prep

Which of the following objects has the most potential energy?

**A** a lemon on a tree
**B** a lemon on the ground
**C** a lemon falling off a desk
**D** a lemon falling from a tall building

SPI 0507.10.1

### Go Digital Technology

Visit **www.eduplace.com/tnscp** to learn more about kinetic and potential energy.

# EXtreme Science

# EXTREME DROP!

Imagine getting a speeding ticket for going 73 miles per hour over the speed limit! At speeds of up to 128 miles per hour, the Kingda Ka roller coaster in New Jersey is one of the fastest roller coasters in the world! It is also one of the tallest roller coasters an has one of the largest drops. It may possibly give you one of the most thrilling minutes of your life.

Roller coasters cars have both potential energy and kinetic energy, depending upon where they are on the track. When the cars are at the top of an incline, they have potential energy, but when they go racing down a hill, that potential energy is converted into kinetic energy.

Kingda Ka launches riders from 0 to 128 miles per hour in under 4 seconds!

**GLE 0507.10.1** Design an experiment to illustrate the difference between potential and kinetic energy.

**EXTEND**

When the roller coaster cars reach the peak of the roller coaster, they have potential energy due to their position.

When the cars begin to go down the slope, their potential energy is converted into kinetic energy as the cars speed up.

**TENNESSEE STANDARDS**

GLE 0507.Inq.1 Explore different scientific phenomena by asking questions, making logical predictions, planning investigations, and recording data.
GLE 0507.10.2 Conduct experiments on the transfer of heat energy through conduction, convection, and radiation.

Guiding Question

# How Does Thermal Energy Spread?

## Why It Matters...

Sometimes you want things hot, and sometimes you want things cold. Many devices control the transfer of thermal energy. Some examples include refrigerators, toasters, hair dryers, blankets, ovens, and fans.

## PREPARE TO INVESTIGATE

### Inquiry Skill

**Use Variable** When you use variables, you change one factor of the experiment to see how that change affects the results. The controls of the experiment do not change.

### Materials
- plastic knife
- stick of butter
- ruler
- thin metal rod
- low, wide bowl
- hot water
- stopwatch

### Science and Math Toolbox
For step 3, review **Measuring Elapsed Time** on pages H14–H15.

# Directed Inquiry

## The Melting Point

### Procedure

**Safety:** Be careful when using hot water.

**1** **Collaborate** Work in a small group. Create a chart like the one shown in your *Science Notebook*.

| Sample | Placement | Melting Time |
|---|---|---|
| 1 | end of rod | |
| 2 | 8 cm from end | |
| 3 | 16 cm from end | |

**2** **Use Variables** Use the plastic knife to cut three equal pats of butter. Use the ruler to measure distances along the metal rod. Place the first pat of butter at one end of the rod. Place the second pat 8 cm from that end, and place the third pat 16 cm from the same end.

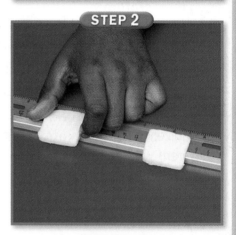

**3** **Experiment** Fill the bowl to a height of 3 cm with hot tap water. As one group member holds the bowl in place, carefully slide the unbuttered end of the metal rod into the bowl. Cover as much of the rod as possible with water, but keep the butter out of the water. Start the stopwatch when the rod enters the water.

**4** **Observe** Time how long it takes for each butter pat to begin to melt and slide off the rod.

**5** **Record Data** Record the times in your *Science Notebook*.

## Think and Write

1. **Infer** Why did the butter pats begin to melt at different times?

2. **Use Variables** What part of the experiment could you change to test your inference?

0507.10.5

### Guided Inquiry

**Design an Experiment**
Will using cardboard, plastic, or cloth melt a butter pat as quickly as using a metal rod? Form a hypothesis, then test it with an experiment. Test several materials and look for a pattern.

# Thermal Energy

## GRAPHIC ORGANIZER

**Main Idea and Details**
Complete the graphic organizer to show the different ways thermal energy can be transferred.

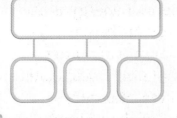

GLE 0507.10.2 Conduct experiments on the transfer of heat energy through conduction, convection, and radiation.

## Temperature and Thermal Energy

All matter is made up of tiny particles, such as atoms and molecules. These particles are constantly moving, which means they have kinetic energy. **Thermal energy** is the total kinetic energy due to the random motion of the particles that make up a material.

Each cup below contains the same amount of soup, but the cup of hot soup contains much more thermal energy. This is because the particles of the hot soup are moving faster than those of the cold soup. The faster particles have more kinetic energy.

Words such as hot and cold describe temperature. **Temperature** describes the average kinetic energy of the particles that make up a material. The temperature of the hot soup is higher because its particles have a greater kinetic energy.

**Comparing Thermal Energy**

◄ **Cold Soup**
Slow-moving particles have little kinetic energy.

**Hot Soup** ▲
Fast-moving particles have lots of kinetic energy.

▲ Although temperature is the same in the small cup and the large urn, the cocoa in the urn has 30 times more thermal energy.

## Heat

Thermal energy is often produced when other forms of energy go through a transformation. For example, a large amount of thermal energy is produced when solar energy, or sunlight, strikes objects and warms them. Other sources of thermal energy include chemical reactions, friction, and electricity.

Look at the large urn of hot cocoa and the cup of hot cocoa next to it. The cocoa in the cup was just poured from the urn, so it has the same temperature as the cocoa in the urn. However, the urn contains more cocoa, which means it has more particles in motion. Thus, it has more

thermal energy than the cocoa in the cup.

Thermal energy can move through matter. The movement, or transfer, of thermal energy from warmer regions of matter to cooler regions is called **heat**.

Because the liquid in the cup has less thermal energy, it will cool more quickly than the liquid in the urn. The liquid cools as its thermal energy is transferred as heat to the air, the cup, and the table.

Before a hot liquid is poured into a cup, the cup will feel cool to the touch. After the hot liquid is poured, the cup will feel warm. That change in temperature is a result of the transfer of thermal energy.

Recall that thermal energy is the total kinetic energy of the particles that make up a sample of matter. Particles of the hot liquid will collide with particles in the cold cup, transferring some of their kinetic energy to the cup. So, the average kinetic energy of the particles of the cup increases. The cup gets warmer. The liquid loses some thermal energy and gets cooler.

Just as thermal energy of the liquid is passed on to the cup, this energy can be transferred to all matter in contact with the cup, including the air. Eventually, the liquid, the cup, the air, and the part of the tabletop touching the cup will all have the same temperature.

**FOCUS CHECK** Compare hot soup and cold soup.

# Conduction

Thermal energy is spread, or transferred, through three different processes: conduction, convection, and radiation. Transfer of thermal energy through direct contact is called **conduction**. Conduction occurs mainly in solids, when rapidly vibrating particles cause nearby particles to vibrate more rapidly. Materials that easily allow conduction are called **conductors**. Those that resist conduction are called **insulators**.

Remember that particles in a solid do not move from place to place, but vibrate back and forth. As they vibrate, they collide with and pass some of their kinetic energy to nearby particles. In this way, thermal energy can spread throughout a solid object or among solid objects in contact with each other.

In the picture below, thermal energy from the burner is transferred to the bottom of the pan through conduction. As the process continues, thermal energy is conducted throughout the pan and into the food it contains. The pan and its contents become warmer.

**Conduction**
Thermal energy from the burner is transferred through the metal by the process of conduction. Conduction happens when particles transfer their vibrations to neighboring particles. ▼

◀ **Convection**
Currents of water or air created by the process of convection are called convection currents.

## Convection

As you have learned, gases and liquids are not rigid like solids. Their particles move much more freely. When a gas or liquid is in contact with a hot object, it expands and becomes less dense as its temperature increases. A warmer, less dense liquid will rise, while the surrounding cooler, denser liquid will sink.

This process is called **convection**. Convection is the process for transfer of thermal energy in liquids and gases.

The aquarium above uses a heater to warm the water. Water becomes warmer as it touches the heater, causing it to expand and rise. As the warm water rises to the top of the aquarium, it carries thermal energy with it. Some of that energy is transferred to other water particles by collisions.

When the warm water reaches the surface, it continues to lose thermal energy to the surrounding water and the air. As the water cools, it becomes denser and sinks. Eventually, it reaches the heater and starts the journey again.

▲ The heater at the bottom of the balloon creates convection currents that fill the balloon with hot air, causing it to rise.

**FOCUS CHECK** How do conduction and convection compare?

**Activity Card**
*Transfer Thermal Energy*

339

## Radiation

Thermal energy can also be transferred by radiation. **Radiation** is the transfer of energy by electromagnetic waves. All objects emit thermal radiation. Even Earth's polar ice caps emit a little. Living things emit some radiation. A hot burner on a stove emits much more.

When an object absorbs thermal radiation, its particles vibrate faster. This increases their kinetic energy and raises the temperature.

Here on Earth, the most important source of radiation is the Sun. The Sun emits radiation of different wavelengths. Some are waves of visible light. Others are infrared (ihn fruh REHD) light, which have a longer wavelength. Most of the heating power of the Sun comes from infrared radiation.

A campfire is similar in some ways to the Sun, only on a smaller scale. Both emit waves of visible light and infrared light. After sunset, the campers will use the fire as a source of light and heat.

You feel infrared radiation as heat because the specific wavelengths of this radiation affect the motions of the particles of your body. Longer infrared wavelengths cause particles to move faster and increase their thermal energy.

Unlike convection and conduction, radiation can travel through empty space.

**◎ FOCUS CHECK** How is radiation different than conduction?

### Radiation
The fire emits infrared waves, which radiate in all directions and warm the campers. ▼

The special bulb in the picture emits infrared light. These light waves heat the inside of an incubator, helping to keep newly hatched chicks warm. ▼

## Lesson Wrap-Up

### Visual Summary

Thermal energy is transferred through solids by conduction. In liquids and gases both conduction and convection occur.

Electromagnetic radiation can change into thermal energy. Radiation may travel through empty space.

Conductors easily transfer thermal energy. Insulators transfer thermal energy poorly.

### ✓ Check for Understanding

**MOVEMENT OF THERMAL ENERGY**
Make a chart with three columns. List one way that thermal energy can move at the top of each column. Beneath the labels, describe the differences among the three.

✔ 0507.10.2

## Review

❶ **MAIN IDEA** Name and describe the three ways that thermal energy is transferred.

❷ **VOCABULARY** What is the difference between conduction and convection?

❸ **READING SKILL: Main Idea and Details** Why do some materials make good conductors while others make good insulators?

❹ **CRITICAL THINKING: Apply** How might you determine if a material is a conductor or an insulator?

❺ **INQUIRY SKILL: Use Variables** How would you design an experiment that shows which of three materials is the best conductor of thermal energy? Identify the variables in your experiment.

### TCAP TCAP Prep

Infrared rays emitted by a fire are an example of

**A** radiation
**B** convection
**C** insulation
**D** conduction

SPI 0507.10.2

### Go Digital Technology

Visit **www.eduplace.com/tnscp** to learn more about conduction, convection, and radiation.

# Space Blankets

The lowest temperature ever recorded in Tennessee was −36°C in Mountain City. The highest temperature ever recorded in Tennessee was 45°C in Perryville. These temperatures may seem extreme, but outside of Earth's atmosphere, the temperatures can be a lot more extreme.

Satellites and other spacecraft that orbit Earth can face temperatures from −100°C to 120°C. In order for the electronics on spacecraft to continue working properly, they must be protected from extreme temperatures. Scientists have developed space blankets and thermal tiles to protect spacecraft.

Space blankets are made of several layers of different materials, including silver. The shiny layers in the blanket reflect the light from the sun, which helps keep the temperature inside from getting too high. Other layers don't conduct thermal energy well, so they help keep the temperature of the electronic system from getting too high or too low. This enables the delicate electronics inside satellites to function properly.

The underside of the space shuttle is covered with thermal tiles that protect the shuttle when it returns to Earth.

◢◤ **GLE 0507.T/E.1** Describe how tools, technology, and inventions help to answer questions and solve problems.

EXTEND

Space blankets help keep electronics safe from getting too hot or too cold.

## Sharing Ideas

1. **READING CHECK** Describe how a space blanket protects the electronic system in a spacecraft.

2. **WRITE ABOUT IT** Compare the high and low temperatures outside of Earth's atmosphere to those in Tennessee.

3. **TALK ABOUT IT** What ways of heat transfer does a space blanket reduce?

**GLE 0507.10.1** Design an experiment to illustrate the difference between potential and kinetic energy.
**Math GLE 0506.2.5** Develop fluency in solving multi-step problems using whole numbers, fractions, mixed numbers, and decimals. **ELA GLE 0501.3.2** Write in a variety of modes and genres, including narration, literary response, personal expression, description, and imaginative.

## Math Home Heating

Adding insulation to a home can reduce heat loss in winter and heat gain in summer. That means less fuel is needed to heat the home and less electricity is needed to run an air conditioner. Using less energy means spending less money.

Suppose that adding insulation to a home costs $3,000. Adding the insulation saves an average of $8 per day in energy costs.

1. How many days will it take before the homeowner breaks even?

2. How much money will be saved after 2 years?

3. How much money will be saved after 10 years?

**Writing** **Narrative**

Write a story about a time you went to a park. Tell what kinds of games you played and what playground equipment you used. Include a description of when you had potential energy and when you had kinetic energy.

## Thermal Engineer

If you've ever been in a building that stayed cool inside while it was hot outside, or kept a drink hot in a thermos, you can thank a thermal engineer. Thermal engineers develop materials that help prevent heat from moving from one place to another. They solve many types of problems, from how to insulate buildings to keep them warmer in the winter to how to keep the space shuttle safe.

**What It Takes!**

- A college degree
- A desire to solve problems
- A good background in chemistry and physics

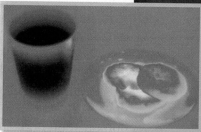

▲ Thermogram of milk and cookies

## Demolition Specialist

Sometimes, old buildings need to be demolished, or destroyed. This is the job of a demolition specialist. They make sure that the building is demolished safely so that it doesn't harm anyone or any nearby buildings. Demolition specialists need to know how to correctly use special tools and sometimes explosives.

**What It Takes!**

- High school diploma
- On the job experience
- Ability to pay attention to detail

## Vocabulary

**Complete each sentence with a term from the list.**

1. The transfer of thermal energy through the movement of a liquid or a gas is _____.

2. The transfer of thermal energy from warmer regions to cooler regions is _____.

3. A material that easily transfers thermal energy is a(n) _____.

4. Mechanical and chemical are both forms of _____.

5. The average kinetic energy of the particles in a sample of matter is its _____.

6. A material that transfers thermal energy poorly is a(n) _____.

7. The transfer of thermal energy from one particle to another is _____.

8. A book resting on a shelf has _____.

9. Infrared light is a form of _____.

10. The total kinetic energy due to the random motion of the particles of a substance is its _____.

★ conduction
★ conductor
★ convection
  energy
  heat
★ insulator
★ kinetic energy
★ potential energy
★ radiation
  temperature
  thermal energy

## TCAP Inquiry Skills

11. **Measure** What tool would you use to measure the average kinetic energy of particles in a sample of matter?
    GLE 0507.Inq.2

12. **Use Variables** Create an experiment that would test the ability of different materials to prevent heat loss. Identify the variables in the experiment. GLE 0507.10.2

## Map the Concept

Write the terms from the Word Bank in their proper position in the concept map.

conduction          insulator
conductor           radiation
convection          thermal energy

easily transfers          poorly transfers

transfers by

GLE 0507.10.2

## Critical Thinking

**13. Apply** How are potential and kinetic energy used together to make a roller coaster work? **GLE 0507.10.1**

**14. Synthesize** What could you conclude from an experiment that measured the temperature of three amounts of the same substance and showed each to have the same temperature?

**GLE 0507.10.2**

**15. Evaluate** How might you decide if a material would make a good conductor? Describe a test you might perform. **GLE 0507.10.2**

**16. Analyze** How are conduction, radiation, and convection similar? How are they different? Give examples to support your answer. **GLE 0507.10.2**

 **Check for Understanding**

**Make a Poster**

Make a poster that illustrates the major forms of energy. Beside each form of energy, list several examples of that energy type. Draw three pictures that illustrate your examples for each form of energy you listed.

✓ **0507.10.4**

## TCAP TCAP Prep

Answer the following questions.

**17** Which of the following does a falling leaf have?

**A** potential energy only

**B** kinetic energy only

**C** both potential and kinetic energy

**D** no energy **SPI 0507.10.1**

**18** Which answer shows one form of kinetic energy and one form of potential energy?

**F** chemical; elastic

**G** elastic; thermal

**H** electrical; sound

**J** sound; thermal **SPI 0507.10.1**

**19** How is thermal energy often transferred in gases and liquids?

**A** convection

**B** conduction

**C** radiation

**D** electromagnetic waves **SPI 0507.10.2**

**20** Which way can thermal energy move through empty space?

**F** by convection

**G** by conduction

**H** by radiation

**J** by insulation **SPI 0507.10.2**

# Chapter 10

# Forces, Motion, and Work

# Lesson Preview



**LESSON 1**

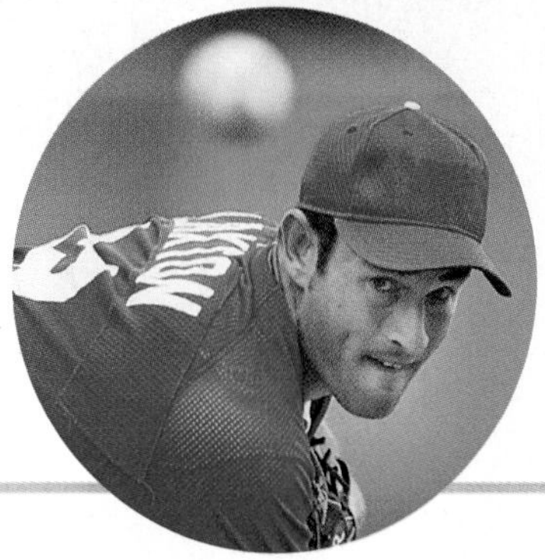

**After the pitcher lets go of the ball, why does the ball continue moving toward home plate?**

**LESSON 2**

**Ramps and levers were used to build the Great Pyramids. How do ramps and levers work?**

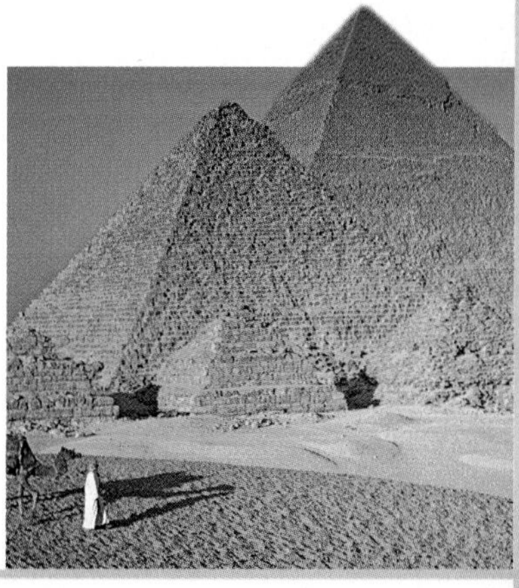

**LESSON 3**

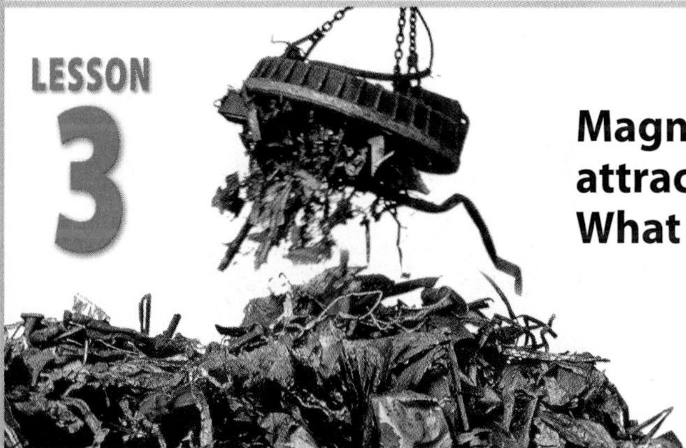

**Magnetism is a force that attracts certain metals. What causes magnetism?**

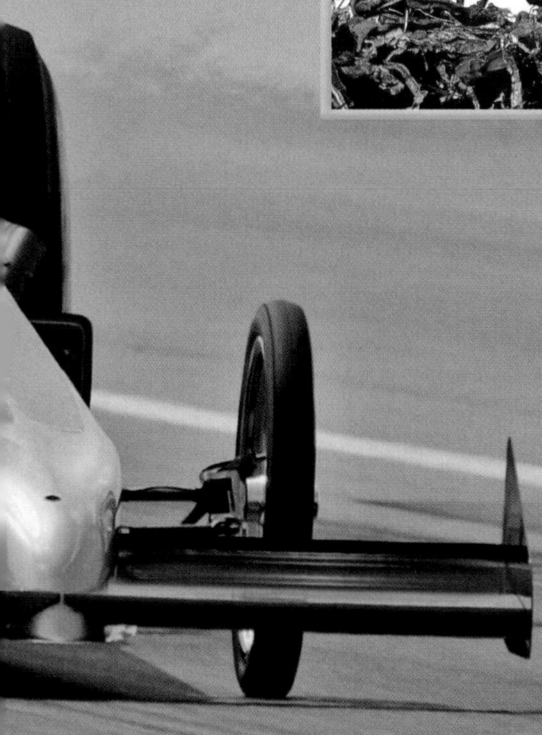

## Fun Facts

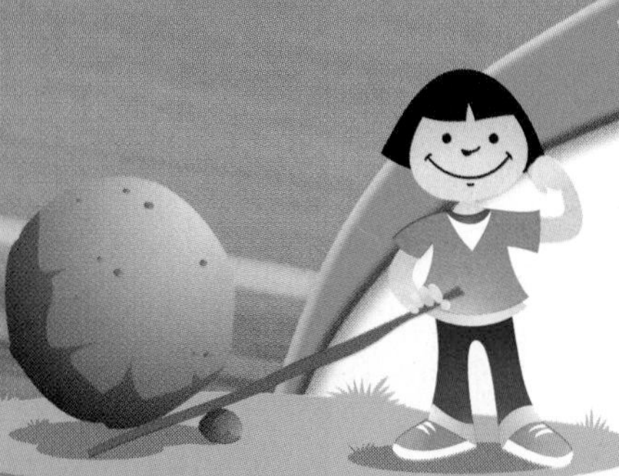

You could easily move a heavy boulder if you had a lever long enough.

acceleration
electromagnet
force
friction
gravity
inertia
motion
newton
simple machines
speed
velocity
work

## Vocabulary Strategies

Have you ever seen any of these terms before? Do you know what they mean?

State a description, explanation, or example of the vocabulary in your own words.

Draw a picture, symbol, example, or other image that describes the term.

**Glossary** p. H18

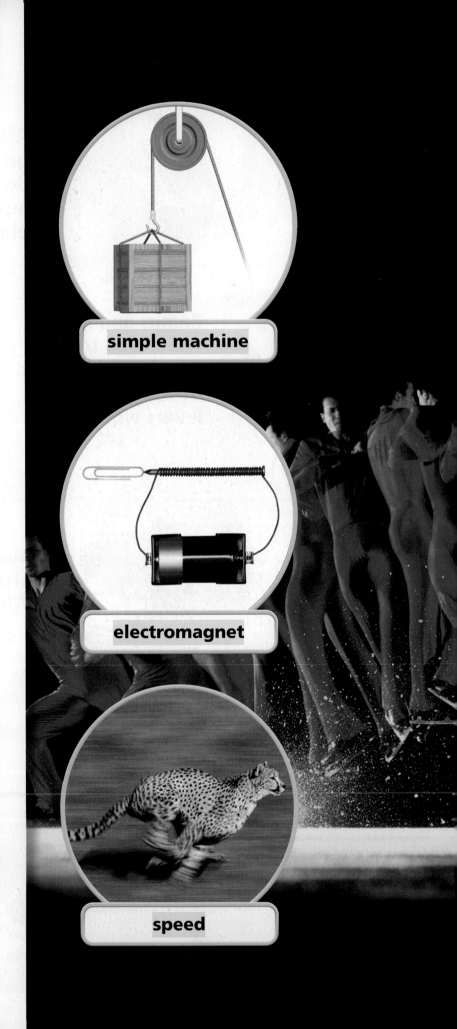

**simple machine**

**electromagnet**

**speed**

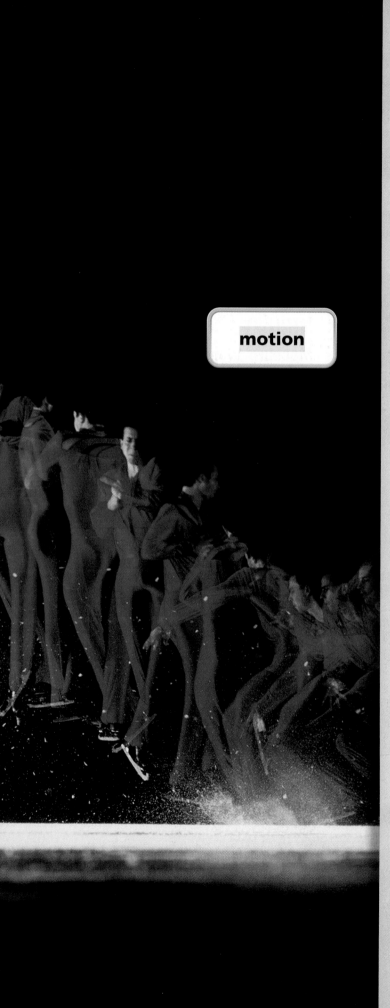

motion

# Start with Your Standards

## Inquiry

**GLE 0507.Inq.3** Organize data into appropriate tables, graphs, drawings, or diagrams.

**GLE 0507.Inq.6** Compare the results of an investigation with what scientists already accept about this question.

## Physical Science

### Standard 11—Motion

**GLE 0507.11.1** Design an investigation, collect data and draw conclusions about the relationship among mass, force, and distance traveled.

### Standard 12—Forces in Nature

**GLE 0507.12.1** Recognize that the earth attracts objects without directly touching them.

**GLE 0507.12.2** Investigate how the shape of an object influences the way that it falls toward the earth.

**GLE 0507.12.3** Provide examples of how forces can act at a distance.

**Interact with this chapter.**

 www.eduplace.com/tnscp

**TENNESSEE STANDARDS**

GLE 0507.Inq.3 Organize data into appropriate tables, graphs, drawings, or diagrams.

GLE 0507.11.1 Design an investigation, collect data and draw conclusions about the relationship among mass, force, and distance traveled.

# What Can Change an Object's Motion?

**Guiding Question**

## Why It Matters...

Almost everything is moving in the world around you. If you understand the physical laws of motion, then you can understand many processes in nature and technology.

## PREPARE TO INVESTIGATE

### Inquiry Skill

**Measure** When you measure something, you compare physical characteristics, such as length, volume, and mass, to a standard unit.

### Materials

- toy truck or car
- shoebox without top
- scissors
- large rubber band
- 2 rulers
- packing tape
- stopwatch
- meterstick or metric measuring tape
- small masses

### Science and Math Toolbox

For step 3, review **Using a Tape Measure or Ruler** on page H6.

# Directed Inquiry

## Monster Trucks

### Procedure

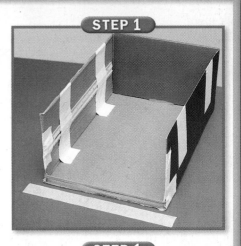

1. **Collaborate** Work with a partner. Cut away one short end of the shoebox. Use packing tape to tape the rulers to the long sides of the box and to attach the rubber band across the open end. In your *Science Notebook*, make a chart like the one shown.

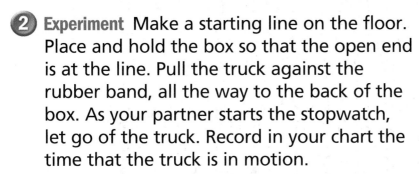

|  |  | Distance | Time | Speed |
|---|---|---|---|---|
| Truck alone | 1 |  |  |  |
|  | 2 |  |  |  |
|  | 3 |  |  |  |
| Truck with mass | 1 |  |  |  |
|  | 2 |  |  |  |
|  | 3 |  |  |  |

2. **Experiment** Make a starting line on the floor. Place and hold the box so that the open end is at the line. Pull the truck against the rubber band, all the way to the back of the box. As your partner starts the stopwatch, let go of the truck. Record in your chart the time that the truck is in motion.

3. **Measure** Use the meterstick or measuring tape to measure the distance that the truck traveled. Record the distance.

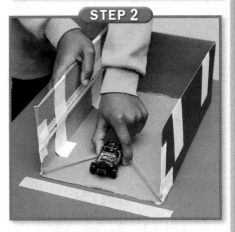

4. **Experiment** Repeat steps 2 and 3 two more times. Record the results of each trial.

5. **Use Numbers** For each trial, find the truck's average speed by dividing the distance traveled by the time elapsed.

6. **Use Variables** Tape a block of wood or other mass to the top of the truck. Do three more trials. Repeat again, using a greater mass.

### Think and Write

1. **Analyze Data** How far did the truck go in the first three trials? How did changing the mass affect the distance traveled or the truck's speed?

2. **Hypothesize** What do you think would happen if you added a second rubber band?

**Guided Inquiry**

**Design an Experiment** How could you use the same equipment to make the truck travel farther? Write your ideas, then test them. What factors affect the truck's motion?

0507.11.2

353

# Change in Motion

## VOCABULARY

acceleration
force
friction
gravity
inertia
motion
newton
speed
velocity

## GRAPHIC ORGANIZER

**Main Idea and Details**
Choose one paragraph of the lesson. Write the main idea and details in a chart.

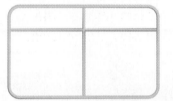

**GLE 0507.11.1** Design an investigation, collect data and draw conclusions about the relationship among mass, force, and distance traveled.

**GLE 0507.12.1** Recognize that the earth attracts objects without directly touching them.

**GLE 0507.12.3** Provide examples of how forces can act at a distance.

## Motion

When something moves, it is in motion. **Motion** is a change in an object's position. A motionless object is at rest, or stationary.

Motion is described relative to a frame of reference. In other words, to describe an object as moving or stationary, you have to compare it to another object.

Consider people standing on the street watching a bus drive past. Their frame of reference includes other objects, such as trees and houses. Relative to these objects, the people on the street are stationary and the people on the bus are moving.

To the bus passengers, their frame of reference is the bus and everything inside it. Relative to the bus, the people on the bus are not moving, unless they get up and walk around.

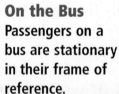

**On the Bus**
Passengers on a bus are stationary in their frame of reference.

**On the Ground**
Observers on the street see a bus moving in their frame of reference.

## Newton's First Law

In any discussion of motion, the name of English scientist Sir Isaac Newton usually comes up. He was one of history's greatest scientists and mathematicians. In 1687, he presented his laws of motion. Newton's laws show the relationship between forces and motion. A **force** is a push or a pull that acts on an object.

Newton's first law of motion explains what happens to objects that are at rest or are moving. The law states that an object at rest will remain at rest unless a force acts on it. For example, this page is at rest. It will remain at rest until it is acted upon by an external force, such as your hand lifting it.

Newton's first law also states that an object in motion will continue to move at a constant speed in the same direction if no forces act on it.

This tendency of an object at rest to remain at rest or an object in motion to remain in motion is called **inertia**. So, Newton's first law is also called the principle of inertia.

You can see examples of Newton's first law in a game of soccer. A soccer ball lying on the field will remain at rest until a player kicks it. The force of the kick overcomes the inertia of the ball, setting the ball in motion.

The ball will continue to move at a constant speed until another force acts on it. A ball rolling across the grass will slow down because of friction. A ball kicked into the air will fall back to the ground because of the force of gravity.

The soccer ball will remain at rest until the force of the kicker's foot overcomes the soccer ball's inertia and sets it in motion.

Newton's first law also applies to a game of baseball. A baseball begins at rest in the pitcher's hand. The pitcher then applies a force to the ball, hurling it toward home plate. The ball's inertia keeps it moving forward, although the ball changes direction slightly because of air resistance and the force of gravity.

At home plate, two things may happen. The ball may land in the mitt of the catcher, who applies a force to stop it. Or the batter may strike the ball with a bat. If the batter's force is strong enough, the ball could travel long enough for a home run.

**FOCUS CHECK** What is inertia?

## Speed, Velocity, and Acceleration

Newton's first law means that, without the action of a force, an object will move at a constant speed—the same speed all the time—in a constant direction. The **speed** of an object is a measure of the distance it moves in a given amount of time.

To calculate average speed, divide the distance traveled by the time it took the object to travel that distance. You can use a formula to relate speed (*s*), distance (*d*), and time (*t*):

$$s = \frac{d}{t}$$

For example, if a car travels 160 km (100 mi) in 2 hours, its average speed is

$$s = \frac{160 \text{ km}}{2 \text{ h}}$$

$$s = 80 \text{ km/h}$$

There are many other units of speed, but they all have the same form: units of distance per units of time. Scientists often use meters per second (m/s). Note that speed is a rate. It is the rate of change in distance over time.

**Velocity** is a measure of both an object's speed *and* its direction.

**A jumping ice skater changes both his acceleration and velocity, as this stop-action photograph shows. If a skater moves a distance of 4 meters during 2 seconds, what is his average speed? ▼**

time = 0 sec    time = 1 sec    time = 2 sec

0 meter    1 meter    2 meters    3 meters    4 meters

To understand the difference between speed and velocity, think of the following example. Suppose you are jogging north at a speed of 8 km/h (5 mph) while your friend is jogging east at a speed of 8 km/h. You and your friend have the same speed but your velocities are different. This is because your directions of travel are different.

A force can change the speed of an object, its direction, or both. In each case, a force causes the object's velocity to change. Change in an object's velocity is known as **acceleration**. Since velocity describes both speed and direction, acceleration can be a change in speed, a change in direction, or both.

Acceleration is expressed as a change in velocity over a certain period of time. For example, suppose the velocity of a car changes from 13 m/s to 23 m/s in 5 seconds. The change in the car's velocity is 23 m/s – 13 m/s = 10 m/s. It takes 5 s to make this change, so the acceleration is 10 m/s ÷ 5 s = 2 m/s per second.

People usually think of acceleration as speeding up. That is why a car's gas pedal is also called an accelerator. When an object slows down, it is commonly called deceleration. In science, however, accelerating can mean speeding up, slowing down, or changing direction. In fact, any change in motion is acceleration.

**FOCUS CHECK** What is the difference between speed and velocity?

Top Animal Speeds

| Cheetah | 100 km/h (60 mph) |
| Blue Whale | 50 km/h (30 mph) |
| Peregrine Falcon | 320 km/h (200 mph) |
| Dragonfly | 60 km/h (35 mph) |

## Balanced and Unbalanced Forces

Newton's first law applies to situations in which no forces are acting upon an object. What happens when forces do act upon an object?

Suppose you are having a tug-of-war with your dog. You are pulling on one end of the rope and your dog is pulling on the other end in the opposite direction. If each of you pulls with equal force, the rope will not move. The two forces are equal in strength, but opposite in direction. The forces are balanced.

Now suppose a friend helps you pull your end of the rope. Together, you pull with a greater force than the dog does. The forces are unbalanced. When forces are balanced, they cancel each other out, and there is no movement. In this case, the dog's force is not great enough to balance the force of two people. The difference between the two forces, called the net force, is acting on the rope. The rope will accelerate in the direction of the net force, toward you and your friend.

An object will accelerate, or change its motion, only when an unbalanced force acts on it. This is Newton's second law of motion.

**Balanced Forces**

The child and the dog apply equal force in the tug-of-war. Their forces are balanced, so neither one accelerates, or changes the motion of the rope.

**Unbalanced Forces**

A second child adds more force to the tug-of-war. Now the forces are unbalanced, so the children are able to accelerate the rope, or change its motion.

## Newton's Second Law

Newton's second law of motion describes the relationship between force, mass, and acceleration. The law can be stated as a formula,

$$F = ma,$$

where $F$ is the applied net force, $m$ is the mass of the object, and $a$ is the amount of acceleration.

Look at the photos at right. In the top photo, a fifth-grader pushes the wagon, causing it to accelerate. In the second photo, an adult pushes on the same wagon. Because the adult pushes the same mass with a greater force, the acceleration is greater. The greater the net force applied to an object, the greater the acceleration of the object.

Now compare the top and bottom pictures. The fifth-grader pushes the wagon with the same force in both cases. But because the adult's mass is much greater than the mass of the child, the acceleration of the wagon is smaller. For the same applied force, an object with a greater mass will have a smaller acceleration than an object with a smaller mass.

Force is measured in a unit called the newton, in honor of Sir Isaac Newton. One **newton (N)** is the force required to accelerate a mass of 1 kg at 1 m/s per second. If you measure any two of the quantities force, mass, and acceleration, you can use the formula $F = ma$ to calculate the third.

**◎ FOCUS CHECK** What is Newton's second law?

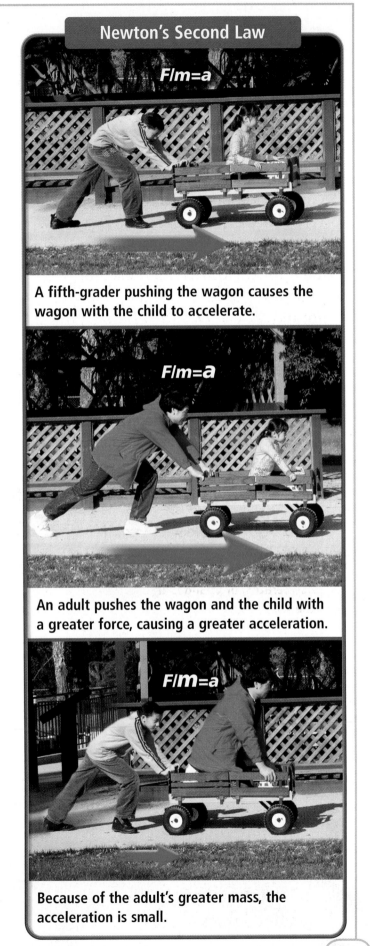

**Newton's Second Law**

$F/m=a$

A fifth-grader pushing the wagon causes the wagon with the child to accelerate.

$F/m=a$

An adult pushes the wagon and the child with a greater force, causing a greater acceleration.

$F/m=a$

Because of the adult's greater mass, the acceleration is small.

# Gravity and Friction

**Gravity** is a force that causes objects with mass to be attracted, or pulled, toward one another. Gravity is a noncontact force, meaning it acts on an object without touching it.

Newton's Law of Universal Gravitation describes the attractive force between two masses. The force increases with the masses of the two objects. However, the farther apart the two objects are, the weaker the force. Earth's mass is much greater than the mass of any object on its surface. That's why you experience gravity as a downward force.

**The force of gravity accelerates the skater as she moves down the hill.** ▼

**Friction** is a force that resists motion of one surface across another surface. Friction is a contact force, which means that two objects or surfaces have to touch one another. Friction is usually greater between rough surfaces than smooth ones.

In the photo, the skater slows down by using friction between the brake and the concrete. Even without the brake, she still will slow down eventually. Friction between her skate wheels and the ground will slow her movement until she stops.

Air resistance will also help slow down the skater. Air resistance, or drag, opposes motion through air. Skydivers use a parachute to increase air resistance and slow down their rate of falling. Air resistance is affected by the shape of an object.

As you have seen, gravity and friction affect motion on Earth. In outer space, however, no air slows down a moving object. And far away from stars and planets there is little gravity. Objects moving through space continue in a straight line at constant velocity.

**⊚ FOCUS CHECK Describe some forces that affect motion on Earth.**

◀ To slow down, the skater uses the friction between the sidewalk and the brake on her skate.

## Express Lab

**Activity Card**
*Test Shapes*

## Lesson Wrap-Up

### Visual Summary

Newton's first law states that an object at rest or in motion will remain at rest or in motion unless a force acts on it.

Newton's second law states that an object will accelerate if the forces acting on it are unbalanced.

The forces of gravity and friction also affect the motion of objects.

### Check for Understanding

**FORCE, MASS, AND DISTANCE**
Predict how the mass of a skateboard, toy car, and roller skate affects the distance each will travel in a specific amount of time when a constant force is applied. Use a spring scale to pull each object with the same force for 10 seconds. Record your observations. Was your prediction correct?

✔ 0507.11.1

## Review

**1 MAIN IDEA** How can an object's speed or direction be changed?

**2 VOCABULARY** What is the difference between velocity and acceleration? Give an example of each. Be sure to use the correct units.

**3 READING SKILL: Main Idea and Details** What are three ways an object may accelerate?

**4 CRITICAL THINKING: Analyze** Explain why the shoulder strap of a car seat belt is important.

**5 INQUIRY SKILL: Measure** In the United States, speed is typically measured in miles per hour (mph). To convert mph to km/h, multiply by 1.6. Calculate in km/h the speed of a train traveling 75 mph.

**TCAP Prep**

Which of the following affects air resistance?

**A** mass
**B** volume
**C** shape
**D** weight

SPI 0507.12.3

### Technology

Visit **www.eduplace.com/tnscp** to learn more about force and motion.

361

**Lesson 2**

TENNESSEE STANDARDS

GLE 0507.Inq.3 Organize data into appropriate tables, graphs, drawings, or diagrams.

GLE 0507.11.1 Design an investigation, collect data and draw conclusions about the relationship among mass, force, and distance traveled.

# How Do We Use Simple Machines?

## Why It Matters...

You perform hundreds of tasks every day, and simple machines make them easier. Imagine how hard it would be to steer a bicycle without handlebars, or to cut meat without a knife. Even your arms and legs are examples of simple machines.

## PREPARE TO INVESTIGATE

### Inquiry Skill

**Compare** When you compare, you describe how two or more things or events are similar and how they are different.

### Materials

- 50-g mass with hook
- spring scale
- stack of books
- tape measure
- 2 large pieces of cardboard
- scissors

### Science and Math Toolbox

For step 2, review Measurements on pages H16–H17.

# Directed Inquiry

## Ramping It Up
## Procedure

**1** **Collaborate** Work with a partner. Make a stack of books. In your *Science Notebook*, make a chart like the one shown.

**2** **Experiment** Hook the mass to the spring scale. Lift the mass straight up to the height of the stack of books. Read the spring scale and record the force needed to lift the mass.

**3** **Record Data** Use a tape measure to carefully measure the distance the mass was lifted. Record the distance.

**4** **Experiment** Lean the cardboard against the stack of books to create a ramp. Align the top edge of the cardboard with the top of the books. While holding the ramp in place, use the spring scale to drag the mass to the top of the ramp. Move the mass smoothly and at a constant speed. Record the force and the length of the ramp.

**Safety:** Be careful using scissors.

**5** **Use Variables** Cut the cardboard in half to shorten it. Repeat step 4 using the shorter ramp.

### Think and Write

1. **Compare** How did using the ramp affect the amount of force needed to lift the mass?

2. **Infer** How did changing the length of the ramp affect the force needed to raise the mass to the top of the stack of books?

✔ 0507.11.3

**STEP 1**

| Distance (cm) | Force (N) |
|---|---|
|  |  |
|  |  |

**STEP 2**

**STEP 4**

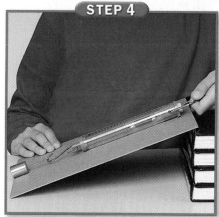

### Guided Inquiry

**Design an Experiment**
Try the experiment using the same length of cardboard but a different-sized stack of books. How does the height of the stack affect the force needed to move the mass the same distance?

# Simple Machines

## Doing Work

What do you think of when you think of work? Perhaps you think of mowing the lawn, washing dishes, or walking the dog. From the last lesson, you know that force is a push or pull on an object. In science, **work** is done when a force moves an object over a distance.

What happens if you apply a force to something, but it does not move? According to Newton's laws of motion, another equal force must be opposing your force. Look at the first photo below. If the person does not move the car, then no work has been done on the car. Even though the person has exerted a force, he has done no work on the car.

Now look at the second photo. If two people apply enough force to the car to move it some distance they will have done work on the car.

One person is not able to apply enough force to move the car. He is unable to do work.

Two people apply enough force to move the car over a distance. Together, they do work.

Work

Gravity

**The force of gravity is doing work on this skydiver, causing him to fall. The work done equals force times distance. ▲**

The greater the distance through which a force is applied, the more work is done. For example, think about picking up a book from the floor. To lift the book, you apply a force equal to its weight. If you raise the book over your head, you do more work than if you just lift it to your waist.

You can use a formula to calculate the work done.

$$W = Fd$$

Work (W) equals the amount of force (F) times the distance (d) that the object is moved.

Work is measured in units of force times units of distance. The standard unit is called a newton-meter (N·m). If you apply a force of 10 N to lift a book a distance of 1 m, you have done 10 N·m of work. Another name for a newton-meter is the joule (J).

## Simple Machines

Machines are tools that make doing the same work easier. **Simple machines** have few or no moving parts. They make work easier by changing the amount of force applied, the direction of the force, or both.

For example, one machine might allow you to use less force to move an object a given distance. Another machine might allow you to use the weight of your body to pull an object rather than push it. Some machines give the user both advantages.

The force used to do work using a machine is called the effort force. The force it overcomes is called the load, or resistance force. There are six types of simple machines, as shown below.

**◎ FOCUS CHECK What problems do machines solve?**

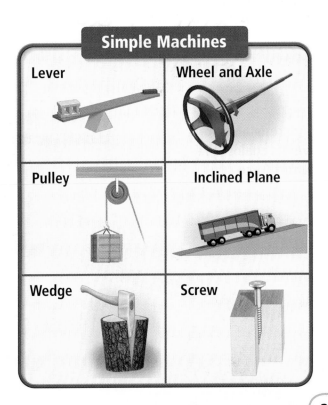

Simple Machines

| Lever | Wheel and Axle |
| Pulley | Inclined Plane |
| Wedge | Screw |

# Levers

Levers are rigid bars that pivot around a point. Levers can change the direction of a force, change the ratio between the force and the distance an object moves, or both.

To understand a lever, consider two different forces: the effort and the load. The effort force is the force that is applied to the lever. The load is the force that works against the effort. Also look at the lever's pivot point, called the fulcrum. Different kinds of levers place the fulcrum in different positions. There are three classes of levers.

**First-Class Levers** Take a look at the diagram below. This lever shows the fulcrum between the effort and the load. This type of lever is called a first-class lever. A small downward force exerted by the brick on the far end of the lever can overcome the weight of the concrete block, which is the load. The block will be balanced, or will rise.

Note that the fulcrum is placed closer to the load than to the effort. With this placement, the effort end of the lever is pushed a long distance to raise the load just a short distance. The advantage is that much less force is used to push the lever down. A first-class lever always changes the direction of the force. Pushing down on the effort end raises the load.

Look at the photo of the pliers on the next page. A pliers is made of two first-class levers joined together at the fulcrum. Squeeze the handles of the pliers, and the pliers squeezes the walnut at the other end. Because of the placement of the fulcrum, the force on the walnut is much greater than the force you exert on the handles.

Other examples of first-class levers include seesaws, crowbars, and fingernail clippers. In all cases, the fulcrum is between the effort and load.

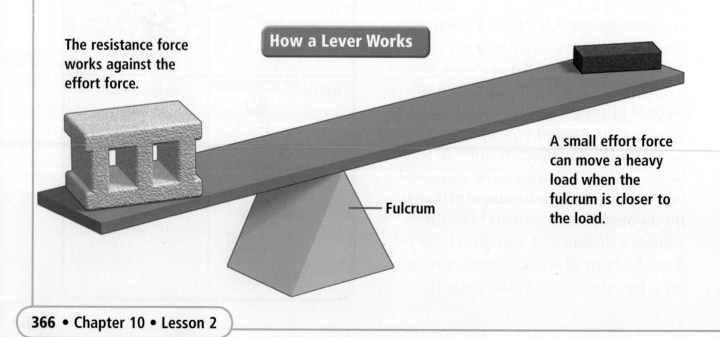

The resistance force works against the effort force.

**How a Lever Works**

Fulcrum

A small effort force can move a heavy load when the fulcrum is closer to the load.

**Second-Class Levers** In a second-class lever, the load is placed between the fulcrum and the effort force. A second-class lever increases the force but doesn't change its direction.

The nutcracker shown here is made of two second-class levers. Squeeze its handles, and the nut will be squeezed even harder. But unlike the forces on a pliers, the direction of the effort force on a nutcracker is the same as the direction of the resistance force.

Other examples of second-class levers are wheelbarrows and bottle openers. As with the nutcracker, these tools allow a small effort force to overcome a large load.

**Third-Class Levers** In a third-class lever, the effort is applied between the fulcrum and the load. This is the only type of lever that always reduces the effort force instead of increasing it.

In the photograph, each chopstick acts as a third-class lever. Notice that a force applied over a tiny distance at the fulcrum—where you hold the chopsticks—moves the food at the other end over a longer distance.

A fishing rod is another example of a third-class lever. The fulcrum is at the end of the rod that you hold steady. The resistance force is the weight of the fish at the other end. By pulling up on the middle of the fishing rod, you can lift the fish out of the water.

A shovel and a stapler are other familiar examples of third-class levers. A pair of tweezers consists of two third-class levers, joined at the fulcrum.

**☉ FOCUS CHECK** List examples of problems a lever could solve.

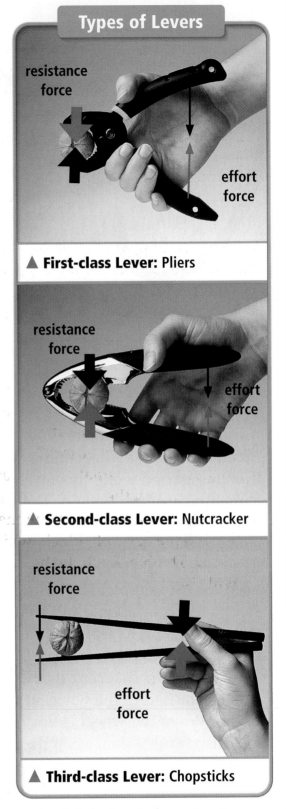

**Types of Levers**

▲ **First-class Lever:** Pliers

▲ **Second-class Lever:** Nutcracker

▲ **Third-class Lever:** Chopsticks

Each of these tools is made of two levers joined together at their fulcrums.

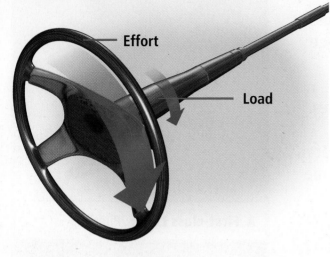

Effort

Load

▲ A car's steering wheel is an example of a wheel and axle. The axle is a cylinder attached to the center of the wheel.

## Wheel and Axles and Pulleys

No one knows exactly who invented the first wheel and axle, but humans started using this machine sometime around 3300 B.C. The wheel and axle is a simple machine that changes the amount of force applied to an object. Wheel and axles are used for many things, including to steer a truck, to open a valve on a water pipe, and to seal a submarine hatch.

Examine the diagram above. The axle is attached to the wheel at the center. When the wheel is turned, the axle also turns. Likewise, if the axle is turned, the wheel turns as well.

A wheel and axle can be used two ways. When the effort force is applied to the wheel, the force is increased. When the effort force is applied to the axle, the distance over which the force acts is increased.

Look at the diagram of the car steering wheel. When a driver turns the wheel, the rim of the steering wheel travels a greater distance than the rim of the steering column. Because the steering column—the axle—travels a shorter distance, the force applied to the axle is increased.

Many other familiar items, such as doorknobs and faucets, work the same way. The wider the wheel, the less effort force required to turn it. However, you need to turn the wider wheel a greater distance to do the same amount of work.

Have you ever watched gears in action? A gear is a wheel with teeth around its rim. The teeth interlock with teeth of other gears, allowing a system of gears to transmit motion. Machines that use gears include cars, bicycles, and window cranks.

A pulley is a wheel with a groove along its edge. A single fixed pulley consists of a pulley attached to a high point, such as a tree branch or a ceiling, with a rope fed through the wheel's groove. You attach one end of the rope to an object and then pull down the other end to lift the object. This is called a fixed pulley because the pulley remains in place.

The fixed pulley changes the direction but not the size of the force needed to move an object. Pulling the rope a distance of 1 m lifts the object 1 m, so the same force must be exerted. The advantage is that you can pull down instead of lifting up. Pulling down is often much easier!

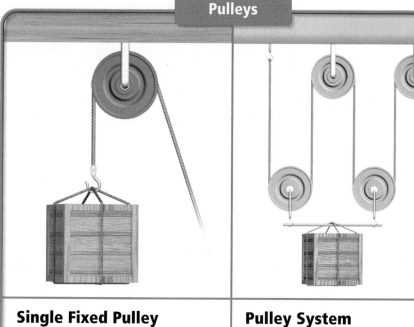

**Pulleys**

**Single Fixed Pulley**
A fixed pulley changes the direction of the force needed to move an object, but not the amount of force needed.

**Pulley System**
In this system of four pulleys, pulling through 4 meters of rope will lift the load 1 meter high.

If you want to reduce the amount of force needed to lift a load, try using a movable pulley. The pulley attaches to the load, which in effect doubles the pulling force upon the load. The drawback is that you need to pull twice as much rope to lift the load.

You can also combine two or more pulleys together, creating a pulley system as shown in above. The more ropes supporting the load, the less force you need to lift a load and the more rope you need to pull through.

**FOCUS CHECK** When would you use a pulley system instead of a single fixed pulley?

A fixed pulley attached to the top of the pole helps raise the flags. Pulling down on one side of the rope raises the other side with the flags attached. ▶

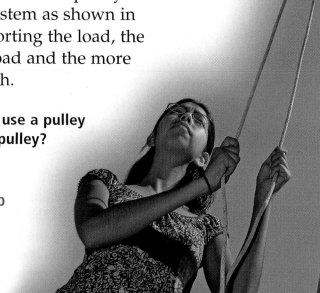

## Inclined Planes

Another simple machine that changes the ratio of force to distance is an inclined plane, or ramp. An inclined plane decreases the amount of force required to raise an object. In exchange, it increases the distance that the object must be moved to reach a given height.

In one picture below, two people are lifting a heavy box into a truck. In the other picture, one person uses an inclined plane to do a similar task. The box must be moved twice the distance, but only half the effort force is needed. If the inclined plane were longer, even less effort force would be needed.

The amount of work done on the box is the same whether it is lifted straight up or slid along the inclined plane. Look again at the example below. To lift the box straight up from the ground, the

two people must apply a force equal to the weight of the box. The amount of work done to lift the 500-N box a distance of 2.0 m is $W = 500 \text{ N} \times 2.0 \text{ m} = 1,000 \text{ N·m}$.

Pushing the 500-N box up the inclined plane requires only half the force, or 250 N. The inclined plane is 4.0 m long. The work done is $W = 250 \text{ N} \times 4.0 \text{ m} = 1,000 \text{ N·m}$.

The example assumes that the inclined plane is frictionless. In the real world, the friction force between the box and the inclined plane would need to be overcome. Using a wheeled cart helps to reduce friction.

🎯 **FOCUS CHECK** What is the advantage of using an inclined plane to move a heavy object?

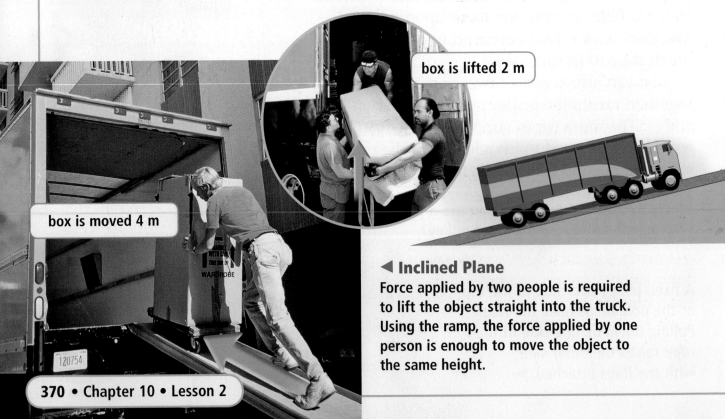

box is lifted 2 m

box is moved 4 m

◀ **Inclined Plane**
Force applied by two people is required to lift the object straight into the truck. Using the ramp, the force applied by one person is enough to move the object to the same height.

**Wedge**
The blade of a log-splitting maul is a wedge. When it is swung, the weight of the head drives the wedge into the wood, splitting the wood into two pieces. ▲

## Wedges and Screws

A wedge is a simple machine that consists of two inclined planes back to back. Like an inclined plane, a wedge changes the direction of the force. An effort force is applied to the thick end of the wedge. As the wedge moves under or through an object, the sides of the wedge exert forces on the object that are at right angles to the direction of the applied force.

Because of its shape, a wedge must move a greater distance through an object to push it apart a much smaller distance. The sideways force exerted by the wedge is greater than the applied force. Many tools, such as chisels, knives, and even doorstops, are wedges.

A screw is an inclined plane wrapped around a cylinder or cone. The plane makes up the threads of a screw. A screw changes both the direction of force and the ratio of force to distance. When force is applied to turn the screw, the threads cause the screw to move.

Look at the car jack shown below. It takes many turns of the screw to move the car up or down only a little. A small effort force is greatly multiplied, allowing a person to slowly lift a car.

⊙ **FOCUS CHECK** List three ways you might use a wedge.

**Screw**
Turning the screw pulls the diagonal pieces closer together, which raises the jack and lifts the car. ▼

**Express Lab**

**Activity Card**
*Use Simple Machines*

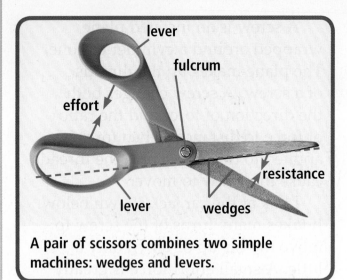

A pair of scissors combines two simple machines: wedges and levers.

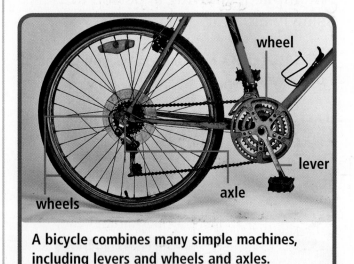

A bicycle combines many simple machines, including levers and wheels and axles.

A piano uses several different types of levers to make music.

## Compound Machines

Many of the devices that you use every day are made of two or more simple machines. Tools that are made of a combination of simple machines are called compound machines. A pair of scissors is one example. The scissors consists of a pair of levers with the fulcrum in the middle. The cutting blades of the scissors are wedges.

Another example of a compound machine is a bicycle. It uses pedals, which are levers, to apply force to the sprocket. The sprocket is a wheel and axle that uses gears to move the chain.

As the chain moves, it transfers force to a smaller sprocket attached to the axle of the rear wheel. So, the force applied to the pedal is converted through a combination of simple machines to make the back wheel turn.

A piano uses a variety of different types of levers to make the hammers strike the strings. The keys are first-class levers. Pushing down on a key causes the other end of the key to lift, pushing on a wooden post. The post pushes up into the end of the hammer, which is another first-class lever. The hammer strikes the string.

**FOCUS CHECK What are compound machines?**

# Lesson Wrap-Up

## Visual Summary

Scientists define work as a force moving an object over a distance, *W = Fd*. Energy can be expended without accomplishing any work.

Simple machines make work easier to do. Some increase the effort force by applying it over a shorter distance. Others decrease the effort force by applying it over a longer distance.

Compound machines combine two or more simple machines. Many useful devices are compound machines.

## ✓ Check for Understanding

### DESIGN AN INVESTIGATION

Design and explain an investigation that explores how simple machines work against Earth's pull on objects. Record your findings about both Earth's pull on these objects and how the simple machines can be used to work against that pull.

✓ 0507.12.3

## Review

**1 MAIN IDEA** How do machines make the same work easier?

**2 VOCABULARY** Explain how it is possible to exert force but accomplish no work.

**3 READING SKILL: Problem and Solution** Explain how three different simple machines other than inclined planes might be used to lift a heavy box.

**4 CRITICAL THINKING: Analyze** A home owner is designing a ramp to connect the driveway to the front door. A person in a wheelchair will use the ramp. What facts must be known to design a useful ramp?

**5 INQUIRY SKILL: Compare** Compare the advantages of a single fixed pulley to a pulley system.

### TCAP TCAP Prep

Using inclined planes has which effect?

**A** work done increases
**B** force used increases
**C** distance moved increases
**D** work done decreases

SPI 0507.11.1

### Go Digital Technology

Visit **www.eduplace.com/tnscp** to learn more about simple machines.

# Transportation

**Transportation is any method of moving from place to place.** Read on to discover how transportation has changed over the past 200 years.

**1840s: Clipper Ships**
Clipper ships traveled faster and carried more cargo than all other ships of their day. Unfortunately, many were wrecked due to poor navigation and inaccurate maps.

## Typical Speeds

| | | | |
|---|---|---|---|
| Speed (miles per hour) | Stagecoach 1830 | Train 1870 | Jet Airplane 1990 |
| 550 | | | 550 mph |
| 500 | | | |
| 400 | | | |
| 300 | | | |
| 200 | | | |
| 100 | | 45 mph | |
| 0 | 5 mph | | |

**1700s**                                    **1800s**

**1790s: Horse and Buggy**
Farmers used the horse and buggy to carry goods to and from town. Horse-powered coaches carried passengers between towns and cities.

GLE 0507.T/E.1 Recognize that new tools, technology, and inventions are always being developed.

EXTEND

Astronaut
Mae Jemison ▶

## 1920s: Automobiles
In 1913, Henry Ford began mass-producing cars on an assembly line. Within a decade, people everywhere were driving Model T's. They cost only $290 each!

## 1950s: Airplanes
Jet-powered airplanes entered passenger service in the 1950s. They quickly became people's first choice for long-distance travel.

## 2000s: Space Shuttle
To travel fast and far today, step aboard the space shuttle! It can orbit Earth about once every 90 minutes.

1900s

2000s

## 1870s: Railroads
Inventions such as the steam-powered locomotive and vacuum brakes made trains fast, safe, and popular.

Note Book

# Sharing Ideas

1. **READING CHECK** Compare the different modes of transportation.

2. **WRITE ABOUT IT** When would each mode of transportation be your choice for a trip?

3. **TALK ABOUT IT** How does transportation affect people's lives?

**TENNESSEE STANDARDS**

GLE 0507.Inq.6 Compare the results of an investigation with what scientists already accept about this question.
GLE 0507.12.3 Provide examples of how forces can act at a distance.

Guiding Question

# What Forces Come from Magnets?

## Why It Matters...

Did you know that you use a magnet every time you ring a doorbell? From refrigerator magnets to doorbells to bullet trains, magnets are an important part of today's fast-paced, technology-filled world.

## PREPARE TO INVESTIGATE

### Inquiry Skill

**Infer** When you infer, you use data and observations to draw conclusions.

### Materials

- bar magnet
- iron filings
- plastic tray
- horseshoe magnet
- wax paper
- disc magnet
- goggles

# Directed Inquiry

## Exploring Magnets

### Procedure

**Safety**: Wear goggles for this activity.

STEP 1

**1** **Experiment** Place the bar magnet in the tray. Cover the magnet with a sheet of wax paper. Sprinkle iron filings onto the paper and observe what happens.

**2** **Record Data** In your *Science Notebook*, sketch the pattern of the filings around the magnet. Include a written description of how the filings are arranged.

**3** **Use Variables** Pick up the wax paper with the filings. Be careful not to spill any. Replace the bar magnet with the horseshoe magnet. Put the wax paper, with the filings, on top of the horseshoe magnet.

STEP 3

**4** **Compare** Sketch the pattern of the filings and include a written description. Note any differences between the two patterns.

**5** **Use Variables** Repeat steps 3 and 4, replacing the horseshoe magnet with the disc magnet. Draw and record your observations.

### Think and Write

1. **Compare** How were the iron filing patterns different for each magnet? How were they similar?

2. **Infer** What can you infer from the patterns about how each type of magnet attracts filings?

✔ 0507.12.1

### Guided Inquiry

**Research** Research how a battery, an iron nail, and a wire can be used to make a simple electromagnet. With your teacher's approval, build the electromagnet. Use iron filings to investigate the magnetic field it creates.

# Magnets

## Magnets and Magnetic Fields

Prehistoric people discovered magnetism when they found magnetic rocks, called lodestones. Lodestones, which are mostly iron, are able to attract or repel certain metals. They must have seemed very unusual to ancient peoples.

Today, scientists know that magnetism is a force created by the motion of electrons in atoms. Moving electrons produce magnetic fields, or areas in which a magnetic force can be observed. When electrons are aligned in the same direction, the fields around them combine to create a strong magnet. Metals such as iron, nickel, and cobalt are some materials that can act as magnets.

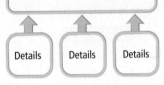
**Nonmagnetic**
The atoms of paper and other nonmagnetic materials have tiny magnetic fields. However, they all point in different directions. They cancel each other out and do not create a strong magnetic field.

**Magnetic**
The atoms of a magnet have tiny magnetic fields that are aligned in the same direction. They combine to create a strong magnetic field.

Because the atoms in a magnet are aligned in the same direction, they form two regions called poles. The poles are named north and south.

All magnets have a north pole and a south pole. Even if you break a magnet in half, each half would still have a north pole and a south pole.

What happens if you bring the north pole of one magnet near the north pole of another magnet? Without touching, the two magnets will strongly repel, or push away from, each other. This repulsion occurs because the atoms of the first magnet are aligned in the opposite direction from the atoms in the second magnet. The same is true if you put two south poles together.

However, if you bring the north pole of one magnet near the south pole of another magnet, the magnets will strongly attract each other. In this case, the atoms of both magnets will be aligned in the same direction. They create one big magnetic field.

Each pole of a magnet is attracted to a magnetic pole of Earth. If you hang a magnet on a string, the north pole of the magnet will point to Earth's North Pole and the south pole will point to Earth's South Pole. To make a compass needle easy to understand, the north pole of the needle is labeled "N." This is a way of saying "North is this way."

When you put a magnet close to an iron object without the magnet touching it, you will see or feel a magnetic attraction. The magnet temporarily aligns the atoms in the

**Like Poles Repel**
The iron filings show the attraction and repulsion of the magnets' magnetic fields. With the two north poles face to face, the magnets repel each other.

**Opposite Poles Attract**
With opposite poles facing one another, the magnets attract each other.

iron in the same direction as the atoms in the magnet.

On the other hand, if you bring a magnet near an object that contains no magnetic material, nothing will happen. The atoms in the nonmagnetic material will not be affected.

**FOCUS CHECK** What are some magnetic materials?

## Making Magnets

There are several ways to change the alignment of atoms in magnetic materials. As you have seen, bringing a permanent magnet close to a magnetic material will temporarily change the alignment of its atoms. When you take the magnet away, however, the atoms of the magnetic material lose their alignment.

For example, if you rub a magnet along an iron nail, the nail's atoms will begin to align. Continue rubbing for a few minutes, and the nail's atoms will stay aligned for a short time after you take the magnet away. The nail itself will become a magnet for a little while. A magnet that is created this way is called a temporary magnet.

The alignment of atoms in magnets can also be changed. If you strike or heat a magnet, some of the magnet's atoms will move out of alignment. For example, if you drop a magnet on the floor, it will become weaker.

Another way to change the alignment of atoms in a magnetic material is by using an electric current. Electrons moving through a wire create a magnetic field around the wire. When magnetic materials are placed within these fields, some of their atoms will align. The greater the electric current that runs through the wire, the stronger the magnetic field will be.

A magnet created by using an electric current is called an **electromagnet**. You can construct a simple electromagnet by using a flashlight battery, a coil of insulated wire, and an iron core, such as a nail. First, coil the wire around the nail, as shown in the picture below. Make sure that the coils are all wrapped in the same direction.

Next, carefully tape one bare end of the wire to the positive terminal on the battery and the other bare end to the negative terminal. The nail will act as a magnet as long as an electric current passes through the coil.

**An electric current passing through a wire coiled around an iron nail turns the nail into an electromagnet.** ▶

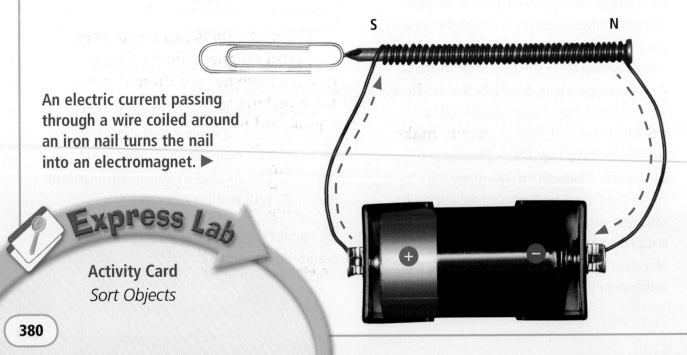

Express Lab

**Activity Card**
*Sort Objects*

380

When a doorbell button is pressed, a coil of wire is magnetized, attracting the rod and causing it to hit the bell.

You can increase the strength of an electromagnet by wrapping more coils around the core, and by using a stronger battery. Be careful, however! In addition to creating magnetic fields, an electric current running through a wire can generate heat. Too much electric current could make the wire or the nail too hot to touch. Only use flashlight batteries that provide 1.5 volts.

You can conduct different experiments to create electromagnets. For example, you can try magnetic materials other than a nail, such as a paper clip, a pair of scissors, or a piece of silverware. Check the item with a magnet first to see if would make a good electromagnet. If the item is strongly attracted to the magnet, then it will probably make a good electromagnet.

Another experiment you can try is to change the number of turns on the wire coil. Test three different numbers of turns and record how many paper clips you can pick up in each case.

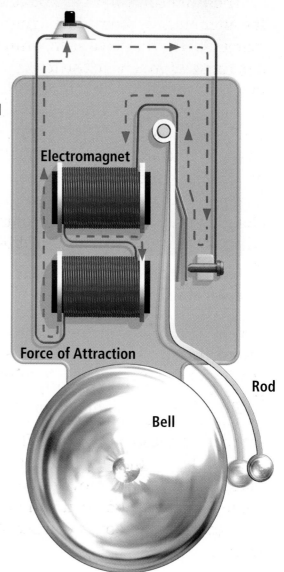

**How a Doorbell Works**

Switch (doorbell button)

Electromagnet

Force of Attraction

Bell

Rod

Electromagnets can create very powerful magnetic fields. These devices have many different uses, from picking up and moving cars at a junkyard to sending bullet trains speeding across the countryside. Electromagnets are also used in electric motors found in many household appliances.

**FOCUS CHECK** What causes the atoms in an electromagnet to align?

The arrows represent solar wind. These fast-moving electrons distort Earth's magnetic field and can cause auroras in the skies above both magnetic poles. ▼

▲ Aurora Borealis is Latin and means "dawn of the north."

## Auroras

If you are far enough north and go outside on a dark night, you might see ribbons and curtains of green or red light chase across the sky. This is the aurora borealis (aw RAWR uh bawr ee AL ihs) or northern lights.

What causes the aurora? Recall that Earth is like a giant magnet. Like a bar magnet, Earth has a north magnetic pole and a south magnetic pole. The magnetic lines of force are closest together at the magnetic poles and Earth's magnetic field surrounds the planet.

Fast electrons from space are guided by Earth's magnetic field into Earth's upper atmosphere. There, at altitudes of 100 km (60 mi) or higher, the fast electrons collide with atoms and molecules of oxygen and nitrogen that make up Earth's atmosphere. In the collisions, the electrons give up their energy to the atoms and molecules, which emit light you see as an aurora.

The color of the aurora depends on the type of gas molecules that are hit by the electrons. This is just like in a neon sign, where the color of the light depends on the type of gas the sign is filled with.

Where do the fast electrons come from? They come from the Sun! The Sun continuously sends out a stream of charged particles in all directions, called the solar wind.

Auroras are also produced near Earth's South Pole. As you might have guessed, these auroras are called southern lights.

**FOCUS CHECK** Why do auroras occur in Earth's polar regions?

# Lesson Wrap-Up

## Visual Summary

Atoms have small magnetic fields. In magnets, these fields all point in the same direction, one larger, stronger magnetic field.

Electrons moving through a wire create a magnetic field around the wire. When a magnetic material is placed within this field, its atoms are temporarily aligned, creating a strong magnetic field.

Technologies that use magnets and electromagnets include doorbells, bullet trains, and electric motors.

## Check for Understanding

### AT A DISTANCE

Research how a mag-lev train works. Prepare a poster to show how magnets are used and how it works. Include which forces act on the train from a distance.

✓ 0507.12.1

## Review

❶ **MAIN IDEA** What gives magnets their magnetic properties?

❷ **VOCABULARY** What is an electromagnet? Describe its properties and how it works.

❸ **READING SKILL: Draw Conclusions** Suppose that two electromagnets attract each other, then suddenly repel each other. What conclusion could explain this observation?

❹ **CRITICAL THINKING: Apply** While on a hike, you notice that the needle of your compass suddenly points to a new direction. Aside from moving the compass, what might cause such a change?

❺ **INQUIRY SKILL: Infer** Suppose you have a magnet that is losing some of its strength. What might have happened to it?

### TCAP Prep

Which force causes Earth to attract objects without touching them?

**A** gravity
**B** friciton
**C** magnetism
**D** electromagnetism

SPI 0507.12.1

 **Technology**

Visit **www.eduplace.com/tnscp** to learn more about magnetism.

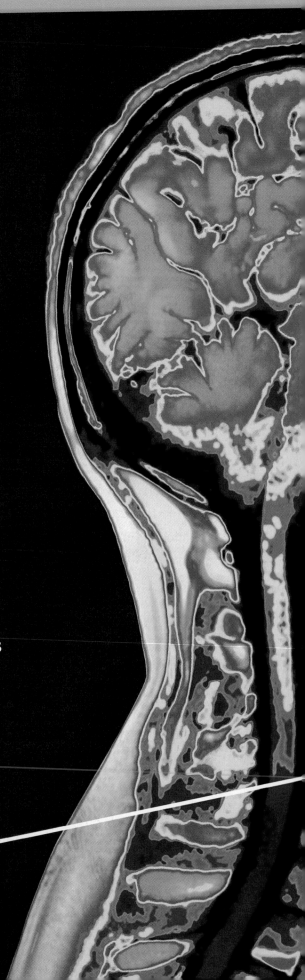

# From the Inside Out!

Brain surgery has a long history dating back to possibly 7,000 B.C.! Those early brain surgeons, however, worked at a disadvantage. They couldn't see the brain without opening the skull.

Today's doctors can look at any part of the brain from the inside out using a Magnetic Resonance Imaging (MRI) machine. First a patient's head is placed in an MRI machine. The hydrogen atoms in that patient's head line up with the MRI's strong magnetic field.

Then a radio frequency is applied to the patient's body. This causes the hydrogen atoms to shift out of alignment with the magnetic field. Finally the radio frequency is turned off. The atoms give off energy which is used to produce a picture of the head.

In this image, you can see the spinal cord and the vertebrae that surround it.

**GLE 0507.T/E.4** Recognize the connection between scientific advances, new knowledge, and the availability of new tools and technologies.

EXTEND

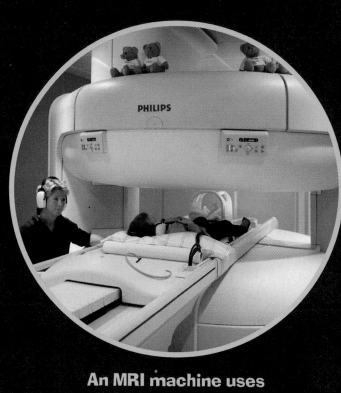

An MRI machine uses magnets to take images of what is inside a body.

This part of the brain is called the cerebrum.

MRI images show much more detail than an image made with an x-ray machine.

GLE 0507.11.1 Design an investigation, collect data and draw conclusions about the relationship among mass, force, and distance traveled. **Math GLE 0506.1.2** Apply and adapt a variety of appropriate strategies to problem solving, including estimation, and reasonableness of the solution. **Math GLE 0506.5.1** Make, record, display and interpret data and graphs that include whole numbers, decimals, and fractions. **ELA GLE 0501.4.1** Conduct research to access and present information.

## Math Speedy Animals

For most of the animals, the table shows maximum speeds measured over a distance of about 400 meters. For the cheetah and the lion, the distance was shorter.

1. Use the information in the table to make a bar graph showing the speed of each of the five animals.

2. How do you think the speeds would change if the measure were the average speed over a distance of a kilometer (1,000 m)?

3. Explain your answer to question 2.

| Speed of Land Animals | |
|---|---|
| **Animal** | **Speed (km/hour)** |
| Cheetah | 113 |
| Pronghorn anelope | 98 |
| Lion | 80 |
| Greyhound | 63 |
| Elephant | 40 |

 **Informational**

Choose two animals from the table above. Research more information about them, and find out why one can run faster than the other. Write a report that explains the factors that determine how fast the two animals can run.

## Amrutur V. Anilkumar

Have you ever fallen down and bruised your knee or arm? What if you could fall and never hit the ground? That's exactly what objects that orbit Earth do. Objects in orbit seem weightless because they are in freefall. Another word for this is *microgravity*.

Dr. Amrutur Anilkumar studies microgravity and its unusual effects on matter. On Earth, liquids take the shape of their containers because of gravity, and we can also pour liquids from an open container. In microgravity, liquids will only come out of a container if they're pumped. Through experiments on the shuttle and International Space Station, he has studied how liquid drops and bubbles in microgravity respond to forces, for example, how to move a bubble through a liquid.

The water came out of this bottle after it was squeezed by the person holding it. ▶

Dr. Anilkumar was born and went to school in India. He became interested in science because he liked knowing how and why things happen. His father's career as an engineer led to his own interest in aerospace technology. The space race in the 1960s also captured his imagination. Dr. Anilkumar is a Professor of the Practice in Mechanical Engineering at Vanderbilt University.

## Vocabulary

**Complete each sentence with a term from the list.**

1. Anything that causes an object to change velocity is a _____.

2. The rate at which an object changes speed is _____.

3. When an object changes its position _____ happens.

4. A tool that changes the amount of force applied, the direction of that force, or both is a _____.

5. The measure of an object's speed and direction is _____.

6. A _____ is a unit of force.

7. A ratio of distance over time is _____.

8. A force that attracts all matter to other matter is _____.

9. When two objects rub together, there is _____.

10. When a force moves an object through a distance, _____ is performed.

**acceleration**
**electromagnet**
**force**
**friction**
**gravity**
**inertia**
**motion**
**newton**
**simple machine**
**speed**
**velocity**
**work**

## TCAP Inquiry Skills

11. **Infer** What are some effects of Earth's magnetic field?  GLE 0507.12.3

12. **Communicate** How would you describe the difference between Newton's first and second laws of motion?  GLE 0507.Inq.4

## Map the Concept

Use a concept map to show the relationship between the following terms.

mass            distance
work            object
force           simple machines
motion                  GLE 0507.11.1

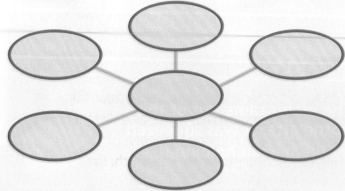

## Critical Thinking

13. **Apply** What might happen if an astronaut floating in space moved the north poles of two magnets together, then let go of the magnets?

GLE 0507.12.3

14. **Synthesize** How would you use a pulley to decrease the amount of force required to lift an object? Include a diagram in your answer. GLE 0507.11.1

15. **Evaluate** Is it accurate to say that the shape of an object influences the way that it falls toward earth? Explain.

GLE 0507.12.2

16. **Analyze** How are gravity and magnetic forces similar? Describe ways they affect objects. GLE 0507.12.1

### Make a Poster

Make a poster that shows the relationship between mass, applied force, and distance traveled. Place a caption by each of the images on the poster to explain them.

 0507.11.2

## TCAP Prep

Answer the following questions.

**17** Which two forces attract objects without touching them?

**A** magnetism and gravity

**B** gravity and friction

**C** magnetism and inertia

**D** friction and inertia     SPI 0507.12.1

**18** Which force affects a falling object based on its shape?

**F** gravity

**G** magnetism

**H** air resistance

**J** inertia     SPI 0507.12.3

**19** Which will result in the most work being done?

**A** a strong force on a heavy object

**B** a strong force on a light object

**C** a light force on a heavy object

**D** a light force on a light object

SPI 0507.11.1

**20** Which force causes objects to fall to the earth?

**F** inertia

**G** friction

**H** magnetism

**J** gravity     SPI 0507.12.2

### 9 Matter

**Performance Indicator:**  **SPI 0507.9.1 Distinguish between physical and chemical properties.**

**1**  Which observation shows that a chemical change occurred?

   **A**  A substance melted.

   **B**  A substance crumbled into smaller pieces.

   **C**  A substance changed color and gave off heat.

   **D**  A substance turned from a liquid to a gas.

### 9 Matter

**Performance Indicator:**  **SPI 0507.9.3 Describe factors that influence the rate at which different types of material freeze, melt, or evaporate.**

**2**  Which factor will <u>not</u> cause a cup of water to evaporate faster?

   **F**  The water in the cup spills and forms a large puddle.

   **G**  The wind begins to blow quickly across the surface of the water.

   **H**  The sun warms the air temperature around the cup by 5°C.

   **J**  A lid with a small hole is placed on top of the cup.

### 11 Motion

**Performance Indicator:**  **SPI 0507.11.1 Explain the relationships that exist among mass, force, and distance traveled.**

**3**  Which thrown ball will travel farthest?

   **A**  Ball A

   **B**  Ball B

   **C**  Ball C

   **D**  Ball D

**Motion Investigation**

| Ball | Mass of Ball (kg) | Speed (mph) |
|------|-------------------|-------------|
| A | 15 | 20 |
| B | 32 | 20 |
| C | 18 | 20 |
| D | 50 | 20 |

## 10 Energy

**Performance Indicator:** **SPI 0507.10.1 Differentiate between potential and kinetic energy.**

**4** Look at the drawing below. At which point does the skier have the most potential energy?

**F** The skier has the most potential energy at Point A.

**G** The skier has the most potential energy at Point B.

**H** The skier has the most potential energy at Point C.

**J** The skier is moving, so he doesn't have any potential energy.

## 12 Forces in Nature

**Performance Indicator:** **SPI 0507.12.3 Use data to determine how shape affects the rate at which a material falls to earth.**

**5** A student folded a piece of paper into three shapes. She tested how long it took each shape to hit the ground, and she made a bar graph with her data. Predict how long it will take a piece of paper crumpled into a ball to reach the ground.

**A** 5 seconds

**B** 8 seconds

**C** 10 seconds

**D** 15 seconds

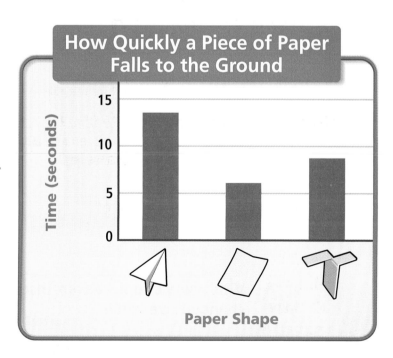

# Discover More

**Chemical Changes** The Statue of Liberty has welcomed people to the United States for more than 115 years. In that time, the statue has been exposed to precipitation, pollution, and salty ocean air. All of these substances caused changes to the statue's copper surface.

When the copper combined with oxygen in air, chemical changes turned the new copper surface dark brown. Over many years, more chemical changes produced a layer of a new substance on the statue's surface. This new substance changed the dark surface to the light green it is today.

The statue had a bright copper surface when it was built in France in the early 1880s. Copper is a pinkish-brown metal.

The statue was put on an island in New York Harbor in 1886. By that time, the shiny copper surface had turned dark brown.

Substances in the environment caused more chemical changes. The dark brown copper started to turn green.

Today, the statue is light green. The new substance that coats the surface of the copper is called a patina.

Visit **www.eduplace.com/tnscp** to see how the statue has changed over time.

# Science and Math Toolbox

Using a Microscope. . . . . . . . . . . . . . . . . . . . . . H2

Making a Bar Graph . . . . . . . . . . . . . . . . . . . . . H3

Using a Calculator. . . . . . . . . . . . . . . . . . . . . . H4

Finding an Average . . . . . . . . . . . . . . . . . . . . . H5

Using a Tape Measure or Ruler. . . . . . . . . . . . . . H6

Measuring Volume . . . . . . . . . . . . . . . . . . . . . H7

Using a Thermometer . . . . . . . . . . . . . . . . . . . H8

Using a Balance. . . . . . . . . . . . . . . . . . . . . . . H9

Using an Equation or Formula . . . . . . . . . . . . . . H10

Making a Chart to Organize Data. . . . . . . . . . . . . H11

Reading a Circle Graph . . . . . . . . . . . . . . . . . . H12

Making a Line Graph. . . . . . . . . . . . . . . . . . . . H13

Measuring Elapsed Time . . . . . . . . . . . . . . . . . . H14

Measurements. . . . . . . . . . . . . . . . . . . . . . . . H16

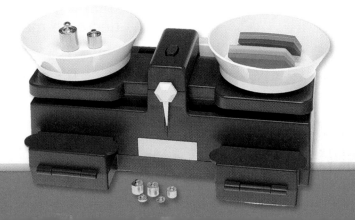

# Using a Microscope

A microscope makes it possible to see very small things by magnifying them. Some microscopes have a set of lenses that magnify objects by different amounts.

## Examine Some Salt Grains

Handle a microscope carefully; it can break easily. Carry it firmly with both hands and avoid touching the lenses.

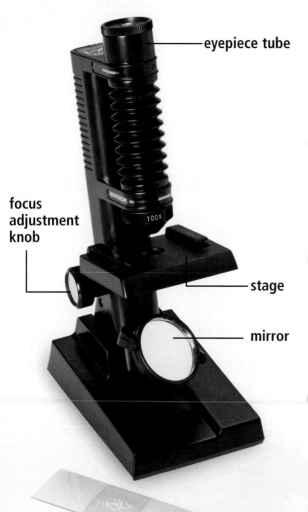

eyepiece tube

focus adjustment knob

stage

mirror

microscope slide

1. Turn the mirror toward a source of light. **NEVER** use the Sun as a light source.

2. Place a few grains of salt on the slide. Put the slide on the stage of the microscope.

3. Bring the salt grains into focus. Turn the adjustment knob on the back of the microscope as you look through the eyepiece.

4. Raise the eyepiece tube to increase the magnification; lower it to decrease magnification.

# Making a Bar Graph

A bar graph helps you organize and compare data. For example, you might want to make a bar graph to compare weather data for different places.

## Make a Bar Graph of Annual Snowfall

For more than 20 years, the cities listed in the table have been recording their yearly snowfall. The table shows the average number of centimeters of snow that the cities receive each year. Use the data in the table to make a bar graph showing the cities' average annual snowfall.

| Snowfall | |
|---|---|
| **City** | **Snowfall (cm)** |
| Atlanta, GA | 5 |
| Charleston, SC | 1.5 |
| Houston, TX | 1 |
| Jackson, MS | 3 |
| New Orleans, LA | 0.5 |
| Tucson, AZ | 3 |

1. Title your graph. The title should help a reader understand what your graph describes.

2. Choose a scale and mark equal intervals. The vertical scale should include the least value and the greatest value in the set of data.

3. Label the vertical axis *Snowfall (cm)* and the horizontal axis *City*. Space the city names equally.

4. Carefully graph the data. Depending on the interval you choose, some amounts may be between two numbers.

5. Check each step of your work.

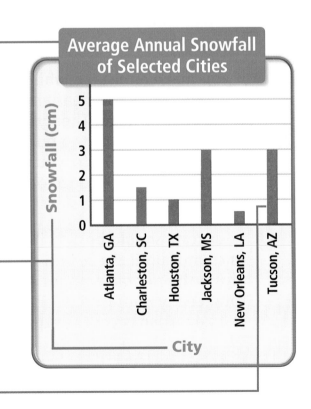

Average Annual Snowfall of Selected Cities

# Using a Calculator

After you've made measurements, a calculator can help you analyze your data. Some calculators have a memory key that allows you to save the result of one calculation while you do another.

## Add and Divide to Find Percent

The table shows the amount of rain that was collected using a rain gauge in each month of one year. You can use a calculator to help you find the total yearly rainfall. Then you can find the percent of rain that fell during January.

| Rainfall | |
|---|---|
| **Month** | **Rain (mm)** |
| Jan. | 214 |
| Feb. | 138 |
| Mar. | 98 |
| Apr. | 157 |
| May | 84 |
| June | 41 |
| July | 5 |
| Aug. | 23 |
| Sept. | 48 |
| Oct. | 75 |
| Nov. | 140 |
| Dec. | 108 |

1. Add the numbers. When you add a series of numbers, you need not press the equal sign until the last number is entered. Just press the plus sign after you enter each number (except the last).

2. If you make a mistake while you are entering numbers, press the clear entry (CE/C) key to erase your mistake. Then you can continue entering the rest of the numbers you are adding. If you can't fix your mistake, you can press the (CE/C) key once or twice until the screen shows 0. Then start over.

3. Your total should be 1,131. Now clear the calculator until the screen shows 0. Then divide the rainfall amount for January by the total yearly rainfall (1,131). Press the percent (%) key. Then press the equal sign key.

214 ÷ 1131 % =

The percent of yearly rainfall that fell in January is 18.921309, which rounds to 19%.

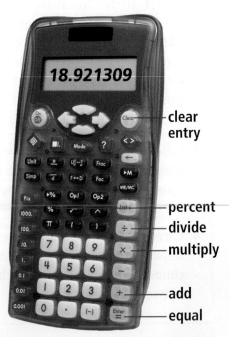

clear entry

percent

divide

multiply

add

equal

# Finding an Average

An average is a way to describe a set of data using one number. For example, you could compare the surface temperature of several stars that are of the same type. You could find the average surface temperature of these stars.

## Add and Divide to Find the Average

Suppose scientists found the surface temperature of eight blue-white stars to be those shown in the table. What is the average surface temperature of the stars listed?

**Surface Temperature of Selected Blue-White Stars**

| Blue-White Star | Surface Temperature (°F) |
|---|---|
| 1 | 7,200 |
| 2 | 6,100 |
| 3 | 6,000 |
| 4 | 6,550 |
| 5 | 7,350 |
| 6 | 6,800 |
| 7 | 7,500 |
| 8 | 6,300 |

**1** First find the sum of the data. Add the numbers in the list.

```
  7,200
  6,100
  6,000
  6,550
  7,350
  6,800
  7,500
+ 6,300
-------
 53,800
```

**2** Then divide the sum (53,800) by the number of addends (8).

```
       6,725
    8 ) 53,800
      - 48
        58
      - 56
         20
       - 16
          40
        - 40
           0
```

**3** 53,800 ÷ 8 = 6,725
The average surface temperature of these eight blue-white stars is 6,725°F.

H5

# Using a Tape Measure or Ruler

Tape measures, metersticks, and rulers are tools for measuring length. Scientists use units such as kilometers, meters, centimeters, and millimeters when making length measurements.

## Use a Meterstick

1. Work with a partner to find the height of your reach. Stand facing a chalkboard. Reach up as high as you can with one hand.

2. Have your partner use chalk to mark the chalkboard at the highest point of your reach.

3. Use a meterstick to measure your reach to the nearest centimeter. Measure from the floor to the chalk mark. Record the height.

## Use a Tape Measure

1. Use a tape measure to find the circumference of, or distance around, your partner's head. Wrap the tape around your partner's head.

2. Find the line where the tape begins to wrap over itself.

3. Record the distance around your partner's head to the nearest millimeter.

# Measuring Volume

A graduated cylinder, a measuring cup, and a beaker are used to measure volume. Volume is the amount of space something takes up. Most of the containers that scientists use to measure volume have a scale marked in milliliters (mL).

▲ This measuring cup has marks for each 25 mL.

▲ This beaker has marks for each 50 mL.

▲ This graduated cylinder has marks for every 1 mL.

## Measure the Volume of a Liquid

1. Measure the volume of some juice. Pour the juice into a measuring container.

2. Move your head so that your eyes are level with the top of the juice. Read the scale line that is closest to the surface of the juice. If the surface of the juice is curved up on the sides, look at the lowest point of the curve.

3. Read the measurement on the scale. You can estimate the value between two lines on the scale to obtain a more accurate measurement.

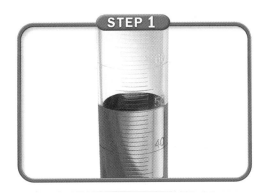

STEP 1

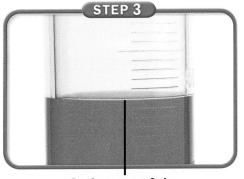

STEP 3

The bottom of the curve is at 35 mL.

# Using a Thermometer

A thermometer is used to measure temperature. When the liquid in the tube of a thermometer gets warmer, it expands and moves farther up the tube. Different scales can be used to measure temperature, but scientists usually use the Celsius scale.

## Measure the Temperature of a Liquid

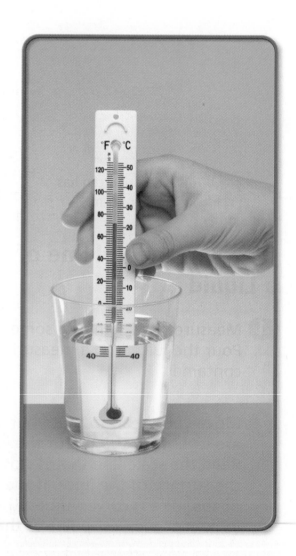

1. Half fill a cup with water or another liquid.

2. Hold the thermometer so that the bulb is in the center of the liquid. Be sure that there are no bright lights or direct sunlight shining on the bulb.

3. Wait until you see the liquid in the tube of the thermometer stop moving. Read the scale line that is closest to the top of the liquid in the tube. The thermometer shown reads 22°C (about 71°F).

# Using a Balance

A balance is used to measure mass. Mass is the amount of matter in an object. To find the mass of an object, place the object in the left pan of the balance. Place standard masses in the right pan.

## Measure the Mass of a Ball

1 Check that the empty pans are balanced, or level with each other. When balanced, the pointer on the base should be on the middle mark. If it needs to be adjusted, move the slider on the back of the balance a little to the left or right.

2 Place a ball in the left pan. Then add standard masses, one at a time, to the right pan. When the pointer is at the middle mark again, each pan is holding the same amount of matter, and the same mass.

3 Each standard mass is marked to show its number of grams. Add the number of grams marked on the masses in the pan. The total is the mass of the ball in grams.

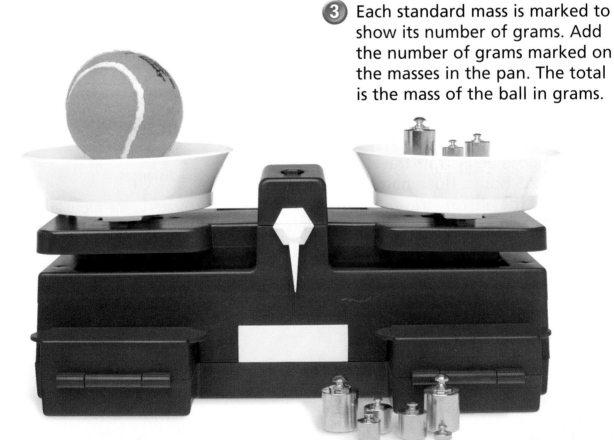

# Using an Equation or Formula

Equations and formulas can help you to determine measurements that are not easily made.

## Use the Diameter of a Circle to Find Its Circumference

**1** Find the circumference of a circle that has a diameter of 10 cm. To determine the circumference of a circle, use the formula below.

$C = \pi d$

$C = 3.14 \times 10$ cm

$C = 31.4$ cm

The circumference of this circle is 31.4 cm.

> $\pi$ is the symbol for pi. Always use 3.14 as the value for $\pi$, unless another value for pi is given.

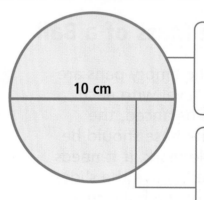

10 cm

> The circumference (C) is a measure of the distance around a circle.

> The diameter (d) of a circle is a line segment that passes through the center of the circle and connects two points on the circle.

## Use Rate and Time to Determine Distance

**2** Suppose an aircraft travels at 772 km/h for 2.5 hours. How many kilometers does the aircraft travel during that time? To determine distance traveled, use the distance formula below.

> d = distance
>
> r = rate, or the speed at which the aircraft is traveling.
>
> t = the length of time traveled

$d = rt$

$d = 772$ km/h $\times 2.5$ hours

$d = 1{,}930$ km

The aircraft travels 1,930 km in 2.5 hours.

# Making a Chart to Organize Data

A chart can help you record, compare, or classify information.

## Organize Properties of Elements

Suppose you collected the data shown at the right. The data presents properties of silver, gold, lead, and iron.

You could organize this information in a chart by classifying the physical properties of each element.

**My Data**

Silver (Ag) has a density of 10.5 g/cm³. It melts at 961°C and boils at 2,212°C. It is used in dentistry and to make jewelry and electronic conductors.

Gold melts at 1,064°C and boils at 2,966°C. Its chemical symbol is Au. It has a density of 19.3 g/cm³ and is used for jewelry, in coins, and in dentistry.

The melting point of lead (Pb) is 328°C. The boiling point is 1,740°C. It has a density of 11.3 g/cm³. Some uses for lead are in storage batteries, paints, and dyes.

Iron (Fe) has a density of 7.9 g/cm³. It will melt at 1,535°C and boil at 3,000°C. It is used for building materials, in manufacturing, and as a dietary supplement.

Create categories that describe the information you have found.

Give the chart a title that describes what is listed in it.

Make sure the information is listed accurately in each column.

### Properties of Some Elements

| Element | Symbol | Density g/cm³ | Melting Point (°C) | Boiling Point (°C) | Some Uses |
|---|---|---|---|---|---|
| Silver | Ag | 10.5 | 961 | 2,212 | jewelry, dentistry, electric conductors |
| Gold | Au | 19.3 | 1,064 | 2,966 | jewelry, dentistry, coins |
| Lead | Pb | 11.3 | 328 | 1,740 | storage batteries, paints, dyes |
| Iron | Fe | 7.9 | 1,535 | 3,000 | building materials, manufacturing, dietary supplement |

# Reading a Circle Graph

A circle graph shows the whole divided into parts. You can use a circle graph to compare parts to each other or to compare parts to the whole.

## Read a Circle Graph of Land Area

The whole circle represents the approximate land area of all of the continents on Earth. The number on each wedge indicates the land area of each continent. From the graph you can determine that the land area of North America is 16% × 148,000,000 km², or about 24 million square kilometers.

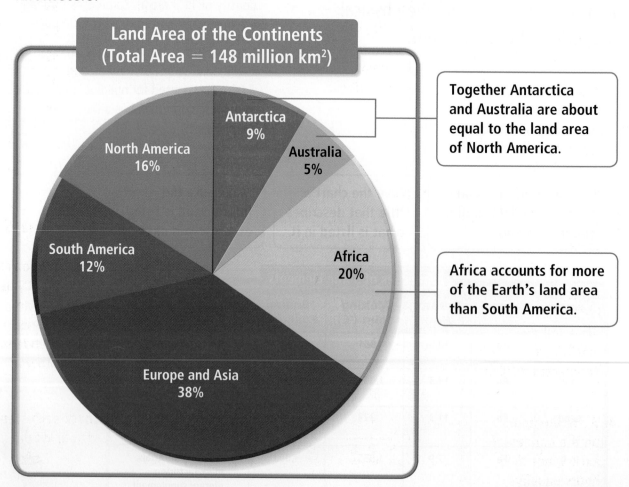

**Land Area of the Continents
(Total Area = 148 million km²)**

Antarctica 9%
Australia 5%
North America 16%
South America 12%
Africa 20%
Europe and Asia 38%

Together Antarctica and Australia are about equal to the land area of North America.

Africa accounts for more of the Earth's land area than South America.

# Making a Line Graph

A line graph is a way to show continuous change over time. You can use the information from a table to make a line graph.

## Make a Line Graph of Temperatures

The table shows temperature readings over a 12-hour period at the Dallas-Fort Worth Airport in Texas. This data can also be displayed in a line graph that shows temperature change over time.

| Dallas-Fort Worth Airport Temperature | |
|---|---|
| **Hour** | **Temp. (°C)** |
| 6 A.M. | 22 |
| 7 A.M. | 24 |
| 8 A.M. | 25 |
| 9 A.M. | 26 |
| 10 A.M. | 27 |
| 11 A.M. | 29 |
| 12 noon | 31 |
| 1 P.M. | 32 |
| 2 P.M. | 33 |
| 3 P.M. | 34 |
| 4 P.M. | 35 |
| 5 P.M. | 35 |
| 6 P.M. | 34 |

**1.** Choose a title. The title should help a reader understand what your graph describes.

**2.** Choose a scale and mark equal intervals. The vertical scale should include the least value and the greatest value in the set of data.

**3.** Label the horizontal axis *Time* and the vertical axis *Temperature* (°C).

**4.** Write the hours on the horizontal axis. Space the hours equally.

**5.** Carefully graph the data. Depending on the interval you choose, some temperatures will be between two numbers.

**6.** Check each step of your work.

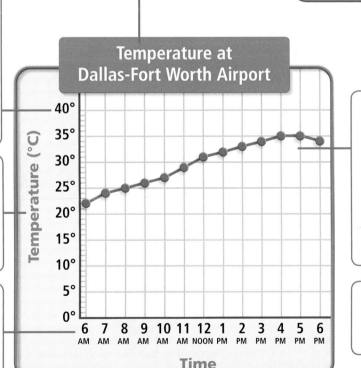

Temperature at Dallas-Fort Worth Airport

# ...g Elapsed Time

...u may need to find out how much time has passed, or
...ock is often used to find elapsed time. You can also change
...d add or subtract to find out how much time has passed.

## Using a Clock to Find Elapsed Minutes

You need to time an experiment for 20 minutes. It is 1:30.

- Start at 1:30.
- Count ahead 20 minutes, by fives to 1:50.
- Stop the experiment at 1:50.

## Using a Clock or Stopwatch to Find Elapsed Seconds

You need to time an experiment for 15 seconds. You can use a second hand on a clock.

1. Wait until the second hand is on a number. Then start the experiment.
2. Stop the experiment when 15 seconds have passed.

You can also use a stopwatch to figure out elapsed seconds.

1. Press the reset button on the stopwatch so you see 0:0000.
2. Press the start button to begin.
3. When you see 0:1500, press the stop button on the watch.

# Changing Units and Then Adding or Subtracting to Find Elapsed Time

If you know how to change units of time, you can use addition and subtraction to find elapsed time.

**1** To change from a larger unit to a smaller unit, multiply.

2 d = ▪ h

2 × 24 = 48

2 d = 48 h

**2** To change from a smaller unit to a larger unit, divide.

78 wk = ▪ yr

$78 ÷ 52 = 1\frac{1}{2}$

$78 \text{ wk} = 1\frac{1}{2} \text{ yr}$

## Another Example

Suppose it took juice in an ice-pop mold from 6:40 A.M. until 10:15 A.M. to freeze. How long did it take for the juice to freeze? To find out, subtract.

|  9 h | 75 min |
|------|--------|
| ~~10 h~~ | ~~15 min~~ |
| − 6 h | 40 min |
| 3 h | 35 min |

Rename 10 h 15 min as 9 h 75 min, since 1 hr = 60 min.

| **Units of Time** |
|-------------------|
| 60 seconds (s) = 1 minute (min) |
| 60 minutes = 1 hour (h) |
| 24 hours = 1 day (d) |
| 7 days = 1 week (wk) |
| 52 weeks = 1 year (yr) |

You can also add to find elapsed time.

|   | 3 h | 30 min | 14 s |
|---|-----|--------|------|
| + | 1 h | 40 min | 45 s |
|   | 4 h | 70 min | 59 s = 5 h 10 min 59 s |

# Measurements

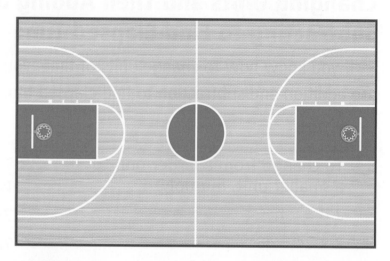

### Volume

1 L of sports drink is a little more than 1 qt.

### Area

A basketball court covers about 4,700 ft². It covers about 435 m².

## Metric Measures

### Temperature

- Ice melts at 0 degrees Celsius (°C)
- Water freezes at 0°C
- Water boils at 100°C

### Length and Distance

- 1,000 meters (m) = 1 kilometer (km)
- 100 centimeters (cm) = 1 m
- 10 millimeters (mm) = 1 cm

### Force

- 1 newton (N) =
  1 kilogram × 1 (meter/second) per second

### Volume

- 1 cubic meter (m³) = 1 m × 1 m × 1 m
- 1 cubic centimeter (cm³) =
  1 cm × 1 cm × 1 cm
- 1 liter (L) = 1,000 milliliters (mL)
- 1 cm³ = 1 mL

### Area

- 1 square kilometer (km²) = 1 km × 1 km
- 1 hectare = 10,000 m²

### Mass

- 1,000 grams (g) = 1 kilogram (kg)
- 1,000 milligrams (mg) = 1 g

## Temperature

The temperature at an indoor basketball game might be 27°C, which is 80°F.

## Length/Distance

A basketball rim is about 10 ft high, or a little more than 3 m from the floor.

# Customary Measures

### Temperature

- Ice melts at 32 degrees Fahrenheit (°F)
- Water freezes at 32°F
- Water boils at 212°F

### Length and Distance

- 12 inches (in.) = 1 foot (ft)
- 3 ft = 1 yard (yd)
- 5,280 ft = 1 mile (mi)

### Weight

- 16 ounces (oz) = 1 pound (lb)
- 2,000 pounds = 1 ton (T)

### Volume of Fluids

- 8 fluid ounces (fl oz) = 1 cup (c)
- 2 c = 1 pint (pt)
- 2 pt = 1 quart (qt)
- 4 qt = 1 gallon (gal)

# Metric and Customary Rates

- km/h = kilometers per hour
- m/s = meters per second
- mph = miles per hour

# Glossary

## A

**acceleration** (ak sehl uh RAY shuhn), change in velocity (357)

**acquired trait** (uh KWYRD trayt), characteristic that an organism develops after it is born (124)

**adaptation** (ad ap TAY shuhn), a trait or characteristic that helps an organism survive in its environment (88, 142)

**air mass**, a huge volume of air responsible for types of weather (258)

**amphibian** (am FIHB ee uhn), a kind of vertebrate, most of which begin life in water and live part of the time on land (31)

**asexual reproduction** (ay SEHK shoo uhl ree pruh DUHK shuhn), production of offspring from only one parent (136)

**asteroid** (AS tuh royd), a small, rocky object that orbits the Sun (172)

**atmosphere** (AT muh sfihr), the mixture of gases that surrounds Earth (256)

**atom**, the smallest particle of matter that has the properties of that matter (289)

## B

**biome** (BY ohm), a large group of similar ecosystems (54)

**boiling point** (BOY lihng point), the temperature at which a substance changes rapidly from a liquid to a gas (299)

## C

**cell**, the basic structural unit of a living thing (16)

⭐**chemical property** (KEHM ih kuhl PRAP ur tee), a characteristic of matter that can be observed only when that matter is changed into a new kind of matter (297, 301)

**chromosome** (KROH muh sohm), a thick coil of DNA (126)

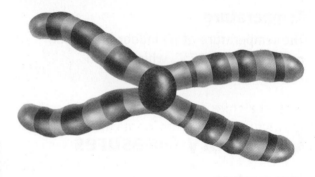

**climate** (KLY miht), the normal pattern of weather that occurs in an area over a long period of time (54, 247)

**cnidarian** (ny DAIR ee ehn), a type of invertebrate with radial symmetry, a saclike body, a true mouth, and the ability to digest food (28)

**comet** (KAHM iht), a small, orbiting body made of dust, ice, and frozen gases (173)

**community** (kuh MYOO nih tee), a group of living things of different species found in an ecosystem (49)

**condensation** (kahn dehn SAY shuhn), a change of state from a gas to a liquid as energy is removed (309)

⭐ = Tennessee Academic Vocabulary

**conduction** (kuhn DUHK shuhn), the transfer of thermal energy between two substances or between two parts of the same substance (338)

**conductivity** (kuhn duhk TIV ih tee), the ability to carry energy (300)

⭐**conductor** (kuhn DUHK tuhr), a material that easily transfers thermal energy or electricity (338)

⭐**convection** (kuhn VEHK shuhn), the transfer of thermal energy by the flow of liquids or gases (339)

**core**, Earth's innermost structure (207)

**crust**, the thin, rocky outer layer of Earth that makes up the continents and the ocean floor (206)

**density** (DEHN sih tee), a measure of the mass per unit volume of a substance (298)

**deposition** (dehp uh ZIHSH uhn), the change of state from a gas to a solid (310)

**desert** (DEHZ uhrt), a very dry area (56)

**DNA**, a molecule found in the nucleus of a cell and shaped like a double helix; associated with the transfer of genetic information (126)

**dome mountains** (dohm MOWN tuhnz), mountains that form when magma pushes up on Earth's crust but does not break through (230)

**dominant trait** (DAHM un nuhnt trayt),

the trait that is expressed when an organism receives genes for two different forms of a trait (139)

**earthquake** (URTH kwayk), a violent shaking of Earth's crust as built-up energy is released (216)

⭐**ecosystem** (EHK oh sihs tuhm), all the living and nonliving things that interact with one another in a given area (48)

**El Niño** (ehl NEE nyo), a periodic change in the direction of warm ocean currents across the Pacific Ocean (250)

**electromagnet** (ih lehk troh MAG niht), a magnet that is powered by electricity (380)

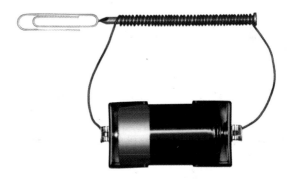

**endangered species** (ehn DAYN juhrd SPEE sheez), a species close to becoming extinct (107)

**energy** (EHN uhr jee), the ability to do work (326)

**epicenter** (EHP ih sehn tuhr), the point on Earth's surface directly above the focus of an earthquake (216)

**evaporation** (ih VAP uhr ay shuhn), show or gradual vaporization that takes place at the surface of a liquid (309)

**extinction** (ihk STIHNGK shuhn), when all the members of a species die out (99)

⭐ = Tennessee Academic Vocabulary

Glossary

## F

**fault** (fawlt), a crack in Earth's crust along which movement takes place (214)

**fault-block mountains** (fahwt blahk MOWN tuhnz), mountains that form along fault lines where blocks of rock fall, are thrust up, or slide (229)

**focus** (FOH kuhs), the point underground where the faulting in an earthquake occurs (216)

**fold mountains** (fohld MOWN tuhnz), mountains that form where two plates collide and force layers of rock into folds (228)

**food chain**, a description of how energy in an ecosystem flows from one organism to another (69)

**food web**, a description of all the food chains in an ecosystem (70)

**force**, a push or a pull acting on an object (355)

★ **fossil** (FAH suhl), the physical remains or traces of a plant or an animal that lived long ago (210)

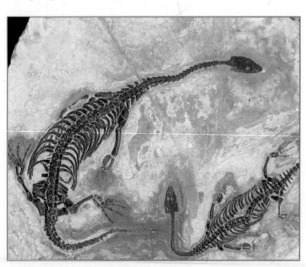

**friction** (FRIHK shuhn), a force that resists the motion of one surface across another (360)

**front**, a narrow region between two air masses that have different properties (259)

## G

**gene** (jeen), a short segment of DNA that determines one of an organism's inherited traits (127)

**grasslands** (GRAS landz), land covered by grasses with few trees (56)

**gravity** (GRAV ih tee), the pulling force between two objects (360)

## H

**habitat** (HAB ih tat), the natural environment where an organism lives (86)

**heat**, the transfer of thermal energy from warmer areas to cooler areas (337)

**heredity** (huh REHD ih tee), the genetic transfer of characteristics from parent to offspring (124)

**hybrid** (HY brihd), an organism that has two different genes for the same trait (139)

★ = Tennessee Academic Vocabulary

**inertia** (ih NUR shuh), the resistance to a change in motion (355)

**inner planets** (IHN uhr PLAN ihtz), the four planets of the solar system that are closest to the sun—Mercury, Venus, Earth, and Mars (178)

⭐ **insulator** (IHN suh lay tuhr), a material that does not easily transfer thermal energy or electricity (338)

**invertebrates** (ihn VUR tuh brihtz), animals that have no internal skeletons or bones (28)

⭐ **kinetic energy** (kih NEHT ihk EHN uhr jee), the energy of a moving object (328)

**light-year**, a unit of measurement for distances outside the solar system and equal to the distance light travels in one year—about 9.5 trillion km (189)

**lithosphere** (LIHTH uh sfihr), the shell formed from Earth's solid upper mantle and crust (207)

**magma** (MAG muh), melted rock below Earth's surface; called lava at the surface (218)

**magnitude** (MAG nih tood), the brightness of a star as perceived from Earth (189)

**mantle** (MAN tl), the thick layer of Earth's structure just below the crust (207)

**matter**, anything that has mass and takes up space (288)

**melting** (MEHL tihng), the change of state from a solid to a liquid as energy is added (308)

**melting point** (MEHL tihng point), the temperature at which a substance changes from a solid to a liquid (299)

**mesosphere** (MEHZ oh sfihr), the layer of Earth's atmosphere above the stratosphere and below the thermosphere (257)

**meteor** (MEE tee uhr), a streak of light in the night sky caused by a meteoroid (174)

**meteorite** (MEE tee uh ryt), chunks of meteor matter that fall to the ground (174)

**meteoroid** (MEE tee uh royd), a chunk of matter that enters Earth's atmosphere and is heated by interaction with the air (174)

**molecule** (MAHL ih kyool), two or more atoms joined by chemical bonds (289)

**motion**, a change in an object's position (354)

**mutation** (myoo TAY shuhn), a change in the genes of an organism (129)

⭐ = Tennessee Academic Vocabulary

**newton** (NOOT n), a unit to measure force; one newton (N) is equal to the force required to accelerate a 1 kg mass by 1 m/s2 (359)

**niche** (NIHCH), the role of an organism in its habitat (87)

**nucleotide** (NOO klee uh tyd), the basic structural unit of DNA (127)

**nucleus** (NOO klee uhs), the storehouse of the cell's most important chemical information, DNA (18)

**ocean current** (OH shuhn KUR uhnt), a moving stream of water in the ocean created by winds pushing against the ocean's surface (250)

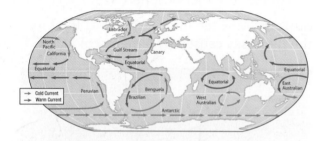

**organelles** (AWR guh nehlz), cell structures that perform specific functions (18)

**outer planets** (OW tuhr PLAN ihtz), the four planets of the solar system farthest from the Sun—Jupiter, Saturn, Uranus, and Neptune (180)

**physical property** (FIHZ ih kuhl PRAHP uhr tee), a characteristic of matter that can be detected by the senses and that does not involve the changing of matter into something new (292)

**planet** (PLAN iht), large bodies in space that revolve around the Sun (170)

**plate tectonics** (playt tehk TAHN ihks), the theory that giant plates of Earth's crust and upper mantle are moving slowly across Earth's surface (208)

**pollution** (puh LOO shuhn), harmful substances that have been added to the environment (108)

**population** (pahp yuh LAY shuhn), all the members of the same type of organism living in an ecosystem (50, 94)

⭐ **potential energy** (puh TEHN shuhl EHN uhr jee), energy stored in an object (328)

**predator** (PREHD uh tuhr), an animal that hunts and eats other animals (95)

**prey** (pray), an animal that is hunted and eaten by predators (95)

⭐ **radiation** (ray dee AY shuhn), the transfer of thermal energy through electromagnetic waves (340)

**recessive trait** (rih SEHS ihv trayt), a trait that is not expressed when an organism received genes for two different forms of a trait (139)

⭐ = Tennessee Academic Vocabulary

**seismic waves** (SYZ mihk wayvz), waves of energy sent through Earth when parts of the crust move suddenly during an earthquake (215)

**selective breeding** (suh LEHK tihv BREE ding), the practice of breeding plants and animals for desired traits (140)

**sexual reproduction** (SEHK shoo uhl ree pruh DUHK shuhn), the production of offspring by the union of male and female gametes (138)

**simple machine** (SIHM puhl muh SHEEN), a machine that has few or no moving parts (365)

**solar system** (SOH luhr SIHS tuhm), the Sun and all the bodies in space that revolve around it (170)

**solubility** (sahl yoo BIHL ih tee), the measure of how much of one substance can dissolve in another substance (300)

**speed**, the measure of the distance an object moves in a given unit of time (356)

**star**, a giant sphere of glowing gases (188)

⭐ **state of matter**, a physical form that matter takes; solid, liquid, and gas are states of matter (290)

**stratosphere** (STRA tuh sfihr), the layer of Earth's atmosphere above the troposphere and below the mesosphere (257)

**sublimation** (suhb luh MAY shuhn), the change of state from a solid to a gas (310)

**symbiosis** (sihm bee OH sis), a close, long-lasting relationship between two species (90)

**symmetry** (SIHM uh tree), matching body form, such as across opposite sides of a dividing line (28)

**taiga** (TY guh), an area that has long, severe winters and short, cool summers (57)

**temperate forest** (TEM puhr uht FAWR uhst), forests that experience four distinct seasons: summer, fall, winter, and spring (55)

**temperature** (TEHM puhr uh chuhr), the measure of the average kinetic energy of the particles that make up a substance (336)

**thermal energy** (THUHR muhl EHN uhr jee), the kinetic energy of the particles that make up a material (336)

**thermal expansion** (THUHR muhl ihk SPAN shuhn), an increase in the size of a substance due to a change in temperature (312)

**thermosphere** (THUHR muh sfihr), the outermost layer of Earth's atmosphere, above the mesosphere (257)

**threatened species** (THREHT nd SPEE sheez), a species close to becoming endangered (107)

**tropical rain forest** (TRAHP ih kuhl rayn FAWR uhst), a forest in a region that is very hot and very rainy (55)

⭐ = Tennessee Academic Vocabulary

**troposphere** (TROH puh sfihr), the layer of Earth's atmosphere closest to Earth's surface and containing about three-quarters of the atmosphere's gases (257)

**tundra**, Earth's coldest biome (57)

**vaporization** (vay puh rih ZAY shuhn), the change of state from a liquid to a gas as energy is added (309)

**velocity** (vuh LAHS ih tee), the measure of an object's speed and direction (356)

**vertebrates** (VUR tuh brihtz), animals that have backbones or a nerve cord running down their back (30)

**work**, the result of a force moving an object a certain distance (364**)**

**Acceleration,** 358, 359
   friction and, 360
   gravity and, 360
**Acid rain,** 108
**Acquired traits,** 124–125
**Adaptations,** 88, 142–143
   to changes in ecosystems, 98
   to climate, 100
   for open ocean zone, 58, 59
   speed of, 144
**African Plate,** 208
**Aftershocks,** 216
**Air bladders,** 142
**Air, composition of,** 256
**Air masses,** 258
   fronts between, 259
**Airplanes,** 375
**Air pollution,** 108
**Air pressure,** 257
   measuring, 262
   on weather maps, 260
**Air resistance,** 360
**Algae,** 59, 60
   in EcoSphere™, 112
   as producers, 69
**Alien species,** 96
**Alioth,** 189
**Alkaid,** 189
**Alligator snapping turtles,** 119
**Alligators,** 31, 49
**Amino acids,** 128
**Amphibia,** 34
**Amphibians,** 31
**Analyze data**
   climates, 52-53
   earthquake and volcano locations, 212–213
   as inquiry skill, 52-53, 122-123, 212–213
   traits, 122–123
**Andes Mountains,** 228, 230
**Anemometers,** 262
**Anilkumar, Amrutur,** 387
**Animal cells,** 18–20
   mitochondria in, 133
   organelles of, 18
**Animalcules,** 22

**Animals**
   adaptations of, 88, 142–143
   alien species of, 96
   characteristics of, 27
   classifying, 24–27, 34
   cold-blooded vertebrates, 30–31
   in deserts, 56
   in energy pyramids, 72
   extinction of, 100
   in food chains, 69
   in forest biomes, 55
   in freshwater ecosystems, 60
   in grasslands, 56
   invertebrates, 27–29
   in last ice age, 100
   in marine biomes, 58–59
   perishing of, 98, 99
   predators and prey, 95
   regeneration in, 137
   selective breeding of, 140–141
   sexual reproduction in, 138–139
   species of, 27
   of taiga, 57
   of tundra, 57
   warm-blooded vertebrates, 32–33
   in wetlands, 107
**Antarctic Plate,** 208
**Anti-Atlas Mountains,** 232
**Antibiotics,** 144
**Appalachian Mountains,** 160, 161, 230, 232
**Appalachian Plateau,** 160, 161
**Area, measuring,** H16
**Argon, in air,** 256
**Ariel,** 172
**Arthropods,** 27, 29
**Asexual reproduction,** 136–137
**Ash,** 301
**Asian long-horned beetles,** 96
**Ask questions,** in scientific inquiry, S6, S8
**Asteroid belt,** 172, 174
**Asteroids,** 170–172, 185
**Astronauts,** 182, 195
   in microgravity, 387
**Atmosphere**

   conditions in the (See Weather)
   of Earth (See Earth's atmosphere)
   of moons, 172
   of Venus, 179
   views of space and, 182
**Atoms,** 289, 297
   of magnets, 378–380
**Attraction** (magnets), 379
**Aurora borealis,** 382
**Auroras,** 382
**Automobiles,** 375
**Average,** H5

**Backbones,** 30
   animals with (See Vertebrates)
   animals without (See Invertebrates)
**Bacteria**
   asexual reproduction of, 136, 137
   near ocean vents, 59
   as producers, 69
   speed of adaptations in, 144
**Balanced forces,** 358
**Balances,** 298
**Bar graphs,** H3
   speedy animals, 386
**Barometers,** 262
**Barringer impact crater,** 174
**Basalt,** 206
**Baseball, forces in,** 355
**Base pairs (DNA),** 127, 128
**Bats,** 3, 33
**Beaks,** 32
   adaptations of, 142
**Bears,** 33
**Beavers,** 6
**Bees,** 4–5, 143
**Beetles,** 96
**Behavioral adaptations,** 88
**Behaviors, inherited,** 124, 146
**Big Dipper,** 189
**Bilateral symmetry,** 26, 29
**Biodegradable bottles,** 304–305
**Biomes,** 52, 54

deserts, 56
forest, 55
freshwater, 60
grasslands, 56
marine, 58–59
taiga, 57
tundra, 57
**Biospheres,** 112, 113
**Birds,** 32
adaptations of, 142
courting beh aviors of,
146–147
natural selection among,
89
in savanna, 87
**Bison,** 104, 107
**Black Hills,** 231
**Blacksmiths,** 277
**Blue-footed booby,** 146–147
**Blue Ridge Mountains,** 232
**Blue Spring Cave,** 2
**Blue whales,** 357
**Body waves,** 217
**Boiling point,** 299, 309
**Bombs** (from volcanoes), 219
**Botanists,** 39
**Bottles,** biodegradable,
304–305
**Brain surgery.** *See* Magnetic
Resonance Imaging
**Breathing**
by amphibians, 31
by fish, 30
oxygen for, 27
**Bridger, Jim,** 204
**Bridges,** 312
**Bristleworms,** 29
**Bristol Dragway,** 274–275
**Bristol Motor Speedway,**
274–275
**Budding,** 136, 137
**Bug-eating plants,** 70
**Burning,** 297, 301, 302
**Butterflies,** 143

**Cacti,** 88
**Calculators,** H4
**Camouflage,** 143
**Carbon dioxide,** in air, 256

**Careers in science**
astronaut, 195
botanist, 39
chef, 39
computer systems techni-
cian, 195
demolition specialist, 345
meteorologist, 267
oceanographer's assistant,
267
thermal engineer, 345
wetlands ecologist, 115
zookeeper, 115
**Caribbean Plate,** 208
**Carnivora,** 34
**Carnivores,** 33, 70
**Cars,** pollutants from, 109
**Catnip,** S10
**Cats,** chromosomes of, 126
**Cat's Eye Nebula,** 193
**Catskill Mountains,** 231
**Cattle egrets,** 90
**Caves,** 2–3
**Cell membranes,** 18, 19
**Cell theory,** 17
**Cell walls,** 18, 19
**Cells**
animal, 18
as building blocks of life,
16–17
DNA in, 126
parts of, 4–5, 18–20
plant, 18
proteins in, 128
**Centromeres,** 126
**Ceres,** 181
**Charon,** 181
**Charts,** H11
**Cheetahs,** 357
**Chefs,** 39
**Chemical changes,** 301-302
**Chemical energy,** 327
in batteries, 328
potential, 329
**Chemical properties,** 297, 301
changed by cooking, 302
**Chloroplasts,** 18, 20, 133
**Chordata,** 34
**Chromatids,** 126
**Chromatin,** 126
**Chromosomes,** 126–127
of gametes, 138

separation of, 130
in sexual reproduction, 138
**Cinder cone volcanoes,** 219
**Cinders** (from volcanoes), 219
**Circle graphs,** H12
**Clams,** 29, 159
**Classes** (of animals), 34
**Classifying animals,** 24–27, 34
**Clean Air Act,** 109
**Cleaner shrimp,** 90
**Climate change,** 100
**Climates,** 54, 247
comparing, 52–53
of deserts, 56
of forest biomes, 55
of grasslands, 56
land and sea breezes, 248
ocean currents and, 250
of taiga, 57
of tundra, 57
uneven heating of Earth
and, 246
**Climate zones,** 246, 247
**Clingman's Dome,** 232
**Clipper ships,** 374
**Clownfish,** 84
**cm³** (cubic centimeters), 298
**Cnidarians,** 27, 28
**Coal,** burning, S11
**Cocos Plate,** 208
**Cold-blooded vertebrates,**
30–31
**Cold fronts,** 259, 260
**Collaborate**
air pressure, 254–255
as inquiry skill, 254–255
**Coloration,** 143
**Coma,** 173
**Comets,** 170, 171, 173, 185
orbits of, 169
**"Comets, Meteors, and Aster-
oids"** (Seymour Simon), 185
**Commensalism,** 90
**Communication**
animal classification, 24–25
as inquiry skill, 14–15,
24–25
of investigations, S3
science results, 14–15
in scientific inquiry, S6
**Communities,** 49
in ecosystems, 50

in Everglades, 49
formation of, 46
**Compare**
factors affecting climate, 244–245
as inquiry skill, 244–245, 362–363
ramps, 362–363
**Compasses,** 379
**Composite volcanoes,** 219
**Compound machines,** 372
**Computer systems technicians,** 195
**Condensation,** 309
mountain effect precipitation and, 248
**Conduction,** thermal, 338
**Conductivity,** 300
**Constellations,** 189
apparent movement of, 190
Big Dipper, 189
mapping, 156, 157
**Consumers,** 68–72
classifying, 70
zebras as, 87
**Continental air masses,** 258
**Continental drift,** 208
**Continental plates,** 208, 209
**Continental polar air masses,** 258
**Continental tropical air masses,** 258
**Continents,** movement of, 208
**Convection,** 339
**Converging boundaries,** 209
faults at, 215
mountain building at, 229
volcanic mountains at, 230
**Cooking,** chemical properties changed by, 302
**Coon Creek Formation,** Adamsville, Tennessee, 159
**Coral,** 28
**Coral snake,** 143
**Core** (Earth), 206, 207
**Cows,** 141
**Crab Nebula,** 192–193
**Crabs,** 29, 58
**Craters**
on Mercury, 178
from meteors, 174
of volcanoes, 218

**Crick, Francis,** 132
**Critical thinking,** S5
**Crocodiles,** 31
**Crucibles,** 279
**Crust** (Earth), 206
plate movement in, 161
**Cubic centimeters** (cm³), 298
**Cumberland Plateau,** 160, 161
**Currents,** ocean, 250
**Customary measures,** H16
**Cycles,** in nature, 70
**Cystic fibrosis,** 130
**Cytoplasm,** 18, 19

**Dams in Tennessee,** 6–7
**Darwin, Charles,** 89
**Data,** charts of, H11
**Death Valley,** 229
**Deceleration,** 357
**Decision making,** S14–S15
**Decomposers,** 69
**Delaware Water Gap,** 231
**Demolition specialists,** 345
**Density,** 298
**Deoxyribonucleic acid.** *See* DNA
**Deposition,** 310
**Desert biomes,** 56
**Desert climates,** 249
**Desert tortoise,** 88
**Digestion,** in great white sharks, 74–75
**Dinosaurs,** fossils of, 98, 99
**Directed Inquiry**
Air Pressure, 254–255
Chromosome Combinations, 134–135
Comet Orbits, 168–169
Compare Climates, 52–53
Compare Matter, 286–287
Exploring Magnets, 376–377
Get Closer!, 14–15
Lighten Up!, 244–245
Limits to Growth, 92–93
Look at Life, 46–47
Make a Mountain, 226–227
Making Rain, 306–307
The Melting Point, 334–335

Model Energy Flow, 67
A Model World, 202–203
Monster Trucks, 352–353
Oil and Water, 294–295
Organizing Animals, 24–25
Picking Out a Pattern, 212–213
Ramping It Up, 362–363
Rising Sea Level, 104–105
Rollerball, 324–325
Scaling the Solar System, 176–177
Star Search!, 186–187
Trait Tabulation, 122–123
Worm and Fish Habitats, 84–85
**Direction,** acceleration and, 357
**Distance**
measuring, H16,–H17
work and, 365
**Distance traveled,** formula for, 356
**Diverging boundaries,** 209
faults at, 215, 220
mountain building at, 229
volcanic mountains at, 230
**DNA** (deoxyribonucleic acid), 126–129
in asexual reproduction, 136, 137
of mitochondria, 133
x-ray pictures of, 132
**DNA replication,** 128, 129
**Dogs,** chromosomes of, 126
**Dollywood Craft Preservation School,** Pigeon Forge, Tennessee, 276–277
**Dolphins,** 33, 59
**Dome mountains,** 230, 231
**Dominant genes,** 139
**Down syndrome,** 130
**Dragonflies,** 357, 360
**Draw conclusions,** in scientific inquiry, S6, S8
**Droughts**
dams for control of, 7
ecosystems changed by, 97
in Tennessee, 264–265
**Dry ice,** 310
**Dubhe,** 189
**Duck-billed platypus,** 33
**Dwarf planets,** 181

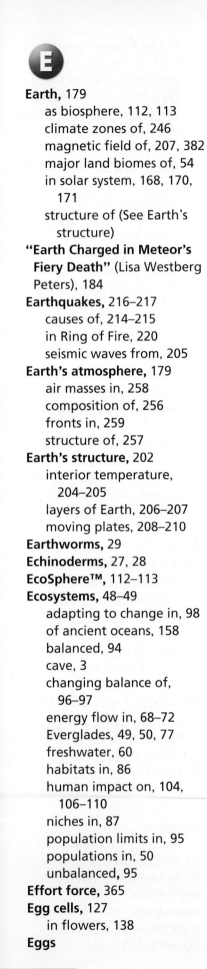

Index

## E

**Earth,** 179
    as biosphere, 112, 113
    climate zones of, 246
    magnetic field of, 207, 382
    major land biomes of, 54
    in solar system, 168, 170, 171
    structure of (See Earth's structure)
**"Earth Charged in Meteor's Fiery Death"** (Lisa Westberg Peters), 184
**Earthquakes,** 216–217
    causes of, 214–215
    in Ring of Fire, 220
    seismic waves from, 205
**Earth's atmosphere,** 179
    air masses in, 258
    composition of, 256
    fronts in, 259
    structure of, 257
**Earth's structure,** 202
    interior temperature, 204–205
    layers of Earth, 206–207
    moving plates, 208–210
**Earthworms,** 29
**Echinoderms,** 27, 28
**EcoSphere™,** 112–113
**Ecosystems,** 48–49
    adapting to change in, 98
    of ancient oceans, 158
    balanced, 94
    cave, 3
    changing balance of, 96–97
    energy flow in, 68–72
    Everglades, 49, 50, 77
    freshwater, 60
    habitats in, 86
    human impact on, 104, 106–110
    niches in, 87
    population limits in, 95
    populations in, 50
    unbalanced, 95
**Effort force,** 365
**Egg cells,** 127
    in flowers, 138
**Eggs**

    amphibian, 31
    mammal, 33
    reptile, 31
**El Niño,** 250
**Elastic energy,** potential, 329
**Electrical conductivity,** 300
**Electrical energy,** 326, 327
    as kinetic energy, 329
**Electromagnetic energy,** 326, 327
**Electromagnets,** 380–381
**Electron microscopes** (EMs), 17, 23
**Electrons,** in space, 382
**Elements,** 289
**Ellipses,** 171
**Emeagwali, Dale Brown,** S2–S3
**EMs** (electron microscopes), 17
**Enceladus,** 172
**Endangered species,** 107
    gray bat, 3
**Endangered Species Act,** 109
**Endoplasmic reticulum** (ER), 18–20
**Endosymbiont hypothesis,** 133
**Energy,** 326
    changes in, 324
    and changes in state of matter, 308–309
    chemical, 327, 328
    conductivity of, 300
    elastic, 329
    electrical, 326, 327, 329
    electromagnetic, 326, 327
    from food, 68
    in food chains, 69
    forms of, 326–327
    kinetic, 328–329
    mechanical, 327–330
    oceans' absorption of, 250
    potential, 328–329
    solar, 337
    sound, 327, 329
    sunlight as, 3
    thermal, 326, 329, 336–340
**Energy Beads,** S9
**Energy pyramid,** 67, 72
**Engineering projects**
    Build a Fish Transport, 8
    Build a Safe Clubhouse, 162

    Build a Solar Oven, 280
**Environment**
    adaptations to changes in, 98
    effect of dams on, 6–7
**Environmental legislation,** 110
**Environmental Protection Agency** (EPA), 110
**Environmental traits,** 125
**EPA** (Environmental Protection Agency), 110
**Epicenter** (earthquakes), 216–217
**Equations,** H10
**ER.** See Endoplasmic reticulum
**Eris,** 181
**Erosion**
    on Mars, 179
    of mountains, 161
    mountains shaped by, 229
**Erosion mountains,** 231
**Eskimo Nebula,** 193
**Eurasian Plate,** 208
**Evaporation,** 309
    mountain effect precipitation and, 249
**Evaporation rate,** 311
**Everglades,** 49, 50, 77
**Exoskeletons,** 29
**Expansion,** thermal, 312
**Expansion joints,** 312
**Experiment**
    with colors in light, S7
    with Energy Beads, S9
    in scientific inquiry, S6, S8
**Exploring space,** 182
**Express Labs**
    Analyze a Food Web, 69
    Compare Adaptations, 144
    Compare the Outer Planets, 180
    Compare Parents and Offspring, 129
    Compare Regions, 259
    Compare Sponges, 291
    Explore Distant Planets, 171
    Identify Interspecific Relationships, 90
    Investigate Climate, 249
    Investigate Scents, 291
    Make an Earth Model, 210

Make a Model Fossil, 100
Make a Mountain Type, 231
Model Cells, 20
Model Interactions in Ecosystems, 49
Model Plate Motion, 218
Observe an Animal, 32
Observe Chemical Reactions, 301
Observe Condensation, 311
Observe Ecosystems, 58
Protect Wildlife, 109
Sort Objects, 380
Store and Release Energy, 329
Test Shapes, 360
Transfer Thermal Energy, 339
Use Simple Machines, 371
Use a Star Chart, 190
**Extinction,** 99
from clearing rain forests, 106
of ice age animals, 100
mass, 99
**Extreme Science**
balanced ecosystems, 112–113
biodegradable bottles, 304–305
great white sharks, 74–75
living fossils, 36–37
magnetic resonance imaging, 384–385
mating behaviors, 146–147
Mount St. Helens, 234–235
roller coasters, 332–333
supernovas, 192–193
tornadoes, 252–253

**F**

**Facts,** S5
**Fall Creek Falls State Park,** Pikeville, Tennessee, 156
**Families** (of animals), 34
**Fangtooth fish,** 59
**Fault-block mountains,** 229
**Faulting,** 215, 220
mountains formed by, 229
**Fault lines,** 209
**Faults,** 214–215

**Feathers,** bird, 32
**Ferns,** fossil, 99, 210
**Fertilizers,** 108
**Fire,** thermal radiation by, 340
**First-class levers,** 366
**First-level (primary) consumers,** 68–70, 72
**Fish**
fossil, 99
in marine biomes, 58–59
**Fishing,** 107
**Fish ladders,** 6, 30
**Fission,** 136
**Fixed pulleys,** 368, 369
**Flamingos,** 124
**Flatworms,** 29, 137
**Floods**
dams for control of, 7
ecosystems changed by, 97
**Florida Everglades,** 49, 50, 77
**Florida panther,** 49
**Flowering plants,** reproduction in, 138
**Flowers,** bees and, 5
**Focus** (of earthquake), 216–217
**Fold mountains,** 228–229
**Food**
adaptations for finding, 142
for animals, 26
for birds, 32
in caves, 3
energy from, 68
in energy pyramid, 72
for mammals, 33
in ocean ecosystems, 50
**Food chains,** 69
in caves, 3
gray bat, 3
**Food webs,** 70, 71
**Forces**
balanced and unbalanced, 358
definition of, 355
effort, 365
first law of motion and, 355
friction, 360
gravity, 360
with inclined planes, 370, 371
with levers, 366–367

load, 365
measuring, 359, H16
opposing, 364
with pulleys, 368–369
and race cars, 275
resistance, 365
with screws, 371
second law of motion and, 359
with wedges, 371
with wheel and axles, 368
in work, 364
**Forest biomes,** 55
**Forest ecosystems,** 48
**Forest fires,** ecosystems changed by, 97
**Forges,** 277
**Formulas,** H10
**Fossil fuels,** 108
**Fossils,** 210
age of, 99
as evidence of changes, 99
of fern, 210
information from, 98
of Tennessee, 102–103, 159
**Frame of reference,** for motion, 354
**Franklin, Rosalind,** 132
**Freezing point,** 308
**Freezing rate,** 311
**Freshwater ecosystems,** 60
**Friction,** 360
affecting race cars, 275
with inclined planes, 370
**Frogs,** 31, 94
warning coloration of, 143
**Fronts,** 259, 260
**Frost,** 310
**Fruit flies,** chromosomes of, 126
**Fujita Scale,** 253
**Fulcrum** (levers), 366, 367
**Fungi,** reproduction of, 137

**G**

**g** (grams), 298, 312
**Galaxies,** Milky Way, 170, 171
**Gametes,** 127
in sexual reproduction, 138
yeast, 137
**Garbage,** 108

**Gases,** 290, 299
  in Earth's atmosphere, 256
  properties of, 292
  transfer of thermal energy
    in, 339
  volcanic, 219
**Gas giants,** 180, 181
**Gears,** 368
**Genes,** 127, 130
  disappearance of, 144
  dominant and recessive,
    139
  in selective breeding, 140
**Genetic disorders,** 130
**Genetic heredity,** 149
**Genus** (of animals), 34
**Geologic age,** 99
**Geologic events**
  earthquakes, 216–217, 220
  erosion, 160–161, 231, 232
  faulting, 214–215, 228–229
  plate movements, 208–210
  volcanic eruptions, 218–
    219, 220, 230
  weathering, 160–161, 231,
    232
**Geologic features**
  mountains, 228–232
  ocean ridges, 220
  ocean trenches, 220
  plateau, 160–161, 231
  valleys, 231, 232
  volcanoes, 218–219,
    234–235
**Geysers,** 204, 205
  on moons, 172
**Giant anteaters,** 36–37
**Gills,** 30
**Giraffes,** 134
**Glaciers,** 100
  valley formation and, 231
**Glass,** properties of, 297
**Glassmaking,** 278–279
**g/mL** (grams per milliliter),
  298
**Golgi apparatus,** 18, 19
**Grams** (g), 298, 312
**Grams per milliliter** (g/mL),
  298
**Granite,** 206
**Graphs**
  circle, H12
  line, H13

**Grassland biomes,** 56
**Gravitational force**
  holding moons in orbits,
    172
  of Sun, 171
**Gravity,** 360
  formation of solar system
    and, 171
  microgravity, 195, 387
  work done by, 365
**Gray bats,** 3
**Great Red Spot** (Jupiter), 180
**Great white sharks,** 74–75
**Green anoles,** 98
**Gross, Lou,** 77

**H**

**Habitats,** 86
  human impact on, 107
  worm and fish, 84–85
**Hair,** of mammals, 33
**Hale-Bopp comet,** 173
**Halley's comet,** 173
**Hawaii,** 230
**Health,** inherited conditions
  and, 130
**Heat,** 337
  infrared radiation felt as,
    340
**Helium,** in air, 256
**Hemoglobin,** sickle cell ane-
  mia and, 130
**Hemophilia,** 130
**Herbivores,** 33, 70
**Heredity,** 124
  chromosomes and genes,
    126–127
  DNA, 126–129
  genes and health, 130
  genetic, 149
  mutations, 129
**Herring,** 58
**Herschel,** 181
**High-pressure systems,** 260
**History of science**
  Rosalind Franklin, 132
  Lynn Margulis, 133
  microscopes, 22–23
  transportation, 374–375
**Honeybees,** in Tennessee, 4–5
**Hooke, Robert,** 16, 22

**Hookworms,** 90
**Horse and buggy,** 374
**Horses,** 33
**Horseshoe crabs,** 36–37
**Host** (parasitism), 90
**Hot spots,** 230
**Hot springs,** 204, 205
**Hubbard's Cave,** McMinnville,
  Tennessee, 2–3
**Human activities**
  ecosystems changed by,
    104
  impact on ecosystems,
    106–110
  pollution from, 108–110
**Humans**
  in animal kingdom, 26
  chromosomes of, 126
**Hummingbirds,** 142
**Hunting,** 107
**Hurricane Charley,** 261
**Hybridization,** 140
**Hybrid organisms,** 139, 140
**Hydra,** 137
**Hypothesize**
  as inquiry skill, 92–93
  limits to growth, 92–93
  in scientific inquiry, S6, S8

**I**

**Ice ages,** 100, 291
**Iceboxes,** 314
**iGNiS Glass Studio,** Chatta-
  nooga, Tennessee, 278–279
**Impact craters,** 174
**Inbreeding,** 141
**Inclined planes,** 365, 370–371
**Indian-Australian Plate,** 208
**Inertia,** 355
**Infer**
  as inquiry skill, 376–377
  magnets, 376–377
**Infrared light,** 340
**Inherited behaviors,** 146
**Inherited disorders,** 130
**Inherited traits,** 124, 138–143
**Inner core** (Earth), 206, 207
**Inner planets,** 178–179
**Inquiry.** See Scientific inquiry
**Inquiry skills,** S8
  analyze data, 52–53,

122–123, 212–213
collaborate, 254–255
communicate, 14–15, 24–25
compare, 244–245, 362–363
hypothesize, 92–93
infer, 376–377
measure, 352–353
observe, 46–47, 84–85, 226–227, 286–287, 306–307
predict, 104–105, 324–325
research, 168–169
use models, 66–67, 134–135, 176–177, 202–203
use numbers, 186, 294–295
use variables, 334–335
**Insects,** 29
as bird food, 32
camouflaged, 143
red, 143
**Insulators,** 300
**Intensity,** of earthquakes, 216
**Intertidal zone,** 58
**Inventors,** S10–S13
**Invertebrates,** 27–29
**Investigations,** communication of, S3
**Io,** 172
**Iron**
in Earth's core, 207
making products from, 277
**Isle Royale,** 95

**Jacobs-Young, Chavonda,** 317
**Jellyfish,** 28, 59
**Jemison, Mae,** 375
**Jupiter,** 180
asteroids' origin and, 172
moons of, 172
in solar system, 170

**Kangaroos,** 33
**Kelp,** 58
**Kilograms** (kg), 298

**Kinetic energy,** 328–329
in roller coasters, 332, 333
thermal, 336, 337, 340
**Kingda Ka roller coaster,** New Jersey, 332–333
**Kingdom Animalia,** 26, 27
**Kingdom** (animals), 34
**Kingfishers,** 60
**King snake,** 143

**l** (liters), 298
**Lake ecosystems,** 60
**Land breezes,** 248
**Landfills,** 108
**Landforms**
formation of, 161
on Mars, 179
**Land pollution,** 108
**Late Cretaceous,** 159
**Lava,** 218, 219
**Lava dome,** 235
**Learned traits,** 125
**Leeuwenhoek, Anton van,** 16, 22
**Leeward side of mountains,** 249
**Length,** measuring, H16, H17
**Lenses,** of microscopes, 17
**Levers,** 365–367
**Light**
as energy, 327
infrared, 340
from stars, 188
wavelengths of, 340
**Light microscopes,** 17
**Light-year** (Ly), 189
**Line graphs,** H13
**Lions,** 86, 87
**Liquids,** 290, 299
properties of, 292
transfer of thermal energy in, 339
**Literature**
"Earth Charged in Meteor's Fiery Death," 184
"Meteors," 185
**Liters** (L), 298
**Lithosphere,** 207, 208
**Living things**

adaptations by, 98
cells of, 16, 17
in ecosystems, 48, 49
ecosystems changed by, 96
interactions among, 84
*See also* Animals; Humans; Organisms; Plants
**Lizards,** 30, 31, 159
adaptations of, 98
**Load force,** 365
**Lobsters,** 29
**Long-period comets,** 173
**"Look Out! It's an Earthquake!",** 222–225
**Low-pressure systems,** 260
**L waves,** 217
**Ly** (light-year), 189
**Lysosomes,** 18, 19

**Machines**
compound, 372
simple, 365–371
**Magma,** 218–220, 230
**Magnetic fields,** 378, 379
of atoms, 378
of Earth, 207, 382
of nonmagnetic materials, 378
**Magnetic Resonance Imaging** (MRI), 384–385
**Magnets,** making, 380–381
**Magnification,** 288, 289
with microscopes, 17
**Magnitude**
of earthquakes, 216
of stars, 189
**Malin, Peter,** 237
**Mammalia,** 34
**Mammals,** 33
**Manatees,** S14–S15
**Mangrove trees,** 49
**Manipulated traits,** 125
**Mantle** (Earth), 206, 207
**Margulis, Lynn,** 133
**Marine biomes,** 58–59
**Maritime air masses,** 258
**Maritime polar air masses,** 258
**Maritime tropical air masses,**

258
**Mars,** 170, 179
**Mars Expedition rovers,** 179, 182
**Marsupials,** 33
**Mass(es)**
    acceleration and, 359
    attractive force between, 360
    measuring, H9, H16
    as physical property, 298
**Mass extinction,** 99
**Math in science**
    bird population, 114
    calculators, H4
    earthquake totals, 236
    finding averages, H5
    home heating, 344
    melting point, 316
    mouse maze, 148
    planet circumferences, 194
    precipitation chart, 266
    tables, 38, 76
    using an equation or formula, H10
**Mating behaviors,** 146–147
**Matter,** 286
    changing states of, 299, 308–312
    observing, 288–289
    properties of, 288, 289, 292, 296–302
    states of, 290–291, 299
**Measuring**
    customary, H17
    elapsed time, H14–H15
    as inquiry skill, 352–353
    metric, H16
    motion, 352–353
    tools for, H6–H9
**Mechanical energy,** 327
    calculating, 330
    kinetic, 329
    potential, 328, 329
**Meerkats,** 27
**Megalodon,** 75
**Megrez,** 189
**Melting point,** 299, 308
**Melting rate,** 311
**Mendel, Gregor,** 149
**Merak,** 189
**Mercury** (planet), 171, 178, 179

**Mesosphere,** 257
**Metals,** conductivity of, 300
**Meteorites,** 174
**Meteoroids,** 170, 171, 174
**Meteorologists,** 260, 267
**Meteors,** 174, 185
**Meteor showers,** 174
**Meters per second** (m/s), 356
**Metersticks,** H6
**Metric measures,** H16
**Microbiologists,** S2–S3
**Microgravity,** 195, 387
**Microorganisms,** S2, S3
**Microscopes,** 288, H2
    development of, 17
    electron, 17
    history of, 22–23
    invention of, 16
**Microtubules,** 19
**Mid-ocean ridges,** 215, 230
**Milky Way galaxy,** 170, 171
**Milliliters** (mL), 298
**Mimicry,** 143
**Mites,** 5
**Mitochondria,** 18–20, 133
**Mizar,** 189
**mL** (milliliters), 298
**Models**
    of Earth's structure, 202–203
    energy flow, 66–67
    of genes on chromosomes, 134–135
    of solar system, 176–177
    *See also* Use models
**Moisture,** in air masses, 258
**Molecules,** 289, 297
**Mollusks,** 27, 29
**Monitor lizards,** 159
**Moons**
    formation of, 171
    of Jupiter, 180
    of Neptune, 181
    of Pluto, 181
    in solar system, 170, 172
    of Uranus, 181
**Moose,** 95
**Mosasaurs,** 159
**Mosey, Chris,** 278, 279
**Moths,** 3
**Motion,** 354–360
    acceleration, 357
    balanced and unbalanced

    forces, 358
    friction and, 360
    gravity and, 360
    as kinetic energy, 328
    Newton's first law of, 355
    Newton's second law of, 359
    speed, 356, 357
    velocity, 356–357
**Mountain City, Tennessee,** 342
**Mountain effect precipitation,** 248–249
**Mountains**
    formation of, 161, 226–232
    in Georgia, 232
    underwater, 230
    volcanoes, 218
**Mount Minsi, Pennsylvania,** 231
**Mount St. Helens,** 97, 234–235
**"Mr. Wayne's Way Cool Science Podcast",** 62–65
**MRI.** *See* Magnetic Resonance Imaging
**m/s** (meters per second), 356
**Mudpots,** 205
**Muscular dystrophy,** 130
**Mussels,** 58, 96
**Mutagens,** 129
**Mutations,** 129
    with asexual reproduction, 136
**Mutualism,** 90
    of bees and flowers, 5

**N**

**N** (newton), 359
**NASA,** 195
**NASCAR** (National Association of Stock Car Auto Racing), 275
**Natural cycles,** 70
**Natural disasters**
    droughts, 264–265
    earthquakes, 216–217
    ecosystems changed by, 97
    tornadoes, 252–253
    volcanic eruptions, 218–219

**Natural resources**
    limits on, 94
    organisms' different uses of, 87
**Natural selection,** 89
**Nazca Plate,** 208
**Near-shore zone, 58**
**Neon,** in air, 256
**Neptune,** 170, 180, 181
**Newton, Sir Isaac,** 355, 359
**Newton-meter (N-m),** 365
**Newton (N),** 359
**Newton's first law of motion,** 355, 358
**Newton's Law of Universal Gravitation,** 360
**Newton's second law of motion,** 359
**Newts,** 31
**Niches,** 87
    of lions, 86
    of zebras, 87
**Nickel,** in Earth's core, 207
**Night sky,** star positions in, 190
**Nitrogen,** in air, 256
**Nitrogen bases** (in DNA), 127, 128
**Nitrogen cycle,** 70
**N·m** (newton-meter), 365
**Noncontact forces,** 360
**Nonliving things**
    in ecosystems, 48, 49
    ecosystems changed by, 97
**Nonmagnetic materials,** 378
**Norris Dam,** 6–7
**North America**
    during ice age, 100
    typical air masses in, 258
**North American Plate,** 208
**Northern elephant seals,** 144
**Northern Hemisphere**
    glaciers in, 100
    stars seen from, 190
**Northern lights,** 382
**North Pole,** 379
**Nuclear reactions**
    causing starlight, 188
    Sun produced by, 171
**Nucleotides,** 127
**Nucleus,** cell, 18

**Observe**
    earthworms, 46–47
    as inquiry skill, 46–47, 84–85, 226–227, 286–287, 306–307
    making rain, 306–307
    matter, 286–287
    mountain formation, 226–227
    in scientific inquiry, S6, S8
    worm and fish habitats, 84–85
**Ocean currents,** 250
**Ocean ecosystems,** 50
**Ocean ridges,** 220
**Ocean-floor crust,** 206
**Oceanic plates,** 208, 209
**Oceanographers,** 267
**Oceans**
    climate and, 248, 250, 258
    prehistoric, 158
**Ocean trenches,** 209, 220
**Octopuses,** 29
**Oil spills,** 108
**Olympus Mons** (Mars), 179
**Omnivores,** 33, 70
**Open ocean zone,** 59
**Opinions,** S5
*Opportunity* Mars rover, 179, 182
**Optical telescopes,** 182
**Orbits**
    of asteroids, 172
    of comets, 169, 173
    of moons, 172
    of Pluto, 181
    in solar system, 171
**Orders** (of animals), 34
**Organelles,** 18–20, 128
**Organisms**
    adaptations of, 88
    alien species of, 96
    cells of, 126
    in ecosystems, 49
    habitats of, 86
    hybrid, 139, 140
    in marine biomes, 59
    natural selection and, 89
    niches of, 87
    perishing of, 98, 99
    populations of, 50, 94
    purebred, 139, 141
    reproduction in, 126–127
    symbiotic relationships between, 90
    traits of, 124–125
    *See also* Living things
**Ostriches,** 32
**Ouachita Mountains, Arkansas,** 229
**Outer core** (Earth), 206, 207
**Outer planets,** 180–181
**Ovens,** for glassmaking, 279
**Overfishing,** 106, 107
**Overhunting,** 107
**Oxygen**
    in air, 256
    in Earth's core, 207
**Oxygen cycle,** 70
**Oysters,** 29
**Ozone,** 257

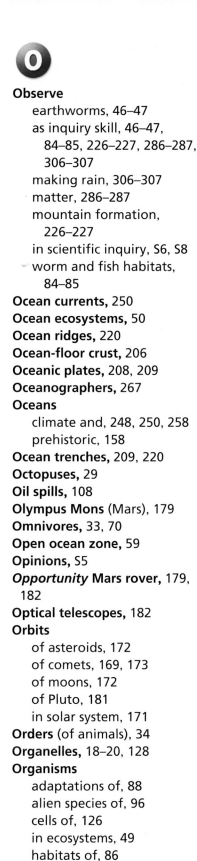

**Pacific Ocean:** El Niño, 250
**Pacific Plate,** 208, 220
**Paper making,** 317
**Parasitism,** 5, 90
    worms, 29
**Parrots,** 142
**Peacocks,** 147
**Pea plants,** 149
**Pelicans,** 142
**People in Science**
    Amrutur V. Anilkumar, 387
    Lou Gross, 77
    Chavonda Jacobs-Young, 317
    Peter Malin, 237
    Gregor Mendel, 149
**Peregrine falcons,** 357
**Perishing** (dying), 98, 99
**Permanent magnets,** 380
**Perryville, Tennessee,** 342
**Peters, Lisa Westberg,** 184
**Phecda,** 189
**Philippi Plate,** 208
**Phosphates** (in DNA), 127
**Photosynthesis,** 20, 68
**Phyla** (of animals), 34
**Physical adaptations,** 88

**Physical properties**, 292, 297–300
  boiling point, 299
  conductivity, 300
  density, 298
  mass, 298
  melting point, 299
  solubility, 300
  volume, 298
**Piedmont**, 232
**Pistils**, 138
**Planaria**, 137
**Planets**
  dwarf, 181
  formation of, 171
  inner, 178–179
  outer, 180–181
  in solar system, 170, 171
**Plankton**, 60, 96
**Plant cells**, 18–20
**Plantlets**, 136, 137
**Plants**
  adaptations of, 88, 142
  alien species of, 96
  asexual reproduction in, 136
  in deserts, 56
  as food, 69
  in food chains, 69
  in forest biomes, 55
  in freshwater ecosystems, 60
  in grasslands, 56
  in marine biomes, 58–59
  as producers, 69
  in rain forests, 106
  regrowth after volcanic eruptions, 97
  reproduction of, 137
  selective breeding of, 140–141
  sexual reproduction in, 138–139
  of taiga, 57
  of tundra, 57
  in wetlands, 107
**Plastics**, biodegradable, 304–305
**Plateaus**, 160–161
  formation of, 161
**Plate boundaries**, 208, 209
  faults at, 214–215
  volcanic mountains at, 230

**Plates**, 161, 208–209
  evidence for movement of, 210
  hot spots in, 230
**Plate tectonics**, 208
**Pluto**, 180, 181
**Poisonous organisms**, adaptations of, 143
**Polar air masses**, 258
**Polar bears**, 33
**Polar climates**, 246, 247
**Poles**, magnetic, 379
**Pollen**, 4, 5, 138
**Pollination**, 138
**Pollution**, 108–110
**Pond ecosystems**, 60
**Pond plants**, 142
**Populations**, 50, 94
  in balanced ecosystems, 94
  limits on, 95
  size of, 92
**Porcupine quills**, 142
**Potential energy**, 328–329
  in roller coasters, 332–333
**Power tools**, S12
**Prairie chickens**, 147
**Prairies**, 56
**Precipitation**
  in climate zones, 247
  measuring, 262
  mountain effect, 248–249
  on weather maps, 260
**Predator-prey relationships**, 95
**Predators**, 94, 95
  camouflage to protect from, 143
**Predict**
  as inquiry skill, 104–105, 324–325
  rising sea level, 104–105
  rollerball, 324–325
  weather (See Weather forecasting)
**Prey**, 95
**Primary consumers.** *See* First-level consumers
**Producers**, 68, 72
**Properties of materials**, 294, 297
**Properties of matter**, 288, 289, 292, 296–302
  chemical, 297, 301–302

  physical, 292, 297–300
**Proteins**, 19, 128
  amino acids of, 129
  mutations of, 129
**Protein synthesis**, 128
**Protists**, asexual reproduction of, 136
**Proxima Centauri**, 189
*Pterotrigonia thoracica*, 159
**Pulleys**, 365, 368–369
**Purebred organisms**, 139, 141
**P waves**, 217

**Quinolones**, 144

**Race cars**, 275
**Racetracks**, 274
**Radar**, weather, 261
**Radial symmetry**, 26, 28
**Radiation**, thermal, 340
**Radioactive dating**, 99
**Radio waves**, 326
**Railroads**, 375
**Rain**, fronts and, 259
**Rain forests**, destruction of, 106
**Rain gauges**, 262
**Rain shadows**, 249
**Readers' Theater**
  "Look Out! It's an Earthquake!", 222–225
  "Mr. Wayne's Way Cool Science Podcast," 62–65
**Recessive genes**, 139
**Red winter wheat**, 140
**Refrigerators**, 314–315
**Regeneration**, 137
**Relocation**, as adaptation, 98
**Reproduction**
  by amphibians, 30
  asexual, 136–137
  DNA in, 126–127
  by mammals, 33
  mating behaviors and, 146–147
  by reptiles, 31

selective breeding, 140–141

sexual, 138–139

**Reptiles,** 31

**Reptilia,** 34

**Repulsion** (magnets), 379

**Research**

comet orbits, 168–169

as inquiry skill, 168–169

**Resistance force,** 365

**Ribosomes,** 19, 128

**Richter scale,** 216, 217

**Rift valleys,** 209

**Ring Nebula,** 193

**Ring of Fire,** 220

**Rings,** of outer planets, 180, 181

**River ecosystems,** 60

**Rocks**

in Earth's inner layers, 206, 207

evidence of changes in, 99

at faults, 214, 215

formation of, 161

on Mars, 182

melting of, 218

**Rocky Mountains,** 229, 230

**Roller coasters,** 332–333

**Roseate spoonbill,** 49

**Rough endoplasmic reticulum,** 20

**Roundworms,** 29

**Rulers,** H6

**Rust,** 301, 302

**S**

**Safety in science,** S16

**SAFOD.** *See* San Andreas Fault Observatory at Depth

**Salamanders,** 31

**San Andreas Fault,** 214, 215

**San Andreas Fault Observatory at Depth** (SAFOD), 225, 237

**Sandhill cranes,** 147

**Sandpipers,** 89

**Satellites**

moons as, 172

temperatures around, 342

weather, 262, 342

**Saturn,** 171, 172, 180

**Savanna habitat,** 86–87

**Savannas,** 56

**Scales** (for measuring), 298

**Scales** (of reptiles), 31

**Scanning electron microscopes** (SEMs), 17, 22

**Scanning probe microscopes,** 23

**Schleiden, Matthias,** 17

**Science safety,** S16

**Scientific inquiry,** S4, S6–S9

**Scientists,** S2–S3

technology used by, S11

thinking like, S4–S9

**Scorpions,** 29

**Scottish Highlands,** 232

**Screws,** 365, 371

**Sea anemones,** 84

**Sea breezes,** 248

**Sea cucumbers,** 28

**Sea-floor spreading,** **209**

**Sea level,** during ice ages, 100

**Seals,** 144

**Sea stars,** 58

**Sea turtles,** 88

**Sea urchins,** 28

**Seaweed,** 142

**Second-class levers,** **367**

**Second-level consumers,** **69,** 70, 72

**Sedimentary rocks,** fossils in, 210

**Sediments,** 60

**Seismic waves,** 214–217

information about Earth's interior from, 205

**Seismographs,** 214–216

**SEMs.** *See* Scanning electron microscopes

**Senses,** observing properties with, 296

**Sensory systems,** of fish, 30

**Sexual reproduction,** 138–139

**Sharks,** 74–75

**Shells,** fossil, 99

**Shield volcanoes,** 219

**Shooting stars,** 174

**Short-period comets,** **173**

**Shrimp,** 90

in EcoSphere™, 112, 113

**Sickle cell anemia,** 130

**Sierra Nevada Mountains,** 231

**Simon, Seymour,** 185

**Simple machines,** **365–371**

in compound machines, 372

inclined planes, 370–371

levers, 366–367

pulleys, 368–369

screws, 371

wedges, 371

wheels and axles, 368

**Skeletons,** fish, 30

**Sliding boundaries,** 209

faults at, 215

mountain building at, 229

**Smooth endoplasmic reticulum,** 20

**Snails,** 29

**Snakes,** 30, 31, 143

**Soccer,** forces in, 355

**Solar energy,** 337

**Solar system,** 168, 170–171

asteroid belt in, 172

asteroids in, 172

comets in, 173

exploring, 182

inner planets in, 178–179

meteors in, 174

moons in, 172

outer planets in, 180–181

**Solar wind,** 382

**Solids,** 290, 299

properties of, 292

thermal conduction by, 338

**Solid waste,** 108

**Solubility,** 300

**Solutions,** 300

**Sound energy,** 327

as kinetic energy, 329

**South American Plate,** 208

**Southern Hemisphere,** stars seen from, 190

**Southern lights,** 382

**South Pole,** 379, 382

**Space,** movement of objects through, 360

**Spacecraft,** 182

space probes, 182, 343

space shuttle, 182, 343, 375, 387

space station, 182

temperatures around, 342

**Space exploration,** 182

**Space probes,** 182, 343

**Space shuttle,** 182, 343, 375, 387

**Space station,** 182

**Species,** 34
alien, 96
endangered, 107
extinct, 99
natural selection in, 89
threatened, 107

**Speeds**
of forms of transportation, 374
of roller coasters, 332–333

**Sperm cells,** 127, 138

**Spiders,** 29

**Spines,** 142

**Spiny anteaters,** 33

*Spirit* Mars rover, 179, 182

**Sponges,** 27, 28

**Spores,** 136

**Spring Star Party,** 156

**Squids,** 29

**Stamens,** 138

**Star charts,** 156, 190

**Star wheels,** 156, 157

**Starfish,** 28

**Stars**
movement of, 157, 190
patterns of (constellations), 189
positions in night sky, 190
Sun, 188–189
supernovas, 192–193
in Tennessee, 156

**State fossil** (Tennessee), 159

**States of matter,** 290–291
changing, 299, 308–312
as physical properties, 299

**Stationary fronts,** 259

**Steam plume** (volcanoes), 235, 292

**Stinging rays,** 142

**Storms,** forecasting, 261

**Stratosphere,** 257

**Stream ecosystems,** 60

**Subduction**
faulting during, 220
and trenches, 209

**Sublimation,** 310

**Sugars** (in DNA), 127

**Sulfur,** 207

**Sun**
in food chains, 69

formation of, 171
orbit of comets around, 169
as radiation source, 340
in solar system, 170, 171
as star, 186, 188–189

**Sunlight**
as energy, 3
energy from, 69
in marine biomes, 58, 59

**Supercells,** 252

**Super-giants** (stars), 192

**Supernovas,** 192–193

**Super Outbreak** (tornadoes), 252

**Surface currents,** 250

**Surface waves,** 217

**Survival**
adaptations for, 88
natural selection for, 89

**S waves,** 217

**Swim bladders,** 30

**Symbiosis,** 90

**Symmetry**
in animals, 26
of invertebrates, 28

**T**

**Tadpoles,** 31

**Taiga biome,** 57

**Taipei, Taiwan,** 216

**Tape measures,** H6

**Tarnishing,** 302

**Technology,** S11
build a fish transport, 8
build a safe clubhouse, 162
build a solar oven, 280
for pollution reduction, 110
refrigerators, 314-315
in selective breeding, 141
space blankets, 342–343

**Teeth**
of great white sharks, 74–75
of mammals, 33

**Telescopes**
atmosphere affecting, 182
optical, 182

**Temperate climates,** 246, 247

**Temperate forests,** 55

**Temperatures**
of air masses, 258
in climate zones, 247
definition of, 336
in Earth's atmosphere, 257
of Earth's interior, 205
on Earth's surface, 179
extremes of, 342
measuring, H8, H16, H17
on Mercury, 178
of Sun, 188
thermal energy and, 336
on Venus, 179
on weather maps, 260

**Temporary magnets,** 380

**Tennessee**
ancient ocean covering, 158–159
Blue Spring Cave, 2
Bristol Dragway, 274–275
Bristol Motor Speedway, 274–275
Clingman's Dome, 232
Coon Creek Formation, Adamsville, 159
Cumberland Plateau, 160, 161
Dollywood Craft Preservation School, Pigeon Forge, 276–277
droughts in, 264–265
Fall Creek Falls State Park, Pikeville, 156
fossils of, 102–103, 159
honeybees in, 4–5
Hubbard's Cave, McMinnville, 2–3
iGNiS Glass Studio, Chattanooga, 278–279
lowest and highest temperatures in, 342
mountains in, 232
Norris Dam, 6–7
Spring Star Party, 156
stars in, 156
state fossil, 159
West Tennessee Agricultural Museum, Milan, 4

**Thermal conductivity,** 300

**Thermal energy,** 326, 336–340
devices controlling, 334
heat as transfer of, 337
as kinetic energy, 329

in shaping iron objects, 277
sources of, 337
temperature and, 336
transfer of, 337–340
**Thermal engineers, 345**
**Thermal expansion, 312**
**Thermometers,** 262, H8
**Thermosphere, 257**
**Third-class levers, 367**
**Third-level consumers,** 69, 70, 72
**Thorns, 142**
**Threatened species, 107**
**Tigers, 34**
**Time,** elapsed, H14–H15
**Toads, 31**
**Tools**
balances, H9
calculators, H4
electric-powered, S12
for measuring, H6–H9
metersticks, H6
microscopes, H2
radar, 261
rulers, H6
tape measures, H6
technology and, S11
thermometers, H8
weather instruments, 262
**Tornadoes, 252–253**
**Tortoises,** 31, 88
**Traits,** 122, 124–125
acquired, 124–125
adaptations of, 142–143
asexual reproduction and, 136–137
genes controlling, 127
inherited, 124
predicting, 149
selective breeding for, 140–141
sexual reproduction and, 138–139
**Transmission electron micrograph, 23**
**Transportation, 374–375**
**Trash, 108**
**Triton, 181**
**Tropical air masses, 258**
**Tropical climates,** 246, 247
**Tropical rain forests, 55**

destruction of, 106
**Troposphere, 257**
air masses in, 258
**Tubeworms, 59**
**Tuna, 58**
**Tundra biome, 57**
**Turtles,** 31, 88

## U

**Unbalanced forces, 358**
**Universal Gravitation,** Newton's Law of, 360
**Uranus,** 180, 181
moons of, 172
in solar system, 170
**Use models,** 66–67, 134–135, 176–177, 202–203
**Use numbers**
as inquiry skill, 186, 294–295
mixing oil and water, 294–295
star search, 186–187
**Use variables, 334–335**

## V

**Vacuoles,** 18, 19
**Vaporization, 309**
**Variables,** in melting points, 334–335. See also Use variables
**Venomous organisms,** adaptations of, 143
**Vents,** ocean, 59
**Venus,** 171, 178, 179
**Venus flytraps, 70**
**Vertebrates,** 27, 30
cold-blooded, 30–31
warm-blooded, 32–33
**Virchow, Rudolf, 17**
**Visible light, 340**
**Volcanic eruptions, 230**
**Volcanic mountains, 230**
**Volcanoes,** 212, 218–219
ecosystems changed by, 97
on Mars, 179
on moons, 172
Mount St. Helens, 234–235

in Ring of Fire, 220
**Volume**
measuring, H7, H16, H17
as physical property, 298
**Vulcan, 218**

## W

**Wagner, Cassandra** "Cassie," S10
**Warm-blooded vertebrates, 32–33**
**Warm fronts,** 259, 260
**Warning coloration, 143**
**Water**
convection by, 339
density of, 298
expansion of, 312
properties of, 297
states of, 290–292, 306
**Water birds, 32**
**Water cycle, 70**
**Water pollution, 108**
**Water vapor,** 291
in air, 256
**Watson, James,** 132
**Weather,** 260
fronts and, 259
observing, 260
**Weather forecasting,** 254, 260–261
maps for, 260
radar in, 261
tools for, 262
**Weathering,** of mountains, 161, 231
**Weather instruments,** 262
**Weather maps,** 259, 260
**Weather satellites,** 262, 342
**Weather vanes,** 262
**Wedges,** 365, 371
**Wegener, Alfred,** 208
**Weight,** measuring, H17
**West Tennessee Agricultural Museum,** Milan, Tennessee, 4
**Wetlands**
as ecosystems, 60
human impact on, 107
protecting, 110
**Wetlands ecologists, 115**

**Whales,** 33, 59

**Wheels and axles,** 365, 368

**Wildlife refuges,** 109

**Wilkins, Maurice,** 132

**Wind**
  creation of, 250
  on Jupiter, 180
  measuring speed of, 262
  on Neptune, 181
  solar, 382
  in tornadoes, 252

**Windward side of mountains,** 249

**Wolves,** 92, 95

**Work,** 328, 364–365
  force used to do, 365

**Worms,** 27, 29

**Writing Links**
  informational, 76, 266, 386
  narrative/tell a story, 38,
    148, 236, 344
  persuasive essay, 114
  response to literature, 194,
    316

**Yaks,** 89

**Yeasts, reproduction in,** 136,
  137

**Yellowstone National Park,
  Wyoming,** 204, 205

**Yuji Hyakutake comet,** 173

**Zebra mussels,** 96

**Zebras,** 87

**Zookeepers,** 115

**Index**